UNDER-STANDING
DANIEL AND REVELATION

MARK FINLEY

Pacific Press®
Publishing Association
Nampa, Idaho | www.pacificpress.com

Cover design by Gerald Lee Monks
Cover design resources from iStockphoto.com | DNY59
Inside design by Aaron Troia

p. 8 © GoodSalt.com—Lars Justinen, p. 24 © GoodSalt.com—Steve Creitz, p. 40 © Review and Herald
Publishing—Russ Harlan, p. 80 © GoodSalt.com—Darrel Tank, p. 88 © GoodSalt.com—Phil McKay, p. 106
© Review and Herald Publishing—artist unknown, p. 128 © Review and Herald Publishing—Russ Harlan,
p. 160 © GoodSalt.com—Steve Creitz, p. 167 © Review and Herald Publishing—artist unknown, p. 186 ©
GoodSalt.com—Steve Creitz, p. 209 © GoodSalt.com—Steve Creitz, p. 234 © Goodsalt.com—Lars Justinen,
p. 242 © GoodSalt.com—Steve Creitz, p. 265 © GoodSalt.com—Steve Creitz, p. 273 © GoodSalt
.com—Steve Creitz, p. 290 © Review and Herald Publishing—Clyde Provonsha, p. 297 © GoodSalt.com—
Lars Justinen, p. 313 © Pacific Press Publishing—Lars Justinen, p. 328 © Goodsalt.com—Phil McKay, p. 336
© GoodSalt.com—Steve Creitz, p. 346 © Review and Herald Publishing—Jim Padgett, p. 376 © Goodsalt.
com—Lars Justinen, p. 384 © GoodSalt.com—Steve Creitz, p. 399 © Goodsalt.com—Lars Justinen, p. 408
The Blessed Hope by Nathan Greene, © 2010, all rights reserved, used by permission, www.nathangreene.com

Additional copies of this book are available for purchase by calling toll-free 1-800-765-6955 or by visiting
adventistbookcenter.com.

Library of Congress Cataloging-in-Publication Data

Names: Finley, Mark, 1945- author.
Title: Understanding Daniel and Revelation / Mark Finley.
Description: Nampa, Idaho : Pacific Press Publishing Association, 2020. |
    Summary: "This is a commentary on the Biblical books of Daniel and Revelation"— Provided by publisher.
Identifiers: LCCN 2020006732 (print) | LCCN 2020006733 (ebook)
Subjects: LCSH: Bible. Revelation—Commentaries. | Bible. Daniel—Commentaries.
Classification: LCC BS2825.53 .F55 2020 (print) | LCC BS2825.53 (ebook) | DDC 224/.507—dc23
LC record available at https://lccn.loc.gov/2020006732
LC ebook record available at https://lccn.loc.gov/2020006733

ISBN 9780816367139 (hardcover) | ISBN 9780816367146 (kindle edition)

July 2020

DEDICATION

This book is dedicated to those faithful, committed, tireless Adventist evangelists that night after night preach the prophetic Word. At times, their audiences are large, and at other times, they are small. They preach in civic auditoriums, churches, tents, schools, or any other venue where they can get an audience. At times, they preach in large metropolitan city centers, and at other times, in small country villages.

They are fearless preachers of God's Word. Their messages are shaped by the prophecies of Daniel and Revelation, not by popular culture. Their one goal is to proclaim the Christ of prophecy to a world on the verge of eternity. They are not out to win a popularity contest; they are out to preach the Word.

I salute these stalwart preachers whose minds are captive to the Word, who nightly proclaim the Word, and who unashamedly call people to make eternal decisions. To these—my colleagues in evangelistic ministry—this book is dedicated.

CONTENTS

INTRODUCTION

The twenty-first century might be dubbed "The Era of Uncertainty." As we gaze across the horizon of history, we see only a few periods that have been as uncertain as the present. This world is facing some extremely serious issues. The instability of the Middle East, the rising nuclear threats of Iran and North Korea, the tensions between the United States, Russia, and China, the shaky world economy, global warming, rapidly spreading worldwide pandemics and international food shortages, and a host of other regional and global problems lead millions to nervously ask, "What does the future hold? Where is this world headed? How can we face the future with greater confidence?"

The prophecies of Daniel and Revelation provide answers for honest-hearted people seeking to understand the uncertainties of our time. These prophetic revelations are filled with hope for today, tomorrow, and forever. Although this world may seem out of control, prophecy reveals a God who is still in control. As you read these pages, you will discover the secret to unlock these ancient predictions. Your faith will be strengthened. Your understanding will be enlarged. Your relationship with God will be deepened.

These prophecies are not merely about mystic symbols, strange beasts, and cryptic images. Every chapter focuses on the living Christ and His ability to change lives. Daniel and Revelation will come alive to you as you carefully study each chapter. The Holy Spirit will enable you to see truth from a new perspective and in a fresh way. You will understand the deep spiritual principles behind every prophecy and discover your place in the conflict of the ages.

A crisis of enormous proportions will soon break upon our planet. You can be ready for those earth-shaking events set to overtake the world with overwhelming surprise. The same God that inspired Daniel to pen His prophetic messages and visited John on the Isle of Patmos with angelic revelations will lift your vision, inspire your heart, and prepare you for what is coming. I pray that as you read *Understanding Daniel and Revelation*, you will be drawn preciously near to Jesus Christ—the Author and Center of all prophecy.

Understanding Daniel

THE GOD WHO TURNS DEFEAT INTO VICTORY

Daniel 1

1 In the third year of the reign of Jehoiakim king of Judah, Nebuchadnezzar king of Babylon came to Jerusalem and besieged it. **2** And the Lord gave Jehoiakim king of Judah into his hand, with some of the articles of the house of God, which he carried into the land of Shinar to the house of his god; and he brought the articles into the treasure house of his god.

3 Then the king instructed Ashpenaz, the master of his eunuchs, to bring some of the children of Israel and some of the king's descendants and some of the nobles, **4** young men in whom there was no blemish, but good-looking, gifted in all wisdom, possessing knowledge and quick to understand, who had ability to serve in the king's palace, and whom they might teach the language and literature of the Chaldeans. **5** And the king appointed for them a daily provision of the king's delicacies and of the wine which he drank, and three years of training for them, so that at the end of that time they might serve before the king. **6** Now from among those of the sons of Judah were Daniel, Hananiah, Mishael, and Azariah. **7** To them the chief of the eunuchs gave names: he gave Daniel the name Belteshazzar; to Hananiah, Shadrach; to Mishael, Meshach; and to Azariah, Abed-Nego.

8 But Daniel purposed in his heart that he would not defile himself with the portion of the king's delicacies, nor with the wine which he drank; therefore he requested of the chief of the eunuchs that he might not defile himself. **9** Now God had brought Daniel into the favor and goodwill of the chief of the eunuchs. **10** And the chief of the eunuchs said to Daniel, "I fear my lord the king, who has appointed your food and drink. For why should he see your faces looking worse than the young men who are your age? Then you would endanger my head before the king."

11 So Daniel said to the steward whom the chief of the eunuchs had set over Daniel, Hananiah, Mishael, and Azariah, **12** "Please test your servants for ten days, and let them give us vegetables to eat and water to drink. **13** Then let our appearance be examined before you, and the appearance of the young men who eat the portion of the king's delicacies; and as you see fit, so deal with your servants." **14** So he consented with them in this matter, and tested them ten days.

15 And at the end of ten days their features appeared better and fatter in flesh than all the young men who ate the portion of the king's delicacies. **16** Thus the steward took away their portion of delicacies and the wine that they were to drink, and gave them vegetables.

17 As for these four young men, God gave them knowledge and skill in all literature and wisdom; and Daniel had understanding in all visions and dreams.

18 Now at the end of the days, when the king had said that they should be brought in, the chief of the eunuchs brought them in before Nebuchadnezzar. **19** Then the king interviewed them, and among them all none was found like Daniel, Hananiah, Mishael, and Azariah; therefore they served before the king. **20** And in all matters of wisdom and understanding about which the king examined them, he found them ten times better than all the magicians and astrologers who were in all his realm. **21** Thus Daniel continued until the first year of King Cyrus.

⚜

Although it was written centuries ago, the book of Daniel is not just a musty, historical document filled with dates and facts. The more we study this book, the more Christ will appear in its pages, coming close to us to help us in the problems and challenges we face in our own lives each day. The more we understand the prophecies of Daniel, the better we will understand our place in earth's history and how to fill the role Jesus has for us in these last days.

Daniel's book has a message that speaks to us in our generation, but we are not the only ones who have found meaning in its prophecies. In the fifteenth century, Christopher Columbus (1451–1506), the early discoverer of the Americas, was a diligent student of the book of Daniel. One of the things that compelled Columbus to set out on his discovery of the New World was his study of the prophecies of Daniel. Columbus believed that Daniel predicted end-time events. He believed that as the world came to an end, God would open up new continents for the preaching of the gospel. His understanding of Daniel was one of the factors that led Columbus to find the New World, where the gospel could be preached to those who had never heard of Jesus.

Sir Isaac Newton (1643–1727), the famous British mathematician and scholar, was also a student of the book of Daniel. As he studied Daniel's prophecies, their mathematical precision confirmed his belief that the Bible was truly God's inspired Word.

Timothy Dwight (1752–1817) was the eighth president of Yale College (later, Yale University). During the time of the French Revolution, a number of students at Yale began to accept the arguments of European scholars that questioned the existence of God and doubted the truthfulness of the Bible. These atheistic students challenged professors on the campus with their unbelief.

Timothy Dwight announced, "I'd like to meet all the students in the chapel."

The students filed into the chapel, including those who had been outspoken about their unbelief. Timothy Dwight came into the room carrying a large load of history books. He put them on a table, and then he asked these students to present all their arguments against the Bible. So the unbelieving students presented their arguments. After they had given their most persuasive reasons for unbelief, Professor Dwight opened his Bible to the book of Daniel and began to read its prophecies—some of the same prophecies we will be studying as we explore this book. As Professor Dwight read Daniel's prophecies, he then turned to the stack of history books on the table at the front of the room. He read from Daniel, and then he compared Daniel's words with the history books. As he presented the facts of history compared with Bible prophecy, the students were amazed. History confirmed the prophecies of this ancient Bible book.

In the end, the students stood up and applauded Professor Dwight. That chapel meeting led to a magnificent spiritual revival at Yale College.

You are not alone in your desire to study the book of Daniel. Bible students down through the centuries have found meaning and comfort in its pages for their lives and their day. And as we, here in the twenty-first century, study Daniel together, God Himself will reveal amazing truths to us.

Daniel's book is divided into two segments: prophecies and stories. The first six chapters are mostly stories, and the last six are mostly prophecies. The prophecies deal with the great sweep of history down through the ages. They reveal time periods that lead us from Daniel's day, some six hundred years before Jesus was born in Bethlehem, down to the time of the end and Jesus' second coming. The stories illustrate how we are to prepare for the time of the end. They talk about faith, courage, and hope. The prophecies tell us *when*; the stories tell us *how*.

The importance of the book

Of all the books of the Bible, Daniel is the only one that Jesus Himself specifically counsels us to study. In Matthew 24, Jesus describes what the world will be like just before He returns. He talks about rising crime and violence, earthquakes and famines, and social conflicts. He pictures a world in which nation is rising against nation and kingdom against kingdom. Then He says, "Therefore when you see the 'abomination of desolation' spoken of by Daniel the prophet, standing in the holy place (whoever reads, let him understand) . . ." (Matthew 24:15).

> Prophecy enables us to understand that the Bible is not just myth, allegory, or historical drama. Prophecy and its fulfillment show us that the Bible is indeed true and that it really is God's Word.

Jesus points us to the book of Daniel in the context of a world in turmoil just before He returns. And He tells us two things we should be doing. He says (1) read Daniel's prophecies, and (2) understand them. If Jesus says to read Daniel's prophecies, and if Jesus says to understand them, it must be important to spend time studying this book.

Have you ever wondered why God gave Daniel the prophecies that appear in his book? And have you ever wondered why Daniel wrote them out for us to read and study so many hundreds of years later? What really is the purpose of prophecy? Is it just to demonstrate that God knows the future? Is it just to satisfy our curiosity?

In Matthew 24, Jesus warns us about false prophets that will arise in the days before His coming. They will try to deceive those who are waiting for His return. Then Jesus says,

"See, I have told you beforehand.
"Therefore . . . do not believe [their deceptive lies]" (verses 25, 26).

One purpose for prophecies such as those we find in Daniel is to enable us to know what's coming in order not to be deceived by Satan's deceptions. Knowing what lies ahead helps us see clearly when we are surrounded by confusion and deception.

The more we study prophecy and see its fulfillment, the more it builds our confidence in the Bible. Prophecy enables us to understand that the Bible is not just myth, allegory, or historical drama. Prophecy and its fulfillment show us that the Bible is indeed true and that it really is God's Word.

Of course, there are Bible scholars who say Daniel was not a prophet at all. Some have said that he simply made up the visions he recorded and that they were just the figment of his imagination. But many of these scholars are largely silent today because the prophecies of Daniel have been confirmed historically. They are accurate history.

Some critical Bible scholars have changed the argument against Daniel's prophecies. Before, they used to say the prophecies were just myths and allegories—that there is no archeological or historical evidence that they came true. But today, there is such an abundance of historical and archeological evidence supporting the accuracy of Daniel's prophecies that these scholars have come up with a new objection. They say, "Daniel's prophecies are so accurate that he must have written them *after* the events took place. He wasn't really a prophet; he just wrote what had already happened as if he were predicting it beforehand."

But what does Jesus say? Jesus called Daniel a "prophet" (verse 15). Jesus said we should read and understand his prophecies.

Before we get into the book of Daniel and begin studying the first chapter, we need to ask: To what specific time period do Daniel's prophecies apply? If we are to read and understand them, we need to know when they are pointing to in earth's history. In the last chapter of Daniel, God Himself answers this question. He says, "But you, Daniel, shut up the words, and seal the book *until the time of the end*" (Daniel 12:4; emphasis added). And verse 9 says, "The words are closed up and sealed till the time of the end."

The prophecies of Daniel apply to "the time of the end." To the days we are living in. To the days of social instability, warring nations, rising crime and violence, and the earthquakes and famines that Jesus described in Matthew 24 as a description of what the world would be like just before His return.

The theme of the book

The title of the book is simply *Daniel*, named for the prophet who wrote it, recording his experiences and the prophecies God gave him. Names in the Bible usually have meaning. What does the name Daniel mean? It comes from two Hebrew words. *Dan* was one of the twelve tribes of Israel—the tribe of judges. The short word, *el*, attached to *Dan*, refers to the name of God, *Elohim*. So interpreted literally, Daniel's name means "the God of judgment."

Today, when we think of a judge, we often think of someone who passes sentence on us, someone who condemns us. But that was not the Old Testament concept of judgment. In the Old Testament, a judge is the one who sets all things right, the one who pronounces righteous judgment. A judge is the one who vindicates and exonerates. One major theme of the book of Daniel is "the God of judgment and justice." The book of Daniel presents the God of the universe, who will ultimately set all things right. Kingdoms rise and fall, but God sits upon His throne, holding the destiny of the nations in His hand. In the controversy between good and evil, in the panorama between right and wrong, in the battle for the throne of the universe, the God of justice, the God of judgment, the God of righteousness will set all things right. That is the overarching theme of Daniel's book.

The controversy of good versus evil

"In the third year of the reign of Jehoiakim, king of Judah, Nebuchadnezzar king of Babylon came to Jerusalem and besieged it" (Daniel 1:1). The book begins with two cities and two kings—Babylon and Jerusalem; Nebuchadnezzar and Jehoiakim. Babylon was the center of rebellion against God, the center of confusion, the center of error, the center of apostasy. Babylon, that mighty city, attacked Jerusalem, God's city, the city of truth, the city of obedience. Right away, we are introduced to the great controversy of good versus evil. Wrong attacks right.

And in this case, wrong triumphs. Nebuchadnezzar of Babylon attacks Jerusalem and is victorious. Sometimes we hear people ask, "If God is good, why does evil so often seem to triumph?" "If God is good, why did my husband get cancer?" "If God is so good, why did my parents get divorced?" "If God is so good, why was my daughter killed by a drunk driver who walked away from the accident unhurt?" "If God is so good, why does wrong so often seem to triumph?"

There is a well-known poem by James Russell Lowell that contains these lines: "Truth forever on the scaffold, Wrong forever on the throne,—yet that scaffold sways the future, and, behind the dim unknown, standeth God within the shadow, keeping watch above his own."

Daniel chapter 1 begins with a great defeat for the true God. God's city, Jerusalem, is in ruins. God's people are in captivity and bondage. The very first verse of Daniel 1 introduces the great controversy theme—the conflict between Christ and Satan, good and evil, right and wrong. That conflict unfolds all through this first chapter. After besieging and taking Jerusalem, King Nebuchadnezzar looked at the Jewish youths and chose a few of the best of them to bring back to Babylon as captives. There they would be educated in the university of Babylon, brainwashed, and sent back to their homeland as puppet rulers. That was standard practice in the ancient world, and nations still follow that practice today.

When the Russians invaded Afghanistan, they took Afghani youth and put them in special schools in Russia, where they were taught the philosophies of Marxism and Communism. The idea was to send them back to Afghanistan to be puppet rulers for the Kremlin. Hitler often did the same with youth from the nations that he overran in World War II. After inculcating them with the philosophies of Nazi Germany, they were to return to their own countries and propagate what they had learned in Germany. And that is what King Nebuchadnezzar did as well.

The first chapter of Daniel tells us about the young people Nebuchadnezzar brought back to Babylon following his conquest of Jerusalem.

"Then the king instructed Ashpenaz, the master of his eunuchs, to bring some of the children of Israel and some of the king's descendants and some of the nobles, young men in whom there was no blemish, but good-looking, gifted in all wisdom, possessing knowledge and quick to understand, who had ability to serve in the king's palace, and whom they might teach the language and literature of the Chaldeans" (verses 3, 4).

The word translated "children" is a special Hebrew word better translated as "teenagers" or "young adults." Daniel was probably seventeen or eighteen years old when he was taken captive along with Hananiah, Mishael, and Azariah (verse 6). Notice the characteristics of these young men:

- *"No blemish, but good-looking."* Physically, they were handsome, muscular, and physically fit.
- *"Gifted in all wisdom, possessing knowledge and quick to understand."* They were intelligent, educated, and fast learners.
- *"Ability to serve in the king's palace."* These were young men who were capable of assuming responsibility, who knew how to handle themselves and fit in with those in positions of power.
- *"Whom they might teach the language and literature of the Chaldeans."* The plan was to indoctrinate them in the language and ways of Babylon.

These young men were to be enrolled in a three-year training program, at the end of which they would be tested before the king. Nebuchadnezzar appointed them a daily provision of the same food and wine that he ate and drank. They were to be educated in the culture and religion of Babylon (verse 5).

Why names matter

To complete this brainwashing process of Daniel and his three friends, the king changed their Hebrew names to Babylonian ones. He gave them names that would correspond with the heathen gods of Babylon. Daniel's name became Belteshazzar;

Hananiah was now called Shadrach; Mishael was renamed Meshach, and Azariah became Abed-Nego (verse 7).

The king wanted to change their names because he wanted to change their identities. As we have already noted, names meant something in Bible times; they were not just names. In Genesis, Jacob, whose name means "deceiver," deceived his father regarding the birthright (Genesis 27). But when Jacob met God and struggled with Him for a blessing, his name was changed from "Jacob" to "Israel" (Genesis 32). The name Israel means "one who has prevailed." A change of names means a change of character. Jacob, the deceiver, had become Israel, the one who prevails with God.

By changing the names of these Hebrew captives, Nebuchadnezzar indicated that their characters were to be changed. They were to become "Babylonians" in their outlook and loyalties. We've already noted that Daniel's name meant "the God who judges" or "God is my judge." All through his captivity in Babylon, all through this brainwashing process, all through the time that Nebuchadnezzar was trying to influence his mind, Daniel would say to himself, "My name is Daniel. God is my judge. God is on the throne. God is going to set all things right—not King Nebuchadnezzar."

What did Daniel's new name mean? The name Belteshazzar means "the keeper of the hidden treasures of Bel." In connection with Daniel's new name, there is something very interesting. In describing Nebuchadnezzar's victory over Jerusalem, Daniel 1:2 says, "The Lord gave Jehoiakim king of Judah into his [Nebuchadnezzar's] hand, with some of the articles of the house of God, which he carried into the land of Shinar to the house of his god; and he brought the articles into the treasure house of his god."

Nebuchadnezzar ordered his soldiers to take some of the sacred objects from the temple in Jerusalem and place them in the pagan temple of the Babylonian god Bel. This signified that the god of Babylon was superior to the God of the Hebrews.

Bel, sometimes known also as Marduk, was the chief deity of the thirteen gods of Babylon. Daniel's new name, Belteshazzar, means "the keeper of the hidden treasures of Bel." By this name change, the king was saying, "Daniel, God is not your judge. Jerusalem is in ruins. We have the sacred vessels from His temple that you Hebrews use in your worship of Him. Our god, Bel, is in charge of those sacred vessels now. And you are no longer 'Daniel,' but 'Belteshazzar,' the one who cooperates with Bel, the keeper of the sacred, hidden treasures that I have taken from Jerusalem."

The king did the same thing with Daniel's three friends. Hananiah's name means "the Lord is gracious to me." Growing up, every time the child said, "My name is Hananiah," he was reminded, "The Lord is gracious to me." Every time his mother called him, he was reminded, "The Lord is gracious to me." Nebuchadnezzar declared, "Your name will be 'Shadrach,' which means 'inspiration of the sun.' It is the sun god who shines graciously on you."

The name Mishael means "one who is God-like." We have a similar name in English—Michael. Mishael's name denoted one who has patience and kindness and love in a godlike way. Nebuchadnezzar changed Mishael's name to Meshach, meaning "the servant of the goddess of Sheba." Every name change Nebuchadnezzar made represented a change of focus from the God of heaven to a focus on a pagan god of Babylon. He changed Azariah's name to Abed-Nego, meaning "the servant of the god, Nebo." Azariah means "the Lord is my helper." Nebuchadnezzar was saying, "The Lord is no longer your helper. You are a captive in Babylon; you will never see your mother or father again. Your God cannot help you. You are to serve the Babylonian gods now."

Resisting the pressure to conform

Can you imagine what life was like for Daniel, Hananiah, Mishael, and Azariah during those early days in Babylon? Torn from their homes in Judah, they were confused and perplexed regarding why God had allowed the pagan Babylonians to defeat their city and carry them off to a strange, foreign land. They were just teenagers, facing incredible pressures to conform to the materialistic, sex-centered, morally jaded, thrill-seeking society all around them. All they had to do was to go along with the king's program, and a rich, secure future lay ahead. It would be so easy. To resist would be so difficult.

Why, do you think, did God begin Daniel's book with a story and not a prophecy?

God knows that at the time of the end, the days in which we live, society will attempt to brainwash His people just as the king of Babylon tried to brainwash Daniel and his friends. God doesn't start out this book with some spectacular prophecy that predicts events in the future. He starts out telling the story of a young man and his friends who are far from home. Four young men whose hearts are not in the society in which they find themselves physically. Four young men in a foreign country. Four young men who are under unbelievable pressure to go along with evil.

Some young people today say, "You know, it's impossible to really be a Christian and serve God because everybody in my high school is having premarital sex. Everybody in my high school is involved in drugs. Everybody in my high school is going to parties and drinking alcohol. It's impossible to serve God in this kind of environment." Daniel and his friends could have said the same thing. But they didn't.

Some men say, "I work in a very rough factory where everyone curses and swears, and everybody tells off-color jokes. In the environment I work in, it is impossible to serve God." Some businessmen say, "Look, you can't serve God and be completely honest. If you are going to get ahead in business, you have to cut corners here and there." Daniel and his friends could have said the same thing. But they didn't.

The battle for your mind

God begins the book of Daniel with the story of a young man in a corrupt, godless society whose mind could easily have been shaped by that society. In fact, this young man was under almost incomprehensible pressure to conform to the pressures of Babylon. But Daniel 1:8 says, "Daniel purposed in his heart that he would not defile himself with the portion of the king's delicacies, nor with the wine which he drank; therefore he requested of the chief of the eunuchs that he might not defile himself."

"Daniel *purposed* in his heart." What does that mean? It means that Daniel *decided*. It means that he *determined*. It means that he *chose*. Daniel *decided* in his heart. He *determined* in his heart. He *chose* in the inner recesses of his heart. In the Bible, particularly in the Old Testament, the "heart" is used in a special way to refer to the seat of both the intellect and the emotions. It is the center of the thought processes. Proverbs 4:23 says, "Keep your heart with all diligence." Proverbs 23:7 says, "As [a person] thinks in his heart, so is he."

The book of Daniel begins with the story of a young man who makes a settled choice in the depths of his mind and emotions that he will not defile himself by conforming to the evil around him. And it does so because the real battle at the time of the end, in the last days of earth's history, is not some battle in the Middle East. The real battle just before Jesus returns is the battle for your mind. The devil will do everything he can through this godless, secular society to influence your thought processes because the mind is the seat of your thoughts and emotions. Satan was there in Babylon, doing everything he possibly could to influence Daniel's mind and emotions through the enticements of the pagan culture around him. But Daniel "purposed in his heart that he would not defile himself." The story in Daniel chapter 1 illustrates how God would have us react to the culture in which we live. Like Daniel, we need to purpose in our hearts that we will follow God's way, not the world's way. In these remaining days of earth's history before Jesus returns, it's important that we determine that by His grace, we will remain faithful to Him and to His will for our lives.

The power to choose

You see, we are not merely highly evolved animals. We can choose. We can exercise our power to make decisions about how we will live. And if we ask Him, God will help us to carry out those decisions. The will is the governing power in our human nature that brings all other faculties under its sway. Human beings are different from the animal creation.

For example, some years ago, scientists at one of the great East Coast universities were conducting experiments with monkeys. They noted that there was an area in their brains that controlled pleasure. So these scientists connected an electrode to this "pleasure center" deep within the monkey's brain. Monkeys operate on a physical, biological level, not on the human level of reason or choice. The scientists rigged up a button that could be pushed, and every time that button was pushed, an electrical stimulation went into

> Like Daniel, we need to purpose in our hearts that we will follow God's way, not the world's way. In these remaining days of earth's history before Jesus returns, it's important that we determine that by His grace, we will remain faithful to Him and to His will for our lives.

the area of the monkey's brain that controlled pleasure. It gave the monkey a sense of feeling really happy. They put the monkey in a cage with the button to see how strong the desire would be for the monkey to experience pleasure. It wasn't long until the monkey figured out the relationship of the button to that happy feeling. It began pushing the button repeatedly.

They put a female monkey in the cage with him. He didn't even look at her; he just kept pressing the button. They put food in the cage, but he was more interested in the button. Nothing they did could distract him from the button and the pleasure it provided.

That's what the devil tries to do with us. He tries to keep us so focused on the pleasures and attractions of this world that we will have little interest in the world to come. But human beings are not monkeys. Neither are we evolved monkeys. However, there are some people who act as that monkey did. They keep returning to the things that bring them temporary, fleeting pleasures. These things may be destroying their lives even here on earth, but they continue pressing the pleasure button again and again.

God blesses Daniel's faithfulness

All the pleasures of the most powerful kingdom on earth at the time lay within

Daniel's grasp. They were his for the taking, but verse 8 says he made a decision: he decided not to defile himself with the king's food and drink. Furthermore, he decided to give God an opportunity to show His power. Daniel proposed a test.

"Daniel said to the steward whom the chief of the eunuchs had set over Daniel, Hananiah, Mishael, and Azariah, 'Please test your servants for ten days, and let them give us vegetables to eat and water to drink. Then let our appearance be examined before you, and the appearance of the young men who eat the portion of the king's delicacies; and as you see fit, so deal with your servants' " (verses 11–13).

One reason Daniel decided he would not eat the king's food and drink his wine was that it was rich, unhealthful food, much of which was "unclean" according to the regulations God had laid down for Israel. But even more important, Daniel knew that this food had been offered to the idols of the Babylonian gods before it was served to the royal household. To eat this food was to participate in the ceremony of idolatry. Daniel would not eat food that had been offered to idols. Doing so would be acknowledging the deity of these pagan gods. It would be repudiating the God of heaven.

When Daniel purposed in his heart to serve God, God purposed in His heart to bless Daniel. What was the result of this ten-day test?

> At the end of ten days their features appeared better and fatter in flesh than all the young men who ate the portion of the king's delicacies. Thus the steward took away their portion of delicacies and the wine that they were to drink, and gave them vegetables.
>
> As for these four young men, God gave them knowledge and skill in all literature and wisdom; and Daniel had understanding in all visions and dreams.
>
> Now at the end of the days, when the king had said that they should be brought in, the chief of the eunuchs brought them in before Nebuchadnezzar. Then the king interviewed them, and among them all none was found like Daniel, Hananiah, Mishael, and Azariah; therefore they served before the king. And in all matters of wisdom and understanding about which the king examined them, he found them ten times better than all the magicians and astrologers who were in all his realm (verses 15–20).

God blessed Daniel's faithfulness with health and wisdom. As the king examined the captives he had brought from his conquest of Jerusalem, Daniel and his friends who had remained faithful to God stood out in stark contrast to the young men who had compromised their principles by eating the king's idolatrous food.

God will bless you as He did Daniel

During the three years of training, the steward "took away their portion of delicacies and the wine that they were to drink" (verse 16). When a person decides to remain faithful to what he or she knows is right, there will always be things that will be taken away. But God will replace them with things that are better. He will pour out His blessings "pressed down, shaken together, and running over" (Luke 6:38). Unless you allow God to take away the things that separate you from Him, you cannot receive the rich blessings He has in store for you.

There are three steps to receiving God's blessings in your life, as did Daniel and his friends.

First, determine to please God. Like Daniel, purpose in your heart to do nothing that you consciously know displeases God.

Second, allow God to take away the obstacles. When God puts His finger on some sin in your life, no matter how much you cherish that thing, no matter how much pleasure it gives you to push that button, recognize that God knows how to please you even more than you know how to please yourself. If you do that, you will be much happier in life. Allow God to take away any obstacles in your life and open your heart to receive His rich blessings.

Third, rely on God's power and grace to enable you to follow through on the decision you have made to be faithful to Him. It's true that we are weak and that in our own strength, we often are unable to do the things we know we should—the things we *want* to do. Even the great apostle Paul had this problem. He says, "The good that I will to do, I do not do; but the evil I will not to do, that I practice" (Romans 7:19). We can all identify with Paul on that! What is the answer? The apostle goes on to say, "O wretched man that I am! Who will deliver me . . . ? I thank God—through Jesus Christ our Lord!" (verses 24, 25). When we purpose in our heart to be faithful to God, He will help us. He will give us the power to resist temptation and do what is right.

Good triumphs over evil

Daniel chapter 1 begins with a great defeat for the true God. God's city, Jerusalem, is in ruins. God's man, Daniel, and his friends are in captivity. Evil seems to have triumphed over good. But when we come to the end of this first chapter, Daniel and his friends have triumphed over the temptations of Babylon. They have stood up faithfully for the God of heaven, and God has demonstrated His power in their lives.

"None was found like Daniel, Hananiah, Mishael, and Azariah; therefore they served before the king. And in all matters of wisdom and understanding about which

21

the king examined them, he found them ten times better than all the magicians and astrologers who were in all his realm" (verses 19, 20).

Daniel graduated with his PhD from the university of Babylon, untarnished. God's man stood as a stalwart witness of honesty and integrity.

Tucked away in the last verse of chapter 1 are words that are filled with meaning— "Thus Daniel continued until the first year of King Cyrus" (verse 21). Kings rise and fall. Empires rise and fall. Babylon was the dominant world empire from 605 to 539 B.C. Nebuchadnezzar was followed on the throne by his son and grandson. But the Bible says that Daniel continued from the kingdom of Babylon to the kingdom of Media-Persia. Through all the long years of his life, Daniel served God. Like Daniel, there are men and women in our world today who have one overriding desire in life—a passion in their hearts to serve God. And, like Daniel, they will continue. The Babylons of this world will collapse like a deck of cards. The cheap tinsel of secularism and godlessness is soon to crumble like a sandcastle before the waves, but there is a new King coming. God's men and God's women who purpose in their hearts to serve Him will pass from one kingdom to the next, and live forever and ever and ever.

That's the message that Daniel chapter 1 has for us today. God will bless those who purpose in their hearts to remain faithful to Him, and they will live with Him forever.

THE GOD WHO REVEALS THE FUTURE

Daniel 2

1 Now in the second year of Nebuchadnezzar's reign, Nebuchadnezzar had dreams; and his spirit was so troubled that his sleep left him. **2** Then the king gave the command to call the magicians, the astrologers, the sorcerers, and the Chaldeans to tell the king his dreams. So they came and stood before the king. **3** And the king said to them, "I have had a dream, and my spirit is anxious to know the dream."

4 Then the Chaldeans spoke to the king in Aramaic, "O king, live forever! Tell your servants the dream, and we will give the interpretation."

5 The king answered and said to the Chaldeans, "My decision is firm: if you do not make known the dream to me, and its interpretation, you shall be cut in pieces, and your houses shall be made an ash heap. **6** However, if you tell the dream and its interpretation, you shall receive from me gifts, rewards, and great honor. Therefore tell me the dream and its interpretation."

7 They answered again and said, "Let the king tell his servants the dream, and we will give its interpretation."

8 The king answered and said, "I know for certain that you would gain time, because you see that my decision is firm: **9** if you do not make known the dream to me, there is only one decree for you! For you have agreed to speak lying and corrupt words before me till the time has changed. Therefore tell me the dream, and I shall know that you can give me its interpretation."

10 The Chaldeans answered the king, and said, "There is not a man on earth who can tell the king's matter; therefore no king, lord, or ruler has ever asked such things of any magician, astrologer, or Chaldean. **11** It is a difficult thing that the king requests, and there is no other who can tell it to the king except the gods, whose dwelling is not with flesh."

12 For this reason the king was angry and very furious, and gave the command

to destroy all the wise men of Babylon. **13** So the decree went out, and they began killing the wise men; and they sought Daniel and his companions, to kill them.

14 Then with counsel and wisdom Daniel answered Arioch, the captain of the king's guard, who had gone out to kill the wise men of Babylon; **15** he answered and said to Arioch the king's captain, "Why is the decree from the king so urgent?" Then Arioch made the decision known to Daniel.

16 So Daniel went in and asked the king to give him time, that he might tell the king the interpretation. **17** Then Daniel went to his house, and made the decision known to Hananiah, Mishael, and Azariah, his companions, **18** that they might seek mercies from the God of heaven concerning this secret, so that Daniel and his companions might not perish with the rest of the wise men of Babylon. **19** Then the secret was revealed to Daniel in a night vision. So Daniel blessed the God of heaven.

20 Daniel answered and said:

"Blessed be the name of God forever
  and ever,
For wisdom and might are His.
21 And He changes the times and the
  seasons;
He removes kings and raises up kings;
He gives wisdom to the wise
And knowledge to those who have
  understanding.

22 He reveals deep and secret things;
He knows what is in the darkness,
And light dwells with Him.

23 "I thank You and praise You,
O God of my fathers;
You have given me wisdom and might,
And have now made known to me
  what we asked of You,
For You have made known to us the
  king's demand."

24 Therefore Daniel went to Arioch, whom the king had appointed to destroy the wise men of Babylon. He went and said thus to him: "Do not destroy the wise men of Babylon; take me before the king, and I will tell the king the interpretation."

25 Then Arioch quickly brought Daniel before the king, and said thus to him, "I have found a man of the captives of Judah, who will make known to the king the interpretation."

26 The king answered and said to Daniel, whose name was Belteshazzar, "Are you able to make known to me the dream which I have seen, and its interpretation?"

27 Daniel answered in the presence of the king, and said, "The secret which the king has demanded, the wise men, the astrologers, the magicians, and the soothsayers cannot declare to the king. **28** But there is a God in heaven who reveals secrets, and He has made known to King Nebuchadnezzar what will be in the latter days. Your dream, and the visions of your head upon your bed, were these: **29** As for you, O king, thoughts came to your mind while on your bed, about what would come to pass after this; and He who reveals secrets has made known to you what will be. **30** But as for me, this secret has not been revealed to me because I have more wisdom than anyone living, but for our sakes who make known the interpretation to the king, and that you may know the thoughts of your heart.

31 "You, O king, were watching; and behold, a great image! This great image, whose splendor was excellent, stood before you; and its form was awesome. **32** This image's head was of fine gold, its chest and arms of silver, its belly and thighs of bronze, **33** its legs of iron, its feet partly of iron and partly of clay. **34** You watched while a stone was cut out without hands, which struck the image on its feet of iron and clay, and broke them in pieces. **35** Then the iron, the clay, the bronze, the silver, and the gold were crushed together, and became like chaff from the summer threshing floors; the wind carried them away so that no trace of them was found. And the stone that struck the image became a great mountain and filled the whole earth.

36 "This is the dream. Now we will tell the interpretation of it before the king. **37** You, O king, are a king of kings. For the God of heaven has given you a kingdom, power, strength, and glory; **38** and wherever the children of men dwell, or the beasts of the field and the birds of the heaven, He has given them into your hand, and has made you ruler over them all—you are this head of gold. **39** But after you shall arise another kingdom inferior to yours; then another, a third kingdom of bronze, which shall rule over all the earth. **40** And the fourth kingdom shall be as strong as iron, inasmuch as iron breaks in pieces and shatters everything; and like iron that crushes, that kingdom will break in pieces and crush all the others. **41** Whereas you saw the feet and toes, partly of potter's clay and partly of iron, the kingdom shall be divided; yet the strength of the iron shall be in it, just as you saw the iron mixed with ceramic clay. **42** And as the toes of the feet were partly of iron and partly of clay, so the kingdom shall be partly strong and partly fragile. **43** As you saw iron mixed with ceramic clay, they will mingle with the seed of men; but they will not adhere to one another, just as iron does not mix with clay. **44** And in the days of these kings the God of heaven will set up a kingdom which shall never be destroyed; and the kingdom shall not be left to other people; it shall break in pieces and consume all these kingdoms, and it shall stand forever. **45** Inasmuch as you saw that the stone was cut out of the mountain without hands, and that it broke in pieces the iron, the bronze, the clay, the silver, and the gold—the great God has made known to the king what will come to pass after this. The dream is certain, and its interpretation is sure."

46 Then King Nebuchadnezzar fell on his face, prostrate before Daniel, and commanded that they should present an offering and incense to him. **47** The king answered Daniel, and said, "Truly your God is the God of gods, the Lord of kings, and a revealer of secrets, since you could reveal this secret." **48** Then the king promoted Daniel and gave him many great gifts; and he made him ruler over the whole province of Babylon, and chief administrator over all the wise men of Babylon. **49** Also Daniel petitioned the king, and he set Shadrach, Meshach, and Abed-Nego over the affairs of the province of Babylon; but Daniel sat in the gate of the king.

❧

In the second chapter of Daniel, God reveals to us a dream He gave to Nebuchadnezzar—a dream that predicted the future some 2,500 years in advance. We have trouble today predicting the weather even a few days ahead. Every year in January, the supermarket tabloids headline their predictions for the coming months—and they are almost always wildly wrong. But the amazing thing about the predictions found in Daniel 2 is that they have been accurately fulfilled for the last 2,500 years! Many details of this prophetic dream have already come to pass. And that gives us confidence that the parts remaining to be fulfilled will happen just as God has said they would. So let's look at this amazing dream and what it means for us today.

Remember, Daniel 1 leaves us with Daniel firmly in place in the royal palace in Babylon, as an advisor to the king. He is one of a group of counselors and advisors to the court. God had given him "understanding in all visions and dreams" (Daniel 1:17). That understanding is about to be put to the test.

God speaks in a dream

"In the second year of Nebuchadnezzar's reign, Nebuchadnezzar had dreams; and his spirit was so troubled that his sleep left him. Then the king gave the command to call the magicians, the astrologers, the sorcerers, and the Chaldeans to tell the king his dreams. So they came and stood before the king. And the king said to them, 'I have had a dream, and my spirit is anxious to know the dream' " (Daniel 2:1–3).

In ancient times, dreams were considered an important way through which the gods communicated with humans. Today, we don't look at dreams like that. We think of dreams as the mind pulling together a variety of thoughts and experiences and other things into a convoluted, often confusing, mix. We don't think of them as God trying to tell us something, but that was not the way people looked at dreams in Daniel's day.

King Nebuchadnezzar had a dream that troubled him greatly. It woke him up, and he couldn't go back to sleep. He also couldn't remember what he had dreamed. He knew it was important, but he couldn't recall the dream. So he called his team of advisors—the magicians and the astrologers and the sorcerers. "I've had a dream," he told them, "and I'm anxious to know what it means."

They replied, "O king, live forever! Tell your servants the dream, and we will give the interpretation" (verse 4). Of course, Nebuchadnezzar couldn't tell them the dream, because he couldn't remember it.

Now, it might seem to you that the king was being unreasonable. How could he expect his advisors to know what he had dreamed?

But that was exactly what these "magicians" and "astrologers" and "sorcerers" were supposed to be able to do. They were supposed to be in touch with the gods. They were supposed to be able to know things that ordinary people had no way of knowing. The gods were supposed to speak to them and give them special insight and knowledge. So when they asked to know his dream before they could interpret it for him, Nebuchadnezzar knew exactly what they were doing. Once they knew the dream, they would be able to come up with an interpretation that they thought would please him.

"The king answered and said, 'I know for certain that you would gain time, because you see that my decision is firm: if you do not make known the dream to me, there is only one decree for you! For you have agreed to speak lying and corrupt words before me till the time has changed. Therefore tell me the dream, and I shall know that you can give me its interpretation' " (verses 8, 9).

Daniel becomes involved

If his brain trust couldn't tell the king what he dreamed the night before, how could they tell him what would happen in the future? As they continued negotiating back and forth, the king became furious. He gave the command "to destroy all the wise men of Babylon. So the decree went out, and they began killing the wise men; and they sought Daniel and his companions, to kill them" (verses 12, 13).

Daniel was not one of these magicians and astrologers and sorcerers. He was not a psychic, but he was part of the educated elite. He was one of the king's advisors, and the death decree applied to him as well. Apparently, Daniel was not in the room when the back and forth was going on between the king and these magicians because the king's soldiers came looking for him as they carried out the decree to put these advisors to death (verse 13). He didn't know what was going on (verse 15). But when he learned why the king was so angry and how urgently Nebuchadnezzar wanted to know what he had dreamed and what it meant, "Daniel went in and asked the king to give him time, that he might tell the king the interpretation" (verse 16).

Think about what this verse implies. Think about the faith required on Daniel's part to do what he did. When he went to ask Nebuchadnezzar for time, did Daniel have any idea what the king had dreamed? No, he did not. Did he have any idea what the interpretation of the dream might involve? No. But *he had faith* that God would make all this known to him. And Nebuchadnezzar, also, must have believed that Daniel could fulfill what he promised.

"Then Daniel went to his house, and made the decision known to Hananiah, Mishael, and Azariah, his companions, that they might seek mercies from the God of heaven concerning this secret, so that Daniel and his companions might not perish with the rest of the wise men of Babylon. Then the secret was revealed to Daniel in a night vision. So Daniel blessed the God of heaven" (verses 17–19).

Daniel didn't know what the king had dreamed, but he knew Someone who did. He didn't know the interpretation, but he knew Someone who did. And he knew what to do. In the secret place of prayer, Daniel and his friends found the answer to the dilemma they faced. "The secret was revealed to Daniel in a night vision" (verse 19).

In the crisis at the close of this earth's history, we are going to face many problems that we will never be able to go through unless we know how to pray. There are problems that we all face every day right now—problems in our marriages, problems in our homes with our kids, financial problems, health problems. We need to bring these to the Lord in prayer. Yes, sometimes there are individuals who can help with our everyday problems. There are doctors and financial advisors and family counselors. We need to take advantage of all these human resources. But rather than waiting until we come to the end of our ability to deal with things, it is important to recognize that God is always there. Day by day in the secret place of prayer, we can receive strength from God so that when the problems come, we have the inner resolve to thrive in the midst of life's challenges.

There was no human being who could solve Daniel's problem. And when we go into the crisis of the end time, we, too, will find that God is the only solution to the issues we face. Like Daniel and his friends, we will need to "seek mercies from the God of heaven" (verse 18). In the crisis of his life, Daniel found the answer in the secret place of prayer, and that is where you will find answers too.

Daniel explains the dream

Armed with the knowledge he had received from God, Daniel went in before the king and said: "The secret which the king has demanded, the wise men, the astrologers, the magicians, and the soothsayers cannot declare to the king. But there is a God in heaven who reveals secrets, and he has made known to King Nebuchadnezzar what will be in the latter days" (verses 27, 28).

Daniel was careful not to take personal credit for being able to reveal the king's dream (see verse 30). "There is a God in heaven," he said, "who reveals secrets." It would have been easy to build up his credibility and power with the king by pointing to himself as the one who was able to do what none of the other of the king's advisors could do. But Daniel pointed, instead, to the God of heaven. With certainty and assurance, he announced, "There *is* a God in heaven." Not "maybe." Not "perhaps." Not "I think so." There *is* a God in heaven.

Notice, too, what Daniel says about the focus of the dream. God "has made known to King Nebuchadnezzar *what will be in the latter days*" (verse 28; emphasis added.) So wherever this dream may begin, it ends "in the latter days." This is a dream that takes us down the corridors of time to the final days of earth's history. Let's take a look at the king's dream.

> "You, O king, were watching; and behold, a great image! This great image, whose splendor was excellent, stood before you; and its form was awesome. This image's head was of fine gold, its chest and arms of silver, its belly and thighs of bronze, its legs of iron, its feet partly of iron and partly of clay. You watched while a stone was cut out without hands, which struck the image on its feet of iron and clay, and broke them in pieces. Then the iron, the clay, the bronze, the silver, and the gold were crushed together, and became like chaff from the summer threshing floors; the wind carried them away so that no trace of them was found. And the stone that struck the image became a great mountain and filled the whole earth" (verses 31–35).

Can't you just imagine how Nebuchadnezzar must have reacted when he heard Daniel describe his dream? "Yes! That's just what I saw. I remember now this huge image of different metals and the rock that came and smashed it all to pieces! It's all coming back to me now." The Bible doesn't tell us the king's reaction, but it must have been something like that. He had been so troubled by this dream that he couldn't remember. He knew it was important, but it remained tantalizingly out of reach of his memory. Now Daniel had brought it all back to him. But, of course, the really important question was, What does it mean? What is the interpretation?

Now, some people say that Bible prophecy is just a matter of personal interpretation—that we can make a prophecy mean whatever we think it should mean. We can read into it anything we like. But doesn't it make sense that the God who gave the prophecy would also provide the correct interpretation of the prophecy? Wouldn't that be a logical conclusion? If God gave Nebuchadnezzar a dream that applied to the last days, wouldn't Daniel's explanation of that dream be the one that God gave him? So let's see how God interpreted the dream He gave to Nebuchadnezzar and explained to Daniel.

Babylon, the head of gold

Daniel begins by saying, "You, O king, are a king of kings. For the God of heaven has given you a kingdom, power, strength, and glory; and wherever the children of men dwell, or the beasts of the field and the birds of the heaven, He has given them into your hand, and has made you ruler over them all—you are this head of gold" (verses 37, 38).

Who was represented by the head of gold—Nebuchadnezzar or Nebuchadnezzar's kingdom? The text says, "*You* are this head of gold" (verse 38; emphasis added), referring to Nebuchadnezzar. But let's look further. As we will see in the succeeding verses of the interpretation, the remaining metals of the image represent kingdoms—not the individual rulers of those kingdoms. So it makes sense to understand that when Daniel told Nebuchadnezzar, "You are this head of gold," he was referring primarily to the kingdom of Babylon over which Nebuchadnezzar ruled. God was giving Nebuchadnezzar a summary of world history and of the successive kingdoms that would be world powers from his day down to the very end of time. The four metals of the image, in descending value, represent four great world kingdoms. The first, the head of gold, represents Babylon. Daniel's interpretation of the image doesn't name the kingdoms that would follow Babylon on the world stage. But Daniel chapter 8 identifies two of them as Media-Persia and Greece.

As Nebuchadnezzar listened with rapt attention, Daniel continued the interpretation he had received from God. "You, O king, are a king of kings. . . . But after you shall arise another kingdom inferior to yours; then another, a third kingdom of bronze, which shall rule over all the earth" (verses 37, 39).

The head of gold represents Babylon. The image's silver chest and arms represent the next world kingdom after Babylon, and that kingdom was Media-Persia. The thighs of bronze represent Greece, the nation that would follow Media-Persia. Then the Bible says there would be a fourth world kingdom represented by the iron legs and feet of the image.

"The fourth kingdom shall be as strong as iron, inasmuch as iron breaks in pieces and shatters everything; and like iron that crushes, that kingdom will break in pieces and crush all the others. Whereas you saw the feet and toes, partly of potter's clay and partly of iron, the kingdom shall be divided; yet the strength of the iron shall be in it, just as you saw the iron mixed with ceramic clay. And as the toes of the feet were partly of iron and partly of clay, so the kingdom shall be partly strong and partly fragile. As you saw iron mixed with ceramic clay, they will mingle with the seed of men; but they will not adhere to one another, just as iron does not mix with clay" (verses 40–43).

What kingdom does history tell us followed Greece as a world power? Rome. The iron empire of Rome ruled the world following Greece. History has unfolded just as Nebuchadnezzar's dream predicted, following the blueprint God gave centuries in advance. Let's review the miraculous accuracy of this prophecy.

Babylon, represented by the head of gold, ruled the world from 605 to 539 B.C. Gold was a very apt symbol of Babylon. Babylon's wealth was unparalleled. In fact, Marduk, the god of Babylon, sat on a golden throne beside a golden table next to a golden candlestick in a golden-domed temple. The prophet Jeremiah pictured Babylon as "a golden cup in the LORD's hand" (Jeremiah 51:7).

Media-Persia, the chest and arms of silver

But then another empire was to follow Babylon—Media-Persia, symbolized by the chest and arms of silver. The Medes and Persians overthrew Babylon in 539 B.C.

Babylon was such a mighty empire that it seems unthinkable it could be overthrown. Its capital city had walls over 100 feet high and wide enough for two chariots to race along the top side-by-side. The Euphrates River ran through the city of Babylon, providing it with a constant water supply. In those days, when one nation attacked another, its soldiers would surround the enemy's city and lay siege to it, preventing food from coming in. Reliable historians tell us that Babylon had a twenty-year food supply within the city. It was a well-fortified city that seemed invincible. The river Euphrates supplied it with its fresh water. Its armies comprised one of the largest and strongest fighting forces in the ancient world. Its wealth was unparalleled, and its fortifications appeared unconquerable.

So how did Babylon fall to Media-Persia? Let's look at an amazing prophecy in the book of Isaiah. In this prophecy, God not only named the leader who would overthrow Babylon but also the strategy that he would use to overcome the city.

> "Thus says the LORD to His anointed,
> To Cyrus, whose right hand I have held—
> To subdue nations before him
> And loose the armor of kings,
> To open before him the double doors,
> So that the gates will not be shut:
> 'I will go before you . . .
> I will break in pieces the gates of bronze' " (Isaiah 45:1, 2).

> "Thus says the LORD . . .
> '. . . I will dry up your rivers';
> Who says of Cyrus, 'He is My shepherd,
> And he shall perform all My pleasure' " (Isaiah 44:24–28).

More than a hundred years before Cyrus was born, God named him as the man who would overthrow Babylon! The psychics may make guesses; the astrologers and magicians may throw out their idle speculations, but God *knows*! Prophecy doesn't guess because it looks into the future with the eyes of the all-seeing God.

In 539 B.C. Cyrus, the Persian ruler, and Darius the Mede, of the joint Medo-Persian Empire, led their armies to overthrow Babylon. Over a century earlier, God had said this would happen. He knows the future. How did the fall of Babylon take place?

The Euphrates River ran through Babylon. And where it entered and exited the city, there were huge gates that could be closed to seal off the city from invaders. But Cyrus dug large tributaries, or canals, upriver from the city. He diverted the river into these channels, which stopped the water flow of the river. He then marched his soldiers down the empty riverbed and under the city gates.

But Babylon also had walls along the river within the city for just such an emergency. Anyone who pierced the main city walls, where the river entered, still had to get past these inner walls along the riverbanks within the city. The night of Cyrus's attack, the "double doors" of these inner walls had been left open because a drunken feast was going on. And so the river was dried up, the doors were left open, and

Cyrus marched into the city and overthrew it.

God had foretold all this more than a century earlier—even mentioning Cyrus by name! Prophecy does not guess. Media-Persia followed Babylon as the dominant world empire just as Daniel told King Nebuchadnezzar it would. It ruled from 539 to 331 B.C.

Greece, the belly and thighs of bronze

Daniel continued his interpretation of the king's dream. A third world kingdom would arise, he said, symbolized by the bronze belly and thighs of the image. The nation of Greece ruled the world from 331 to 168 B.C.

The powerful Greek leader Alexander the Great, at thirty-two years old, expanded the Greek Empire throughout the Mediterranean region. A brilliant military strategist, ruthless warrior, and relentless fighter, Alexander himself often led his soldiers into combat. By the time Alexander was thirty-three, Greece was a dominant world power. Nation after nation fell before its attacks. One historian states that Alexander lamented because there were no more worlds to conquer. History was following this prophecy like a blueprint.

Alexander planned to rebuild the temple tower at Babylon. He wanted to make Babylon a provincial capital. For two months, ten thousand men worked to clear away the debris from Babylon. Then Alexander died suddenly, weakened by malaria and overcome with alcohol, and the project was abandoned.

Alexander and Jesus both died at thirty-three. When Jesus was thirty-three years old, He hung on a cross with nails through His hands and feet and a crown of thorns on His head. One had all the kingdoms of this world but died having nothing of real value; the other had nothing in this world but died victorious, having everything of real value. When we come to our last day and are staring death in the face, only one thing really matters—knowing God. The only thing that matters then is the assurance that your life is safe in His hands and that you will live forever with Him in His kingdom. Alexander didn't have that assurance. He went to his grave not knowing the peace that comes only from this personal, intimate relationship with the Creator of the universe. There is a sense of inner contentment and deep joy in the assurance that there is a God in heaven who is guiding the affairs of your life. When you have the certainty that you are not some speck of cosmic dust in the universe but are created in the image of God and have untold value in His sight, your life takes on a new depth of meaning.

Rome, the legs of iron

Greece, in turn, would fade away and give place to another world kingdom. In 168

B.C., the "iron empire" of Rome conquered Greece at the battle of Pydna, marking its rise to world dominion. World history had reached the place in Nebuchadnezzar's dream represented by the iron portion of the great image. The Romans united their empire with a system of Roman roads, the worship of Roman gods, Roman culture, Roman governors, and a strong, ruthless Roman military that immediately suppressed all opposition. Rome ruled with an iron fist.

Edward Gibbon wrote in his world-renowned book *The Decline and Fall of the Roman Empire*, "The images of gold, or silver, or brass, that might serve to represent the nations and their kings, were successfully broken by the iron monarchy of Rome." Isn't it amazing that the historian uses the very words of Bible prophecy to describe these legs of iron?

It's noteworthy that the image the king saw in his dream was composed of different metals—gold, silver, bronze, and iron—in descending order of value. The feet of the image were made of iron mixed with clay. Could this be telling us that the world is becoming increasingly unstable? Economically, nations teeter on the verge of financial disaster. Global warming seriously impacts our environment. Killer storms are becoming more frequent. Crime and violence are increasing, and school shootings have become commonplace. The nations possessing nuclear weapons are gradually and increasingly making our world less safe.

Additionally, moral values and ethical principles are rapidly deteriorating. The Bible warns of just such a time in the last days. The apostle Paul says, "Know this, that in the last days perilous times will come: For men will be lovers of themselves, lovers of money, boasters, proud, blasphemers, disobedient to parents, unthankful, unholy, unloving, unforgiving, slanderers, without self-control, brutal, despisers of good, traitors, headstrong, haughty, lovers of pleasure rather than lovers of God, having a form of godliness but denying its power" (2 Timothy 3:1–5).

The prophecy of Daniel 2 predicts a succession of four world kingdoms that will follow each other—Babylon, Media-Persia, Greece, and Rome. Four kingdoms—not five, not six, but four. This prophecy is not some general, vague prediction like many of the ones we find in the supermarket tabloids. It is exact and specific—four world kingdoms. The book of Daniel even names three of them—Babylon, Media-Persia, and Greece (Daniel 2:36–38; 8:19–21). What does the prophecy say will happen following the iron empire of Rome?

"The fourth kingdom shall be as strong as iron, inasmuch as iron breaks in pieces and shatters everything; and like iron that crushes, that kingdom will break in pieces and crush all the others. Whereas you saw the feet and toes, partly of potter's clay and partly of iron, the kingdom shall be divided; yet the strength of the iron shall be in it, just as you saw the iron mixed with ceramic clay. And as the toes of the feet were partly of iron and partly of clay, so the kingdom shall be partly strong and partly fragile. As you saw iron mixed with ceramic clay, they will mingle with the seed of men; but they will not adhere to one another, just as iron does not mix with clay" (Daniel 2:40–43).

The feet of iron and clay

Notice this prophecy says there would *not* be a fifth world-ruling empire that would follow Rome. But what does the prophecy reveal would take place after Babylon, the head of gold; Persia, the chest and arms of silver; Greece, the thighs of brass, and Rome, the legs of iron? If we made an educated guess, based on simple logic, we would probably predict more of the same. We might surmise that additional nations described by additional metals would arise. It is only logical to assume that after four ruling nations, there would be a fifth, a sixth and a seventh, and so on. The march of history would continue. But here we are in for a surprise.

What do we know about the fall of the fourth nation in the sequence, Rome? Was Rome conquered by a fifth great empire? No! It was broken up and divided. This is exactly what Nebuchadnezzar's dream predicted. The iron was not followed another powerful metal, but by feet and toes of clay and iron, two things that will absolutely not stick together. Daniel 2:41 declares, "Whereas you saw the feet and toes, partly of potter's clay and partly of iron, the kingdom shall be divided."

Contrary to logic? Yes, most definitely, but it happened just as the Bible predicted: barbarian tribes invaded from the north, attacked the Roman Empire, and tore it apart. The Franks conquered and then settled in the area that we now know as France. The Anglo-Saxons invaded England. The Alemanni overran Germany. The Heruli occupied Italy. The Visigoths dominated southern Spain. The Suevi established themselves in Portugal, and the Vandals settled in Northern Africa. The old Roman Empire was divided just as the prophecy forecast, and the map of Europe today reflects in part these ancient divisions. Although the borders of the countries have shifted due to additional wars through the centuries, the divided state of Europe still reflects the accuracy of this ancient prophecy.

Daniel's prophecy declares that the iron kingdom would be divided, and that is just what happened. From A.D. 351 to A.D. 476, Rome fell apart through laziness, corruption, and immorality within. Rome would fracture into numerous kingdoms symbolized by the ten toes. During the fourth and fifth centuries (351 to 476), barbaric invaders from the north poured down on the decaying Roman Empire, delivering blow after blow. Eventually, numerous independent nations established themselves within the boundaries of what today is western Europe. Some of these were strong like iron; others were brittle and weak like clay, just as the prophecy predicted. These became the forerunners of the modern nations of Europe. The statue's toes of iron mixed with clay represent these nations into which the Roman Empire was divided. The prophecy was literally fulfilled, and history again harmonizes with what God foretold. History is following the Bible like a blueprint.

Notice verse 43. "As you saw iron mixed with ceramic clay, they [the nations of the divided Roman Empire] will mingle with the seed of men; but they will not adhere to one another, just as iron does not mix with clay." There would be attempts to bring together these nations of a divided Rome and reunite them into a single world power. They would mingle themselves "with the seed of men." The history of Europe is a history of kings arising and attempting to marry off their sons and daughters to the children of kings of other powerful nations in order to unite and form major family units that could dominate all Europe. At times in history, many of the rulers of Europe were closely related to one another. Others, such as Napoleon and Hitler, tried to unite the nations of Europe into a single empire through war and conquest. But all these attempts to bring about a fifth world empire have failed. God's Word said, "They will not adhere to one another, just as iron does not mix with clay" (verse 43).

> We are living the days just before the rock strikes the kingdoms of this world and breaks them all in pieces so that the God of heaven can establish His everlasting kingdom of peace and righteousness.

Those words have stopped every would-be ruler of a fifth world empire. For a time, it looked as though Communism was spreading beyond the bounds of Russia down into Ukraine, out into Hungary, Poland, Romania, Bulgaria, and Yugoslavia. But it, too, was stopped. Why? Because God's Word says, "They will not adhere to one another." Prophecy doesn't guess or wish or hope. It is certain because God is guiding the destiny of the nations.

The rock that breaks in pieces

Now notice the great climax of the prophecy of Daniel 2: "In the days of these kings the God of heaven will set up a kingdom which shall never be destroyed; and the kingdom shall not be left to other people; it shall break in pieces and consume all these kingdoms, and it shall stand forever. Inasmuch as you saw that the stone was cut out of the mountain without hands, and that it broke in pieces the iron, the bronze, the clay, the silver, and the gold—the great God has made known to the king what will come to pass after this. The dream is certain, and its interpretation is sure" (verses 44, 45).

The rock cut out of the mountain without hands clearly represents the eternal, everlasting kingdom of Jesus Christ. The prophecy says that God's kingdom will be set up "in the days of these kings"—the nations of modern Europe that formed out of the divisions of the Roman Empire. We are living today—not in the head of gold, not in the chest and arms of silver, not in the thighs of brass, not in the legs of iron, not even in the days of the feet of iron and clay. We are living in the very toenails of history! We are living the days just before the rock strikes the kingdoms of this world and breaks them all in pieces so that the God of heaven can establish His everlasting kingdom of peace and righteousness.

This world will not end in some great nuclear holocaust. This world will not end in some overwhelming famine. This world will not end with some massive earthquake. It will not end with some human catastrophe. Babylon rose and fell. Media-Persia rose and fell. Greece rose and fell. Rome rose and fell. The Roman Empire was divided. Political leaders attempted to unite Europe. They didn't succeed. For 2,500 years, this prophecy has been accurate in each precise detail. For 2,500 years, prophecy has been fulfilled in each minute detail. And God says that the next event in the prophecy is the rock cut out without hands—His everlasting kingdom.

Throughout the Bible, Jesus Christ is symbolized as the great Rock of Ages. He is solid and immovable. He is permanent and eternal. Babylon had its moment in the sun of fame and glory. So did Media-Persia and Greece and Rome. But those kingdoms have come and gone. Christ's eternal kingdom is on the way. We are living at the end of time. Daniel's words to the ancient Babylonian king speak in trumpet tones to this generation, "The dream is certain. The interpretation is sure." To a generation seeking for answers regarding the future, God's Word presents certainty. The kingdom of God will soon be established. Suffering will soon be over. The kingdoms of this earth will give way to the kingdom of God.

When Daniel finished interpreting the king's dream, Nebuchadnezzar "fell on his face" before the prophet and proclaimed, "Truly your God is the God of gods, the Lord of kings, and a revealer of secrets" (verse 47). He made Daniel "chief administrator of over all the wise men of Babylon" (verse 48). To his credit, Nebuchadnezzar accepted this word from the God of heaven. Once again, Daniel's faithfulness to his God had made an impact on the pagan ruler of Babylon, although it would not be a lasting one, as we shall see in Daniel chapter 3.

THE GOD WHO DELIVERS HIS PEOPLE

Daniel 3

1 Nebuchadnezzar the king made an image of gold, whose height was sixty cubits and its width six cubits. He set it up in the plain of Dura, in the province of Babylon. **2** And King Nebuchadnezzar sent word to gather together the satraps, the administrators, the governors, the counselors, the treasurers, the judges, the magistrates, and all the officials of the provinces, to come to the dedication of the image which King Nebuchadnezzar had set up. **3** So the satraps, the administrators, the governors, the counselors, the treasurers, the judges, the magistrates, and all the officials of the provinces gathered together for the dedication of the image that King Nebuchadnezzar had set up; and they stood before the image that Nebuchadnezzar had set up. **4** Then a herald cried aloud: "To you it is commanded, O peoples, nations, and languages, **5** that at the time you hear the sound of the horn, flute, harp, lyre, and psaltery, in symphony with all kinds of music, you shall fall down and worship the gold image that King Nebuchadnezzar has set up; **6** and whoever does not fall down and worship shall be cast immediately into the midst of a burning fiery furnace."

7 So at that time, when all the people heard the sound of the horn, flute, harp, and lyre, in symphony with all kinds of music, all the people, nations, and languages fell down and worshiped the gold image which King Nebuchadnezzar had set up.

8 Therefore at that time certain Chaldeans came forward and accused the Jews. **9** They spoke and said to King Nebuchadnezzar, "O king, live forever! **10** You, O king, have made a decree that everyone who hears the sound of the horn, flute, harp, lyre, and psaltery, in symphony with all kinds of music, shall fall down and worship the gold image; **11** and whoever does not fall down and worship shall be cast into the midst of a burning fiery furnace. **12** There are certain Jews whom you have set over

the affairs of the province of Babylon: Shadrach, Meshach, and Abed-Nego; these men, O king, have not paid due regard to you. They do not serve your gods or worship the gold image which you have set up."

13 Then Nebuchadnezzar, in rage and fury, gave the command to bring Shadrach, Meshach, and Abed-Nego. So they brought these men before the king. **14** Nebuchadnezzar spoke, saying to them, "Is it true, Shadrach, Meshach, and Abed-Nego, that you do not serve my gods or worship the gold image which I have set up? **15** Now if you are ready at the time you hear the sound of the horn, flute, harp, lyre, and psaltery, in symphony with all kinds of music, and you fall down and worship the image which I have made, good! But if you do not worship, you shall be cast immediately into the midst of a burning fiery furnace. And who is the god who will deliver you from my hands?"

16 Shadrach, Meshach, and Abed-Nego answered and said to the king, "O Nebuchadnezzar, we have no need to answer you in this matter. **17** If that is the case, our God whom we serve is able to deliver us from the burning fiery furnace, and He will deliver us from your hand, O king. **18** But if not, let it be known to you, O king, that we do not serve your gods, nor will we worship the gold image which you have set up."

19 Then Nebuchadnezzar was full of fury, and the expression on his face

changed toward Shadrach, Meshach, and Abed-Nego. He spoke and commanded that they heat the furnace seven times more than it was usually heated. **20** And he commanded certain mighty men of valor who were in his army to bind Shadrach, Meshach, and Abed-Nego, and cast them into the burning fiery furnace. **21** Then these men were bound in their coats, their trousers, their turbans, and their other garments, and were cast into the midst of the burning fiery furnace. **22** Therefore, because the king's command was urgent, and the furnace exceedingly hot, the flame of the fire killed those men who took up Shadrach, Meshach, and Abed-Nego. **23** And these three men, Shadrach, Meshach, and Abed-Nego, fell down bound into the midst of the burning fiery furnace.

24 Then King Nebuchadnezzar was astonished; and he rose in haste and spoke, saying to his counselors, "Did we not cast three men bound into the midst of the fire?"

They answered and said to the king, "True, O king."

25 "Look!" he answered, "I see four men loose, walking in the midst of the fire; and they are not hurt, and the form of the fourth is like the Son of God."

26 Then Nebuchadnezzar went near the mouth of the burning fiery furnace and spoke, saying, "Shadrach, Meshach, and Abed-Nego, servants of the Most High God, come out, and come here."

Then Shadrach, Meshach, and Abed-Nego came from the midst of the fire. **27** And the satraps, administrators, governors, and the king's counselors gathered together, and they saw these men on whose bodies the fire had no power; the hair of their head was not singed nor were their garments affected, and the smell of fire was not on them.

28 Nebuchadnezzar spoke, saying, "Blessed be the God of Shadrach, Meshach, and Abed-Nego, who sent His Angel and delivered His servants who trusted in Him, and they have frustrated the king's word, and yielded their bodies, that they should not serve nor worship any god except their own God! **29** Therefore I make a decree that any people, nation, or language which speaks anything amiss against the God of Shadrach, Meshach, and Abed-Nego shall be cut in pieces, and their houses shall be made an ash heap; because there is no other God who can deliver like this."

30 Then the king promoted Shadrach, Meshach, and Abed-Nego in the province of Babylon.

There is a huge disconnect between the closing verses of chapter 2 and the first verse of chapter 3. We don't know how much time elapsed between these accounts. It probably wasn't a lengthy period, but it was long enough for King Nebuchadnezzar to begin having some significant second thoughts about his dream and its meaning as explained to him by Daniel. Listening to Daniel reminding him of the dream he couldn't remember and caught up in the interpretation, Nebuchadnezzar was greatly impressed. He "fell on his face" and declared publicly, "Truly your God is the God of gods, the Lord of kings, and a revealer of secrets" (Daniel 2:46, 47). He seemed to accept that Daniel's God was showing him the future.

But then the king must have started thinking about the fact that his kingdom was going to be replaced by another. He liked the idea of being the head of gold, but having another kingdom supersede Babylon was another matter. We read in the opening verse of chapter 3, "Nebuchadnezzar the king made an image of gold, whose height was sixty cubits and its width six cubits. He set it up in the plain of Dura, in the province of Babylon" (Daniel 3:1).

Nebuchadnezzar challenges God

The difference between the statue Nebuchadnezzar saw in his dream and the one he erected on the plain of Dura is obvious. The statue the king saw in his dream had a golden head, but the rest of it was made up of silver, bronze, iron, and clay. The statue the king set up was *all* gold. The statement Nebuchadnezzar was making was also obvious. Babylon would last forever; no other kingdoms would take its place. Daniel had told the king that the stone he saw in his dream represented God's everlasting kingdom, which would supersede all the kingdoms of the earth. But Nebuchadnezzar didn't want to accept that. God had given him a message in a dream. He had been impressed at the time, but now he determined not to accept it. The statue in Daniel 2 was God's statue. The statue in chapter 3 was Nebuchadnezzar's statue. One was God's accurate description of the future. The other was a man's expression of rebellion and resistance to God's will.

The statue King Nebuchadnezzar set up was sixty cubits high and six cubits wide. In other words, it was ten times as tall as it was wide. That is a rather unusual ratio. The Statue of Liberty is 151 feet tall and 35 feet wide at the waist. That is slightly more than four times as tall as it is wide. The statue of Christ the Redeemer, overlooking Rio de Janeiro, is approximately 98 feet tall and 28 feet wide—or some three and a half times taller than it is wide. Michelangelo's famous statue, David, is a little more than two and a half times taller than it is wide (roughly 17 feet tall and 6.5 feet wide). But Nebuchadnezzar's golden statue is ten times taller than it is wide! A biblical cubit, it is estimated, equaled 18 to 21 inches. So the king's statue would have measured some 90 to 105 feet in height—and only 9 to 10.5 feet wide. It would have been an unusually skinny statue with one exception. The measurements given in the Bible most likely included the base of the statue. Factoring in a base of approximately 30 feet would make the statue perfectly proportionate.

Nebuchadnezzar signaled his defiance of God's message with an all-gold statue. But that wasn't all.

King Nebuchadnezzar sent word to gather together the satraps, the administrators, the governors, the counselors, the treasurers, the judges, the magistrates, and all the officials of the provinces, to come to the dedication of the image which King Nebuchadnezzar had set up. So the satraps, the administrators, the governors, the counselors, the treasurers, the judges, the magistrates, and all the officials of the provinces gathered together for the dedication of the image that King Nebuchadnezzar had set up; and they stood before the image that Nebuchadnezzar had set up. Then a herald cried aloud: "To you it is commanded, O peoples, nations, and languages, that at the time you hear the sound of the horn, flute, harp, lyre, and psaltery, in symphony with all kinds of music, you shall fall down and worship the gold image that King Nebuchadnezzar has set up" (verses 2–5).

Everyone who was anyone in the kingdom and its provinces was commanded to attend the grand dedication of the golden image—and to bow down and worship it. If you didn't get an invitation, you were a nobody with no position of prominence whatsoever in the empire. Worshiping Nebuchadnezzar's golden image signified the person's allegiance to the king. It also signified that the person was joining the king in his defiance of God's message about the future and that he or she was choosing to worship an idol rather than the God of heaven.

The counterfeit was an image of gold set up by a man and not by God, and all the rulers representing their people had come to the plain of Dura at the command of the king. The plain of Dura was flat—you could see for miles—and this massive golden image stood out against the skyline in stark relief, shimmering as the sun glanced off the gleaming gold. No one could miss this monument to the king's glory—not a statue with a golden head, but a whole statue made of gold from head to foot.

God had said to Nebuchadnezzar, "Your kingdom is represented by the head of gold, but another kingdom will replace you." By his actions, Nebuchadnezzar declared, "No way. I don't accept Your interpretation. My way is better than Your way. My kingdom, Babylon, will last forever."

In fact, recent archeological discoveries in Babylon have uncovered a clay tablet signed by Nebuchadnezzar. Archeologists consider it to be authentic. The tablet says, "O Babylon, the delight of mine eyes, the excellency of the kingdoms, may it, my kingdom Babylon, last forever." Once again, the archeologist's spade has corroborated the testimony of Scripture. Nebuchadnezzar was determined that God's prophecy concerning Babylon would not come to pass.

Notice verse 6: "Whoever does not fall down and worship shall be cast immediately into the midst of a burning fiery furnace."

Let's examine carefully the issues that were going on here on the plain of Dura. A powerful world ruler, Nebuchadnezzar, passed a universal decree of forced obedience. He declared, "To you it is commanded, O peoples, nations, and languages" (verse 4). The central issue was worship. Everyone was compelled to worship the image. For Daniel's three Hebrew friends, Shadrach, Meshach, and Abed-Nego, this counterfeit image stood in direct opposition to the truth of God. For them, this was a great time of trouble, greater than any they had ever experienced. Their lives were at stake. To fail to bow down meant certain death. But, as we will see, these three Hebrews had a death-defying faith.

A political-religious confederacy
In Daniel 3, we find a powerful world leader who commands and compels the

worship of a counterfeit image. In Babylon, church and state were united. Nebuchadnezzar not only ruled politically, but he also exercised religious authority. He commanded absolute allegiance from the populace. As we study the prophecies in the latter half of Daniel's book, we will see the divine predictions that a religious-political power will arise at the end time and will also exercise spiritual authority and demand allegiance in opposition to God. The prophecies predict a crisis in the last days over the issue of worship and spiritual authority. God's people will face a deadly test of allegiance.

The story we read here in Daniel 3 not only really happened but also illustrates the issues God's people will face at the end of time. The book of Revelation in the New Testament is the prophetic counterpart, the complement, to Daniel's book in the Old Testament. Revelation declares that the issues described in Daniel will be repeated at the end of time. Speaking of this religious-political power that will arise, John wrote, "He exercises all the authority of the first beast in his presence, and causes the earth and those who dwell in it to worship the first beast, whose deadly wound was healed. . . . He was granted power to give breath to the image of the beast, that the image of the beast should both speak and cause as many as would not worship the image of the beast to be killed" (Revelation 13:12–15).

We will study these verses and their symbols in more detail when we come to the book of Revelation. But we can see from Revelation 13 that it depicts a powerful authority that causes the earth to worship an image that it has established—and that decrees death to anyone who refuses to do as it commands. The issues here are the same as those on the plain of Dura—worship the power opposed to God or be put to death. A distinct parallel exists between Daniel 3 and Revelation 13. One describes an image to Nebuchadnezzar's power; the other describes an image to the beast's power. Both describe counterfeit, forced worship, representing disobedience to God. And in both cases, those who won't fall down in worship will be killed.

There was a test over worship, obedience, and the commandments of God in Daniel's day. A similar test concerning worship, obedience, and the commandments of God will occur in the last days. Once again, a powerful world ruler will pass a universal decree uniting church and state. The golden image on the plain of Dura was a sign of Babylon's authority, and worship of that image constituted worship of Babylon. So also, at the time of the end, there will be a sign, or mark, of the authority of a church-state power. And those who refuse to go along with this church-state and worship the image it sets up will face death. At that time, God's people will need to have a death-defying faith and unswerving loyalty to God like that shown by Shadrach, Meshach, and Abed-Nego.

On the plain of Dura, Nebuchadnezzar commanded, "When the band plays, when you hear the music, fall on your face and worship."

"When all the people heard the sound of the horn, flute, harp, and lyre, in symphony with all kinds of music, all the people, nations, and languages fell down and worshiped the gold image which King Nebuchadnezzar had set up" (Daniel 3:7).

Everyone in that vast crowd surrounding the golden image fell on their faces in obedience to the king's command and worshiped the image except for three young Hebrew men—Shadrach, Meshach, and Abed-Nego. The officials standing near them were more than happy to report their disobedience to the king.

They spoke and said to King Nebuchadnezzar, "O king, live forever! You, O king, have made a decree that everyone who hears the sound of the horn, flute, harp, lyre, and psaltery, in symphony with all kinds of music, shall fall down and worship the gold image; and whoever does not fall down and worship shall be cast into the midst of a burning fiery furnace. There are certain Jews whom you have set over the affairs of the province of Babylon: Shadrach, Meshach, and Abed-Nego; these men, O king, have not paid due regard to you. They do not serve your gods or worship the gold image which you have set up" (verses 9–12).

The Bible says that Nebuchadnezzar's reaction to this information was rage and fury. But he wasn't willing to take the accusation of his officials at face value. Perhaps he suspected they were jealous of these Hebrew captives whom he had elevated to positions of responsibility. Perhaps he recalled the test these three young men had undergone when they were being prepared to serve—and the way they had passed that test and turned out "ten times better" (Daniel 1:20) than those who ate his food and drank his wine. Maybe Nebuchadnezzar was uneasy enough about defying God's dream that he wanted to give Shadrach, Meshach, and Abed-Nego a second chance. At any rate, he decided to hear for himself what they had to say in their defense.

In this, the king showed more judgment than we sometimes do. Have you ever heard that someone said that somebody else had said something less than positive about you? It's so easy to believe the rumor and so difficult to go to that person and find out the truth. Many problems in human relations would be solved if we followed Nebuchadnezzar's example in this.

Death-defying faith

So the king, full of rage and fury, brought Shadrach, Meshach, and Abed-Nego before him and looked them in the eyes and said, "Is true . . . that you do not serve my gods or worship the gold image which I have set up?" (Daniel 3:14). He was giving them the benefit of the doubt. "I gave you a chance once, but don't push me. Don't try my patience. When the band strikes up, you had better fall down this time and worship the image!"

Their reply contains a valuable lesson for us today. "Shadrach, Meshach, and Abed-Nego answered and said to the king, 'O Nebuchadnezzar, we have no need to answer you in this matter' " (verse 16).

Some decisions in life need to be settled before we're brought to the test. Shadrach, Meshach, and Abed-Nego obeyed the king as far as they could. They went to the dedication because he commanded them to. But they had already decided that they were not going to yield their conscientious convictions and worship the image. They would be loyal to God. So they replied, "O king, we don't need to think about this. You don't have to give us a second chance. We've already given this situation a great deal of thought, and we've made up our minds. We will remain faithful to God. You can throw us into the fiery furnace, but we will not worship your image of gold."

I don't think they said this with an arrogant, defiant tone of voice. I think they were trying to help the king see the dilemma he had put them in and why they couldn't obey him. They explained the reasoning behind their decision: "If that is the case, our God whom we serve is able to deliver us from the burning fiery furnace, and He will deliver us from your hand, O king. But if not, let it be known to you, O king, that we do not serve your gods, nor will we worship the gold image which you have set up" (verses 17, 18). Shadrach, Meshach, and Abed-Nego would rather die believing in God than yield their conscientious convictions.

Some people have the idea that faith is kind of like magic or a good luck charm, that if you pray and believe strongly enough, you never get sick, you're never in debt, or you never get discouraged. Their whole idea is that faith is kind of like a "get out of jail free" card that you can present, and God will grant you whatever you ask. Shadrach, Meshach, and Abed-Nego had no doubt that God *could* deliver them, but they didn't automatically assume that He *would*. They recognized that their faithfulness to God might lead them into the burning, fiery furnace. Faith doesn't always deliver us *from* the fire, but it will always take us *through* the fire trusting in God. Faith is not a good luck charm that ensures things will always turn out right. It is a strong belief that God is in control even if things do not turn out the way we anticipated.

A woman went to her pastor and said, "I am a Christian, and I believed that if I had enough faith, I would never get cancer. But then I went to my doctor because I noticed I was losing weight and was a little nauseated and had some other symptoms. My doctor diagnosed my problem as a malignant cancer that was rapidly growing. So

I began treatments. That was about six months ago, and I have been in chemotherapy and radiation therapy, but my cancer has metastasized, and the medical prognosis is not good. My physicians have indicated that I have a short time to live.

"One of my friends said, 'If you only have enough faith, God will deliver you from the cancer.' "

The woman told her pastor, "Now I have two problems. I have cancer, and I don't have enough faith. Although I earnestly prayed, my cancer got worse. I went back to my friend and told her that my cancer was getting worse even though I had been asking God to deliver me from it. And she said, 'Maybe there is some sin in your life, and that's the reason God can't heal you.'

"Now, I have three problems. I have cancer, I don't have enough faith, and there is some sin in my life." And she said, "By this time, I was really depressed and discouraged. I felt that I must be a terrible sinner and that God had given up on me. Then I read Daniel 3 about Shadrach, Meshach, and Abed-Nego and how they weren't sure God would deliver them from the flames. But they were sure that God was with them as they went into the flames. Now I understand that having faith doesn't mean that things will always go well. Faith is believing that God is there even when things don't go well." That's an important lesson to learn from the experience of Daniel's three friends.

When Shadrach, Meshach, and Abed-Nego refused the king's offer of a second chance to bow down and worship the image, he was even more furious than before.

"Then Nebuchadnezzar was full of fury, and the expression on his face changed toward Shadrach, Meshach, and Abed-Nego. He spoke and commanded that they heat the furnace seven times more than it was usually heated. And he commanded certain mighty men of valor who were in his army to bind Shadrach, Meshach, and Abed-Nego, and cast them into the burning fiery furnace. Then these men were bound in their coats, their trousers, their turbans, and their other garments, and were cast into the midst of the burning fiery furnace" (verses 19–21).

Divine deliverance

The fire was so hot it killed the men who threw them into it! But what about Shadrach, Meshach, and Abed-Nego? They "fell down bound into the midst of the burning fiery furnace" (verse 23). But God worked a miracle on their behalf. He honored their faith and delivered them from a horrible death. Jesus Himself came down and stood in the fire with them! The fire that killed the men who came close enough to throw them into it merely burned away the ropes that bound them!

Then King Nebuchadnezzar was astonished; and he rose in haste and spoke, saying to his counselors, "Did we not cast three men bound into the midst of the fire?"

They answered and said to the king, "True, O king."

"Look!" he answered, "I see four men loose, walking in the midst of the fire; and they are not hurt, and the form of the fourth is like the Son of God" (verses 24, 25).

When you go through the flames of life, God is there. He is the God who delivers us. There is a time of trouble coming on the whole earth before Jesus comes, and it will require loyalty to God like that of Shadrach, Meshach, and Abed-Nego. But sometimes we face a time of trouble, not in the future, but right now. And when that happens, God is there as well. He is the God who rescues us in the flames of life. When your heart is broken, God is there. When your marriage has fallen apart, God is there. When your doctor tells you that you have a terminal illness, God is there. When you're going through the flames of life and it seems that you're going to be consumed by discouragement and depression, God is there. In every heartache, every disappointment, God is there. He is the God who delivers.

This doesn't mean that He will always put your marriage back together or heal your terminal illness. The three Hebrews told the king, "Our God whom we serve is able to deliver us from the burning fiery furnace. . . . But if not . . ." (verses 17, 18). They realized God's plan might be that their lives would end in the flames. But even so, they would still trust Him. They would still be faithful because He is the God who delivers. He may choose to deliver us by quenching the flames, or He may choose to deliver us by standing in the flames with us and giving us the courage and loyalty to keep our hand in His no matter the cost.

When Shadrach, Meshach, and Abed-Nego went through their fiery trial and stayed faithful to God, God was teaching them to trust Him in the darkness. He was teaching them to have greater faith and greater courage. It was not because God did not love them that they went through the fire. It was because He saw in them something valuable and precious that had to be refined by the flames of difficulty. Maybe you're not going through any flames right now. Your life may be moving along on an easy path. But sooner or later, you will experience the flames of adversity. Every life has its sorrows and heartaches. The world we are living in is not always kind. But when we are thrown into the flames, there is Someone who enters the furnace with us. When Shadrach, Meshach, and Abed-Nego went into the furnace, they did not go in alone. Nebuchadnezzar saw the "Son of God" walking about in the furnace with them. And when we are in the furnace of life, we can look with the eye of faith through the smoke and the flames and the tears and see the Son of God with His arms around us, whispering courage in our ears as He walks with us in the furnace of affliction.

Changed by God's power

Daniel 3 ends in a magnificent show of glory—a heathen king is impacted by the faith of Shadrach, Meshach, and Abed-Nego. Nebuchadnezzar called the three Hebrews to come out of the furnace. Notice that, apparently, they didn't leave the furnace until the king told them they could! I think I would have been rushing out of the furnace as soon as I realized I wasn't going to be burned alive! But Shadrach, Meshach, and Abed-Nego were content to remain in the furnace with Jesus. When they finally did emerge from the furnace, the king and all the officials nearby "saw these men on whose bodies the fire had no power; the hair of their head was not singed nor were their garments affected, and the smell of fire was not on them" (verse 27). What a testimony to the God who delivers! The fire had killed those men who threw them into the furnace, but it wasn't able even to singe the hair on their heads!

"Nebuchadnezzar spoke, saying, 'Blessed be the God of Shadrach, Meshach, and Abed-Nego, who sent His Angel and delivered His servants who trusted in Him, and they have frustrated the king's word, and yielded their bodies, that they should not serve nor worship any god except their own God! Therefore I make a decree that any people, nation, or language which speaks anything amiss against the God of Shadrach, Meshach, and Abed-Nego shall be cut in pieces, and their houses shall be made an ash heap; because there is no other God who can deliver like this' " (verses 28, 29).

Nebuchadnezzar had looked into the flames and had seen the Son of God, Christ, the mighty Deliverer. Nebuchadnezzar saw that these three Hebrews had something that he didn't have—a God who was able to deliver. He still had his old autocratic tendencies. He still didn't understand the God of love and free will. He switched from demanding that the people worship his golden image to demanding that they worship the God of Shadrach, Meshach, and Abed-Nego. He had threatened anyone who failed to worship the golden image with death in the fiery furnace. Now he threatened anyone who failed to worship the God of heaven with being cut in pieces. He didn't fully understand; nevertheless, he was filled with a sense that God delivers.

God was speaking to Nebuchadnezzar's heart. Perhaps one day in a place where there is no suffering, pain, or death, the king will be walking on streets of gold with Shadrach, Meshach, and Abed-Nego, remembering that long-ago time on the plain of Dura when he had them thrown into the fiery furnace—and how God had delivered them. If so, it will be because of their faithful witness and their loyalty to God. We need to have the courage of our convictions, like them, to serve God no matter the cost.

THE GOD WHO RULES OVER ALL

Daniel 4

1 Nebuchadnezzar the king,

To all peoples, nations, and languages that dwell in all the earth:

Peace be multiplied to you.

2 I thought it good to declare the signs and wonders that the Most High God has worked for me.

3 How great are His signs,
And how mighty His wonders!
His kingdom is an everlasting kingdom,
And His dominion is from generation to generation.

4 I, Nebuchadnezzar, was at rest in my house, and flourishing in my palace. **5** I saw a dream which made me afraid, and the thoughts on my bed and the visions of my head troubled me. **6** Therefore I issued a decree to bring in all the wise men of Babylon before me, that they might make known to me the interpretation of the dream. **7** Then the magicians, the astrologers, the Chaldeans, and the soothsayers came in, and I told them the dream; but they did not make known to me its interpretation. **8** But at last Daniel came before me (his name is Belteshazzar, according to the name of my god; in him is the Spirit of the Holy God), and I told the dream before him, saying: **9** "Belteshazzar, chief of the magicians, because I know that the Spirit of the Holy God is in you, and no secret troubles you, explain to me the visions of my dream that I have seen, and its interpretation.

10 "These were the visions of my head while on my bed:

I was looking, and behold,
A tree in the midst of the earth,
And its height was great.
11 The tree grew and became strong;
Its height reached to the heavens,

And it could be seen to the ends of all
    the earth.
12 Its leaves were lovely,
Its fruit abundant,
And in it was food for all.
The beasts of the field found shade
    under it,
The birds of the heavens dwelt in its
    branches,
And all flesh was fed from it.

13 "I saw in the visions of my head
while on my bed, and there was a
watcher, a holy one, coming down from
heaven. **14** He cried aloud and said thus:

'Chop down the tree and cut off its
    branches,
Strip off its leaves and scatter its fruit.
Let the beasts get out from under it,
And the birds from its branches.
15 Nevertheless leave the stump and
    roots in the earth,
Bound with a band of iron and bronze,
In the tender grass of the field.
Let it be wet with the dew of heaven,
And let him graze with the beasts
On the grass of the earth.
16 Let his heart be changed from that
    of a man,
Let him be given the heart of a beast,
And let seven times pass over him.

17 'This decision is by the decree of
    the watchers,
And the sentence by the word of the
    holy ones,

In order that the living may know
That the Most High rules in the king-
    dom of men,
Gives it to whomever He will,
And sets over it the lowest of men.'

18 "This dream I, King Nebuchadnezzar, have seen. Now you, Belteshazzar, declare its interpretation, since all
the wise men of my kingdom are not
able to make known to me the interpretation; but you are able, for the Spirit of
the Holy God is in you."
19 Then Daniel, whose name was
Belteshazzar, was astonished for a time,
and his thoughts troubled him. So the
king spoke, and said, "Belteshazzar, do
not let the dream or its interpretation
trouble you." Belteshazzar answered and
said, "My lord, may the dream concern
those who hate you, and its interpretation concern your enemies!
20 "The tree that you saw, which
grew and became strong, whose height
reached to the heavens and which could
be seen by all the earth, **21** whose leaves
were lovely and its fruit abundant, in
which was food for all, under which the
beasts of the field dwelt, and in whose
branches the birds of the heaven had
their home— **22** it is you, O king, who
have grown and become strong; for your
greatness has grown and reaches to the
heavens, and your dominion to the end
of the earth.
23 "And inasmuch as the king saw a
watcher, a holy one, coming down from

heaven and saying, 'Chop down the tree and destroy it, but leave its stump and roots in the earth, bound with a band of iron and bronze in the tender grass of the field; let it be wet with the dew of heaven, and let him graze with the beasts of the field, till seven times pass over him'; **24** this is the interpretation, O king, and this is the decree of the Most High, which has come upon my lord the king: **25** They shall drive you from men, your dwelling shall be with the beasts of the field, and they shall make you eat grass like oxen. They shall wet you with the dew of heaven, and seven times shall pass over you, till you know that the Most High rules in the kingdom of men, and gives it to whomever He chooses.

26 "And inasmuch as they gave the command to leave the stump and roots of the tree, your kingdom shall be assured to you, after you come to know that Heaven rules. **27** Therefore, O king, let my advice be acceptable to you; break off your sins by being righteous, and your iniquities by showing mercy to the poor. Perhaps there may be a lengthening of your prosperity."

28 All this came upon King Nebuchadnezzar. **29** At the end of the twelve months he was walking about the royal palace of Babylon. **30** The king spoke, saying, "Is not this great Babylon, that I have built for a royal dwelling by my mighty power and for the honor of my majesty?"

31 While the word was still in the king's mouth, a voice fell from heaven: "King Nebuchadnezzar, to you it is spoken: the kingdom has departed from you! **32** And they shall drive you from men, and your dwelling shall be with the beasts of the field. They shall make you eat grass like oxen; and seven times shall pass over you, until you know that the Most High rules in the kingdom of men, and gives it to whomever He chooses."

33 That very hour the word was fulfilled concerning Nebuchadnezzar; he was driven from men and ate grass like oxen; his body was wet with the dew of heaven till his hair had grown like eagles' feathers and his nails like birds' claws.

34 And at the end of the time I, Nebuchadnezzar, lifted my eyes to heaven, and my understanding returned to me; and I blessed the Most High and praised and honored Him who lives forever:

> For His dominion is an everlasting dominion,
> And His kingdom is from generation to generation.
> **35** All the inhabitants of the earth are reputed as nothing;
> He does according to His will in the army of heaven
> And among the inhabitants of the earth.
> No one can restrain His hand

Or say to Him, "What have You done?"

36 At the same time my reason returned to me, and for the glory of my kingdom, my honor and splendor returned to me. My counselors and nobles resorted to me, I was restored to my kingdom, and excellent majesty was added to me. **37** Now I, Nebuchadnezzar, praise and extol and honor the King of heaven, all of whose works are truth, and His ways justice. And those who walk in pride He is able to put down.

There is something unique about the fourth chapter of Daniel. It is the only chapter in the book that was *not* written by Daniel—at least Daniel didn't write most of it. Most of this chapter was written by a heathen king—Nebuchadnezzar.

The chapter begins:

Nebuchadnezzar the king,
To all peoples, nations, and languages that dwell in all the earth:
Peace be multiplied to you. (Daniel 4:1).

In the previous chapter, this brutal, arrogant king erected a giant statue of gold on the plain of Dura in defiance of God and the message God had given him. He commanded everyone to bow down to that image in recognition of his power or be burned alive in a fiery furnace! Now he writes to "all peoples, nations, and languages that dwell in all the earth." And what is his message?

Peace be multiplied to you.

I thought it good to declare the signs and wonders that the Most High God has worked for me (verses 1, 2).

The conversion of a king

What brought about such a dramatic change? Chapter four is Nebuchadnezzar's conversion story. It's the story of a heathen king transformed by God's power. God's miraculous deliverance of Shadrach, Meshach, and Abed-Nego made a profound impression on Nebuchadnezzar. Now it's as if he is saying, "I have to speak. God transformed my life. God changed me. God radically did something in my heart, mind, and soul." This heathen king is glowing with God's grace. He is filled with God's goodness. God tapped Nebuchadnezzar on the shoulder, and his life was radically changed.

If God can take an idolatrous, cruel, wicked head of state like Nebuchadnezzar and radically transform him and place peace within his heart, then there is hope for you and me. No matter how hopeless you may feel, no matter how much you have disobeyed God, no matter how guilty you feel because of some sin you've committed, if God can take someone like King Nebuchadnezzar and change his life, then God can reach out to you and change your life as well.

Daniel chapter 4 is Nebuchadnezzar's testimony of how God turned his life around. He was the mighty king of Babylon. He lived a life of luxury, opulence, popularity, and fame. He had hundreds of servants who catered to his every wish. He was rich and powerful. He testified, "I, Nebuchadnezzar, was at rest in my house, and flourishing in my palace" (verse 4). But all that was about to change.

Nebuchadnezzar's second dream

You see, in spite of Nebuchadnezzar's acknowledgment of God's greatness in chapter 3, in spite of being impressed by the wonders and signs God had shown him, Nebuchadnezzar still had an unconverted heart. He was still a proud, despotic ruler. So God spoke to him again in a dramatic dream. The king says, "I, Nebuchadnezzar, was at rest in my house, and flourishing in my palace. I saw a dream which made me afraid, and the thoughts on my bed and the visions of my head troubled me" (verses 4, 5).

Once again, God broke through Nebuchadnezzar's complacency with a troubling dream. How did the king react? He reacted just as he had earlier when God sent him the dream of the metallic image. He called his brain trust—the magicians, the astrologers, and the soothsayers. This, in itself, shows that Nebuchadnezzar didn't really understand Daniel's God. In spite of his words extolling the God of heaven and His power, Nebuchadnezzar hadn't really let God have full control of his life.

> Often as we drift from His plan and purpose for our lives, God taps us on the shoulder. Something happens to warn us that we are no longer following His plan. God loves us so much that He would rather have us go through some disappointment or sorrow, if necessary, than to lose us for all eternity.

He fell back into the same old patterns—with the same old results as before.

"Therefore I issued a decree to bring in all the wise men of Babylon before me, that they might make known to me the interpretation of the dream. Then the magicians, the astrologers, the Chaldeans, and the soothsayers came in, and I told them the dream; but they did not make known to me its interpretation" (verses 6, 7).

The "Nebuchadnezzar syndrome"

Notice what verse 8 says: "At last Daniel came before me." *At last?* Hadn't Nebuchadnezzar been through this before? Had he forgotten how all his wise men had failed to interpret his earlier dream and that Daniel, alone, was able to tell him the message God had for him? Wouldn't you think that Daniel would be the first person who would come to the king's mind in this situation? But how often do we exhibit the "Nebuchadnezzar syndrome"? We worry about some seemingly unsolvable problem. Our stomach is in knots. We're filled with tension and anxiety, and we do everything we can to solve the problem—everything except turn it over to the One who can solve any problem. We do everything humanly possible, and when that doesn't work, *at last*, we turn to God. We need to get on our knees and call God first!

So finally, Daniel appeared to listen to the king's dream. This time, Nebuchadnezzar remembered what he dreamed. It was vivid in his mind. But he didn't know what it meant. "I saw a great tree in my dream," he told Daniel. "It was tall, and as I watched, it grew even taller, so tall it touched the heavens. It could be seen all over the world. It bore abundant fruit and animals sheltered under its shade. It was such a beautiful tree" (verses 10–12, author's paraphrase).

> "I saw in the visions of my head while on my bed, and there was a watcher, a holy one, coming down from heaven. He cried aloud and said thus:
>
> > 'Chop down the tree and cut off its branches.
> > Strip off its leaves and scatter its fruit.
> > Let the beasts get out from under it,
> > And the birds from its branches.
> > Nevertheless leave the stump and roots in the earth,
> > Bound with a band of iron and bronze.
> > In the tender grass of the field.
> > Let it be wet with the dew of heaven,
> > And let him graze with the beasts
> > On the grass of the earth.

Let his heart be changed from that of a man,
Let him be given the heart of a beast,
And let seven times pass over him.

'This decision is by the decree of the watchers,
And the sentence by the word of the holy ones,
In order that the living may know
That the Most High rules in the kingdom of men' " (verses 13–17).

"That's what I dreamed," Nebuchadnezzar told Daniel. "What does it mean?"

Daniel explains the king's second dream

God's purpose in sending this dream to the king is found in the dream itself. In his dream, Nebuchadnezzar heard "a watcher, a holy one" from heaven say that the dream was given "in order that the living may know that the Most High rules in the kingdom of men, [and] gives it to whomever He will" (verse 17). So whatever is the meaning of this dream, its purpose is to reveal that God rules, that God is in control.

In Daniel 1, we saw the God who, as Daniel was taken into captivity, turned his defeat into victory. Daniel 1 teaches us that God is to be praised because He can take our shattered lives, our broken dreams, our frustrated hopes and turn them into victory.

In Daniel 2, in the great dream of the metallic image, we saw a God who reveals the future. And we saw that we can safely trust Him because we can put our future in His hands.

In Daniel 3, we saw the God who delivers. He is our Savior and our Redeemer too. Shadrach, Meshach, and Abed-Nego went into the flames in order to remain faithful to God, and Jesus descended into the furnace with them to deliver them from certain death. So in the flames of our life, when there is no hope, He is our Savior. When we come to the end of the road, and there is no place to turn, He is the Savior.

Here in Daniel 4, we see God as the true King of the universe. He rules in the kingdoms of men. He is in control. God reveals Himself as worthy to be praised because He is the King of kings, and He wants to be the King of our hearts.

Nebuchadnezzar was in his palace. He had acknowledged God's wisdom and power, but he had not acknowledged the God of the universe as the King of his heart. So God gave him a wake-up call. God gave him this dream of a great tree that sheltered and provided for the whole world. Then a decree came from heaven, "Chop down the tree, but leave the stump in the earth and fasten a band of iron and bronze around it." What did the dream mean?—that's what Nebuchadnezzar wanted to know. When Daniel heard the king describe his dream, he "was astonished for a time, and his thoughts troubled him. So the king spoke and said, 'Belteshazzar [Daniel's Babylonian name, remember], do not let the dream or its interpretation trouble you.' Belteshazzar answered and said, 'My lord, may the dream concern those who hate you, and its interpretation concern your enemies!' " (verse 19).

Nebuchadnezzar noticed from Daniel's reaction to his dream that the interpretation was not going to be a positive one for him. Nevertheless, he encouraged Daniel to hold nothing back. "Don't be troubled," he urged. "I want to know what the dream means, even if it isn't good news."

Notice Daniel's reply. He didn't tell Nebuchadnezzar, "You're going to get yours now. You overthrew my city, Jerusalem. You took me captive. This serves you right. You're going to get what's coming to you. Your kingdom is going to be chopped down to the ground. Praise to the God of heaven!" Daniel knew that he could never influence Nebuchadnezzar unless he demonstrated genuine care, concern, and love for the king. Daniel is a sterling example of one whom captivity, mistreatment, and injustice did not make bitter, but better. Daniel had been taken captive and separated from his homeland when he was about seventeen years old, never to see his home or his family again. Now God had shown Daniel the interpretation of the king's dream, and it wasn't good news for Nebuchadnezzar. But Daniel had such love for this heathen king that he was troubled by what the dream implied.

That is an example for us. We will never be able to reach that husband or wife who has treated us so poorly if we treat them like they have treated us. We'll never influence that business partner who cheated us out of the money he owes us if we return hatred for his evil conduct toward us. You see, God never treats us like we deserve. He always treats us with love, no matter how unlovely we have treated Him. God is love, and it is impossible for Him to be unloving.

Daniel was so astonished and overwhelmed by the meaning of the dream that he didn't want to say anything to Nebuchadnezzar. Nebuchadnezzar had to draw it out of him. In verse 20, Daniel began to explain the dream. "The tree that you saw, which grew and became strong, whose height reached to the heavens and which could be seen by all the earth, whose leaves were lovely and its fruit abundant . . . is you, O king, who have grown and become strong" (verses 20–22).

The dream turns dark

That tree represented Nebuchadnezzar personally. In the dream of chapter 2, the head of gold symbolized the kingdom of Babylon, not Nebuchadnezzar himself. But this dream involved the king as an individual. Nebuchadnezzar had grown and

58

become strong like the tree in his dream. But then the dream turned dark. Daniel continued with the interpretation.

> "Inasmuch as the king saw a watcher, a holy one, coming down from heaven and saying, 'Chop down the tree and destroy it, but leave its stump and roots in the earth, bound with a band of iron and bronze in the tender grass of the field; let it be wet with the dew of heaven, and let him graze with the beasts of the field until seven times pass over him'; this is the interpretation, O king, and this is the decree of the Most High, which has come upon my lord the king. They shall drive you from men, your dwelling shall be with the beasts of the field, and they shall make you eat grass like oxen. They shall wet you with the dew of heaven, and seven times shall pass over you till you know that the Most High rules in the kingdom of men, and gives it to whomever He chooses" (verses 23–25).

Cutting down the tree represented God's judgment on Nebuchadnezzar's pride. We aren't told how Nebuchadnezzar reacted to Daniel's words. He was prepared for bad news. Did he believe Daniel? Did he believe the dream was from the God of heaven? Did he believe it would really come true? Perhaps he was encouraged as Daniel went on to explain that just as the stump of the tree was to remain in the ground, so his kingdom would remain, and he would be restored to the throne one day.

What about this mysterious band of iron and bronze that was to be placed around the stump of the tree? In the Bible, iron always represents authority and rulership (see Psalm 2:9). Bronze is a symbol of salvation or cleansing.

The laver in the sanctuary was made of bronze, and the priests washed in it before going into the Holy Place because it was a symbol of salvation. So the band of iron and bronze symbolized authority and salvation. God would protect the king during his time of judgment. God's authority and rulership would keep someone else from taking over the kingdom. But Nebuchadnezzar would lose his kingdom and his dominion until "seven times shall pass over you [and] you know that the Most High rules" (verse 25).

God appeals to Nebuchadnezzar's heart

God's message to Nebuchadnezzar was actually an appeal to his heart. The dream showed him what would happen if he continued on his course of pride, arrogance, and independence from God. He would be driven from human habitation and live with the animals. He would eat grass like oxen. The rain and dew would fall on him. But a stump would remain in the ground. God's rulership and protection would remain over his kingdom. God was saying to Nebuchadnezzar, "All this doesn't have to happen. You don't have to lose your kingdom. You don't have to be removed from your throne. Turn to Me and save yourself from the results of your pride and selfishness."

Daniel made God's appeal clear to the king: "Inasmuch as they gave the command to leave the stump and roots of the tree, your kingdom shall be assured to you, after you come to know that Heaven rules. Therefore, O king, let my advice be acceptable to you; break off your sins by being righteous, and your iniquities by showing mercy to the poor. Perhaps there may be a lengthening of your prosperity" (verses 26, 27).

God was giving King Nebuchadnezzar an opportunity to repent even at this late hour. There are times when God taps us on the shoulder. He taps us once, He taps us twice, and we begin walking away from Him, living careless lives, prayerless lives, occupied by the things of time rather than the things of eternity. As we walk away from Him, we feel His gentle tap on our shoulder. A minor crisis comes into our life. God does not cause it, but He doesn't keep it from happening because He knows it can draw us to Him. But if we continue on a course of neglect and rejection, God allows the volume of His voice to be turned up. His purpose is to teach us in times of sorrow what we failed to learn in a more peaceful time. God loves you so much that He wants you to learn the lessons needed to be ready for heaven.

> Nebuchadnezzar's dream was fulfilled exactly as Daniel had said it would be. But how much sorrow and grief and pain the king could have avoided if he had only listened to God's warning and followed Daniel's advice!

When you were born into this world, God had a plan for your life. Through life, as you follow that plan and make choices to be in harmony with God's will, He guides your life. His plan for your life is to give you happiness and joy in abundance. There are times that bad things happen to good people. Through no fault of our own, our life suddenly changes. Even in those instances, God is there to lead us closer to Him and teach us deeper dependence.

Often as we drift from His plan and purpose for our lives, God taps us on the shoulder. Something happens to warn us that we are no longer following His plan. God loves us so much that He would rather have us go through some disappointment or sorrow, if necessary, than to lose us for all eternity.

God looked down upon Nebuchadnezzar, and He said, "Nebuchadnezzar, I do not want you to lose your throne. That's not My choice. But if you do not repent, the only way I can reach you is to allow circumstances to occur that will bring you to see your need of Me."

God gives Nebuchadnezzar time to repent

Notice the next two verses here in Daniel 4. They are some of the most powerful texts in the Bible. "All this came upon King Nebuchadnezzar. At the end of twelve months he was walking about the royal palace of Babylon" (verses 28, 29).

God gave Nebuchadnezzar time. Twelve months after his dream of the tree that was to be cut down, Nebuchadnezzar was still walking around his royal palace unconcerned! Can you imagine that? The king understood the dream. He understood its prediction that he would lose his kingdom if he didn't make changes in his life. "Repent of your sins," Daniel had urged him. "This doesn't have to happen." And nothing did happen—for one month, two months, three months, six months. Nothing happened for twelve months. A year after the dream, Nebuchadnezzar was still living the same way he had lived before.

We may wonder why the king didn't pay attention. We may think, "If God warned me as He did Nebuchadnezzar, I'd listen and make changes." But is that really true? How often does God tap us on the shoulder and say, "Look, I'm giving you an opportunity. I don't want to withdraw My blessings from your life and allow some dramatic thing to happen"? How often, like Nebuchadnezzar, do we plunge right on anyway, living just as we always have?

A year after his dream, the king was walking around the royal palace, looking at its splendor and thinking about the greatness of his kingdom. "The king spoke, saying, 'Is not this great Babylon, that I have built for a royal dwelling by my mighty power and for the honor of my majesty?' " (verse 30). Filled with pride as he surveyed his kingdom, Nebuchadnezzar voiced his boastful claim. And truly, Babylon was great.

Archeologists have uncovered ancient Babylon. It is located in modern Iraq, more than a hundred miles south of Bagdad. The avenue leading to Nebuchadnezzar's palace, "Procession Way," is paved with thousands of bricks—every one of them has Nebuchadnezzar's name stamped on it! Thousands of them, and they all say, "Nebuchadnezzar." "Nebuchadnezzar." "Nebuchadnezzar."

In the height of his arrogance, this ancient king boastfully proclaimed, "Is not this great Babylon that I have built?" And Scripture says, "While the word was still in the king's mouth, a voice fell from heaven: 'King Nebuchadnezzar, to you it is spoken: the kingdom is departed from you! And they shall drive you from men, and your dwelling shall be with the beasts of the field. They shall make you eat grass like oxen; and seven times shall pass over you, until you know that the Most High rules' " (verses 31, 32).

Nebuchadnezzar failed to heed God's warning. He failed to listen to God's invitation to repent. He failed to accept God's mercy, and he lost his throne and his reason in an instant. He lived outdoors with the animals. The Bible says that his hair grew like eagles' feathers and his nails were like a bird's claws. In my imagination, I can see him. He's on all fours. His filthy hair is long and matted. He's bearded, and his body stinks. His hands are gnarled; his fingernails are like claws. This is the man who was once the king of Babylon. He sat on a throne with the royal scepter in his hand. Once armies marched at his command. He was wealthy beyond understanding. He had winter palaces and summer palaces. Everything to delight the eye and tempt the taste was his. But now, his eyes are vacant; he looks and wanders like an animal. He's lost it all.

There is a scientific name for Nebuchadnezzar's condition. It's a mental disease called lycanthropic insanity. If you are interested, you can look it up in *Webster's Modern Dictionary*. Lycanthropic insanity occurs when an individual perceives himself to be an animal, usually a part of the cat family. There is a neglect of personal hygiene. The individual walks on all fours, associates with the animal kingdom, and behaves like an animal. Lycanthropic insanity comes on suddenly. Persons suffering from this condition don't care how they look; they don't care how they smell. They begin wandering around on all fours. It's a very rare condition but well known by medical specialists in the field of mental health.

God allowed this strange disease to come upon Nebuchadnezzar. Seven "times," or years, were to pass over him while he lived like an animal. One year went by. Two years went by. Three years, and he was still wandering around with the animals: four, five, six years—no change.

Nebuchadnezzar's story is our story

The truth of the matter is that Nebuchadnezzar's story is our story—yours and mine. It's the story of the human race. When God created the earth, he gave Adam and Eve dominion. They were the rulers of earth. They were clothed with a royal robe of righteousness. They were part of the royal family of heaven. Adam and Eve were the son and daughter of God. They ruled this new planet. But through sin, rebellion, pride, and arrogance, they lost it. Their nature was changed so that it became easier to do wrong than right. We can identify with Nebuchadnezzar. We too have lost our way. We too have a changed human nature. Sin has caused us to lose our inner peace.

Have you ever wondered why it is easier to be angry than it is to be patient? Have you ever wondered why it easier to be selfish than it is to be kind? Have you ever wondered why you have to fight those lustful thoughts constantly? Have you ever wondered why you have to struggle constantly to hold back those critical words? It is because our nature has been changed, fundamentally, at our core. There is something basically wrong with us. The prophet Jeremiah states it clearly: "The heart is deceitful above all things, and desperately wicked" (Jeremiah 17:9).

Scripture shows that there is hope for those who have defiled natures. There is hope for those who have corrupt hearts.

> At the end of the time I, Nebuchadnezzar, lifted my eyes to heaven, and my understanding returned to me, and I blessed the Most High and praised and honored Him who lives forever. . . .
>
> At the same time my reason returned to me. . . . I was restored to my kingdom, and excellent majesty was added to me. Now I, Nebuchadnezzar, praise and extol and honor the King of heaven, all of whose works are truth, and His ways justice. And those who walk in pride He is able to put down (verses 34–37).

God did for Nebuchadnezzar what he could never do for himself. God changed Nebuchadnezzar's heart. And He can do the same for you and me. The Bible says, "If anyone is in Christ, he is a new creation; old things have passed away; behold all things have become new" (2 Corinthians 5:17). This is a transformation so complete and far-reaching that it is like being born all over again (John 3:1–7). We become a new person entirely.

Nebuchadnezzar was miraculously transformed as he looked to heaven. The impossible took place. Nebuchadnezzar could not change himself, and neither can we. None of our trying to be patient will make us patient. None of our trying to be pure will make us pure. None of our trying to be honest will make us honest, because there is something fundamentally wrong inside. Change comes when, like Nebuchadnezzar, we look to heaven. There is no other place to look. There is no one else to look to. Looking inside, we see only our fallen human nature. But looking to Jesus, His strength becomes our strength, His righteousness becomes our righteousness, His wisdom becomes our wisdom, and by faith, His life becomes our life.

Nebuchadnezzar's dream was fulfilled exactly as Daniel had said it would be. But how much sorrow and grief and pain the king could have avoided if he had only listened to God's warning and followed Daniel's advice!

THE GOD OF JUSTICE AND JUDGMENT

Daniel 5

1 Belshazzar the king made a great feast for a thousand of his lords, and drank wine in the presence of the thousand. **2** While he tasted the wine, Belshazzar gave the command to bring the gold and silver vessels which his father Nebuchadnezzar had taken from the temple which had been in Jerusalem, that the king and his lords, his wives, and his concubines might drink from them. **3** Then they brought the gold vessels that had been taken from the temple of the house of God which had been in Jerusalem; and the king and his lords, his wives, and his concubines drank from them. **4** They drank wine, and praised the gods of gold and silver, bronze and iron, wood and stone.

5 In the same hour the fingers of a man's hand appeared and wrote opposite the lampstand on the plaster of the wall of the king's palace; and the king saw the part of the hand that wrote. **6** Then the king's countenance changed, and his thoughts troubled him, so that the joints of his hips were loosened and his knees knocked against each other. **7** The king cried aloud to bring in the astrologers, the Chaldeans, and the soothsayers. The king spoke, saying to the wise men of Babylon, "Whoever reads this writing, and tells me its interpretation, shall be clothed with purple and have a chain of gold around his neck; and he shall be the third ruler in the kingdom." **8** Now all the king's wise men came, but they could not read the writing, or make known to the king its interpretation. **9** Then King Belshazzar was greatly troubled, his countenance was changed, and his lords were astonished.

10 The queen, because of the words of the king and his lords, came to the banquet hall. The queen spoke, saying, "O king, live forever! Do not let your thoughts trouble you, nor let your countenance change. **11** There is a man in your kingdom in whom is the Spirit of the Holy God. And in the days of your father, light and understanding and wisdom, like the wisdom of the gods, were found in him; and King Nebuchadnezzar your father—your father the king—made him chief of the magicians, astrologers, Chaldeans, and soothsayers. **12** Inasmuch as an excellent spirit, knowledge, understanding, interpreting dreams, solving riddles, and explaining enigmas were found in this Daniel, whom the king named Belteshazzar, now let Daniel be called, and he will give the interpretation."

13 Then Daniel was brought in before the king. The king spoke, and said to Daniel, "Are you that Daniel who is one of the captives from Judah, whom my father the king brought from Judah? **14** I have heard of you, that the Spirit of God is in you, and that light and understanding and excellent wisdom are found in you. **15** Now the wise men, the astrologers, have been brought in before me, that they should read this writing and make known to me its interpretation, but they could not give the interpretation of the thing. **16** And I have heard of you, that you can give interpretations and explain enigmas. Now if you can read the writing and make known to me its interpretation, you shall be clothed with purple and have a chain of gold around your neck, and shall be the third ruler in the kingdom."

17 Then Daniel answered, and said before the king, "Let your gifts be for yourself, and give your rewards to another; yet I will read the writing to the king, and make known to him the interpretation. **18** O king, the Most High God gave Nebuchadnezzar your father a kingdom and majesty, glory and honor. **19** And because of the majesty that He gave him, all peoples, nations, and languages trembled and feared before him. Whomever he wished, he executed; whomever he wished, he kept alive; whomever he wished, he set up; and whomever he wished, he put down. **20** But when his heart was lifted up, and his spirit was hardened in pride, he was deposed from his kingly throne, and they took his glory from him. **21** Then he was driven from the sons of men, his heart was made like the beasts, and his dwelling was with the wild donkeys. They fed him with grass like oxen, and his body was wet with the dew of heaven, till he knew that the Most High God rules in the kingdom of men, and appoints over it whomever He chooses.

22 "But you his son, Belshazzar, have not humbled your heart, although you knew all this. **23** And you have lifted yourself up against the Lord of heaven. They have brought the vessels of His house before you, and you and your lords, your wives and your concubines, have drunk wine from them. And you have praised the gods of silver and gold, bronze and iron, wood and stone, which do not see or hear or know; and the God who holds your breath in His hand and owns all your ways, you have not glorified. **24** Then the fingers of the hand were sent from Him, and this writing was written.

25 "And this is the inscription that was written:

MENE, MENE, TEKEL,
UPHARSIN.

26 This is the interpretation of each word. MENE: God has numbered your kingdom, and finished it; **27** TEKEL: You have been weighed in the balances, and found wanting; **28** PERES: Your kingdom has been divided, and given to the Medes and Persians." **29** Then Belshazzar gave the command, and they clothed Daniel with purple and put a chain of gold around his neck, and made a proclamation concerning him that he should be the third ruler in the kingdom.

30 That very night Belshazzar, king of the Chaldeans, was slain. **31** And Darius the Mede received the kingdom, being about sixty-two years old.

Chapter 5 of Daniel takes place after Nebuchadnezzar has died and moved off the stage of action. Belshazzar is now the king of Babylon. Belshazzar was the son of Nabonidus. The Nabonidus Chronicle describes Belshazzar as the grandson of Nebuchadnezzar. In the entire Bible, Belshazzar is mentioned only in this chapter. And he's known for only one thing. "Belshazzar the king made a great feast for a thousand of his lords, and drank wine in the presence of the thousand" (Daniel 5:1).

That's Belshazzar's claim to fame—he's a great eater and a great drinker. The only time he's mentioned in the Bible is in the context of throwing a marvelous party! Someone has said that great eaters and great drinkers are seldom great at anything else. And Belshazzar seems to bear this out.

Knowing and doing

Belshazzar's problem was not that he didn't have information. His problem was that he didn't follow through on the information he had. That's another characteristic of Belshazzar that becomes apparent in this story. He knows, but he doesn't do anything about what he knows.

Let's imagine the scene as we go back to ancient Babylon on the night described in chapter 5. We're walking down the streets of Babylon. The moon is shining in a cloudless sky. The stars look like diamonds scattered across the heavens. Moonlight dances off the gates and buildings of Babylon. As we approach Belshazzar's palace, we hear music through the open windows. Looking in, we can see the magnificent banquet hall where the band is playing. Handsome men and beautiful women are dancing. They've been drinking; minds are fuzzy. We hear laughter. The wine is flowing. It's a drunken feast where anything goes. In a half-drunken state, Belshazzar stands and begins to speak. "Belshazzar gave the command to bring the gold and silver vessels which his father Nebuchadnezzar had taken from the temple which had been in Jerusalem, that the king and his lords, his wives, and his concubines might drink from them. Then they brought the gold vessels that had been taken from the temple of the house of God which had been in Jerusalem; and the king and his lords, his wives, and his concubines drank from them. They drank wine, and praised the gods of gold and silver, bronze and iron, wood and stone" (verses 2–4).

Belshazzar is drunk. He's not thinking clearly. His conscience is compromised. Some seventy years or so earlier, King Nebuchadnezzar had besieged Jerusalem and conquered it. He had stolen many of the gold and silver utensils used in the sacred ceremonies in the religious services of the ancient Jewish temple. He carried them back to Babylon as symbols of his triumph and as evidence that the gods of Babylon were more powerful than the God of the Hebrews and the temple in Jerusalem. Now in his drunken condition, Belshazzar commands that these gold and silver goblets be brought out so that he and his party guests could drink wine from them.

Belshazzar knew the background of these temple vessels. He knew they came from the temple in Jerusalem. He knew the symbolism of having his party guests drink their wine from them during this pagan, immoral, drunken orgy. He knew that doing this defied the God of heaven and indicated his disdain for Him.

He also knew about the experiences of his grandfather, Nebuchadnezzar. He was well acquainted with the story told in Daniel 4—how because of his pride and self-glorification, Nebuchadnezzar had been banished from human society by God's decree. He knew how and why Nebuchadnezzar had been restored. But he ignored all that and did as he pleased. And mostly, he pleased to indulge himself in pleasure.

The Bible says that as they drank wine from the sacred vessels of God's temple, they "praised the gods of gold and silver, bronze and iron, wood and stone" (verse 4). Where have we seen that sequence before? Gold, silver, bronze, iron, and stone? These are the metals of the great image Nebuchadnezzar saw in his dream in chapter 2. Could it be that Belshazzar and his guests were making fun of the dream God had given to foretell world history?

Crossing the line

Now, as he mocked and defied the true God at this drunken feast before the gathered aristocracy of Babylon, Belshazzar went too far. There is a line in the sand that God has drawn. He is patient and longsuffering with sinners, not wanting any to perish, but all to come to repentance (2 Peter 3:9). But there comes a time when God says, "You've gone too far. You can go this far in your defiance and rebellion, but no farther." God drew a line in the sand for Belshazzar and his guests that night.

A hand writes on the wall

"In the same hour the fingers of a man's hand appeared and wrote opposite the lampstand on the plaster of the wall of the king's palace; and the king saw the part of the hand that wrote. Then the king's countenance changed, and his thoughts troubled him, so that the joints of his hips were loosened and his knees knocked against each other" (verses 5, 6).

One moment, Belshazzar is the life of the party. The next, he's terrified. Horror is written all over his face. It's plain to see. His knees are knocking together in fear. His entire body is trembling. His hands are shaking. His heart races. In the midst of the cheap laughter and the sacrilegious blasphemy, God's hand appears out of nowhere—a bloodless hand, writing strange, mysterious words on the wall in letters that gleam like fire! It's no hallucination; everybody there sees them. No one can read them or knows what these strange words mean. The party has come to an abrupt halt. The music stops. Long-robed Babylonian aristocrats stand stunned at the mysterious writing. Finely gowned, sweetly perfumed Babylonian women quake in fear.

Belshazzar, shaken and terrified, falls back on the standard policy. He calls in the brain trust! "The king cried aloud to bring in the astrologers, the Chaldeans, and the soothsayers. The king spoke, saying to the wise men of Babylon, 'Whoever reads this writing, and tells me its interpretation, shall be clothed with purple and have a chain of gold around his neck; and he shall be the third ruler in the kingdom' " (verse 7).

You'd think Belshazzar would have learned *something* from Nebuchadnezzar's experience. But apparently, he has not learned a thing. The wise men of Babylon enter—a different set of astrologers and soothsayers from their predecessors of Nebuchadnezzar's time. But just like their earlier counterparts, they are no help. They can't read the writing or tell Belshazzar what it means. In Daniel 2, they couldn't tell Nebuchadnezzar what he had dreamed. In Daniel 4, they couldn't tell him the interpretation, even when he told them what he had dreamed. In Daniel 5, they can't even tell Belshazzar the meaning of the writing when they see it for themselves on the wall!

It seems that God is telling us something here. Although we live in an era of scientific advancement, computerization, and educational sophistication, we still haven't completely outgrown our fascination with astrology and fortune-tellers and psychic phenomena. Millions of people still guide their lives by horoscopes, astrology columns, and psychic forecasts. We still have the supermarket tabloids shouting their predictions for the coming year. Popular movies that captivate the minds of our children condition them to accept ghosts and goblins, wizards and warlocks, as a way of life. What is really going on here? Through their longing for the supernatural, multitudes allow their minds to be influenced by the devil. God is the only true source of wisdom, guidance, and truth. God says, "If any of you lacks wisdom, let him ask of God, who gives to all liberally and without reproach, and it will be given to him" (James 1:5). We can come to God and find in Him our source of wisdom. We can come to Him and find direction for our lives.

The queen mother points to Daniel

Belshazzar is desperate to know what the writing means. He's scared and confused. His face has terror written all over it. Not so, the queen. Apparently, she hadn't been at the party, but she enters the banquet hall when everything comes to a standstill and all is in confusion.

"The queen spoke, saying, 'O king, live forever! Do not let your thoughts trouble you, nor let your countenance change. There is a man in your kingdom in whom is the Spirit of the Holy God. And in the days of your father, light and understanding and wisdom, like the wisdom of the gods, were found in him; and King Nebuchadnezzar your father—your father the king—made him chief of the magicians, astrologers, Chaldeans, and soothsayers. . . . Now let Daniel be called, and he will give the interpretation' " (Daniel 5:10–12).

We need to review Nebuchadnezzar's family tree a bit here. The wise men had failed. The astrologers failed. The Chaldeans failed. The magicians failed. The sooth-sayers failed. Then the queen entered with a different suggestion. Who is this queen?

Daniel 5 talks about Nebuchadnezzar as the father of Belshazzar. It sounds like Belshazzar is Nebuchadnezzar's son. But that is not the case. The Bible, like other ancient documents, often uses the word *father* in the sense of *ancestor* or *forefather*. For example, Luke speaks about David being the father of Jesus (Luke 1:32). But David lived about a thousand years before Jesus. Was Jesus the literal son of David? No. If you are going to call anyone Jesus' earthly father, you would have to pick Joseph. It certainly was not David, who lived a thousand years before Jesus was born in Bethlehem.

So here in Daniel 5, when the queen refers to Nebuchadnezzar as "your father" (verse 11), she is using the word in the sense of "forefather." It's not a father-son relationship as we usually think of it. We know the relationship between Nebuchadnezzar and Belshazzar from archeology. Nebuchadnezzar had many children, but one of his daughters married a king named Nabonidus. So Nabonidus was the son-in-law of Nebuchadnezzar. Nabonidus and his wife (Nebuchadnezzar's daughter) had a son, and that son was Belshazzar. So Belshazzar was actually Nebuchadnezzar's grandson.

Now, who is the queen who appears in Daniel 5:10? Most modern translations use the expression *queen mother*. She may have been Belshazzar's mother, not his wife. Numerous Bible commentators believe she was Nitocris, the wife of Evil-Merodach, who lived during the time of Nebuchadnezzar's wild venture in the wilderness wandering around as a beast.[1] Whoever she was, she had an intimate knowledge of Daniel's influence on the Babylonian kingdom. This is interesting because Belshazzar calls in the astrologers. They fail. He calls in the magicians. They fail. He calls in the soothsayers. They fail. Belshazzar is on the verge of a mental breakdown when the aged, wise queen mother appears. Remember, his mother is well acquainted with Daniel and the affairs of the kingdom. She would have known Daniel. She knew that Daniel interpreted Nebuchadnezzar's dream of the metallic image with its head of gold, chest and arms of silver, belly and thighs of bronze, and legs of iron. She knew that Daniel had interpreted his dream about the great tree and how that dream had been fulfilled to the letter.

So the queen mother comes to the banquet hall because the word has gone all through the royal palace that the king, Belshazzar, is in big trouble because of some mysterious hand, writing incomprehensible letters on the palace wall. She reminds her son of what Daniel was able to do for his grandfather, and she says, "Let Daniel be called, and he will give the interpretation" (verse 12).

God's man in Babylon

By this time, Daniel is in his eighties. He has been in Babylon for about seventy years. Daniel knows very well the political intricacies and the history of Babylon for these seven decades. He is an elder statesman. Daniel is wise, intelligent, knowledgeable, and a servant of the Most High God. He has interpreted dreams, solved problems, and provided wise counsel. Daniel is God's man in Babylon. For seventy years, he's had a sterling reputation for his character of honesty and integrity.

If Daniel could be faithful to God in Babylon, that citadel of immorality, drunkenness, and false religion, you and I can be faithful to God where we are. We can be faithful to God in our school, in our home, and in our workplace. We can be faithful to God in our entertainment, in our finances, and in our lifestyle and diets. No matter what others around us are doing, we can be faithful to God. No matter what circumstances we find ourselves in, we can be faithful to God. But remember this: Daniel wasn't in Babylon by his choice. When you are placed in an environment that you do not choose, when the circumstances around you are not under your control, God can still keep you faithful just as He kept Daniel faithful.

The queen mother told the king, "Bring in Daniel if you want to know what the writing on the wall means." And Belshazzar, still half-drunk, called for Daniel.

"The king spoke, and said to Daniel, 'Are you that Daniel who is one of the captives from Judah, whom my father the king brought from Judah? I have heard of you, that the Spirit of God is in you. . . . I have heard of you, that you can give interpretations and explain enigmas. Now if you can read the writing and make known to me its interpretation, you shall be clothed with purple and have a chain of gold around your neck, and shall be the third ruler in the kingdom' " (verses 13–16).

You talk about insulting! Daniel is the elder statesman in the Babylonian Empire. He's been there for some seventy years through all the ups and downs of the kingdom. Belshazzar may be the king, but he is a young, brash, rebellious upstart looking into the eyes of this great man of integrity. "I've heard of you," he tells Daniel condescendingly. "Aren't you that Hebrew captive my grandfather brought from Judah?" Who did he think was running the empire while Nebuchadnezzar was out eating grass for seven years? "I've heard you can interpret mysterious things. If you can interpret the writing on the wall, I'll owe you a favor."

Daniel's finest hour

What was Daniel's response? "Let your gifts be for yourself," he replied, "and give your rewards to another; yet I will read the writing to the king, and make known to him the interpretation" (verse 17).

"I have no interest in your bribes," Daniel told him. "I can't be bought, but I will tell you what you want to know." What would Daniel want with a purple robe and a gold chain? Why would he want to be the third ruler in the kingdom, when he had been the second ruler under Nebuchadnezzar? Daniel wasn't marching to the earthly beat of wealth or power. His goal was to serve God and please Him. There is a well-known quote that aptly summarizes Daniel's inner spiritual strength: "The greatest want of the world is the want of men—men who will not be bought or sold, men who in their inmost souls are true and honest, men who do not fear to call sin by its right name, men whose conscience is as true to duty as the needle to the pole, men who will stand for the right though the heavens fall."[2] Daniel could not be bought or sold. He did not yield his conscientious convictions for a few moments of fame. In his inmost soul, he was true and honest. He stood for the right irrespective of the consequences.

This is Daniel's finest hour. He told the king, "I am going to give you the interpretation of the writing, not because you give me money but because it is the right thing to do."

By now, the supernatural hand has stopped writing and has disappeared. Half-empty wine glasses sit untouched on tables. Beautifully dressed men and women stand like statues in the center of Babylon's dance floor, their arms hanging at their sides. Everyone is looking at the words on the wall. Where there was once laughter, there is now silence. Where there was once revelry, there is now tense anxiety. Where there was once unbridled pleasure-seeking, there is now terror-stricken fear.

Daniel knows that the Medo-Persian armies are marching toward the city at that very moment. He has already read the writing on the wall. He knows what it means. He knows this is Babylon's last night. He already knows that Belshazzar will be dead before morning and that no one standing on that dance floor will get out of the banquet hall alive. And in that knowledge, Daniel makes a final appeal. He begins eloquently tracing the history of Babylon under the rule of Nebuchadnezzar. God gave Nebuchadnezzar his kingdom, Daniel declares. And as long as Nebuchadnezzar followed God, he prospered as did his kingdom. But when he turned away from God, he lost his kingdom and became like an animal.

Then the aged prophet says, "But you his son, Belshazzar, have not humbled your heart, although you knew all this. And you have lifted yourself up against the Lord of heaven. They have brought the vessels of His house before you, and you and your lords, your wives and your concubines, have drunk wine from them. And you have praised the gods of silver and gold, bronze and iron, wood and stone, which do not see or hear or know; and the God who holds your breath in His hand and owns all your ways, you have not glorified" (verses 22, 23).

What an indictment!

"You knew," Daniel declares. "You knew what Nebuchadnezzar went through. You knew that God is mighty. You knew, but you did nothing about it." What will God say to us in this generation who live in the light of fulfilled Bible prophecy? Will He have to say of you or me, "You knew, but you did nothing about it"? What a fool Belshazzar was to turn away from what he knew to be fortune-tellers!

Then Daniel turned toward the writing on the wall and interpreted it for all those standing there. "This is the interpretation of each word. MENE: God has numbered your kingdom, and finished it; TEKEL: You have been weighed in the balances, and found wanting; PERES: Your kingdom has been divided, and given to the Medes and Persians" (verses 26–28).

Belshazzar's last night

It was Babylon's last night. It was Belshazzar's last hour. It was the kingdom's last moment on the landscape of history. Babylon's accumulated sin had reached the point that God said, "It is enough." Belshazzar had crossed God's line in the sand. As Daniel pronounced the nation's doom, the doors of the banquet hall flew open. The swords of the Medo-Persian soldiers flashed in the candlelight. Belshazzar fell to the floor, thrust through by the swords of his enemies. There was a terrible slaughter all through Babylon. God's mercy had reached out to them. In love, He appealed to them, but they had refused. And now, judgment fell. "That very night Belshazzar, king of the Chaldeans, was slain. And Darius the Mede received the kingdom, being about sixty-two years old" (verses 30, 31).

There's a last dance, a last drink, a last party, a last night for everyone and everything on earth. We all will experience our last moments on earth. Time runs out for your life and for mine. No one will be lost because of what they didn't know. Those who are lost will be lost because they didn't do what they knew to be right. They did not respond to the wooing of God's Spirit. They did not accept the salvation He has so freely provided. They did not yield to the appeal of His grace.

God gave Belshazzar time. God gave him the example of Nebuchadnezzar. But Belshazzar ignored God's efforts to save him. He wasted the time God gave him to repent. Like Babylon, this world is rapidly approaching its last night. Like Babylon, the judgments of God will soon fall. The question this chapter brings home to each of us is this: Will we follow in the footsteps of Belshazzar and be lost in earth's final moment because we don't do what we know we should? Or will we stand, like Daniel, faithful to the God of heaven? As you read these pages, the Spirit of God is appealing to you. The hand of God is writing His appeal on the tablets of your heart. He is impressing you to surrender your life fully to Him. If you have already committed your life to this God of everlasting love, will you bow your head and ask Him to keep you faithful to Him always? If you have never responded to His gracious invitation to follow Him, will you make that decision right now? He will fill your heart with joy, peace, and satisfaction that you have never known before. Why not bow your head and pray right now?

---

1. David Bayliss, "Daniel 5 - Nitocris/Belshazzar," *Bible Exposition*, last modified April 17, 2020, http://www.dabhand.org/Essays/OT572%20C5%20Nitocris.htm.

2. Ellen G. White, *Education* (Oakland, CA: Pacific Press® 1903), 57.

THE GOD WHO REWARDS FAITHFULNESS

Daniel 6

1 It pleased Darius to set over the kingdom one hundred and twenty satraps, to be over the whole kingdom; **2** and over these, three governors, of whom Daniel was one, that the satraps might give account to them, so that the king would suffer no loss. **3** Then this Daniel distinguished himself above the governors and satraps, because an excellent spirit was in him; and the king gave thought to setting him over the whole realm. **4** So the governors and satraps sought to find some charge against Daniel concerning the kingdom; but they could find no charge or fault, because he was faithful; nor was there any error or fault found in him. **5** Then these men said, "We shall not find any charge against this Daniel unless we find it against him concerning the law of his God."

6 So these governors and satraps thronged before the king, and said thus to him: "King Darius, live forever! **7** All the governors of the kingdom, the administrators and satraps, the counselors and advisors, have consulted together to establish a royal statute and to make a firm decree, that whoever petitions any god or man for thirty days, except you, O king, shall be cast into the den of lions. **8** Now, O king, establish the decree and sign the writing, so that it cannot be changed, according to the law of the Medes and Persians, which does not alter." **9** Therefore King Darius signed the written decree.

10 Now when Daniel knew that the writing was signed, he went home. And in his upper room, with his windows open toward Jerusalem, he knelt down on his knees three times that day, and prayed and gave thanks before his God, as was his custom since early days.

11 Then these men assembled and found Daniel praying and making supplication before his God. **12** And they went before the king, and spoke concerning the king's decree: "Have you not signed a decree that every man who petitions any god or man within thirty days, except you, O king, shall be cast into the den of lions?"

The king answered and said, "The thing is true, according to the law of the Medes and Persians, which does not alter."

13 So they answered and said before the king, "That Daniel, who is one of the captives from Judah, does not show due regard for you, O king, or for the decree that you have signed, but makes his petition three times a day."

14 And the king, when he heard these words, was greatly displeased with himself, and set his heart on Daniel to deliver him; and he labored till the going down of the sun to deliver him. **15** Then these men approached the king, and said to the king, "Know, O king, that it is the law of the Medes and Persians that no decree or statute which the king establishes may be changed."

16 So the king gave the command, and they brought Daniel and cast him into the den of lions. But the king spoke, saying to Daniel, "Your God, whom you serve continually, He will deliver you." **17** Then a stone was brought and laid on the mouth of the den, and the king sealed it with his own signet ring and with the signets of his lords, that the purpose concerning Daniel might not be changed.

18 Now the king went to his palace and spent the night fasting; and no musicians were brought before him. Also his sleep went from him. **19** Then the king arose very early in the morning and went in haste to the den of lions. **20** And when he came to the den, he cried out with a lamenting voice to Daniel. The king spoke, saying to Daniel, "Daniel, servant of the living God, has your God, whom you serve continually, been able to deliver you from the lions?"

21 Then Daniel said to the king, "O king, live forever! **22** My God sent His angel and shut the lions' mouths, so that they have not hurt me, because I was found innocent before Him; and also, O king, I have done no wrong before you."

23 Now the king was exceedingly glad for him, and commanded that they should take Daniel up out of the den. So Daniel was taken up out of the den, and no injury whatever was found on him, because he believed in his God.

24 And the king gave the command, and they brought those men who had accused Daniel, and they cast them into the den of lions—them, their children, and their wives; and the lions overpowered them, and broke all their bones in pieces before they ever came to the bottom of the den.

25 Then King Darius wrote:

To all peoples, nations, and languages that dwell in all the earth:

Peace be multiplied to you.

26 I make a decree that in every dominion of my kingdom men must tremble and fear before the God of Daniel.

For He is the living God,
And steadfast forever;
His kingdom is the one which shall
  not be destroyed,
And His dominion shall endure to the
  end.
27 He delivers and rescues,
And He works signs and wonders

In heaven and on earth,
Who has delivered Daniel from the
  power of the lions.

28 So this Daniel prospered in the reign of Darius and in the reign of Cyrus the Persian.

The fifth chapter of Daniel 5 leads directly into chapter 6. Chapter 5 ends with the death of Belshazzar and the fall of Babylon to the Medes and Persians. "That very night Belshazzar, king of the Chaldeans, was slain. And Darius the Mede received the kingdom" (Daniel 5:30, 31). So Babylon fell. Nabopolassar, Nebuchadnezzar, Nabonidus, Belshazzar—the great kings of Babylon—were defeated. Their kingdom crumbled in the dust. They became memories on the ash heap of history. Then, Darius the Mede took the kingdom.

Let's summarize what we discovered in these early chapters of Daniel's book. Chapter 1 introduces us to the God who turns defeat into victory. In chapter 2, He is the God who reveals the future. In Daniel 3, He is the God who delivers His people. Chapter 4 portrays Him as the God who rules over all. Then in chapter 5, we see Him as the God of justice and judgment. His love knows no bounds, His mercy is endless, but our choices can harden our hearts so that we no longer are capable of responding to His love. Now here in chapter 6, we will see Him as the God who never leaves or forsakes us. He is the God who is steadfast forever.

Daniel is given authority in the new kingdom

When the Medes and Persians took over the kingdom just as God had predicted they would in the dream He gave Nebuchadnezzar, Darius decided to reorganize the government.

"It pleased Darius to set over the kingdom one hundred and twenty satraps, to be over the whole kingdom; and over these, three governors, of whom Daniel was one. . . . Then this Daniel distinguished himself above the governors and satraps, because an excellent spirit was in him; and the king gave thought to setting him over the whole realm" (Daniel 6:1–3).

Notice what has happened here. Babylon has fallen, and Media-Persia now rules the Middle East. The new king, Darius the Mede, appoints *Babylon's* prime minister, to be one of his trusted officials. He brought Daniel into his government and placed him in charge of all the other officials, second only to Darius himself! That's absolutely incredible! In most countries, even today, when a new administration comes in, it sweeps out the old and puts its own people in positions of power. What Darius did would be like China overthrowing America and then making the American vice president the second most powerful officer in the Chinese government—or vice versa. It just doesn't happen that way. It becomes even more incredible when we remember Daniel's age at this point. Daniel has spent some seven decades in Babylon. He's in his eighties.

Clearly, Darius saw something special in Daniel. Throughout his career in Babylon, Daniel had been a man of integrity. A man of honesty. A man who faithfully carried out his responsibilities both to the kingdom and to his God. The king could depend on Daniel's word. Darius knew that Daniel would serve him just as faithfully as he had served the kings of Babylon.

The world today is in need of Daniels. Even in this materialistic, pleasure-mad, dog-eat-dog world, there are those who admire integrity, authenticity, transparency, and honesty. Perhaps you remember the story that came out of ancient Greece of Diogenes and his lantern. The philosopher Diogenes would walk the streets of Athens at night carrying a lantern. He would go up to people and hold the lantern beside their face. "What are you doing?" they would ask.

And Diogenes would reply, "I'm looking for an honest man." He was trying to make a point.

Today, God is looking for Daniels. He's looking for men and women who determine in their heart to serve Him. God is looking today for men and women of integrity. Darius found such a man in Daniel; that's why he made Daniel second-in-command of the Medo-Persian Empire. It was a thoughtful move on the new king's part. However, as you can imagine, it didn't sit well with those whom Darius had passed over in order to elevate the "foreigner," Daniel!

Envy of Daniel becomes a significant problem

The Bible says Darius set 120 "satraps" over the kingdom. And over these satraps, he placed three governors, of whom Daniel was the head. All the satraps were accountable to the three governors, and two of the governors were accountable to Daniel, the chief governor. Daniel was directly accountable only to Darius, the king. It didn't take long for jealousy to fill the minds of the two governors and the 120 satraps. It did not take long for envy to consume their thoughts. They were threatened by Daniel's sterling character and his unsullied reputation. It is possible that they had thoughts something like this: "Just who does this Daniel think he is? He is a holdover from the Babylonians. And he isn't even a real Babylonian; he's a Jewish captive. How can we trust him? What makes Darius think Daniel is loyal to Media-Persia? What right does Daniel have to rule over us?" No doubt, these were some of the objections they raised. The more they thought about it, the more angry, jealous, and envious they were of Daniel. Hatred filled their hearts. "So the governors and the satraps sought to find some charge against Daniel concerning the kingdom; but they could find no charge or fault, because he was faithful; nor was there any error or fault found in him" (verse 4).

> The world today is in need of Daniels. Even in this materialistic, pleasure-mad, dog-eat-dog world, there are those who admire integrity, authenticity, transparency, and honesty.

They searched in vain to find something they could report to Darius. They tried to find something, anything, for which they could condemn him. They looked for some fault, some mistake, or some inkling of disloyalty. They tried to find something they could pin on Daniel. He must have some skeletons somewhere in his closet! If there had been computers in those days, they would have tried to hack into his email. If there had been cell phones in those days, they would have bugged his phone. No doubt, they snooped around in his office and went over the royal accounts, trying to find evidence of wrongdoing on Daniel's part. Everything they could check, they checked. They scrutinized Daniel's official life, and they couldn't find a single thing they could accuse him of.

What if somebody checked your private life that intensely? What if they checked mine? What if they carefully examined the kind of books and magazines you read, the kind of television programs you watch, the kind of movies you view, the words that you speak, the surfing you do on the internet, and the things you do when no one is looking? What would they find? That's what these jealous officials did to Daniel—and they found that Daniel had nothing to hide.

It's a wonderful thing when you have nothing to hide. There is a wonderful peace when you can go to bed at night and know there is nothing you need to be afraid someone will discover about you. There is a peace that comes with a life like that.

The plot against Daniel's life

They could find nothing wrong in Daniel's official conduct. "Then these men said, 'We shall not find any charge against this Daniel unless we find it against him concerning the law of his God' " (verse 5).

If somebody condemns you for your obedience and allegiance to God, so be it. If somebody condemns you because you are a principled, moral person, so be it. Wear that criticism like a badge of honor.

"So these governors and satraps thronged before the king, and said thus to him: 'King Darius, live forever! All the governors of the kingdom, the administrators and satraps, the counselors and advisors, have consulted together to establish a royal statute and to make a firm decree, that whoever petitions any god or man for thirty days, except you, O king, shall be cast into the den of lions. Now, O king, establish the decree and sign the writing, so that it cannot be changed, according to the law of the Medes and Persians, which does not alter' " (verses 6–8).

Immediately, we recognize that what they told the king was a bald-faced lie. Why? Notice carefully what they said: "*All* the governors of the kingdom have consulted together to propose this decree." They claimed that *all* the governors had agreed not to pray to anyone other than the king for thirty days. Had the first governor agreed to this? Had they consulted with Daniel and secured his support for this law? Of course not! They had hatched this scheme in order to trap Daniel. Of course, he didn't know about it and hadn't been consulted.

Why didn't Darius check with his chief governor before signing the decree? We don't know. Perhaps vanity was one reason. Perhaps he liked the idea of being the only one receiving prayers for thirty days. Whatever his reason, Darius went along without any questions. He signed the law as his officials suggested (verse 9).

Observe what is happening here. The officials were jealous of Daniel. Their jealousy led to lying, and their lying led to the willingness to put to death an innocent man. That is the way sin works. Sin cherished never gets less powerful in the life; it always becomes more powerful. Drug addicts describe cocaine addiction as "the monkey on your back." The monkey starts out small but then grows to a full-grown gorilla. If there is a monkey on your back, it may appear cute at first, but if you feed it, the monkey will become a gorilla and eventually crush you. It starts out small. It doesn't seem like a big deal. But it grows and grows and grows until it kills you. Sin is like that. If we let it remain in our lives, it never gets smaller; it always gets bigger. Once you start knowingly and willingly indulging sin in your mind, it's only going to grow bigger as the years pass until it crushes out your life. For these Medo-Persian officials, jealousy led

to envy, envy led to lying, and lying led to the hope of murdering their rival.

They made it clear to Darius before he signed that the decree couldn't be reversed or annulled. In Media-Persia, when a law was put into practice, even the king did not have veto power over it. Once signed, everyone had to obey it. The decree was fixed. It could not be altered, changed, or retracted. Darius knew this, and he willingly signed what they put before him.

Daniel remains faithful to God

I'm sure the officials lost no time in publishing the law and making sure everyone knew about it. I'm sure that when Daniel learned about the law, he knew exactly who and what was behind it. How did he respond?

"Now when Daniel knew that the writing was signed, he went home. And in his upper room, with his windows open toward Jerusalem, he knelt down on his knees three times that day, and prayed and gave thanks before his God, as was his custom since early days" (verse 10).

Daniel didn't try to hide his disobedience to the new law. He prayed "in his upper room, with his windows open toward Jerusalem." He was not concerned about the king's officials seeing him. He did not worry about the penalty for disobeying the royal decree. He certainly was not saying, "Arrest me, if you can, I'm the second most powerful man in the kingdom. I'm above the law, and I'll show you I'm more powerful than you are."

Some people might view Daniel's actions that way—except that the verse says he prayed in his upper room in front of the open windows *as was his custom since early days.* What Daniel was doing was nothing new. It was what he always did. It was his habit to pray three times a day with his windows open toward Jerusalem, the city of his youth, the city where the temple of his God was located. Daniel was not purposely acting defiant. He was remaining faithful to his God.

Daniel knew that where there is no prayer, there is no power. Daniel would not allow his relationship with Darius to interfere with his loyalty to God. God had been with him for seventy years in Babylon. God had strengthened him as a teenager to purpose in his heart to be faithful to God. God had given him wisdom, knowledge, and skill to interpret the king's dream. God had delivered Shadrach, Meshach, and Abednego from the fiery furnace. God had enabled him to hold the Babylonian Empire together for seven years during the time that Nebuchadnezzar lost his mind and was living like an animal. God had shown him the meaning of the words written on Belshazzar's palace wall. God had given him the position of first governor in the Medo-Persian Empire.

Daniel knew that God had been with him and that He was going to continue to be with him. He was not going to yield to the commands of a heathen king when they collided with his allegiance to God. Daniel knew that God was the source of his strength and that prayer was his connection to God. For Daniel, prayer was not a mere formality. It was not a meaningless ritual. It was a living experience with the King of the universe. In prayer, Daniel opened his heart to God and communed with Him as a friend. Prayer wasn't some memorized formula to recite without thinking too much about it. To Daniel, prayer was the very breath of his soul, the vital connection between him and God. So Daniel wasn't about to stop praying just because these jealous officials were looking for some way to destroy him.

Notice something else about this decree. What does it say about how Daniel's enemies viewed him? It says they *knew* he would disobey the decree! Why would they go to the trouble to convince Darius to sign the law if they thought Daniel would just stop praying to God for thirty days? The decree itself tells us that they knew Daniel would remain faithful to his God—that he would keep on praying as he always had. As soon as his enemies saw Daniel praying, they hastened to the king as quickly as possible to tell him that Daniel was disobeying the new law. They knew Darius held Daniel in high esteem. I'm sure they were delighted to report that he was disregarding the law Darius had signed.

The issue of worship in the last days

Now there are some very significant issues involved in this decree. Let's look at it carefully. The heart of the decree concerns the conflict between loyalty to God and loyalty to the king, between God's law and man's law. The first of God's Ten Commandments says, "You shall have no other gods before Me" (Exodus 20:3). That's pretty clear. The law Darius signed declared, "Don't worship anyone except the king." It's plain that God's law and man's law were in direct conflict.

In the sunset of his life, Daniel faced a conflict over worship. Whom do *you* worship? Do you worship God or man? How do you worship? Do you worship by following God's commandments or the king's decree? When do you worship? Will you put off your worship of God for thirty days? Near the end of Daniel's life, he had to face all these questions about loyalty and worship.

At the end of time, these issues will take center stage for everyone on earth. A test will come that calls men and women back to worship their Creator. In the final hours of earth's history, the issue will, once again, be centered on worship, loyalty, and obedience. In the book of Revelation, the apostle John writes, "I saw another angel flying in the midst of heaven, having the everlasting gospel to preach to those who dwell on the earth—to every nation, tribe, tongue, and people—saying with a loud voice, 'Fear God and give glory to Him, for the hour of His judgment has come; and worship Him who made heaven and earth, the sea and springs of water' " (Revelation 14:6).

This angel's message is a universal one. It leaps across geographical boundaries, going to every country in the world, and penetrating every language group. It's a call to "fear" God—that is, to reverence and respect Him. It doesn't mean that we should be afraid of God. We are to reverence Him and give Him glory. We glorify God by faithfully following Him and obeying His commandments. We reverence and obey Him because He is the Creator. He gives us life. He made our world and everything in it. Here is a call to worship the Creator, to give our loyalty to the One who made us. That's the message of this first angel John saw in the vision. But he also saw a third angel.

"Then a third angel followed them, saying with a loud voice, 'If anyone worships the beast and his image, and receives his mark on his forehead or on his hand, he himself shall also drink of the wine of the wrath of God' " (verse 9).

We will have more to say about these angels and their messages when we explore the book of Revelation. But it's clear from these two verses that there is going to be a conflict in the last days related to worship. Verse 6 says, "Worship the Creator." Verse 9 says, "Don't worship the beast or his image." And verse 12 tells us how to avoid worshiping the beast. "Here is the patience of the saints; here are those who keep the commandments of God and the faith of Jesus." Those who don't worship the beast have faith *in* Jesus and the faith *of* Jesus, and that leads them to obey all of God's commandments.

> Daniel would not allow his relationship with Darius to interfere with his loyalty to God. God had been with him for seventy years in Babylon. God had strengthened him as a teenager to purpose in his heart to be faithful to God.

In the last days, a human authority will unite church and state and pass a decree that forbids genuine worship of the Creator. Daniel 3 and Daniel 6 are parallel experiences. In Daniel 3, a powerful world leader passed a decree that if anyone did not bow down and worship the image the leader had made, that person would be thrown into a fiery furnace. Shadrach, Meshach, and Abed-Nego were loyal and faithful to God. In God's power, they stood obedient to heaven's commands while the Babylonian nation bowed down to the golden image. In Daniel 6, at the end of Daniel's life, Darius passed a decree that unless a person worshiped him in the prescribed, approved way, that person would be put to death in a den of lions. According to the book of Revelation, there will be a similar decree in the last days. Once again, those who are loyal to God will be threatened with death. Again, the issues will be worship, loyalty, and obedience.

What will we do when we face the crisis of the last days? Will we stand firm like Daniel and his three friends? If we cannot stand up for God today in a time of freedom, how will we do so when all the power of a combined church-state union is arrayed against us, commanding us upon pain of death to obey it and disobey God? Do you think Daniel prepared for this crisis in the moments following the decree Darius signed? Or was he able to stand firm for God because he had been making decisions all along the way to serve God no matter the cost? If in those early days as a captive in Babylon, Daniel had not purposed in his heart not to defile himself with the king's food and drink, he would never have been able, near the close of his life, to continue praying to God three times a day in spite of the king's decree.

Darius tries to save Daniel

As soon as the officials reported to Darius that Daniel was disobeying his decree, the king realized what was going on. He saw that he had been tricked into carrying out their jealous plot against their enemy. "The king, when he heard these words, was greatly displeased with himself, and set his heart on Daniel to deliver him; and he labored till the going down of the sun to deliver him" (Daniel 6:14). But try as he might, there was no way out. The officials reminded him that even the king could not annul a duly signed decree. Darius reluctantly gave the command to throw Daniel into the den of hungry lions. But before he did so, the king made a startling statement. He told Daniel, "Your God, whom you serve continually, He will deliver you" (verse 16).

How could Darius be so sure God would deliver Daniel? It could only be because, in the short time his life had intersected with this aged prophet, Daniel had been able to witness to the king both in words and by his life about the God he served. Darius must have seen God in Daniel's life. He must have listened as Daniel told him about the God of heaven. He had faith in Daniel that Daniel was innocent of any wrongdoing. And he had enough faith in Daniel's God to believe that He would save him from being eaten by the lions. What a tremendous statement about Daniel's faithful witness.

Then they threw Daniel into the den with the hungry lions. They closed the mouth of the den with a large stone and sealed it using the king's own signet ring and the signet rings of his officials. Daniel's enemies wanted to take no chances that someone might try to move the stone and save Daniel's life.

Peace versus no peace

"The king went to his palace and spent the night fasting; and no musicians were brought before him. Also his sleep went from him" (verse 18). Darius knew that what he had done was wrong. His stomach was in knots. He couldn't eat. He couldn't sleep. He tossed and turned all night. *Is Daniel dead? Has his God saved his life?* His mind was going in circles. Thoughts of guilt swirled around in his head and tormented him.

While the king spent the night in a magnificent palace with all the splendor and opulence of Babylon, Daniel spent it in the dirty, smelly den of lions. Do you think Daniel slept that night? We don't know. Maybe he went to sleep with his head against a lion for a pillow! Maybe he stayed awake all night praying. Maybe he slept awhile and stayed awake awhile. We just don't know. But we do know this promise: "You will keep him in perfect peace, whose mind is stayed on You, because he trusts You" (Isaiah 26:3). Daniel trusted God; his mind was focused on God. So he spent that night in the lion's den in perfect peace.

The Lord says to us, "Peace I leave with you, My peace I give to you; not as the world gives do I give to you. Let not your heart be troubled, neither let it be afraid" (John 14:27). Peace doesn't come from outside. Peace doesn't come from having a large bank account or wealthy, influential friends. Peace comes from the inside. It comes from knowing and trusting God. Daniel had perfect peace down in that smelly, dirty den of lions because he knew that things were right between him and God. Darius, on the other hand, spent the night in his beautiful palace, but he had no peace at all because he knew what he had done was wrong. Peace doesn't depend on circumstances; peace depends on knowing and following God.

> God is a lion tamer. When the lions of temptation, anger, lust, and discouragement roar in your life, God is able to shut their mouths so that they cannot hurt you.

God shuts the lions' mouths

The king arose very early in the morning and went in haste to the den of lions.

85

And when he came to the den, he cried out with a lamenting voice to Daniel. The king spoke to Daniel, "Daniel, servant of the living God, has your God, whom you serve continually, been able to deliver you from the lions?"

Then Daniel said to the king, "O king, live forever! My God sent His angel and shut the lions' mouths, so that they have not hurt me" (Daniel 6:19, 20).

God is a lion tamer. When the lions of temptation, anger, lust, and discouragement roar in your life, God is able to shut their mouths so that they cannot hurt you.

"Now the king was exceedingly glad for him, and commanded that they should take Daniel up out of the den. So Daniel was taken up out of the den, and no injury whatsoever was found on him, because he believed in his God" (verse 23).

God still shuts lions' mouths. He did it for Daniel, and He can do it for you.

Daniel's accusers were not so fortunate. Darius had them thrown into the den that Daniel had spent the night in. The Bible says that "the lions overpowered them, and broke all their bones in pieces before they ever came to the bottom of the den" (verse 24). A sad ending. But it illustrates the results of sin. The devil, like a roaring lion, goes around seeking whom he can devour (1 Peter 5:8). Those who, like Daniel's accusers, have placed themselves outside God's protection, have no shield against Satan's efforts to destroy them. But, God can shut the mouth of the devil for those who have put their trust in Him. What hope, what glorious assurance, God is steadfast forever. He will never leave or forsake us. Wherever our circumstances find us, in sickness or in health, in poverty or in wealth, alone or surrounded by friends, in sorrow or in joy, God is there. He is the God who cares, the God who listens, the God who strengthens, the God who fills our hearts with hope and gives us the ability to handle whatever the devil throws at us. He is the ever-present, all-powerful Lord, and that is something to rejoice about.

KINGDOMS IN COLLISION

Daniel 7

1 In the first year of Belshazzar king of Babylon, Daniel had a dream and visions of his head while on his bed. Then he wrote down the dream, telling the main facts.

2 Daniel spoke, saying, "I saw in my vision by night, and behold, the four winds of heaven were stirring up the Great Sea. **3** And four great beasts came up from the sea, each different from the other. **4** The first was like a lion, and had eagle's wings. I watched till its wings were plucked off; and it was lifted up from the earth and made to stand on two feet like a man, and a man's heart was given to it.

5 "And suddenly another beast, a second, like a bear. It was raised up on one side, and had three ribs in its mouth between its teeth. And they said thus to it: 'Arise, devour much flesh!'

6 "After this I looked, and there was another, like a leopard, which had on its back four wings of a bird. The beast also had four heads, and dominion was given to it.

7 "After this I saw in the night visions, and behold, a fourth beast, dreadful and terrible, exceedingly strong. It had huge iron teeth; it was devouring, breaking in pieces, and trampling the residue with its feet. It was different from all the beasts that were before it, and it had ten horns. **8** I was considering the horns, and there was another horn, a little one, coming up among them, before whom three of the first horns were plucked out by the roots. And there, in this horn, were eyes like the eyes of a man, and a mouth speaking pompous words.

9 "I watched till thrones were put in
place,
And the Ancient of Days was seated;
His garment was white as snow,
And the hair of His head was like pure
wool.
His throne was a fiery flame,
Its wheels a burning fire;
10 A fiery stream issued
And came forth from before Him.

A thousand thousands ministered to
Him;
Ten thousand times ten thousand
stood before Him.
The court was seated,
And the books were opened.

11 "I watched then because of the
sound of the pompous words which the
horn was speaking; I watched till the
beast was slain, and its body destroyed
and given to the burning flame. **12** As
for the rest of the beasts, they had their
dominion taken away, yet their lives
were prolonged for a season and a time.

13 "I was watching in the night
visions,
And behold, One like the Son of Man,
Coming with the clouds of heaven!
He came to the Ancient of Days,
And they brought Him near before
Him.
14 Then to Him was given dominion
and glory and a kingdom,
That all peoples, nations, and
languages should serve Him.
His dominion is an everlasting
dominion,
Which shall not pass away,
And His kingdom the one
Which shall not be destroyed.

15 "I, Daniel, was grieved in my
spirit within my body, and the visions
of my head troubled me. **16** I came near
to one of those who stood by, and asked

him the truth of all this. So he told me
and made known to me the interpretation of these things: **17** 'Those great
beasts, which are four, are four kings
which arise out of the earth. **18** But
the saints of the Most High shall receive
the kingdom, and possess the kingdom
forever, even forever and ever.'

19 "Then I wished to know the
truth about the fourth beast, which was
different from all the others, exceedingly
dreadful, with its teeth of iron and its
nails of bronze, which devoured, broke
in pieces, and trampled the residue with
its feet; **20** and the ten horns that were
on its head, and the other horn which
came up, before which three fell, namely,
that horn which had eyes and a mouth
which spoke pompous words, whose
appearance was greater than his fellows.
21 "I was watching; and the same
horn was making war against the saints,
and prevailing against them, **22** until
the Ancient of Days came, and a judgment was made in favor of the saints of
the Most High, and the time came for
the saints to possess the kingdom.
23 "Thus he said:

'The fourth beast shall be
A fourth kingdom on earth,
Which shall be different from all other
kingdoms,
And shall devour the whole earth,
Trample it and break it in pieces.
24 The ten horns are ten kings
Who shall arise from this kingdom.

And another shall rise after them;
He shall be different from the first ones,
And shall subdue three kings.

25 He shall speak pompous words against the Most High,
Shall persecute the saints of the Most High,
And shall intend to change times and law.
Then the saints shall be given into his hand
For a time and times and half a time.

26 'But the court shall be seated,
And they shall take away his dominion,
To consume and destroy it forever.

27 Then the kingdom and dominion,
And the greatness of the kingdoms under the whole heaven,
Shall be given to the people, the saints of the Most High.
His kingdom is an everlasting kingdom,
And all dominions shall serve and obey Him.'

28 "This is the end of the account. As for me, Daniel, my thoughts greatly troubled me, and my countenance changed; but I kept the matter in my heart."

The first six chapters of the book of Daniel highlight the great controversy between God and Satan, specifically relating to God's law and issues of worship. In chapter 1, King Nebuchadnezzar attacked God's temple at Jerusalem and defiled the temple by taking the holy vessels and bringing them to Babylon. In chapter 2, God revealed to Nebuchadnezzar in a dream that He is the King of kings and supreme over all the affairs of earth. In chapter 3, Nebuchadnezzar refused to accept God's supremacy and established a counterfeit image. The powerful world ruler passed a decree commanding men and women to violate the commandments of God by worshiping the image he had made. In chapter 4, God humbled Nebuchadnezzar in order to show him that God is in control. In chapter 5, Belshazzar deliberately defied God by defiling the holy vessels from the Jerusalem sanctuary. Babylon fell that very night as Media-Persia triumphed. And, in chapter 6, the issue revolves around worship and obedience. A death decree is established against those who worship God and are obedient to His commands.

Chapter 7 marks a transition in Daniel's book. The first six chapters are mostly historical; the last six are prophetic. The first six chapters deal with literal kings and the literal temple in Jerusalem. The last six chapters do not focus on the earthly sanctuary; they focus on the sanctuary in heaven. In the last six chapters, a new power arises, combining both religious and political authority. This power tries to cause men and women to defile the sanctuary in heaven. It challenges God's law as established in heaven itself. The lessons we've learned in the first six chapters of Daniel include faithfulness, obedience, and the worship of the true God. The last six chapters apply these lessons at a time when this political and religious power tries to change the very heart of God's law.

The Bible's two sanctuaries

To understand the last six chapters of Daniel, we must first understand something about the Bible's two sanctuaries. After God led the children of Israel out of Egypt and set them on their journey to the Promised Land, He told Moses, "Let them [the Israelites] make Me a sanctuary, that I may dwell among them. According to all that I show you, that is, the pattern of the tabernacle and the pattern of all its furnishings, just so you shall make it" (Exodus 25:8, 9).

He concluded his instruction by saying, "See to it that you make them [the sanctuary and its furnishings] according to the pattern which was shown you on the mountain" (verse 40).

God took Moses up on Mount Sinai, and there He showed him the "pattern"—the dimensions, arrangement, and layout for the earthly sanctuary. The sanctuary Moses built in the wilderness on the way to the Promised Land was a tentlike structure surrounded by a courtyard. Later, after Israel was established in the Promised Land, Solomon built a permanent sanctuary following the same "pattern" as the one Moses built. Solomon's temple was the one in Jerusalem from which Nebuchadnezzar carried off the sacred utensils when he conquered the city.

In the pattern God showed Moses of the sanctuary, the building was divided into two parts—the Holy Place and the Most Holy Place. This earthly sanctuary illustrates the plan of salvation. It was God's way of teaching lessons that the Jewish nation needed to prepare themselves for the coming of Jesus as the Messiah and Savior of the world.

In the Old Testament, if someone sinned, that person was to bring an offering to the sanctuary. For example, if it was a lamb, it must be perfect, without spot or blemish. The sinner must confess his sin over the lamb and slit its throat with a knife, letting its lifeblood run out! This was not easy to do, no doubt. It wasn't meant to be. It was intended to demonstrate the seriousness of sin—that sin results in death. As the apostle Paul states, "The wages of sin is death" (Romans 6:23). The death of the lamb was also intended to illustrate that the Lamb of God, the Messiah, would come to die in the sinner's place. When the sinner confessed his sin, it was symbolically transferred from the sinner to the lamb. The sinner was guilty. The sinner deserved to die, but the lamb died in his place. It was the plan of salvation acted out as a parable. "The wages of sin is death, but the gift of God is eternal life in Christ Jesus our Lord" (Romans 6:23).

When Jesus came, John the Baptist said, "Behold! The Lamb of God who takes away the sin of the world!" (John 1:29). Jesus is our Lamb. We deserve to die. We've broken God's law. We deserve to go into the grave and never ever come out. But God took our sins upon Himself as symbolized by the lamb. In the earthly sanctuary, the little lamb that died when the sinner confessed his sin—that lamb couldn't save anyone. The blood of that lamb couldn't forgive sin. It represented Jesus, the Lamb of God. "The blood of Jesus Christ . . . cleanses us from all sin" (1 John 1:7).

> The lessons we've learned in the first six chapters of Daniel include faithfulness, obedience, and the worship of the true God. The last six chapters apply these lessons at a time when this political and religious power tries to change the very heart of God's law.

Those Israelites in the Old Testament studied the sanctuary and participated in its ceremonies and symbolism. As they did so, they realized that sin could be forgiven. They realized that a Lamb would come who would take their sins upon Himself and die in their place. The priest who officiated in the earthly sanctuary also represented Jesus. The lamb represented the Jesus who dies for us. The priest represented Jesus who lives for us. Everything in the sanctuary—every ceremony, every utensil, every object—represented some aspect of the plan of salvation. In and of themselves, these ceremonies and sacrifices had no power to save or forgive. They were symbols showing God's power to forgive sin and save us from its consequences. The earthly sanctuary was an object lesson of God's great plan of salvation.

The Bible tells us of another sanctuary separate from that of the one on earth during Old Testament times. "We have . . . a High Priest, who is seated at the right hand of the throne of the Majesty in the heavens, a Minister of the sanctuary and of the true tabernacle which the Lord erected, and not man" (Hebrews 8:1, 2).

Remember how God told Moses to build the earthly sanctuary "according to the pattern" he was shown (Exodus 25:40)? He kept referring to a "pattern," which was to be copied by the earthly sanctuary. That is because there is a sanctuary in heaven, the "true tabernacle which the Lord erected, and not man" (Hebrews 8:2). The sanctuary on earth was a scale model of the great original sanctuary in heaven. Hebrews 8 says that the earthly sanctuary and all its ceremonies and sacrifices served as "the copy and shadow of the heavenly things" (verse 5).

The bottom line is this: Two sanctuaries are brought to view in the Bible—one on earth and one in heaven. The one on earth is a copy of the one in heaven. The ceremonies and sacrifices of the earthly sanctuary symbolized and illustrated the realities of what was happening in the sanctuary in heaven.

The heavenly sanctuary is the focus of the conflict

Now all this is the background for understanding the last six chapters of Daniel. The conflict in these chapters involves the sanctuary in heaven. However, because the earthly sanctuary was a copy of the one in heaven, we can understand the conflict going on in heaven by understanding the conflict going on concerning the earthly sanctuary. From what we can see on earth, we can understand what we can't see in heaven.

In the first six chapters of Daniel, the Babylonian kings attacked the earthly sanctuary in Jerusalem. In the last six chapters, Satan works through a counterfeit political and religious power that tries to reach right up into heaven itself and attack God's sanctuary there. Daniel 7 begins to tell us about that power and its attack on God's sanctuary. This is the drama of the ages. This is the conflict between Christ and Satan that is going on throughout the universe.

Daniel receives his first vision

At this time, Daniel is in his sixties. This is his first vision. He has interpreted visions and dreams for Nebuchadnezzar, as we have seen. He read the mysterious writing on the wall for Belshazzar. But this is the first vision he, himself, has received from God. Daniel's spiritual experience became richer as time went on.

In the first year of Belshazzar king of Babylon, Daniel had a dream and visions of his head while on his bed. Then he wrote down the dream, telling the main facts.

Daniel spoke, saying, "I saw in my vision by night, and behold, the four winds of heaven were stirring up the Great Sea. And four great beasts came up from the sea, each different from the other. The first was like a lion, and had eagle's wings. I watched till its wings were plucked off; and it was lifted up from the earth and made to stand on two feet like a man, and a man's heart was given to it.

"And suddenly another beast, a second, like a bear. It was raised up on one side, and had three ribs in its mouth between its teeth. And they said thus to it: 'Arise, devour much flesh!'

"After this I looked, and there was another, like a leopard, which had on its back four wings of a bird. The beast also had four heads, and dominion was given to it.

"After this I saw in the night visions, and behold, a fourth beast, dreadful and terrible, exceedingly strong. It had huge iron teeth; it was devouring, breaking in pieces, and trampling the residue with its feet. It was different from all the beasts that were before it, and it had ten horns" (Daniel 7:1–7).

Daniel's vision began with him looking out at a windy seascape. The wind was lashing the sea into huge waves. Then he saw four "beasts," or animals, coming up out of the waves one after the other. What do these prophetic symbols represent? The windy seascape represents the clash of nations in collision (see Revelation 17:15). In the Bible, "beasts," or animals, represent kingdoms and nations. Daniel 7:17 says, "Those great beasts, which are four, are four kings which arise out of the earth."

In this vision, God is showing Daniel four kings or nations that will arise one after the other, out of conflicts and wars. In Daniel 2, remember, God gave Nebuchadnezzar a dream of a great statue made of four metals—gold, silver, bronze, and iron. And those metals represented the empires of Babylon, Media-Persia, Greece, and Rome. Now in chapter 7, Daniel sees in vision four beasts, representing four kingdoms. Just as gold is the chief of metals, so the lion is the king of beasts. Just as the first metal, gold, represented Babylon, so the first beast, a lion, represents Babylon. In prophecies dealing with time sequences, God always begins at the current time of the prophet. That makes sense, doesn't it? The only place to start is where you are. God starts where Daniel is. He starts in Babylon. Then God goes to the next nation, the next, and the next. So God starts with the lion to represent Babylon. In fact, Jeremiah says that Babylon is like a lion (Jeremiah 50:17). The lion with eagle's wings is a fitting symbol of Babylon. When German archeologists excavated Babylon, they discovered lions with eagle's wings on its walls. You can see those lions in the reconstruction of Babylon's walls with the original tiles in the Pergamon Museum in Berlin today.

Daniel 2 states that after Babylon, which ruled the world from 605 to 539 B.C., another nation would arise. We saw that the nation that overthrew Babylon was

Media-Persia. In Daniel 7, the prophet sees a second beast rise out of the sea—a bear with three ribs in its mouth (Daniel 7:5). When Media-Persia replaced Babylon as a world empire, it did so by conquering the three nations of Babylon, Lydia, and Egypt. Therefore, the bear in Daniel's vision represents Media-Persia. The bear raises itself up on one side, indicating the eventual dominance of the Persians over the Medes.

But there was a third beast—a leopard with four wings on its back (verse 6). The nation that overthrew Media-Persia was Greece. Notice the accuracy of Bible prophecy. Under the leadership of Alexander the Great, Greece conquered the world very rapidly. Now, if you wanted to pick an animal to describe rapid conquest, what animal would you choose? An elephant? No. Certainly not a sheep or cow. You would probably choose a leopard or a cheetah. And if you wanted to describe *really* rapid conquest, you would put four wings on its back!

The leopard representing Greece also had four heads. Alexander died suddenly when he was thirty-three years old. When he died, there were four main generals of his army—Ptolemy, Cassander, Seleucus, and Lysimachus. With Alexander dead, the kingdom was divided into four specific territories. Prophecy does not guess, it knows. God described the rapid conquest of the Greek Empire as a leopard with four wings. And because God knew that Alexander would die young, He put four heads on the leopard, indicating that the Greek Empire would be divided up by his four generals.

Finally, Daniel saw a fourth beast rising up out of the sea following the leopard. What empire ruled the world following Greece? Of course, it was Rome. This fourth beast with great iron teeth that was devouring everything in its path, trampling on them and breaking them in pieces—this beast represented Rome.

The focus is on the great controversy

In the vision, God presented these beasts (nations) rather quickly because He wanted to focus on the great struggle between good and evil, the struggle at the end of time over truth, righteousness, and His law. The historical portion of the prophecy is just to position us for the earth's last conflict. So let's look more carefully at this fourth beast.

Daniel says, "After this I saw in the night visions, and behold, a fourth beast, dreadful and terrible, exceedingly strong. It had huge iron teeth; it was devouring, breaking in pieces, and trampling the residue with its feet. It was different from all the beasts that were before it, and it had ten horns" (verse 7).

Although similar in some respects, this beast was different from the beasts that were before it. Remember, in the prophecy of Daniel 2, the statue had ten toes representing the breakup of the Roman Empire by ten tribes that laid the foundation for the modern nations of Europe. In Daniel 7, the fourth beast, representing Rome, has ten horns representing the divisions of the Roman Empire. The parallels between Daniel 2 and Daniel 7 are obvious. People sometimes wonder why God used metals in Daniel 2 and animals in Daniel 7 to represent the same kingdoms. In Daniel 2, God wanted to point out that every empire on earth is only temporary; they exist only for a short period before the rock of His eternal kingdom smashes them all to powder, and they vanish away. In Daniel 2, each metal is of descending value, and the clay and iron represent an unstable, crumbling society at the end time. In Daniel 7, however, God is emphasizing the conflict between good and evil that has raged all through earth's history and that will take on greater intensity at the end of time. In chapter 7, He uses wild animals to represent world empires in collision. These fierce, warlike beasts attack each other, and they attack God and His kingdom. But God's kingdom will ultimately rule.

The little horn emerges

Daniel 7 covers the same territory as chapter 2, but it expands its focus on the immediate centuries leading up to the second coming of Christ. It tells us about events that are going to occur before the second coming of Jesus. A new power is introduced in Daniel 7:8: "I was considering the horns, and there was another horn, a little one, coming up among them, before whom three of the first horns were plucked out by the roots. And there, in this horn, were eyes like the eyes of a man, and a mouth speaking pompous words."

A little horn emerges from among the ten horns of the fourth beast and displaces three of them. Remember, the ten horns represent the nations resulting from the breakup of the Roman Empire. What would this little horn do when it emerges among them?

"The ten horns are ten kings
Who shall arise from this kingdom.
And another shall rise after them;
He shall be different from the first ones,
And shall subdue three kings.
He shall speak pompous words against the Most High,
Shall persecute the saints of the Most High,
And shall intend to change times and law.
Then the saints shall be given into his hand

For a time and times and half a time" (verses 24, 25).

Who is this little horn? When does it arise? What does it do? This little horn will be different from the first ten. The other ten horns are political powers. Whatever or whoever this little horn represents, it will be different from the political powers before it.

The prophecy says that this little horn will rise up out of the ten horns that represent the breakup of the Roman Empire. That means that it must arise somewhere in the former Roman Empire, and it has to arise sometime around the breakup of Rome. Historians date the breakup of the Roman Empire to A.D. 351–476. The prophecy says that this little horn would be different from the other horns (verse 24). The other horns are political entities. The little horn is different because it combines religion with politics. It is a political and religious power. It "plucked out" three of the original ten horns. Three of the divisions of Rome would be destroyed because they wouldn't accept the teachings of the little horn. This power has "the eyes of a man" and speaks "pompous words against the Most High" (verses 8, 25). Eyes symbolize wisdom in the Bible. Here a religio-political system arises based on human tradition and man's wisdom rather than the authority of God's Word. Ultimately, this power would persecute God's people and attempt to change the very law of God. Three things characterize this political and religious power growing out of the breakup of Rome—(1) it would speak pompous words against God; (2) it would persecute God's people; and (3) it would try to change God's law.

In the first six chapters of Daniel, the Babylonian kings attacked the earthly sanctuary in Jerusalem. In the last six chapters, Satan works through a counterfeit political and religious power that tries to reach right up into heaven itself and attack God's sanctuary there.

This little horn will speak pompous words against God, "the Most High." It will persecute God's people. It will attempt to change God's "times and law"—not human laws but the very law of God.

History has been following the prophecies of Daniel like a road map. Babylon, Media-Persia, Greece, and Rome rose and fell one after the other, just as the prophecy said they would. The Roman Empire was divided just as the prophecy predicted. Finally, Daniel 7 says that due to the efforts of this little-horn power that would arise out of the breakup of the Roman Empire, there would be an attack on God and His people. There would be attempts to betray truth and change God's law. There would be drift and departure from the principles of God's Word. Does history record anything that corresponds to what the prophecy predicted? We might ask the question, what religio-political power rose out of the ashes of the old Roman Empire and became a dominant force in Western Europe in the fourth and fifth centuries? There is only one power that fits this description: it is papal Rome. The Roman Church replaced the Roman state as Western Europe's supreme power.

When the emperor Constantine (reigned A.D. 306–337) had his so-called conversion, he blended paganism and Christianity. Then, when the barbarian tribes from the north invaded pagan Rome (A.D. 351–476), its power waned, and Rome became the religious capital of the world.

From Abbott's history of Roman puts it this way, "The transfer of the emperor's residence to Constantinople was a sad blow to the prestige of Rome, and at the time one might have predicted her speedy decline. But the development of the Church, and the growing authority of the bishop of Rome, or the pope, gave her a new lease on life, and made her again the capital—this time the religious capital—of the civilized world."[1]

British philosopher Thomas Hobbes adds, "The Papacy is no other than the 'ghost' of the deceased 'Roman empire,' sitting crowned upon the grave thereof."[2]

These political and religious developments led to the union of church and state in the Middle, or Dark, Ages. There was a gradual drift from the principles of Scripture. The teachings of priests and prelates replaced the teachings of the Bible. Form and ritual gradually replaced the simplicity of the gospel. The sacrifice of the Mass overshadowed the sacrifice of Christ, and human religious dogma replaced the commandments of God.

This apostate church-state power rose and perverted the pure gospel of the Bible. It cast truth to the ground and set forth a gospel different from the one taught by the object lesson of the sanctuary.

As we explore this prophecy in Daniel 7, let's consider the clear instruction that the apostle Paul gave in the book of Acts. It will help us put all this into perspective. The keeper of the jail in Philippi, where Paul had been preaching, came to him with an urgent question. He asked Paul, "What must I do to be saved?" Paul replied, "Believe on the Lord Jesus Christ, and you will be saved" (Acts 16:30, 31). Paul pointed to the pure gospel of the sanctuary—salvation comes only from Jesus, the Lamb of God who died for us. That's the gospel of the Bible. That's God's plan of salvation. We are saved only through Jesus as we believe on Him and accept Him as our Savior.

The prophecy in Daniel 7 points to a time when a religio-political power would arise, leading men and women away from that truth about salvation. It would teach that salvation comes through the traditions of the church—through a human system of tradition. It would set up its own institutions on earth. This apostate, corrupt form of Christianity would lead people away from the simple truth that salvation comes through the Lamb of God who died for our sins.

Daniel asked his angel guide the meaning of the little-horn prophecy (Daniel 7:20). The angel replied that the little horn would "intend to change times and law" (verse 25). With this, the historical fulfillment of the little-horn power is confirmed. There is only one power that fits this description. As the Roman Empire declined, the Roman Church was rapidly gaining power and authority.

It didn't happen all at once or on a specific date, but during the second century, some Christians, especially those living in the major cities such as Rome and Alexandria, began to worship on Sunday, the first day of the week. One of the reasons they did this was to disassociate from the Jews. Another was to make Christianity more acceptable to the pagans. But Paul had warned the church that a mysterious "man of sin" would appear, an enemy from within who would presume to speak in God's name. He said that anyone who did not "love the truth" would be deceived (2 Thessalonians 2:8–10). Through compromise, the very law of God identifying the Creator, the Sabbath commandment, would be gradually changed. This seems like an amazing prediction, but it happened just as the Bible warned us it would.

John Eadie gives us this insight: "*Sunday* was a name given by the heathens to the first day of the week, because it was the day on which they worshiped the sun."[3] It was a popular pagan holiday.

Here is a quote from *The Catholic World* on the same subject: "The Sun was a foremost god with heathendom. Balder the beautiful, the White God, the old Scandinavians called him. . . . There is, in truth, something royal, kingly about the sun, making it a fit emblem of Jesus, the Sun of Justice. Hence the church in these countries would seem, to have said, 'Keep that old, pagan name. It shall remain consecrated, sanctified.' And thus the pagan Sunday, dedicated to Balder, became the Christian Sunday, sacred to Jesus."[4]

Please think about what you have just read. Here are two authors, one Protestant and the other Catholic, talking about a day that God sanctified in the Ten Commandments. They are referring to a part of the law that had its origin at the creation of the world (Genesis 2:1–3) and that was repeated by God on Mount Sinai while the mountain quaked and trembled (Exodus 19:18, 19). They are telling the history of human beings changing the law engraved by God Himself on tables of stone (Exodus 31:18). They say that a day dedicated to the sun god came to substitute the Sabbath as the day for worship, even keeping its old pagan name. Why? What was the reason or basis for the change? Sunday was popular as a pagan holiday. In a compromise measure, church leaders united with civil leaders in an attempt to unite the empire. The pagans felt comfortable with Sunday because, for thousands of years, their cultures had worshiped the sun god. Christians joined this compromise measure in honor of Jesus, the Sun of Righteousness, and His resurrection on the first day. Now Christianity became much more acceptable to a pagan population.

It was here that the two streams that had flowed separately for centuries finally met and merged: Creator worship and creature worship, obedience to God and obedience to human decrees, the Bible and tradition, truth and the deceptions of the enemy.

God's loyal followers

Not everyone was swept away and deceived. No one knows their number, but many, perhaps most, Christians at that time did not agree. The change was promoted by the leaders in the large cities, especially Rome and Alexandria. Nevertheless, in many areas, Sabbath keeping continued so much so that at the beginning of the fourth century the emperor Constantine became worried. Influenced probably by the church leaders at Rome, he published a decree he hoped would settle the matter and bring uniformity.

Here, in part, is Constantine's edict, published March 7, 321: "On the venerable Day of the Sun . . ." *Venerable* is something that should be treated with reverence. He, of course, is talking about Sunday, the "Day of the Sun." "On the venerable Day of the Sun, let the magistrates and people residing in the cities rest, and let all the workshops be closed."

The effort failed. The decision of the church leaders in favor of Sunday worship had not convinced the many sincere people to give up the Sabbath, and neither were they persuaded by an imperial decree. During the next decade or so, the leaders who were promoting Sunday observance repeatedly met to discuss the problem and publish new decrees about it. The fact that they felt compelled to make these decrees and edicts is the clearest possible evidence that many people still continued to observe the seventh-day Sabbath at the beginning of the fourth century.

Why? Why didn't these folks want to change their day of worship? Maybe they were like the Christians in old Berea. The book of Acts records that when challenged in their faith, these noble folks "searched the Scriptures daily to find out whether these things were so" (Acts 17:11). Anyone who does that could never be deceived.

In his book *The Faith of our Fathers*, Catholic cardinal James Gibbons wrote: "You may read the Bible from Genesis to Revelation, and you will not find a single line authorizing the sanctification of Sunday."[5] The cardinal is right, of course, and he adds, "The Scriptures enforce the religious observance of Saturday, a day we never sanctify."[6] The cardinal says that the Roman Catholic Church made the change on its own authority, and he recognizes that in doing this, the church is going against what the Bible clearly teaches.

The following is from *The Convert's Catechism of Catholic Doctrine*:

Q. *Which is the Sabbath Day?*
A. Saturday is the Sabbath Day.
Q. *Why do we observe Sunday instead of Saturday?*
A. We observe Sunday instead of Saturday because the Catholic Church transferred the solemnity from Saturday to Sunday.[7]

Notice these two clear statements: "The [Roman Catholic] Church changed the observance of the Sabbath to Sunday by right of the divine, infallible authority given to her by her founder, Jesus Christ. The Protestant, claiming the Bible to be the only guide of faith, has no warrant for observing Sunday. In this matter the Seventh-day Adventist is the only consistent Protestant."[8]

"All of us believe many things in regard to religion that we do not find in the Bible. For example, nowhere in the Bible do we find that Christ or the Apostles ordered that the Sabbath be changed from Saturday to Sunday. We have the commandment of God given to Moses to keep holy the Sabbath Day that is the 7th day of the week, Saturday. Today most Christians keep Sunday because it has been revealed to us by the Church outside the Bible."[9]

Apostate Christianity

Daniel 7 predicted there would be apostasy in Christianity. Did that happen? Looking ahead to Daniel 8, we read of this power, "Because of transgression, an army was given over to the horn to oppose the daily sacrifices; and he cast truth down to the ground. He did all this and prospered" (verse 12). Tradition would take the place of Scripture. Out of Rome, a religious, political power would rise that would substitute human teachings for Scripture and try to change the very law of God.

Very early in the history of the Christian church, the apostle Paul was already greatly concerned about this coming apostasy. He was concerned about the fact that there would be a departure from the principles of God's Word right down to the last days of earth's history. He wrote, "That Day [Jesus' return] will not come unless the falling away comes first, and the man of sin is revealed, the son of perdition, who opposes and exalts himself above all that is called God or that is worshiped, so that he sits as God in the temple of God, showing himself that he is God" (2 Thessalonians 2:3, 4).

> History has been following the prophecies of Daniel like a road map. Babylon, Media-Persia, Greece, and Rome rose and fell one after the other, just as the prophecy said they would.

This apostate religious system would establish a counterfeit temple of God, a sanctuary, on earth with earthly priests offering the sacrifices of the Mass. As that system grew and developed, tradition would take the place of Scripture, and an attempt would be made to change the very law of God. Through the teachings of the medieval church, there would be a departure from the clear teachings of God's Word. The apostle Peter declared, "We ought to obey God rather than men" (Acts 5:29). But the Bible predicted that, in the last days, this power would substitute human traditions, human teachings, human commandments for those of God.

Judgment in the heavenly sanctuary

After verse 8, Daniel's prophecy in chapter 7 shifts our attention from the lion, the bear, the leopard, and the terrible fourth beast. It looks away from the ten horns and the little horn—away from the apostasy on earth with its rebellion against God's law. The prophecy turns our focus from earth and fastens it on heaven.

Daniel says,

"I watched till thrones were put in place,
And the Ancient of Days was seated;
His garment was white as snow,
And the hair of His head was like pure wool.
His throne was a fiery flame,
Its wheels a burning fire;
A fiery stream issued
And came forth from before Him.
A thousand thousands ministered to Him;
Ten thousand times ten thousand stood before Him.

The court was seated,
And the books were opened" (verses 9, 10).

In vision, Daniel looks up to heaven and sees the heavenly sanctuary. He sees God, the Ancient of Days, sitting on His throne. He sees thousands upon thousands upon thousands of glorious angels ministering before God's throne. Daniel sees the court in heaven seated, and the books open. He sees the scene of the final judgment.

God is calling men and women everywhere to come back to the pure principles of the gospel. To return to keeping His commandments. To be obedient to His Word. Just before the coming of Jesus, there will be a final call back to the Bible. A call to worship God in harmony with His law and His Word.

Does it really matter whether we follow God completely? The prophecy of Daniel 7 answers, "Yes." It matters a great deal. It matters whether we are totally committed to Christ. It matters whether we obey the commandments of God or the commandments of men. It matters whether we follow the traditions of men or the Word of God.

God has given us His Ten Commandments. This prophecy tells of a religious and political power that would arise in the early days of Christianity and that would put tradition ahead of the Bible. But in these last days, God is calling us back to obedience. The issue is loyalty to God. The issue if faithfulness to His Word.

The saints inherit God's everlasting kingdom

The prophecy concludes with these words:

"The court shall be seated,
And they shall take away his [the little horn's] dominion,
To consume and destroy it forever.
Then the kingdom and dominion,
And the greatness of the kingdoms under the whole heaven,
Shall be given to the people, the saints of the Most High.
His kingdom is an everlasting kingdom,
And all dominions shall serve and obey Him" (verses 26, 27).

When God created the earth and placed Adam and Eve in the Garden of Eden, He gave them dominion over the marvelous world He had created (Genesis 1:26–28). He designed that they would love and obey Him and have dominion over the earth, caring for it as He would Himself. But, as you know, they listened to Satan and disobeyed their Creator. They forfeited the dominion He had given them and were expelled from their garden home. Their sin opened the door to sickness, suffering, death, disaster, sorrow, and heartache for this world.

Jesus came to this sin-darkened world to change all that. He came to demonstrate that men and women, living in this world amid all the temptations of Satan, can still be loyal and obedient to God. In a world of disobedience, Christ would be obedient. In a world of rebellion, Christ would be loyal. In the conflict between good and evil, Jesus settled it in His heart that He would do nothing that would displease the Father. His victory would restore dominion over this world to God's people.

Daniel 7 ends with the victory of God's everlasting kingdom against Satan's attack through the little-horn power. The prophecy ends with one pulse of harmony and gladness beating throughout the universe. In the end, God triumphs, and

"The kingdom and dominion,
And the greatness of the kingdoms under the whole heaven,
Shall be given to the people, the saints of the Most High.
His kingdom is an everlasting kingdom,
And all dominions shall serve and obey Him" (verse 27).

God's great desire is that you and I live with Him in His eternal kingdom forever and ever. This is our destiny. This is His plan for our lives. This is the reason He died and the reason He intercedes for us in heaven's sanctuary. He wants us home with Him forever.

---

1. Frank Frost Abbott, *A Short History of Rome* (Chicago: Scott, Foresman, 1906), 235, 236, https://babel .hathitrust.org/cgi/pt?id=mdp.39015063637915&view=1up&seq=272.

2. Thomas Hobbes, *Leviathan*, ed. J. Gaskin (Oxford University Press, 1998), 463.

3. John Eadie, ed., *Biblical Cyclopædia; or, Dictionary of Eastern Antiquities, Geography, Natural History, Sacred Annals and Biography, Theology, and Biblical Literature, Illustrative of the Old and New Testaments* (London, 1872), s.v. "Sabbath," https://archive.org/details/biblicalcyclopea00eadiuoft/page/n9/mode/2up.

4. Willliam L. Gildea, "Paschale Gaudium," *The Catholic World* 58, no. 348 (March 1894): 809.

5. James Cardinal Gibbons, *The Faith of Our Fathers: Being a Plain Exposition and Vindication of the Church Founded by Our Lord Jesus Christ*, 50th ed. (London: John Murphy, 1898), 111, 112.

6. Gibbons, *Faith of Our Fathers*, 112.

7. Peter Geiermann, *Convert's Catechism of Catholic Doctrine* (St. Louis, MO: B. Herder, 1946), 50, https:// www.google.com/books/edition/The_Convert_s_Catechism_of_Catholic_Doct/6GokT0Qzo0wC?hl=en& gbpv=1&bsq=Saturday.

8. *Catholic Universe Bulletin*, August 14, 1942, 4.

9. "To Tell You The Truth," *Catholic Virginian* 22, no. 49 (October 3, 1947): 9.

THE CLEANSING OF THE SANCTUARY

Daniel 8

1 In the third year of the reign of King Belshazzar a vision appeared to me—to me, Daniel—after the one that appeared to me the first time. **2** I saw in the vision, and it so happened while I was looking, that I was in Shushan, the citadel, which is in the province of Elam; and I saw in the vision that I was by the River Ulai. **3** Then I lifted my eyes and saw, and there, standing beside the river, was a ram which had two horns, and the two horns were high; but one was higher than the other, and the higher one came up last. **4** I saw the ram pushing westward, northward, and southward, so that no animal could withstand him; nor was there any that could deliver from his hand, but he did according to his will and became great.

5 And as I was considering, suddenly a male goat came from the west, across the surface of the whole earth, without touching the ground; and the goat had a notable horn between his eyes. **6** Then he came to the ram that had two horns, which I had seen standing beside the river, and ran at him with furious power. **7** And I saw him confronting the ram; he was moved with rage against him, attacked the ram, and broke his two horns. There was no power in the ram to withstand him, but he cast him down to the ground and trampled him; and there was no one that could deliver the ram from his hand.

8 Therefore the male goat grew very great; but when he became strong, the large horn was broken, and in place of it four notable ones came up toward the four winds of heaven. **9** And out of one of them came a little horn which grew exceedingly great toward the south, toward the east, and toward the Glorious Land. **10** And it grew up to the host of heaven; and it cast down some of the host and some of the stars to the ground, and trampled them. **11** He even exalted himself as high as the Prince of the host; and by him the daily sacrifices were taken away, and the

place of His sanctuary was cast down. **12** Because of transgression, an army was given over to the horn to oppose the daily sacrifices; and he cast truth down to the ground. He did all this and prospered.

13 Then I heard a holy one speaking; and another holy one said to that certain one who was speaking, "How long will the vision be, concerning the daily sacrifices and the transgression of desolation, the giving of both the sanctuary and the host to be trampled underfoot?"

14 And he said to me, "For two thousand three hundred days; then the sanctuary shall be cleansed."

15 Then it happened, when I, Daniel, had seen the vision and was seeking the meaning, that suddenly there stood before me one having the appearance of a man. **16** And I heard a man's voice between the banks of the Ulai, who called, and said, "Gabriel, make this man understand the vision." **17** So he came near where I stood, and when he came I was afraid and fell on my face; but he said to me, "Understand, son of man, that the vision refers to the time of the end."

18 Now, as he was speaking with me, I was in a deep sleep with my face to the ground; but he touched me, and stood me upright. **19** And he said, "Look, I am making known to you what shall happen in the latter time of the indignation; for at the appointed time the end shall be. **20** The ram which you saw, having the two horns—they are the kings of Media and Persia. **21** And the male goat is the kingdom of Greece. The large horn that is between its eyes is the first king. **22** As for the broken horn and the four that stood up in its place, four kingdoms shall arise out of that nation, but not with its power.

23 "And in the latter time of their kingdom,
When the transgressors have reached their fullness,
A king shall arise,
Having fierce features,
Who understands sinister schemes.
24 His power shall be mighty, but not by his own power;
He shall destroy fearfully,
And shall prosper and thrive;
He shall destroy the mighty, and also the holy people.

25 "Through his cunning
He shall cause deceit to prosper under his rule;
And he shall exalt himself in his heart.
He shall destroy many in their prosperity.
He shall even rise against the Prince of princes;
But he shall be broken without human means.

26 "And the vision of the evenings and mornings
Which was told is true;
Therefore seal up the vision,

For it refers to many days in the future."

27 And I, Daniel, fainted and was sick for days; afterward I arose and went about the king's business. I was astonished by the vision, but no one understood it.

※

The conflict brought to view in Daniel 7 intensifies in Daniel 8 and focuses on events taking place right down at the end of time. The prophet is given another vision in which animals are used as symbols.

Daniel says,

I lifted my eyes and saw, and there, standing beside the river, was a ram which had two horns, and the two horns were high; but one was higher than the other, and the higher one came up last. I saw the ram pushing westward, northward, and southward, so that no animal could withstand him; nor was there any that could deliver from his hand, but he did according to his will and became great.

As I was considering, suddenly a male goat came from the west, across the surface of the whole earth, without touching the ground; and the goat had a notable horn between his eyes. Then he came to the ram that had two horns, which I had seen standing beside the river, and ran at him with furious power (Daniel 8:3–6).

God points to the sanctuary

The animals in Daniel 7 were wild beasts—a lion, a bear, a leopard, and a fierce beast with iron teeth. In Daniel 8, the animals are different—a ram and a goat. This is significant because a ram and a goat were animals used in the ceremonies of the sanctuary. By using a ram and a goat as symbols, God wants to tell us something. He wants to point us to the sanctuary and its services.

In the Old Testament, when a sinner came to the sanctuary and offered a perfect lamb as a sacrifice, he or she was acting out God's plan of salvation in which Jesus, the Lamb of God, would die for the sins of that person—and for the sins of every person who has ever lived on earth. The priest would sprinkle some of the lamb's blood on the veil separating the two rooms of the sanctuary—the Holy Place and the Most Holy Place. The Most Holy Place contained the ark of the covenant, a small gold-covered chest with two golden angels seated on the top of it. This represented

God's throne in heaven. That's why this room was called the "Most Holy Place."

Day after day after day, all year long, the priest would sprinkle some of the blood of the sin offerings on the veil separating the Most Holy Place from the Holy Place of the sanctuary. In symbol, the sins of the people were transferred from themselves to the blood of the lamb, and this blood was sprinkled on the veil inside the sanctuary. Thus, the sins of the people were symbolically accumulating in the sanctuary. Once each year—on the Day of Atonement—the sanctuary was ritually "cleansed" of the year's sins that had been brought there by the blood. There was a special ceremony on that day, and a ram and a goat were special sanctuary sacrifices that were used on the Day of Atonement when the sanctuary was cleansed of sin. That day symbolizes the Judgment Day, when God will cleanse the universe of sin once and for all.

The specific reason that God uses the symbols of the ram and the male goat to represent two mighty nations in this chapter is to direct our attention to the heavenly sanctuary. Daniel is told later that the ram represented Media-Persia, and the goat represented Greece (verses 20, 21). These same empires, we learned, were symbolized in Daniel 7 by a bear and a leopard. God changed symbols from fierce beasts—a bear and a leopard—to a ram and a goat. He did so because He wanted us to know, as soon as we begin studying the prophecy of Daniel 8, that the focus of this prophecy is on the heavenly sanctuary and its cleansing at the end of time.

The prophecy's details are historically accurate

Daniel continues to describe what he saw in the vision. He says that he saw the male goat run toward the ram with "furious power" (verse 6). Then he says,

> I saw him confronting the ram; he was moved with rage against him, attacked the ram, and broke his two horns. There was no power in the ram to withstand him, but he cast him down to the ground and trampled him; and there was no one that could deliver the ram from his hand.
>
> Therefore the male goat grew very great; but when he became strong, the large horn was broken, and in place of it four notable ones came up toward the four winds of heaven (verses 7, 8).

In precise and accurate detail, the prophecy describes what happened historically regarding Media-Persia and Greece. But the use of sanctuary animals—the ram and the goat—as symbols indicates that the prophecy is primarily concerned, not with a political challenge, but with a religious challenge in the last days to God's sanctuary and all that it stands for. Daniel 8 focuses on Satan's attack on God's truth at the end of time.

The ram, representing Media-Persia, had two horns—one higher than the other, and it came up last (verse 3). Notice how precise Bible prophecy is. The ram has two horns because the Medo-Persian Empire was a consolidation of two nations, the Medes and the Persians. Persia was the dominant component of this alliance. It was stronger than the Median kingdom, and it arose later, exactly as the prophecy depicts. Daniel also says that he saw "the ram pushing westward, northward, and southward" (verse 4). This accurately pictures the expansion of the Medo-Persian Empire.

In Daniel's vision, the male goat "came from the west" (verse 5). That, too, is historically accurate. The Greeks attacked Media-Persia from the west and overcame it rapidly. In the vision, Daniel saw the goat rushing toward the ram from the west "without touching the ground" (verse 5), so rapid was its conquest.

The "notable horn" that the prophet saw between the goat's eyes (verse 5) represented its "first king" (verse 21), Alexander the Great. That horn was broken when Alexander died shortly after his conquest of Media-Persia, and four horns came up in its place, representing the four generals Ptolemy, Cassander, Seleucus, and Lysimachus, who divided up the empire following Alexander's death. This was symbolized in Daniel 7, as you remember, by the four wings on the back of the leopard and by its four heads (Daniel 7:6). Speaking of the rise of the four horns and then the appearance of the little horn, prophecy declares, "four notable ones (horns) came up toward the four winds of heaven. And out of one of them (winds) came a little horn which grew exceeding great toward the South, toward the East and toward the pleasant land (Israel)" (verses 8, 9).

The "little horn" comes to view again

The Roman armies struck a decisive blow to the Greeks with their victory in the Battle of Pynda in 148 B.C. Rome continued its conquest of the Greek Empire and finally overcame them in the Battle of Corinth in 146 B.C. According to Daniel's prophecy, the little horn power would rise out of Rome in the west. As predicted, the little horn (the Roman church) arose out of the eventual ruins of the Roman Empire and extended its influence throughout Europe and the world. We saw the same symbolism in Daniel 7. There, a little horn arises out of Rome. Here in Daniel 8, a little horn arises out of the Roman Empire. Now, notice what this little horn does. It wars against the host of heaven and attacks it and tramples on it (verse 10). This cannot be solely a political power. The language of the prophecy describes a religio-political power that establishes a counterfeit religious system by distorting the truth of God's Word. This is a religious power reaching right up to heaven and magnifying itself against "the Prince of the host" (verse 11). Who is the prince of the host? The Prince of the host is Jesus Christ, the "Prince of Peace" (Isaiah 9:6). This power goes up against Jesus Christ and heaven itself. The apostle Paul calls this power "the man of sin" and "the son of perdition" (2 Thessalonians 2:3). He says that in the last days, there will be a "falling away" from Bible truth. He says that this man of sin "opposes and exalts himself above all that is called God or that is worshiped, so that he sits as God in the temple of God, showing himself that he is God" (verse 4). Daniel 8 continues to describe the work of the little horn first brought to view in Daniel 7.

The apostle Paul was very concerned about this little-horn power. He warned the people of God in his day about it and called them to be faithful to Scripture and the pure doctrine of Jesus Christ. He urged the church leaders at Ephesus to minister faithfully to the church there. He warned them, "For I know this, that after my departure savage wolves will come in among you, not sparing the flock. Also from among yourselves men will rise up, speaking perverse things, to draw away the disciples after themselves" (Acts 20:29, 30).

"After I die," Paul is saying, "there are going to be those coming into the church who will attack it from within. They will not spare the flock. These persecutions and false teachings will arise even from among church leaders themselves." The apostle Paul is warning the early church against the very little-horn power that Daniel predicted would arise to oppose the church, God, and His sanctuary.

That is exactly what happened in the early decades and centuries of Christianity. In order to convert pagans, pagan ideas and pagan forms of worship were accepted into the church. There was a departure from Bible truth. The little-horn power that Daniel said would come, did come,

> Daniel predicted that a religious and political power would grow and cast down the real truth about Jesus and His sacrifice. All kinds of rituals and traditions would be introduced rather than relying on Jesus, the Lamb of God.

and it was able to "cast truth down to the ground" and "prosper" (Daniel 8:12). This little-horn power opposed the truth of the sanctuary—God's plan of salvation illustrated through the object lessons of the sacrifices and ceremonies of the sanctuary. The prophecy said it would "oppose the daily sacrifices" (verse 12).

How long until the sanctuary is cleansed?

Then, in his vision, Daniel heard someone asking a question.

"How long will the vision be, concerning the daily sacrifices and the transgression of desolation, the giving of both the sanctuary and the host to be trampled underfoot?"

And he said to me, "For two thousand three hundred days; then the sanctuary shall be cleansed" (verses 13, 14).

How long would this "transgression of desolation" last? The word *sacrifices* in this passage is a supplied word. In other words, it was not in the original text but supplied by the translators in an attempt to make the passage plain. The Hebrew word translated "daily" is *tamid*, which is literally translated "continual" or "continually." *Tamid* is regularly used to describe the varied services of the sanctuary. The sacrifices were offered continually. The priest ministered continually. The incense in the Holy Place ascended continually. The shewbread, or the "bread of the presence," was on the golden table continually. The lamps in the sanctuary burned continually. This passage describes a counterfeit sanctuary service of earthly priests with their priestly garments ministering continually with candles, incense, and wafers in an earthly temple. The prophet's appeal is to focus on Christ's sacrifice, Christ's priestly ministry in the heavenly sanctuary, not an earthly one. When would the truth about the heavenly sanctuary be restored? How long would this opposition to the daily in the sanctuary continue?

Daniel predicted that a religious and political power would grow and cast down the real truth about Jesus and His sacrifice. All kinds of rituals and traditions would be introduced rather than relying on Jesus, the Lamb of God. The truth about the sanctuary and the sacrifice of the Lamb of God would be cast down. The truth about Jesus as our great High Priest, who alone can forgive our sins, would be cast down. The truth about God's law and the importance of obedience would be cast down and replaced by the traditions of men.

How long? That is the question. How long would this little-horn power prosper and trample God's truth and His sanctuary teachings? Verse 14 answers, "For two thousand three hundred days; then the sanctuary shall be cleansed."

At the end of this time period, God's truth about Jesus as the Lamb who died for our sins would be proclaimed to all the world. At the end of this period, the truth will go forth about Jesus, the One who leads us back to obedience to God's law. God's eternal message of last-day truth is His final appeal in light of the Day of Atonement, or God's final judgment. His Word speaks to this generation, appealing to each one of us to examine our hearts in total consecration to His will. The message of the cleansing of the sanctuary is a call to let Jesus cleanse our hearts by His divine grace.

Just as Israel gathered around the earthly sanctuary on the Day of Atonement, we are to gather around the heavenly sanctuary by faith. We are to allow His grace to pardon our sins and His power to transform our lives.

What about this time period of 2,300 days? The text says that after 2,300 days, the sanctuary would be cleansed. If these are actual, literal days, how many years is that? At 365 days per year, that would work out to be just a little more than six years. But if we go to verse 17 where the angel Gabriel is explaining the vision to Daniel, we find him saying, "Understand, son of man, that the vision refers to the time of the end." So this vision of the cleansing of the sanctuary applies to the time of the end. Verse 19 confirms this. "And he [Gabriel] said, 'Look, I am making known to you what shall happen in the latter time of the indignation; for at the appointed time the end shall be.' "

The angel is saying that when this 2,300-day period runs out, then the time of the end begins. So these must not be 2,300 literal days. Literal days would take us only to some six years after Daniel's time. The answer to our problem lies in the fact that a "day" in Bible prophecy represents a year of real time. The Lord told the prophet Ezekiel, "I have laid on you a day for each year" (Ezekiel 4:6). The King James Version says, "I have appointed thee each day for a year." And God told Moses that the children of Israel would wander in the wilderness for forty years after their refusal to enter the Promised Land when He told them to. Caleb and Joshua had spent forty days exploring the land. Now the Israelites were to spend forty years in the wilderness before they would be allowed to enter. God said, "According to the number of the days in which you spied out the land, forty days, for each day you shall bear your guilt one year, namely forty years" (Numbers 14:34). So we find a principle in the Bible that, in prophetic symbolism, a "day" represents a year of real time. Therefore, the 2,300 days represent 2,300 literal years.

At the end of these 2,300 years, "the sanctuary shall be cleansed" (Daniel 8:14). The sanctuary on earth was symbolically cleansed on the Day of Atonement each year. That day represented God's judgment day at the end of time. So the prophecy is telling us that the end-time judgment day of God begins at the close of the 2,300 years. In Daniel 9, we will discover exactly when that takes place.

Is the sanctuary that will be cleansed on earth or in heaven?

The "sanctuary" will be cleansed at the end of the 2,300 years (Daniel 8:14). What sanctuary is this referring to? As we have already studied, the sanctuary on earth was a copy of the original sanctuary, or pattern, in heaven. The sanctuary in heaven is the real sanctuary, the one established by God. The sanctuary on earth was an object lesson to the Israelites of the realities of the plan of salvation carried out in the heavenly sanctuary. After Jesus died as the Lamb of God, He ascended to heaven, where He lives eternally as our High Priest in the heavenly sanctuary. Jesus is both the Lamb who dies and the Priest who lives to make intercession for us.

The Bible says, "We have a great High Priest who has passed through the heavens, Jesus the Son of God. . . . We do not have a High Priest who cannot sympathize with our weaknesses, but was in all points tempted as we are, yet without sin. Let us therefore come boldly to the throne of grace, that we may obtain mercy and find grace to help in time of need" (Hebrews 4:14–16).

What sanctuary is cleansed at the end of the 2,300 years—the one on earth or the one in heaven? It has to be the one in heaven because there was no sanctuary on earth some 2,300 years after the time of Daniel. The sanctuary on earth was destroyed for the last time by the Romans in A.D. 70.

What is involved in the cleansing of the sanctuary?

What does the cleansing of the sanctuary in heaven involve? To answer that question, we need to look at what was involved in the cleansing of the sanctuary on earth. Each year, that cleansing was done symbolically on the Day of Atonement, which represented God's final judgment day.

In the sanctuary ritual on earth, sacrifices were slain in the court every day. Every day sinners came to the court, confessed their sins, and slew their sacrifices. Every day the priest brought the blood of these sacrifices into the first room of the sanctuary, the Holy Place, and sprinkled some of it on the veil separating the first room from the second, the Most Holy Place. The sins of the people were symbolically accumulating in the sanctuary.

Once a year, on the Day of Atonement, the sanctuary was symbolically cleansed of those accumulated sins. On that day, at the end of the Jewish year, all Israelites gathered in the presence of God to examine their hearts and ask Him to cleanse them, as they made a commitment of loyalty and obedience. On that day, and only on that one day, the high priest entered the Most Holy Place to cleanse the sanctuary. As he did so, all Israel gathered around the sanctuary. They knelt and prayed, "O, God, we love You. We want to be done with our sins. We want to be totally obedient to You. We want our hearts to be clean. We want to please You."

On the Day of Atonement, two goats were chosen. Lots were cast over these two animals without spot or blemish, and one was slain and its blood carried by the high priest into the sanctuary. No sins were confessed over this goat. Its blood was pure, cleansing blood. The high priest entered the sanctuary, sprinkling the blood in the Holy Place. He then moved beyond the veil into the Most Holy Place of the sanctuary to sprinkle the cleansing blood over the mercy seat on the ark of the covenant between the two golden angels. The law of God, the Ten Commandments, was contained within the ark. In this symbolic act, the high priest cleansed the sanctuary from all of the confessed sins that had entered it through the blood of the sacrifices throughout the year.

After the high priest left the sanctuary and entered the court, he confessed all the sins of Israel over the live goat. Leviticus 16:21 declares, "Aaron [the high priest] shall . . . confess over it all the iniquities of the children of Israel, and all their transgressions, concerning all their sins, putting them on the head of the goat." Throughout the Jewish year, sin entered the sanctuary through the blood of the sacrifice or through some of the sacrifices that were eaten by the priest. On the Day of Atonement, the sins left the sanctuary and were placed on the head of the live goat. The live goat was then led into the wilderness to be separated from God's people forever, and the sanctuary and camp of Israel were clean. During this service, every Israelite was to confess their sins and ask God to cleanse their hearts. Every Israelite that did not participate in this solemn service of confession and repentance was "cut off," or separated, from the camp of Israel.

That day represented God's day of judgment at the end of time when He makes His final appeal to men and women to open their hearts to Him and make a commitment of loyalty and obedience. In this final judgment, or cleansing of the sanctuary, the destinies of the entire human race will be settled forever. The decisions we have made reveal our response to Jesus' sacrifice on our behalf. In this last-day judgment, Jesus will be revealed as fully loving and fully just. His Name will be exalted before the universe. It will be seen by every heavenly being that in the cosmic conflict between good and evil, Jesus has done everything possible to redeem us.

Jesus will be exalted before the whole world as the Lamb of God who takes away sin. He will be exalted as our High Priest, the one who knows us, the one who understands us, the one who knows every heartache and burden. In these final days, the sanctuary in heaven will be cleansed. All of the pollution established by man-made religion will be gone. All of the errors taught by human traditions will be exposed. The cleansing of the sanctuary in heaven at the end of time is a call by Jesus, our High Priest, to love Him, obey Him, serve Him, and give our lives to Him. Daniel 8 is a call to come to Jesus and accept Him as our Savior and our High Priest. It is a call to open our hearts to Him and to accept His mercy, grace, and forgiveness.

GOD'S DIVINE TIMETABLE

Daniel 9

1 In the first year of Darius the son of Ahasuerus, of the lineage of the Medes, who was made king over the realm of the Chaldeans— **2** in the first year of his reign I, Daniel, understood by the books the number of the years specified by the word of the LORD through Jeremiah the prophet, that He would accomplish seventy years in the desolations of Jerusalem.

3 Then I set my face toward the Lord God to make request by prayer and supplications, with fasting, sackcloth, and ashes. **4** And I prayed to the LORD my God, and made confession, and said, "O Lord, great and awesome God, who keeps His covenant and mercy with those who love Him, and with those who keep His commandments, **5** we have sinned and committed iniquity, we have done wickedly and rebelled, even by departing from Your precepts and Your judgments. **6** Neither have we heeded Your servants the prophets, who spoke in Your name to our kings and our princes, to our fathers and all the people of the land. **7** O Lord, righteousness belongs to You, but to us shame of face, as it is this day—to the men of Judah, to the inhabitants of Jerusalem and all Israel, those near and those far off in all the countries to which You have driven them, because of the unfaithfulness which they have committed against You.

8 "O Lord, to us belongs shame of face, to our kings, our princes, and our fathers, because we have sinned against You. **9** To the Lord our God belong mercy and forgiveness, though we have rebelled against Him. **10** We have not obeyed the voice of the LORD our God, to walk in His laws, which He set before us by His servants the prophets. **11** Yes, all Israel has transgressed Your law, and has departed so as not to obey Your voice; therefore the curse and the oath written in the Law of Moses the servant of God have been poured out on us, because we have sinned against Him.

12 And He has confirmed His words, which He spoke against us and against our judges who judged us, by bringing upon us a great disaster; for under the whole heaven such has never been done as what has been done to Jerusalem. **13** "As it is written in the Law of Moses, all this disaster has come upon us; yet we have not made our prayer before the LORD our God, that we might turn from our iniquities and understand Your truth. **14** Therefore the LORD has kept the disaster in mind, and brought it upon us; for the LORD our God is righteous in all the works which He does, though we have not obeyed His voice. **15** And now, O Lord our God, who brought Your people out of the land of Egypt with a mighty hand, and made Yourself a name, as it is this day— we have sinned, we have done wickedly! **16** "O Lord, according to all Your righteousness, I pray, let Your anger and Your fury be turned away from Your city Jerusalem, Your holy mountain; because for our sins, and for the iniquities of our fathers, Jerusalem and Your people are a reproach to all those around us. **17** Now therefore, our God, hear the prayer of Your servant, and his supplications, and for the Lord's sake cause Your face to shine on Your sanctuary, which is desolate. **18** O my God, incline Your ear and hear; open Your eyes and see our desolations, and the city which is called by Your name; for we do not present our supplications before You because of our righteous deeds, but because of Your great mercies. **19** O Lord, hear! O Lord, forgive! O Lord, listen and act! Do not delay for Your own sake, my God, for Your city and Your people are called by Your name."

20 Now while I was speaking, praying, and confessing my sin and the sin of my people Israel, and presenting my supplication before the LORD my God for the holy mountain of my God, **21** yes, while I was speaking in prayer, the man Gabriel, whom I had seen in the vision at the beginning, being caused to fly swiftly, reached me about the time of the evening offering. **22** And he informed me, and talked with me, and said, "O Daniel, I have now come forth to give you skill to understand. **23** At the beginning of your supplications the command went out, and I have come to tell you, for you are greatly beloved; therefore consider the matter, and understand the vision:

24 "Seventy weeks are determined
For your people and for your holy city,
To finish the transgression,
To make an end of sins,
To make reconciliation for iniquity,
To bring in everlasting righteousness,
To seal up vision and prophecy,
And to anoint the Most Holy.

25 "Know therefore and understand,
That from the going forth of the
     command
To restore and build Jerusalem

Until Messiah the Prince,
There shall be seven weeks and sixty-
two weeks;
The street shall be built again, and the
wall,
Even in troublesome times.

26 "And after the sixty-two weeks
Messiah shall be cut off, but not for
Himself;
And the people of the prince who is
to come
Shall destroy the city and the
sanctuary.

The end of it shall be with a flood,
And till the end of the war desolations
are determined.
27 Then he shall confirm a covenant
with many for one week;
But in the middle of the week
He shall bring an end to sacrifice and
offering.
And on the wing of abominations
shall be one who makes desolate,
Even until the consummation, which
is determined,
Is poured out on the desolate."

After His crucifixion and resurrection, Jesus returned to heaven (Acts 1:9–11). But, before He did, He promised His disciples that He would return to earth. "I will come again," He assured them, "and receive you to Myself; that where I am, there you may be also" (John 14:3). He gave them (and us) numerous signs that would tell us when His coming is near (Matthew 24; Luke 21). However, there is one thing about His return that Jesus has never told us. He has never told us exactly when His second coming will take place. In fact, He has specifically told us that no one knows the day or hour—not even the angels of heaven (Matthew 24:36).

God is always on time

Almost as soon as Jesus went back to heaven, God's people began looking for Him to return at any time. We've waited so eagerly down through the centuries. It seems so long since Jesus left and promised to return. Why the lengthy delay? Why hasn't Jesus come before now?

It seems that way to us. But the delay is only from our perspective, not from God's, because God is always on time. Perhaps more clearly than any other chapter in the Bible, Daniel 9 reveals that God is always on time, that His purposes know no haste or delay. We may think that there is a delay in Jesus' return to this earth, but God has a divine timetable, and He gives us a glimpse into this timetable in Daniel 9. God's prophecies are always fulfilled exactly as He has predicted. Daniel 9 will not show us when Jesus will return, but it will show us exactly when the time of the end began.

"In the first year of Darius the son of Ahasuerus, of the lineage of the Medes, who was made king over the realm of the Chaldeans—in the first year of his reign I, Daniel, understood by the books the number of the years specified by the word of the LORD through Jeremiah the prophet, that He would accomplish seventy years in the desolation of Jerusalem" (verses 1, 2).

The first year of the reign of Darius was 539 B.C. How do we know that? Remember that the Medes and Persians overthrew Babylon just as the prophecy of Daniel 2 predicted. History tells us that this happened in 539 B.C.

Daniel was taken captive by Babylon about 605 B.C., when he was a teenager—perhaps seventeen years old. So how old is Daniel here in chapter 9 in the first year of the reign of Darius the Mede? The math tells us that Daniel would be in his eighties—perhaps eighty-three or eighty-four years old. He's coming toward the end of his life. He understands the importance of knowing God's Word. He is a diligent student of prophecy as recorded in the ancient scrolls. He was extremely knowledgeable in the Scriptures. Specifically, he says he has been studying the writings of the prophet Jeremiah. He states that he had learned from Jeremiah's prophecies that seventy years after the Babylonians had overthrown Jerusalem, God would deliver His people from their captivity. You can find that prophecy in Jeremiah 25:11, 12; 29:10. Daniel knew that it had been almost seventy years since Jerusalem had been overthrown and he was taken captive to Babylon. He knew that the time in Jeremiah's prophecy was coming to an end. He knew that God always keeps His word; His purposes know no haste or delay. But Daniel was concerned because he couldn't see any signs that the prophecy was about to be fulfilled. So he began to pray.

Daniel prays to God

His prayer is recorded in Daniel 9:3–19. He says, "I set my face toward the Lord God to make request by prayer and supplications" (verse 3). He's praying for God to release His people from Babylonian bondage. He's confessing his sins and the sins of the Israelites in Babylonian captivity.

Daniel knew that God keeps His promises. But he also knew that God cannot bless those who refuse to honor and obey Him. The Bible says, "Your iniquities have separated you from your God; and your sins have hidden His face from you, so that He will not hear" (Isaiah 59:2). There is a law of cause and effect. That's why Daniel includes this acknowledgment in his prayer:

"All this disaster has come upon us; yet we have not made our prayer before the LORD our God, that we might turn from our iniquities and understand Your truth. . . . For the LORD our God is righteous in all the works which He does, though we have not obeyed His voice" (Daniel 9:13, 14).

When any individual or nation knowingly and willingly turns away from God, they forfeit His divine blessings. They face heartache, sorrow, and disasters that they wouldn't have had to face if they had not entered into that rebellious attitude. The essential nature of God's character is love; He doesn't cause heartache or sorrow, but there is a natural law of cause and effect that says our rebellion against Him forfeits His blessings, leaving us more vulnerable to Satan's attacks. Satan is then able to do things he otherwise would not be able to do. Sometimes God has to teach us in sorrow what we will not learn any other way. The history of Israel is the history of a nation that God taught in deep sorrow because of its rebellion. Babylon's victory over Jerusalem and God's people came about because Israel was unfaithful to God, thus forfeiting His blessings and protection. That's what Daniel was acknowledging in his prayer. Daniel ends his prayer with these moving words:

"Now therefore, our God, hear the prayer of Your servant, and his supplications, and for the Lord's sake cause Your face to shine on Your sanctuary, which is desolate. . . . O Lord, hear! O Lord, forgive! O Lord, listen and act! Do not delay for Your own sake, my God, for Your city and Your people are called by Your name" (verses 17–19).

Gabriel comes to answer Daniel's prayer

Daniel knew that God had a divine timetable; he knew the seventy years of captivity were coming to an end. Human beings have no idea what the future holds. There is very little we can do to alter the great panorama of events over the centuries. But the great God of heaven is wise enough to know what to do and mighty enough to do it.

As Daniel is praying, the angel Gabriel comes down to him to explain the vision. Daniel says, "While I was speaking in prayer, the man Gabriel, whom I had seen in the vision at the beginning, being caused to fly swiftly, reached me about the time of the evening offering. And he informed me, and talked with me, and said, 'O Daniel, I have now come forth to give you skill to understand. . . . Therefore consider the matter and understand the vision' " (verses 21–23).

What vision did Gabriel come to help Daniel understand? There is no vision recorded in chapter 9. However, Daniel had received a vision in chapter 8, and the angel Gabriel came to explain it to him (see Daniel 8:16–19). But did the prophet understand the vision even after Gabriel's explanation in chapter 8? No. Chapter 8 closes with Daniel worried and confused about what he had seen in the vision. He says, "I, Daniel, fainted and was sick for days. . . . I was astonished by the vision, but no one understood it" (verse 27). So, following Daniel's prayer in chapter 9, Gabriel comes again to explain the vision of chapter 8 further. "Consider the matter," he told Daniel, "and understand the vision" (Daniel 9:23).

He says, "Daniel, I'm going to answer your prayer in a much broader way than you expected. You are concerned about when the captivity of your people, Israel, will end, and they can return to Jerusalem, but I want to show you a bigger picture. I want to show you when the bondage of God's people *to sin* will end. I want to show you when the truth about the sanctuary in heaven will be revealed. I want to show you something beyond the sanctuary on earth and the restoration of worship for the Jewish people. I want to show you what the vision says about the end of time when true worship will be restored in the whole world just before Jesus returns." God was answering Daniel's prayer in a much larger, more significant way than the prophet could even imagine. You will recall that in Daniel 8:17, Gabriel told Daniel that the vision "refers to the time of the end."

Before we look at the details of Gabriel's explanation of the prophecy, there is a little phrase we shouldn't pass by. Gabriel tells Daniel, "You are greatly beloved" (Daniel 9:23). As soon as the prophet began praying, Gabriel was sent to answer his prayer—because he was "greatly beloved" of heaven. When you are on your knees, praying, you are "greatly beloved" of heaven. Have you ever longed for a place very close to God's heart that you could call home? As you pray, God whispers to you, as He did to Daniel, "You are greatly beloved. You have a special place in My heart." Never forget how much God loves you.

Gabriel begins to explain the vision

"Therefore," Gabriel says to Daniel, "consider the matter, and understand the vision" (verse 23). What matter? There was only one aspect of the prophecy in Daniel 8 that Daniel did not understand, and that was the time period. The angel Gabriel had clearly explained the meaning of the ram (Media-Persia) and the male goat (Greece). He explained the fall of Greece, the rise of Rome, and the religious and political church-state power rising out of Rome. Only one portion of the prophecy in chapter 8 was left unexplained—the time period—the prophecy of the 2,300 days (years) at the end of which the sanctuary in heaven would be cleansed.

Gabriel begins to break down this time period as he explains the vision to Daniel.

"Seventy weeks are determined
For your people and for your holy city,

To finish the transgression,
To make an end of sins,
To make reconciliation for iniquity,
To bring in everlasting righteousness,
To seal up vision and prophecy,
And to anoint the Most Holy.

"Know therefore and understand,
That from the going forth of the command
To restore and build Jerusalem until Messiah the Prince,
There shall be seven weeks and sixty-two weeks" (verses 24, 25).

Daniel had been concerned about his people, the Jews. He had been praying for them and for the restoration of Jerusalem. So Gabriel begins by telling him that "seventy weeks" of the 2,300 days are "determined for your people and for your holy city." What does this word *determined* mean? The Hebrew word used is *chathak*, and it means "cut off from" or "separated from." We saw in chapter 8 that one prophetic day represents a literal year of real time. There are seven days in a week, so how many days are there in seventy weeks? Seven times 70 equals 490. Gabriel is saying that 490 years of the 2,300 years brought to view in the prophecy are "cut off," or set aside, for Daniel's people.

When do the seventy weeks and the 2,300 days begin?

This is one of the most exciting prophecies in all the Old Testament. It is accurate in its minute details. It shows that God does things on time and according to His plan. Gabriel explains to Daniel that 2,300 years will take place from his day to the beginning of the time of the end. The first 490 years apply to the Jewish people, and he tells him when these 490 years would begin.

"Know therefore and understand,
That from the going forth of the command
To restore and build Jerusalem
Until Messiah the Prince,
There shall be seven weeks and sixty-two weeks;
The street shall be built again, and the wall" (verse 25).

Remember that at this time, Daniel's people, the Jews, were in captivity. Daniel was very concerned about when his people would leave captivity, rebuild Jerusalem and its wall, and be allowed to restore the worship of God. So the angel Gabriel starts with an event that is really important to Daniel—the command to restore and build Jerusalem so that sacrifices could be offered and the priests could minister in the sanctuary again. According to the prophecy, there would be 69 weeks, or 483 years, from the decree restoring worship in Jerusalem until Messiah the Prince, Jesus Christ.

When did this decree go forth to restore and rebuild Jerusalem? You can find a record of that decree, issued by King Artaxerxes, in Ezra 7. Actually, three such decrees were issued, but the third was the significant one because it not only allowed the Jews to return to Jerusalem and rebuild but also allowed them to be a religious community again and establish the worship of God in the sanctuary. This was a special decree. King Artaxerxes issued it in the fall of 457 B.C.

The coming of Messiah, the Prince

Counting from 457 B.C., 69 weeks, or 483 years along the timeline of history, brings us to the fall of A.D. 27 (remember, there is no year zero when we move from B.C. to A.D.). According to the words of Gabriel, then, the Messiah would appear in A.D. 27. And that is exactly what happened. "Messiah" means "the anointed one." In A.D. 27, in that very year, Jesus Christ, the Messiah, was baptized, or anointed, for His ministry.

> In the fifteenth year of the reign of Tiberius Caesar . . . the word of God came to John the son of Zacharias in the wilderness. And he went into all the region around the Jordan preaching a baptism of repentance for the remission of sins. . . .
>
> . . . John [said] . . . "I indeed baptize you with water; but One mightier than I is coming." . . .
>
> When all the people were baptized, it came to pass that Jesus also was baptized; and while He prayed, the heavens were opened. And the Holy Spirit descended in bodily form like a dove upon Him, and a voice came from heaven which said, "You are My beloved Son; in You I am well pleased" (Luke 3:1–22).

Messiah to be cut off in the middle of the week

Bible prophecy does not guess; it knows. Daniel predicted, hundreds of years in advance, the exact date for the baptism of Christ. But that isn't all. Gabriel's explanation continues. "Messiah shall be cut off, but not for Himself; and the people of the prince who is to come shall destroy the city and the sanctuary" (Daniel 9:26).

123

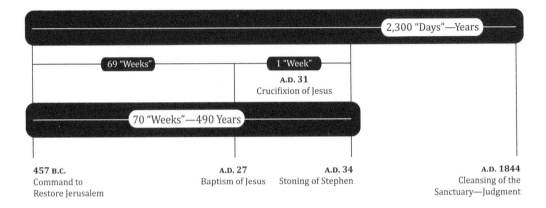

Jesus, the Messiah, "shall be cut off, but not for Himself." Jesus was crucified, not for Himself but for us. He died for you and me. "And the people of the prince who is to come shall destroy the city and the sanctuary." After the Messiah's death, the city of Jerusalem and its sanctuary would be destroyed. That happened in A.D. 70, when the Roman general Titus marched his army into the city and destroyed it. The sanctuary was burned to the ground.

Verse 27 says of Jesus, "He shall confirm a covenant with many for one week; but in the middle of the week He shall bring an end to sacrifice and offering." Notice how precise the prophecy is:

- Seventy weeks (490 years) were cut off from the 2,300 years for the Jewish people.
- Messiah would come after sixty-nine of those weeks (483 years) had ended.
- The decree to restore Jerusalem, marking the beginning of the seventy weeks, went forth in the fall of 457 B.C.
- The 483 years take us to the autumn of A.D. 27, exactly when Christ was baptized.
- Messiah will bring an end to sacrifice and offering in "the middle of the week"—the final, seventieth prophetic week allotted to the Jewish people.
- Three and a half years (half a prophetic week) from the fall of A.D. 27 takes us to the spring of A.D. 31. And what happened at that time?
- Jesus Christ was crucified at Passover time, in the spring of A.D. 31, following a ministry of three and a half years, precisely as the prophecy predicted!

When Jesus Christ, the Lamb of God, died on the cross, there was no more need for sacrifices and offerings in the earthly sanctuary because the reality to which they pointed had taken place. That is why, at the moment He died, the veil in the temple was torn from top to bottom, exposing the Most Holy Place (Matthew 27:51). The sanctuary services were object lessons illustrating the sacrifice of Jesus and the plan of salvation. When He died, they were no longer relevant. They had served their purpose. Now, sinners no longer needed to sacrifice a lamb in the temple; they could come directly to Jesus and accept His blood to cover their sin. Jesus is God's Lamb, slain for us exactly on time as Bible prophecy predicted.

According to Gabriel's explanation, God's covenant with the Jews would cease at the end of the seventy weeks, in A.D. 34. Of course, individual Jews could be saved after that time, just as any individual, Muslim, Hindu, Jew, or Christian, is saved through the blood of Jesus Christ. But after A.D. 34, the Jews would no longer be God's chosen nation. The book of Acts, chapter 7, records the death of the first Christian martyr, Stephen. In A.D. 34 the Jewish high priest broke the everlasting covenant that God had established with His people. This act of terminating the covenant was symbolized by the high priest's tearing his robes and the stoning of Stephen, the first Christian martyr. At this time the gospel was proclaimed powerfully to both Jew and Gentile. The seventy weeks (490 years), allotted to the Jews, came to an end.

The remaining portion of the 2,300 years

Remember, the seventy weeks are only the first 490 years of the 2,300 years of Daniel's prophecy. This is the portion that relates to the Jewish people and their nation. The remaining portion of the 2,300 years has to do with God's people since then, extending down to the time of the end and the second coming of Jesus. The prophecy ties an event we can see (the first coming of Jesus) to an event that has not yet been fulfilled (the second coming of Jesus) to give us confidence that what Bible prophecy predicts is true. We have seen that the events connected with the first part of the prophecy came true with amazing accuracy. That provides assurance that the events of the remaining part of the prophecy will also be fulfilled exactly as predicted.

The prophecy says, "For two thousand three hundred days; then the sanctuary shall be cleansed" (Daniel 8:14). Additionally, Gabriel told Daniel, "Understand, son of man, that the vision refers to the time of the end" (verse 17). Since one prophetic day equals one literal year, the 2,300 days (years) take us down to the time of the end. Can we figure out when the 2,300 years end?

Certainly! They began with the decree to "restore and build Jerusalem" (verse 25). That decree by Artaxerxes was issued, as we have seen, in 457 B.C. If you start at 457

B.C. and go forward 2,300 years on history's timeline, you will come to A.D. 1844 (remember, there is no year zero when moving from B.C. to A.D.). This date, A.D. 1844, ushers in what the Bible calls the time of the end, the time of final judgment just before the coming of Christ. That means that we have been living in the time of the end since 1844! It means that since 1844, the work of cleansing the sanctuary in heaven has been going forward. It means that the truth about the work Jesus is doing as our High Priest in the heavenly sanctuary has been being brought to light since 1844. The truth about God's law is being restored. The cleansing of the sanctuary in heaven and the work of judgment, prefigured by the Day of Atonement each year in the sanctuary on earth, results in God having settled His issues with the nations. Wicked powers and wicked individuals will be judged and found guilty. God's faithful people will be exonerated. They are covered by the righteousness of their Savior, Jesus Christ.

During this time of the end, God's people will be examining their hearts, asking God to forgive their sins and cleanse their hearts and minds from any attitude or practice in their lives not in harmony with His will, just as the Israelites did during the Old Testament Day of Atonement. They will be asking Him to cover them with the robe of Christ's righteousness (Isaiah 61:10).

We are living in the judgment hour. Since the year 1844, God has been restoring the truth of Scripture to the world—truth that has been lost sight of down through the centuries, truth that has been obscured by the traditions and teachings of men. God's last-day message has been going forth, and time is running out. Since 1844, we have been living in the time of the end, the last moments before Jesus returns. What a time in which to be living! This is the time to be faithful to Jesus, our only High Priest and Savior in the heavenly sanctuary. This is the time to make sure there is nothing in our lives that would separate us from Him.

Now is the time to echo Daniel's prayer, recorded here in chapter 9: "O my God, incline Your ear and hear . . . for we do not present our supplications before You because of our righteous deeds, but because of Your great mercies. O Lord, hear! O Lord, forgive! O Lord, listen and act! Do not delay for Your own sake, my God, for . . . Your people are called by Your name" (verses 18, 19).

Will you make Daniel's prayer, your prayer? Will you seek God with all your heart? Will you, right now, surrender everything in your life that is not in harmony with His will? Why not bow your head in a moment of reflection and ask Him through His Holy Spirit to move powerfully in your life at this very moment?

THE GOD WHO LISTENS TO PRAYER

Daniel 10

1 In the third year of Cyrus king of Persia a message was revealed to Daniel, whose name was called Belteshazzar. The message was true, but the appointed time was long; and he understood the message, and had understanding of the vision. **2** In those days I, Daniel, was mourning three full weeks. **3** I ate no pleasant food, no meat or wine came into my mouth, nor did I anoint myself at all, till three whole weeks were fulfilled.

4 Now on the twenty-fourth day of the first month, as I was by the side of the great river, that is, the Tigris, **5** I lifted my eyes and looked, and behold, a certain man clothed in linen, whose waist was girded with gold of Uphaz! **6** His body was like beryl, his face like the appearance of lightning, his eyes like torches of fire, his arms and feet like burnished bronze in color, and the sound of his words like the voice of a multitude.

7 And I, Daniel, alone saw the vision, for the men who were with me did not see the vision; but a great terror fell upon them, so that they fled to hide themselves. **8** Therefore I was left alone when I saw this great vision, and no strength remained in me; for my vigor was turned to frailty in me, and I retained no strength. **9** Yet I heard the sound of his words; and while I heard the sound of his words I was in a deep sleep on my face, with my face to the ground.

10 Suddenly, a hand touched me, which made me tremble on my knees and on the palms of my hands. **11** And he said to me, "O Daniel, man greatly beloved, understand the words that I speak to you, and stand upright, for I have now been sent to you." While he was speaking this word to me, I stood trembling.

12 Then he said to me, "Do not fear, Daniel, for from the first day that you set your heart to understand, and to humble yourself before your God, your words were heard; and I have come

because of your words. **13** But the prince of the kingdom of Persia withstood me twenty-one days; and behold, Michael, one of the chief princes, came to help me, for I had been left alone there with the kings of Persia. **14** Now I have come to make you understand what will happen to your people in the latter days, for the vision refers to many days yet to come."

15 When he had spoken such words to me, I turned my face toward the ground and became speechless. **16** And suddenly, one having the likeness of the sons of men touched my lips; then I opened my mouth and spoke, saying to him who stood before me, "My lord, because of the vision my sorrows have overwhelmed me, and I have retained no strength. **17** For how can this servant of my lord talk with you, my lord? As for me, no strength remains in me now, nor is any breath left in me."

18 Then again, the one having the likeness of a man touched me and strengthened me. **19** And he said, "O man greatly beloved, fear not! Peace be to you; be strong, yes, be strong!"

So when he spoke to me I was strengthened, and said, "Let my lord speak, for you have strengthened me."

20 Then he said, "Do you know why I have come to you? And now I must return to fight with the prince of Persia; and when I have gone forth, indeed the prince of Greece will come. **21** But I will tell you what is noted in the Scripture of Truth. (No one upholds me against these, except Michael your prince. . . .

We left Daniel, in chapter 9, listening to Gabriel explain the vision he had received in chapter 8. The angel told him that the early part of the 2,300-year prophecy related to Jerusalem and the Jewish people, but the prophecy extended far into the future—down to the time of the end. What was the effect of this information on the prophet? Did Daniel fully grasp the significance of this prophecy? Did he understand that a battle over keeping Israel in bondage was going on between the forces of good and evil? The tenth chapter of Daniel pulls aside the curtain and gives us a glimpse of this titanic struggle. It provides the "inside story" of the agelong controversy between angelic forces and demonic forces. Let's view this controversy from Daniel's perspective.

"In the third year of Cyrus king of Persia a message was revealed to Daniel, whose name was called Belteshazzar. The message was true, but the appointed time was long; and he understood the message, and had understanding of the vision. In those days I, Daniel, was mourning three full weeks. I ate no pleasant food, no meat or wine came into my mouth, nor did I anoint myself at all, till three whole weeks were fulfilled" (Daniel 10:1–3).

Daniel was an old man in the third year of Cyrus. He had served God through the Babylonian kingdom and was now serving Him in the kingdom of the Medes and Persians. Media-Persia overthrew Babylon in 539 B.C. So if Daniel had been about seventeen years old when he was taken into captivity by Nebuchadnezzar in 605 B.C., he would be approximately 87 in the third year of the reign of Cyrus. Seventy years have gone by since the Babylonians overthrew Jerusalem. Daniel knew from the writings of Jeremiah that the period of Jewish captivity was coming to an end (Daniel 9:1, 2). But Daniel's people had not yet been released from captivity. "The message was true, but the appointed time was long" (Daniel 10:1). Daniel is longing for deliverance; he's longing for his people to be allowed to go home to Jerusalem and to worship in a rebuilt sanctuary. He's longing for God to fulfill His promise, but the time appointed is long, and Daniel is burdened. That's why he is mourning and fasting and praying.

Waiting for Jesus to return

We can understand how Daniel felt. We have been waiting a long time for Jesus to return. Shortly before His crucifixion, Jesus told the disciples, "Let not your heart be troubled; you believe in God, believe also in Me. . . . I go to prepare a place for you. And if I go and prepare a place for you, I will come again and receive you to Myself; that where I am, there you may be also" (John 14:1–3).

Two thousand years have gone by since Jesus promised to return. The time has been long. This earth groans to be delivered. There are famines, earthquakes, and natural disasters of all kinds. There are increasing crime and civil disorder. There are rampant drug addiction, mass shootings, and broken homes. Like Daniel, we are filled with dismay as we look around us because the appointed time is long. Daniel prayed that the Jews would be delivered from their captivity and return to Jerusalem. We pray that we will be delivered from the bondage of sin and death on this planet and that we will be taken home to the New Jerusalem, where our hearts will be free to worship God. We can identify with Daniel.

For "three whole weeks" (Daniel 10:3), Daniel was in mourning and praying for God to deliver His people. For three whole weeks, as Daniel continues to pray, it seems that nothing is happening. One week goes by. Two weeks go by. Three weeks . . . , and God doesn't seem to be answering at all. Daniel sees no visible evidence that God is even listening.

Have you ever prayed and received no apparent answer? Sometimes it seems like our prayers go up to the ceiling and come right back down! We do not sense that God is present or that He hears us. That's how Daniel felt after three weeks of praying, fasting, and getting no response. Then something amazing occurred.

I lifted my eyes and looked, and behold, a certain man clothed in linen, whose waist was girded with gold of Uphaz! His body was like beryl, his face like the appearance of lightning, his eyes like torches of fire, his arms and feet like burnished bronze in color, and the sound of his words like the voice of a multitude.

And I, Daniel, alone saw the vision. . . . I was left alone when I saw this great vision, and no strength remained in me; for my vigor was turned to frailty in me, and I retained no strength. Yet I heard the sound of his words; and while I heard the sound of his words I was in a deep sleep on my face, with my face to the ground (verses 5–9).

Jesus responds to Daniel's prayers

For three weeks, there has been no apparent answer to Daniel's prayers. Now a being of dazzling brightness appears. This being's brightness is so magnificent that Daniel actually passes out at the sight. Who is this being of dazzling brightness who considered Daniel so beloved that he came down from heaven to be by his side?

The apostle John saw a similar individual in vision. He described this person in these words: "I saw seven golden lampstands, and in the midst of the seven lampstands One like the Son of Man, clothed with a garment down to the feet and girded about the chest with a golden band. His head and hair were white like wool, as white as snow, and His eyes like a flame of fire; His feet were like fine brass, as if refined in a furnace, and His voice as the sound of many waters; . . . His countenance was like the sun shining in its strength" (Revelation 1:12–16).

John's reaction to this glorious sight was much like that of Daniel. John says, "When I saw Him, I fell at His feet as dead" (verse 17). This glorious Being that John

Daniel prayed that the Jews would be delivered from their captivity and return to Jerusalem. We pray that we will be delivered from the bondage of sin and death on this planet and that we will be taken home to the New Jerusalem, where our hearts will be free to worship God.

saw was none other than Jesus Christ. He tells John, "I am the First and the Last. I am He who lives, and was dead, and behold, I am alive forevermore" (verses 17, 18). The description of Jesus in John's vision is almost identical to Daniel's description of the individual he saw in the vision.

Jesus Christ is the heavenly Being who came to Daniel's side in answer to his prayers. Jesus came to encourage Daniel, lift his spirits, and give him hope. Jesus Christ, Himself, came down from heaven to meet with Daniel!

When it seems that our prayers are not being heard, Jesus is there. If our eyes could see eternal realities, we would see Jesus by our side, assuring us that He is listening to our prayers and working out our difficulties. The promises of God are sure. When apparently our prayers go unanswered, we can cling to these promises by faith:

"Fear not, for I am with you;
Be not dismayed, for I am your God.
I will strengthen you,
Yes, I will help you,
I will uphold you with My righteous right hand" (Isaiah 41:10).

For He Himself has said, "I will never leave you nor forsake you" (Hebrews 13:5).

"Lo, I am with you always, even to the end of the age" (Matthew 28:20).

When Daniel had little assurance of God's direct answers to his prayers, he still knew by faith: heaven was working on his behalf. We, too, can have the assurance that every sincere prayer offered in living faith lodges in the heart and mind of God, and it will be answered at the time and in the way He deems best.

Daniel kept praying for three weeks, although it seemed that nothing was happening and God was not listening. But Jesus was listening, and He came to sustain Daniel in his time of need.

In the book of Daniel, Jesus is not pictured sitting on His throne, far away in heaven, and detached from His people on earth. In chapter 2, He is the One who reveals the king's dream to Daniel. In chapter 3, He is the "Son of God" who comes down to stand in the fiery furnace with Shadrach, Meshach, and Abed-Nego. In chapter 5, He writes on Belshazzar's wall. In chapter 6, he shuts the lions' mouths. In chapters 7 and 8, He is the center of the sanctuary—the Lamb who was sacrificed for our sins and our interceding High Priest who provides strength for our every need.

In chapter 9, He is the coming Messiah. And, here in chapter 10, He is the One who listens to prayer. He listened to Daniel's prayer, and He listens to our prayers as well.

Daniel fainted at the sight of Jesus in his vision. He fell on his face to the ground, and all his strength left him (Daniel 10:8, 9). Suddenly he feels a hand on his shoulder, and he manages to get up on his hands and knees (verse 10). An angel has come to explain what Daniel has just seen.

The angel says,

"O Daniel, man greatly beloved, understand the words that I speak to you, and stand upright, for I have now been sent to you." While he was speaking this word to me, I stood trembling.

Then he said to me, "Do not fear, Daniel, for from the first day that you set your heart to understand, and to humble yourself before your God, your words were heard; and I have come because of your words" (verses 11, 12).

What happens behind the scenes when we pray?

Daniel had prayed for three weeks with no apparent response from God. However, the angel tells him that his words had been heard in heaven from the first day that he began to pray! Jesus was listening to Daniel's prayers the whole time! He appeared in a vision to assure Daniel of His love for Him. God loved Daniel, and He loves you and me as well. When you feel depressed and there is nothing but darkness all around you, remember that you are greatly beloved of heaven and that Jesus is listening to your prayers.

Many places in the Bible encourage us to pray. But no other place in the Bible explains so clearly what happens behind the scenes when you pray, as does Daniel chapter 10. It describes the great struggle going on between good and evil and how our prayers affect the impact that struggle has on our personal lives. Chapter 10 reveals the great controversy between Christ and Satan; it unseals the mysteries of prayer.

The angel explains to Daniel why it took so long for heaven to respond to his prayer. Daniel had been praying for three weeks. The angel assures him that his prayers were heard from the very first day he began praying. He wanted to come to Daniel immediately. But there was a problem.

The angel says, "The prince of the kingdom of Persia withstood me twenty-one days; and behold, Michael, one of the chief princes, came to help me, for I had been left alone there with the kings of Persia. Now I have come to make you understand" (verses 13, 14).

The angel tells Daniel, "I am going to explain to you why there was no apparent answer to your prayer. I'm going to give you a behind-the-scenes look at the great controversy going on between good and evil. When you prayed, your prayers went up into heaven. God tried to impress Cyrus, the king of Persia, to help your people. But the problem is that the prince of the kingdom Persia got in the way."

The prince of the kingdom of Persia

Who is this prince of the kingdom of Persia?

Let's look at something Jesus said in John's Gospel. Jesus said, "Now is the judgment of this world; now the ruler of this world ["the prince of this world," KJV] will be cast out" (John 12:31). Who is the ruler, or prince, of this world? Satan. If Satan is the prince of this world, then he was surely the prince of the kingdom of Persia. Satan was resisting Daniel's prayers from being answered by influencing the mind of Cyrus, encouraging him to keep the Israelites from returning home to Jerusalem to rebuild their city.

In his letter to the Ephesians, Paul wrote, "You once walked according to the course of this world, according to the prince of the power of the air, the spirit who now works in the sons of disobedience" (Ephesians 2:2). Satan is the prince of the power of the air, the one who works in those who are disobedient to God.

Satan, the prince of the kingdom of Persia, was fighting against God. He was doing everything he possibly could to keep Daniel's prayers from being answered. God's angel was struggling against Satan. They were both battling for the mind of King Cyrus. God never coerces the will. He never forces us to obey. He influences us through the Holy Spirit. He helps and encourages us. But He doesn't force or manipulate us. We are free, in the end, to make our own decision. God has given us free will, and He continues to respect our freedom of choice even in the crucial issues of the great controversy.

When we pray to God for help, however, our prayers open new channels for God to work. Because of Daniel's prayers, God was able to send greater forces of spiritual power to open Cyrus's mind to the Spirit's leading. He was able to send His angel to struggle directly against Satan. For twenty-one days, the battle raged between Satan and the forces of God.

What would have happened if Daniel had stopped praying after one week or two weeks? The battle might well have been lost. Satan might well have won. We should never give up praying. Keep lifting the hand of faith higher and higher. If we give up praying, we leave the battle open to be won by Satan.

Michael stands up for God's people

The angel tells Daniel that "Michael" came to help him in the struggle with Satan. Who is Michael?

Michael is named only five times in the Bible, and every time, Michael is in conflict with Satan. Revelation 12 says, "War broke out in heaven: Michael and his angels fought with the dragon; and the dragon and his angels fought, but they did not prevail" (verses 7, 8). So Michael has angels who are loyal to Him. Verse 9 identifies the dragon as Satan and says that he and his angels were cast out of heaven. Whoever Michael is, He has the authority to cast Satan out of heaven, and He is powerful enough to cast Satan out of heaven.

Jude, verse 9, speaks of Michael contending with the devil over the body of Moses. You remember that Moses died before he was able to enter the Promised Land. Yet, Moses and Elijah appeared on the mountain with Jesus near the close of His ministry on earth. So Moses was apparently resurrected after he died there on the borders of Canaan. Satan wanted to keep Moses in the grave, but Michael contended with the devil over Moses's body—and prevailed. So whoever Michael is, He has the power to beat back Satan and resurrect Moses from the dead.

Who has the authority to cast Satan out of heaven? Who has the authority and power to raise someone from the dead? Jesus is the One with that authority and power. Michael is one of the names for Jesus Christ. There are many names for Jesus. He is known as the Lamb of God because He is our sacrifice for sin. He is the "Door" to the sheepfold. He is the "Rock of Ages." He is the "Lion of the tribe of Judah." He is the "Prince of Peace," the "Good Shepherd," the "Rose of Sharon," and the "Lily of the Valley." Why are there so many names for Jesus? Because He is everything to us. And Michael is one of Jesus' names.

Some people become confused over the name Michael because Jude 9 uses the expression "Michael the archangel." Here are some things to keep in mind. First, Jesus is certainly not a created being. He is not an angel, but He is the commander and chief of all the angels. In Daniel 10:13, the marginal reading for the expression "one of the chief princes" is "the chief prince." Jesus is eternal. He never had a beginning and will never have an ending. He is the divine Son of God (Micah 5:2; John 1:1–5; 8:58). Angels are created beings. Jesus has existed from the days of eternity. But Jesus has a special function in the divine plan. He is not only our Creator, our Redeemer, and our High Priest but also our coming King. As such, He is the Commander in Chief of all the angels. Jesus declared, "For the Son of Man will come in the glory of His Father with His angels, and then He will reward each according to his works" (Matthew 16:27). The apostle Paul uses the title *archangel*, or commander of the angels, to relate to Jesus when He comes in glory to take us home. "For the Lord Himself will descend from heaven with a shout, with the voice of an archangel, and with the trumpet of God. And the dead in Christ will rise first. Then we who are alive and remain shall be caught up together with them in the clouds to meet the Lord in the air. And thus we shall always be with the Lord" (1 Thessalonians 4:16, 17). Michael, the mighty conqueror, will one day finally defeat Satan, vanquish the powers of hell, and deliver us from this "present evil world" (Galatians 1:4, KJV).

Michael is a special name. It is the name that God uses to describe Christ as the Commander in Chief of all the angels. *Michael* is the name for Jesus that emphasizes His power over Satan. When we need extra strength, Michael comes. When we need extra power, Michael comes. When we need to beat back the forces of hell, Michael comes.

Remember, in the last days, there will be a time of trouble, and all the forces of hell will come against God's people. The Bible says that

"At that time Michael shall stand up,
The great prince who stands watch over the sons of your people;
And there shall be a time of trouble,
Such as never was since there was a nation,
Even to that time.
And at that time your people shall be delivered" (Daniel 12:1).

At the time of the end, when the powers of evil are at their greatest, we need all the help that heaven can provide. That is when Michael will stand up and deliver us from Satan. Every time we read of Michael in the Bible, there is deliverance. When we need power in our life, Michael comes. When the devil is oppressing us, Michael comes.

In the last days, the minds of men and women will be engulfed in darkness. Satan himself will take command of the battle, knowing that the time is short. In the battle between good and evil, in the battle between Christ and Satan, when we feel that Satan's temptations are overwhelming and we cannot go on, that is when Michael stands up and delivers us. We need not fear. Our Lord Jesus Christ is the mighty Deliverer, and soon, He will return to take us home.

THE PROPHETIC CLIMAX

Daniel 11

1 "[(. . .] Also in the first year of Darius the Mede, I, even I, stood up to confirm and strengthen him.) **2** And now I will tell you the truth: Behold, three more kings will arise in Persia, and the fourth shall be far richer than them all; by his strength, through his riches, he shall stir up all against the realm of Greece. **3** Then a mighty king shall arise, who shall rule with great dominion, and do according to his will. **4** And when he has arisen, his kingdom shall be broken up and divided toward the four winds of heaven, but not among his posterity nor according to his dominion with which he ruled; for his kingdom shall be uprooted, even for others besides these.

5 "Also the king of the South shall become strong, as well as one of his princes; and he shall gain power over him and have dominion. His dominion shall be a great dominion. **6** And at the end of some years they shall join forces, for the daughter of the king of the South shall go to the king of the North to make an agreement; but she shall not retain the power of her authority, and neither he nor his authority shall stand; but she shall be given up, with those who brought her, and with him who begot her, and with him who strengthened her in those times. **7** But from a branch of her roots one shall arise in his place, who shall come with an army, enter the fortress of the king of the North, and deal with them and prevail. **8** And he shall also carry their gods captive to Egypt, with their princes and their precious articles of silver and gold; and he shall continue more years than the king of the North.

9 "Also the king of the North shall come to the kingdom of the king of the South, but shall return to his own land. **10** However his sons shall stir up strife, and assemble a multitude of great forces; and one shall certainly come and overwhelm and pass through; then he shall return to his fortress and stir up strife.

11 "And the king of the South shall be moved with rage, and go out and fight with him, with the king of the North, who shall muster a great multitude; but the multitude shall be given into the hand of his enemy. **12** When he has taken away the multitude, his heart will be lifted up; and he will cast down tens of thousands, but he will not prevail. **13** For the king of the North will return and muster a multitude greater than the former, and shall certainly come at the end of some years with a great army and much equipment.

14 "Now in those times many shall rise up against the king of the South. Also, violent men of your people shall exalt themselves in fulfillment of the vision, but they shall fall. **15** So the king of the North shall come and build a siege mound, and take a fortified city; and the forces of the South shall not withstand him. Even his choice troops shall have no strength to resist. **16** But he who comes against him shall do according to his own will, and no one shall stand against him. He shall stand in the Glorious Land with destruction in his power.

17 "He shall also set his face to enter with the strength of his whole kingdom, and upright ones with him; thus shall he do. And he shall give him the daughter of women to destroy it; but she shall not stand with him, or be for him. **18** After this he shall turn his face to the coastlands, and shall take many. But a ruler shall bring the reproach against them to an end; and with the reproach removed, he shall turn back on him. **19** Then he shall turn his face toward the fortress of his own land; but he shall stumble and fall, and not be found.

20 "There shall arise in his place one who imposes taxes on the glorious kingdom; but within a few days he shall be destroyed, but not in anger or in battle. **21** And in his place shall arise a vile person, to whom they will not give the honor of royalty; but he shall come in peaceably, and seize the kingdom by intrigue. **22** With the force of a flood they shall be swept away from before him and be broken, and also the prince of the covenant. **23** And after the league is made with him he shall act deceitfully, for he shall come up and become strong with a small number of people. **24** He shall enter peaceably, even into the richest places of the province; and he shall do what his fathers have not done, nor his forefathers: he shall disperse among them the plunder, spoil, and riches; and he shall devise his plans against the strongholds, but only for a time.

25 "He shall stir up his power and his courage against the king of the South with a great army. And the king of the South shall be stirred up to battle with a very great and mighty army; but he shall not stand, for they shall devise plans against him. **26** Yes, those who eat of the portion of his delicacies shall destroy him; his army shall be swept away, and many shall fall down slain. **27** Both these kings' hearts shall be bent on evil, and they shall speak lies at the same table; but it shall not prosper, for the end will still be at the appointed time. **28** While returning to his land with great riches, his heart shall be moved against the holy covenant; so he shall do damage and return to his own land.

29 "At the appointed time he shall return and go toward the south; but it shall not be like the former or the latter. **30** For ships from Cyprus shall come against him; therefore he shall be grieved, and return in rage against the holy covenant, and do damage.

"So he shall return and show regard for those who forsake the holy covenant. **31** And forces shall be mustered by him, and they shall defile the sanctuary fortress; then they shall take away the daily sacrifices, and place there the abomination of desolation. **32** Those who do wickedly against the covenant he shall corrupt with flattery; but the people who know their God shall be strong, and carry out great exploits. **33** And those of the people who understand shall instruct many; yet for many days they shall fall by sword and flame, by captivity and plundering. **34** Now when they fall, they shall be aided with a little help; but many shall join with them by intrigue. **35** And some of those of understanding shall fall, to refine them, purify them, and make them white, until the time of the end; because it is still for the appointed time.

36 "Then the king shall do according to his own will: he shall exalt and magnify himself above every god, shall speak blasphemies against the God of gods, and shall prosper till the wrath has been accomplished; for what has been determined shall be done. **37** He shall regard neither the God of his fathers nor the desire of women, nor regard any god; for he shall exalt himself above them all. **38** But in their place he shall honor a god of fortresses; and a god which his fathers did not know he shall honor with gold and silver, with precious stones and pleasant things. **39** Thus he shall act against the strongest fortresses with a foreign god, which he shall acknowledge, and advance its glory; and he shall cause them to rule over many, and divide the land for gain.

40 "At the time of the end the king of the South shall attack him; and the king of the North shall come against him like a whirlwind, with chariots, horsemen, and with many ships; and he shall enter the countries, overwhelm them, and pass through. **41** He shall also enter the Glorious Land, and many countries shall be overthrown; but these shall escape from his hand: Edom, Moab, and the prominent people of Ammon. **42** He shall stretch out his hand against the countries, and the land of Egypt shall not escape. **43** He shall have power over the treasures of gold and silver, and over all the precious things of Egypt; also the

Libyans and Ethiopians shall follow at his heels. **44** But news from the east and the north shall trouble him; therefore he shall go out with great fury to destroy and annihilate many. **45** And he shall plant the tents of his palace between the seas and the glorious holy mountain; yet he shall come to his end, and no one will help him.

There is one thing that lifts the human spirit and keeps us going despite the challenges we face. It's called hope. Hope is that intangible quality that looks beyond life's difficulties to a better tomorrow. It leads us to live purposeful lives today because we know a new day is coming. It anticipates the best in life even when we are facing the worst in life. It looks beyond what is to what will be. It keeps believing, trusting, anticipating, and expecting that out of today's darkness, tomorrow's light will shine more brightly.

The Roman statesman Pliny once said, "Hope is the pillar that holds up the world." He was right. Without hope, this world is on a collision course to disaster. Without hope, the foundations of society collapse. Without hope, we live our lives in silent despair.

Rediscovering hope

In a world that seems out of control, how can we rediscover hope? In a world that seems so uncertain, how can we hope again? Is there something certain we can base our hope on? Millions have found hope, assurance, and peace as they have studied the prophecies of Daniel and Revelation. These prophecies speak of hope today, tomorrow, and forever. In the stories and prophecies of Daniel, we discover a God who loves us more than we can imagine and who will strengthen us to face the challenges of today and the trials of tomorrow with incredible courage. He is the God of hope.

The book of Daniel comes to a glorious climax by presenting us with God's ultimate triumph over the principalities and powers of hell. It reveals that one day, the powers of evil will be defeated; one day, the sorrow and suffering of this world will be gone, and the righteous will reign with Christ through the ceaseless ages of eternity.

Chapter 11 of Daniel's book enlarges and expands the great prophecies of chapters 2, 7, 8, and 9. This is God's message for our day that will enable us to safely navigate the end time and meet Jesus when He returns.

Chapter 2 presented a great image outlining four world empires that would rise one after the other—Babylon, Media-Persia, Greece, and Rome. The ten toes of the image represented the nations of Europe that would result from the breakup of the Roman Empire. A rock strikes the image on its feet, smashing it to bits. This scene represents the second coming of Jesus, when He will establish His everlasting kingdom of righteousness.

Chapter 7 covers a similar outline of history but adds details. Once again, we see the four kingdoms. The fourth, Rome, has ten horns instead of ten toes, representing a divided Europe. But chapter 7 introduces a new element—a little horn, representing apostate Christianity, the antichrist power. This power casts the truth of Jesus' complete ministry in the heavenly sanctuary to the ground. It establishes an earthly priesthood and seeks to change God's law regarding time. Then the scene in chapter 7 changes focus—from earth to heaven. In the heavenly courtroom, Jesus represents His obedient people, covered with His righteousness. Daniel declares, "The judgment was set, and the books were opened." In this celestial scene, thousands of heavenly beings gather around the throne of the universe to witness the final judgment. This judgment powerfully reveals that God has done everything He can to save every person possible. The judgment reveals God's justice and mercy. Although we are saved by grace, through faith alone, our works reveal whether our faith is genuine and meets the standard of the judgment.

In chapter 8, the general theme of the previous prophecies continues. However, Daniel 8 presents three kingdoms—not four. Why? Babylon was fading fast and would soon no longer play a significant role in world history. So God didn't present Babylon in chapter 8. In chapters 8 and 9, God once again describes Media-Persia and Greece, the ram and the male goat, as well as Rome. However, this time, He focuses especially on last-day events and the final judgment, the restoration of divine truth, and the cleansing of the heavenly sanctuary. Daniel chapter 9 provides the key to understanding the timing of the 2,300 prophetic days, or literal years, in Daniel 8 by linking it to events in the first coming of Christ.

The prophetic sequence in Daniel's prophecies

We see a repetition of the same sequence in each of these prophetic chapters of Daniel. There is a focus on the great empires of Babylon, Media-Persia, Greece, and Rome. Then we see the breakup of Rome into ten divisions, followed by the rise of a little-horn power representing a union of church and state that obscures the truth about Jesus and His work in the sanctuary of heaven. Then, the focus turns to the judgment that vindicates God and His people and exalts Jesus Christ and His law. Finally comes the return of Jesus and the establishment of God's everlasting kingdom.

When we come to chapter 11, the prophetic climax of Daniel's book, should we expect it to go off in a new direction? Should we expect it to introduce entirely new themes? Certainly not! We would expect it to include all that has gone before and add new details to the larger narrative in Daniel.

In Daniel 11, we again find the three kingdoms—Media-Persia, Greece, and Rome. The last of these kingdoms is broken up and divided. In this chapter, we read about numerous battles back and forth between political powers. We see once more a departure from God and His truth. Human traditions take the place of the Word of God. There is a judgment on this power that exalts itself against God. Daniel 11 ends with earth's final battle between good and evil, God and Satan.

Gabriel outlines the future

In chapter 10, Gabriel came to speak with Daniel and help him better understand a vision. The angel continues to speak to Daniel in chapter 11. In fact, the entire chapter is the angel outlining to Daniel events yet to come. He says, "I will tell you the truth: Behold, three more kings will arise in Persia, and the fourth shall be far richer than them all; by his strength, through his riches, he shall stir up all against the realm of Greece. Then a mighty king shall arise, who shall rule with great dominion, and do according to his will. And when he has risen, his kingdom shall be broken up and divided toward the four winds of heaven" (Daniel 11:2–4).

That happened exactly as the Bible predicted. Four Persian kings stood up—Cambyses, Pseudo-Smerdis, Darius, and Ahasuerus (Xerxes I)—and the last was richer than them all. Then the angel describes a mighty king who would arise in Greece and rule—Alexander the Great. But his kingdom was to be uprooted and divided toward the four winds of heaven (verse 4). We saw this same division in Daniel 7, with the four heads on the leopard representing Greece, and in chapter 8, with four horns that came up from the male goat. Alexander died at thirty-three, and his four generals divided power among themselves—Ptolemy, Cassander, Seleucus, and Lysimachus. Ptolemy dominated the south and ruled Egypt. Verse 5 says, "The king of the South shall become strong. . . . His dominion shall be a great dominion." So chapter 11 introduces Egypt under the Ptolemies as the king of the South.

Egypt down through the centuries was a nation that rebelled against the God of heaven. In the time of Moses, the Egyptian Pharaoh defied God and refused to free the children of Israel from their bondage. When we think of Egypt, we think of this defiance and rebellion against God. Egypt was a power opposed to God. In Daniel

11, when we read about the "king of the South," we are reading about Egypt. But the king of the South denotes something much broader in the conflict between good and evil. The king of the South is a power that shakes its fist in God's face. Egypt represents more than just a nation; it represents rebellion and defiance toward God.

The king of the South and the king of the North

As we go through Daniel 11, we will be reading about the "king of the South" and the "king of the North." These directions are in relation to Israel. Egypt was a southern power in relation to Israel. Babylon was a northern power in relation to Israel. Like Egypt, Babylon was a power opposed to the true God. It signified confusion and religious apostasy. So these terms, "king of the South" and "king of the North," stand for Egypt and Babylon, respectively. But they stand for much more than these literal nations. The king of the South stands for defiance and rebellion against God. The king of the North stands for spiritual confusion and religious apostasy.

So far, in Daniel 11, we've seen that Media-Persia would give way to Greece. Greece would be followed by Rome. One of the four Greek generals, Ptolemy, would settle in Egypt, introducing the idea of the king of the South, or the power that would arise to defy and rebel against God. Verses 6–19 introduce a series of battles and struggles for power among the various factions of the king of the South and the king of the North. Verse 20 introduces Rome, the next world empire following Greece. It says, "There shall arise in his place one who imposes taxes on the glorious kingdom." The "glorious kingdom" is the land of Israel. Luke records, "It came to pass in those days, that there went out a decree from Caesar Augustus, that all the world should be taxed" (Luke 2:1, KJV). It was Augustus's decree imposing taxes that brought Joseph and Mary to Bethlehem.

Daniel 11 says of this imposer of taxes, Caesar Augustus, "within a few days he shall be destroyed" (verse 20). Caesar Augustus died very quickly. Verse 21 says, "In his place shall arise a vile person, to whom they will not give the honor of royalty; but he shall come in peaceably, and seize the kingdom by intrigue. With the force of a flood they shall be swept away from before him and be broken, and also the prince of the covenant."

Tiberius Caesar followed Augustus Caesar, and Tiberius Caesar was a shrewd, cunning ruler willing to destroy anyone he thought might be critical of or opposed to his rule. Tiberius was never honored as was Augustus. The Roman general Titus, during the reign of Tiberius Caesar, attacked Jerusalem and destroyed it. God's people were broken and swept away. The Jews were scattered throughout the Roman Empire. The prophecy says that the "prince of the covenant" also would be broken.

Who is the prince of the covenant? Jesus Christ. According to the prophecy, the Romans would attack Jerusalem and participate with the Jews in putting to death Jesus Christ, the prince of the covenant (see also Daniel 8:11; 9:26). The book of Daniel presents history in advance.

Here is an important key to understanding Bible prophecy. Up until the time of Jesus, the nations mentioned in Daniel and Revelation are literal and local. Egypt and Babylon were citadels of rebellion that oppressed God's people and defied God's law. Literal Israel, on the other hand, were the chosen people of God called to reveal His way of life as lights to the world. When the "prince of the covenant," Jesus Christ, died on the cross, the veil in the sacred Jewish temple was split in two. The presence of God departed from the temple. Christ declared, "Your house is left to you desolate" (Matthew 23:38). Israel was no longer exclusively the chosen people of God. All who accepted the gospel now became spiritual Israelites. The apostle Paul states, "There is neither Jew nor Greek . . . ; for you are all one in Christ Jesus. And if you are Christ's, then you are Abraham's seed, and heirs according to the promise" (Galatians 3:28, 29). The people of the Jewish nation prided themselves that they were of the lineage, or seed, of Abraham. Paul's concept would have been a revolutionary thought. Peter declares that New Testament believers are a "chosen generation, a royal priesthood, a holy nation" (1 Peter 2:9). God's people, His church, have now become spiritual Israel, the chosen of God to share the glorious light of the gospel with the world.

This principle also applies to Babylon and Egypt. By the time of Christ, Babylon had long been destroyed on the ash heap of history. The splendor of Egypt had largely faded into insignificance. Babylon and Egypt were no longer major players on the world scene, but they did powerfully symbolize two ideologies—open defiance against God and spiritual apostasy. We shall consider the significance of these symbols a little later in the chapter. With this background, we return to our study of chapter 11.

A religious and political power arises

Following the sequence we have seen in the prophetic chapters of Daniel, we would now expect chapter 11 to focus our attention on an apostate religious and political power that would arise following the breakup of Rome. We would expect a departure from the truth of God's Word—and that is exactly what we find.

"These kings' hearts shall be bent on evil, and they shall speak lies at the same table; but it shall not prosper, for the end will still be at the appointed time" (verse 27).

Daniel 11 is now beginning to take us down to the time of the end. These verses begin to show us the early centuries after the fall of the Roman Empire and the rise of apostate Christianity. They show us the schemes and the false teachings of the antichrist power. Then they take us down to the end time.

"They shall defile the sanctuary fortress; then they shall take away the daily sacrifices, and place there the abomination of desolation" (verse 31).

As we have seen earlier, the sanctuary was an object lesson illustrating God's plan of salvation. The center of the sanctuary service was the sacrificial lamb that represented Jesus Christ, the Lamb of God, who died for the sins of the world. The sanctuary is polluted by putting any system of human works in the place of the saving grace of Jesus Christ. The priest who officiated in the sanctuary also represented Jesus and His ministry in the plan of salvation. The sanctuary is polluted by putting a human priest between the individual and God, by elevating a human priest to a position reserved for God alone.

"The king shall do according to his own will: he shall exalt and magnify himself above every god, shall speak blasphemies against the God of gods, and shall prosper till the wrath has been accomplished; for what has been determined shall be done" (verse 36).

The "king" in this verse is the antichrist power that would arise to pollute the sanctuary. He will follow his own will in defiance of God's law. He will exalt and magnify himself above God. He will speak blasphemies against God. This antichrist power will grow and prosper as a strong religious power right until the end. This power would lead men and women from the truth that salvation is only through Jesus Christ. It would establish a system of penances and works to earn salvation. Earthly priests would take the place of our great High Priest, Jesus Christ, as the only Mediator between God and humanity. There would be an attempt to change the very law of God.

The apostle Paul saw this power coming in his own day and warned against it. "Let no one deceive you by any means; for *that Day will not come* [the return of Jesus] unless the falling away comes first, and the man of sin is revealed, the son of perdition, who opposes and exalts himself above all that is called God or that is worshiped, so that he sits as God in the temple of God, showing himself that he is God." "The mystery of lawlessness is already at work" (2 Thessalonians 2:3, 4, 7; emphasis added).

In the last days, the issue will be a conflict over worship and loyalty to God, just as it was in Daniel 3 when the king demanded that Shadrach, Meshach, and Abed-Nego bow down and worship the golden image he had made. Church and state will be united in an apostate religious-political power that attempts to change God's law and lead men and women to disobey God and worship the counterfeit it has set up. Nevertheless, God will have a people who will remain loyal, obedient, and true no matter the cost.

"The people who know their God shall be strong, and carry out great exploits. And those of the people who understand shall instruct many; yet for many days they shall fall by sword and flame, by captivity and plundering" (Daniel 11:32, 33).

The final struggle between good and evil

Daniel 11 climaxes with some of the most exciting verses in the entire Bible. It describes this titanic struggle for the control of the world in the battle between the king of the North and the king of the South.

"At the time of the end the king of the South shall attack him; and the king of the North shall come against him like a whirlwind, with chariots, horsemen, and with many ships; and he shall enter the countries, overwhelm them, and pass through" (Daniel 11:40).

Remember where we are in the prophecy. We are beyond the nations of Babylon, Media-Persia, Greece, and Rome. We are in the section of the prophecy that deals with spiritual apostasy. In the book of Daniel, North and South are in relation to God's people Israel. Babylon is northeast, and Egypt is south of Israel. After the time of Christ, what was literal and local now becomes symbolic and universal. Throughout Bible prophecy, Babylon represents spiritual confusion, false religion, and man-made traditions. In Revelation 14, 17, and 18, Babylon represents the same power as the little horn of Daniel 7 and the power that exalts itself above God here in Daniel 11, or papal Rome. The prophecies have a plain progression—Babylon, Media-Persia, Greece, Rome, the breakup of the Roman Empire, the rise of an apostate religious power (papal Rome), the judgment, and the second coming of Christ.

If the king of the North represents the papacy, what does the king of the South represent? Remember, Egypt was a nation of lavish splendor and enormous wealth. Its Pharaoh mocked God by declaring, "Who is the LORD, that I should obey His voice?" (Exodus 5:2). Although Egypt had multiple gods, it rejected the God of heaven. It was, in that sense, a godless, secular, humanistic culture.

The battle between the king of the North and the king of the South for the control of the world is essentially a battle between the forces of false religion under the auspices of the papacy and secular materialism, godlessness, and humanism. These features could be found in Europe at the end of the Middle Ages, in the French Revolution in the eighteenth century, in the teaching of Darwin in the nineteenth century, or the rise of communism in the twentieth century. According to Daniel 11, at a time of international crisis, political turmoil, and worldwide uncertainty, a church-state union under the papacy battles against all the secular powers of this world and dominates them. For a short period, church and state unite under the auspices of the Roman Church. Oppression and persecution follow for those who do not conform to the decrees of the state church. "News from the east and the north shall trouble him; therefore he shall go out with great fury to destroy and annihilate many" (Daniel 11:44). The good news of the gospel will be preached to the ends of the earth in preparation for the coming of Jesus (Matthew 24:14). The earth will be lightened with the glory of God (Revelation 18:1). "The earth will be filled with the knowledge of the glory of the Lord" (Habakkuk 2:14). The antichrist power will "come to his end, and no one will help him" (Daniel 11:45). "As the lightning comes from the east and flashes to the west, so also will the coming of the Son of Man be" (Matthew 24:27). The tidings, or good news, from the east is the proclamation of the gospel to every nation, people, and language group to prepare men and women for the return of our Lord.

Daniel 11 is a clarion call to faithfulness to God in the light of eternity. We live on the knife-edge of eternity, and God invites us by His grace and through His power to be fully committed to Him.

God's people remain faithful

Even in times of great spiritual darkness, God has always had those who remained faithful to Him. During the time of the antichrist power, down through the centuries called the Middle, or Dark, Ages, it seemed that God's truth might die out completely. But there were always those who refused to conform to the demands of the prevailing religious power. They determined, like Daniel, not to defile themselves by disobeying God.

The Waldenses were one such godly group. They copied the Scriptures by hand in secret hideouts in the mountain caves. Their children memorized large sections of the Bible. The state church united all its power and its armies to eradicate them. Many were killed by sword and flame, as Daniel 11 predicted. The Dark Ages were a bloody time when people were massacred for remaining faithful to God.

One such martyr was Jan Huss of Prague, Bohemia (now part of the Czech Republic). He was condemned as a heretic and sentenced to be burned at the stake because he faithfully preached the Word of God and refused to follow human traditions in the place of the commandments of God. At the place of execution, he knelt and prayed aloud. His executioners tied his hands behind his back with ropes and bound his neck to the stake with a chain. Then they stacked wood and straw around his shackled body. Before they set the pile on fire, Huss stated, "God is my witness that I have never taught that of which I have been accused by false witnesses. In the truth of the Gospel which I have written, taught, and preached I will die to-day with gladness."[1] Throughout those long centuries of spiritual apostasy, faithful men and women who lived for God's truth shed their blood rather than disobey God.

Daniel 11 focuses on the end time when this antichrist power and false religion will grow in popularity and prominence. It takes us down to what's going to happen shortly in our day. It focuses on the final crisis between good and evil in our time. The Bible assures us that in that final crisis, God will have a group of people who are true to Him. The apostle John pictured this same crucial time when the history of this world is about to be changed forever by the second coming of Jesus. He points to God's faithful people, saying, "Here is the patience of the saints; here are those who keep the commandments of God and the faith of Jesus" (Revelation 14:12). In the crisis just before Jesus returns, God will have a group of people who love Him and who accept Jesus as their only Savior—a people who are obedient and faithful to His law because they love Him.

---

1. Samuel Macauley Jackson, ed., "Huss, John, Hussites," *New Schaff-Herzog Encyclopedia of Religious Knowledge*, vol. 5 (Grand Rapids, MI: Baker Book House, 1953), 418, https://ccel.org/ccel/schaff/encyc05/encyc05/Page_418.html.

CLOSING THE BOOK

Daniel 12

1 "At that time Michael shall stand up,
The great prince who stands watch
   over the sons of your people;
And there shall be a time of trouble,
Such as never was since there was a
   nation,
Even to that time.
And at that time your people shall be
   delivered,
Every one who is found written in the
   book.
2 And many of those who sleep in the
   dust of the earth shall awake,
Some to everlasting life,
Some to shame and everlasting
   contempt.
3 Those who are wise shall shine
Like the brightness of the firmament,
And those who turn many to
   righteousness
Like the stars forever and ever.

4 "But you, Daniel, shut up the
words, and seal the book until the time
of the end; many shall run to and fro,
and knowledge shall increase."

5 Then I, Daniel, looked; and there
stood two others, one on this riverbank
and the other on that riverbank. **6** And
one said to the man clothed in linen,
who was above the waters of the river,
"How long shall the fulfillment of these
wonders be?"

7 Then I heard the man clothed in
linen, who was above the waters of the
river, when he held up his right hand
and his left hand to heaven, and swore
by Him who lives forever, that it shall
be for a time, times, and half a time;
and when the power of the holy people
has been completely shattered, all these
things shall be finished.

8 Although I heard, I did not understand. Then I said, "My lord, what shall
be the end of these things?"

9 And he said, "Go your way, Daniel,
for the words are closed up and sealed
till the time of the end. **10** Many shall
be purified, made white, and refined,
but the wicked shall do wickedly; and

none of the wicked shall understand, but the wise shall understand.

11 "And from the time that the daily sacrifice is taken away, and the abomination of desolation is set up, there shall be one thousand two hundred and ninety days. **12** Blessed is he who waits, and comes to the one thousand three hundred and thirty-five days.

13 "But you, go your way till the end; for you shall rest, and will arise to your inheritance at the end of the days."

As we have studied the book of Daniel, we've noticed the divinely crafted sequence of the prophetic portions of the book. There is a minutely designed progression in each of the prophecies of Daniel in chapters 2, 7, 8, 9, and 11. Each successive prophecy builds on the earlier prophecies in a pattern of repetition and enlargement. We have already discovered that no matter where it may begin, every prophecy in Daniel ends with the return of Jesus and the establishment of His everlasting kingdom. History is not circular; it doesn't go in endless cycles. The prophecies of Daniel take us through the centuries to the grand finale of all things. The book of Daniel reveals that there is hope for our weary, sin-filled planet. The book of Daniel says, "Let your heart beat with hope!" And the entire book comes to a grand climax in chapter 12 with Christ's final victory over all the forces of evil.

Michael stands up to deliver His people

The focus in chapter 12 is God's deliverance of His people.

"At that time Michael shall stand up,
The great prince who stands watch over the sons of your people;
And there shall be a time of trouble,
Such as never was since there was a nation,
Even to that time.
And at that time your people shall be delivered,
Every one who is found written in the book.
And many of those who sleep in the dust of the earth shall awake,
Some to everlasting life,
Some to shame and everlasting contempt.

Those who are wise shall shine like the brightness of the firmament,
And those who turn many to righteousness
Like the stars forever and ever" (Daniel 12:1–3).

In chapter 10, we discovered that Michael is one of the names for Jesus Christ. Jesus is eternal. He is not a created being like the angels. The word *Michael* literally means "one who is like God." This name is used for Jesus as the mighty God in direct conflict with Satan. In the last days of earth's history, Michael—Jesus Christ—shall *stand up* to deliver His people. He is the mighty warrior who has never lost a battle with Satan. He is the all-powerful conqueror. He is our triumphant Lord. We can have absolute confidence that one day He will defeat the powers of darkness. We have the total assurance that in Christ, through Christ, and because of Christ, we are on the winning side. The phrase "shall stand up" in verse 1 is an interesting choice of words. It implies that Michael has been sitting down before He stands up. Do we have any description in the prophecies of Daniel that there was a time Jesus, the Son of Man, sat down?

In chapter 7, Daniel says,

> In the last days of earth's history, Michael—Jesus Christ—shall *stand up* to deliver His people. He is the mighty warrior who has never lost a battle with Satan. He is the all-powerful conqueror. He is our triumphant Lord.

"I watched till thrones were put in place,
And the Ancient of Days was seated;
His garment was white as snow,
And the hair of His head was like pure wool.
His throne was a fiery flame,
Its wheels a burning fire;
A fiery stream issued
And came forth from before Him.
A thousand thousands ministered to Him;
The court was seated,
And the books were opened" (Daniel 7:9, 10).

This is the prophet's description of the judgment going on in heaven. The Ancient

of Days (God the Father) is seated as the court convenes, and judgment begins. Daniel is telling us that at the end time, just before the coming of Jesus, there will be a cosmic, eternal judgment that examines the books of record and reveals that God is just, fair, and righteous in the way He has dealt with every case in the controversy between good and evil. In the judgment, before a waiting world and a watching universe, the destiny of every person is settled.

Daniel continues describing what he saw in the vision:

"I was watching in the night visions,
And behold, One like the Son of Man,
Coming with the clouds of heaven!
He came to the Ancient of Days,
And they brought Him near before Him" (verse 13).

The Father and Son sit together in judgment. Jesus sits on His throne next to the Father at the beginning of the judgment. Then at the end of the judgment, He stands up to deliver His people. As we have seen, the prophecy of the 2,300 days (years) ended in the year 1844. Since that time, we have been living in what the Bible calls God's judgment hour. The Ancient of Days and Jesus, the Son of Man, sit in the heavenly courtroom, settling the destinies of humanity. At the close of the judgment, Michael will stand up.

Why is Jesus called the Son of Man in Daniel 7 and Michael in chapter 12? Each title, or name of Jesus, reveals a different aspect of His work. He is called the Son of Man in the judgment to show that He understands us. He has been through the trials of earth. He faced temptation in common with all humanity. He overcame, so we can overcome. As the Son of Man, He went to the cross to reveal the Father's unfathomable love for us and to take upon Himself the guilt and shame of our sin. The Son of Man hung upon that cruel cross, condemned as a sinner in our behalf. "For He made Him who knew no sin to be sin for us, that we might become the righteousness of God in Him" (2 Corinthians 5:21) The term *Son of Man* speaks of a Jesus who knows us, lived for us, died for us, redeemed us, empowers us, and is coming again for us. John's Gospel records, "The Father judges no one, but has committed all judgment to the Son" (John 5:22). Jesus is both our lawyer and our judge.

The name Michael is used of Christ as the Commander in Chief of all the angels who will come in glory and vanquish sin and Satan forever. At times, it is also interchangeable with the Son of Man title. Jesus stated, "For the Son of Man will come in the glory of His Father with His angels, and then He will reward each according to his works" (Matthew 16:27).

Christ comes to "reward each according to his works." The judgment must take place before His return to determine who will receive what reward when He returns. The judgment is not for God's sake. He is omniscient and knows everything already. It is for the universe's sake so that every being in the unfallen worlds can see God's justice, mercy, and incredible love.

At the end of this pre-Advent, or investigative, judgment, Jesus arises, signaling to the universe that all have made their final, irrevocable decision on how they will respond to His love and grace. Probation is closed. The destinies of all humanity are settled. Revelation 22:11, 12 emphatically declares,

> "He who is unjust, let him be unjust still; he who is filthy, let him be filthy still; he who is righteous, let him be righteous still; he who is holy, let him be holy still."
>
> "And behold, I am coming quickly, and My reward is with Me, to give to every one according to his work."

The wicked nations and inhabitants of the earth have been judged and condemned in God's throne room. The judgment has shown that God patiently extended His mercy and grace and that He is just in His decisions. The judgment makes it clear that those who are lost are lost because they have turned away from God's love and spurned His grace—not because God has been unmerciful or unjust. The judgment reveals that God has done everything He could to save every human being. The purpose of the judgment is not to condemn people; it is to reveal the choices we made in the light of God's loving initiative to save us. If we have accepted Christ as our Lord and Savior, when our name comes up in the judgment, the Son of Man speaks up on our behalf. He says, "This person belongs to Me. He (she) has accepted my sacrifice and has asked Me to cover their sins with My righteousness." Jesus delivers His people in the judgment from Satan's condemnation.

There is a prominent idea in Christian circles today that somehow Christians are "raptured" away from earth before the time of trouble begins. However, there is no biblical evidence for this belief.

At the close of the judgment, Michael stands up. There is a time of trouble such as has never been known before from the beginning of the world. A crisis of gigantic proportions breaks upon this world. Calamity follows calamity. That is when Michael stands up to ultimately deliver His people—"every one who is found written in the book" (Daniel 12:1).

Delivered, not raptured

There is a prominent idea in Christian circles today that somehow Christians are "raptured" away from earth before the time of trouble begins. However, there is no biblical evidence for this belief. Were Shadrach, Meshach, and Abed-Nego taken from Babylon so that they didn't have to face the flames of the fiery furnace? No! Instead, Jesus came to stand in the flames with them! Was Daniel taken away from the lions' den? No! But he was protected by God from the hungry beasts. When the plagues were poured out on Egypt, were the Israelites taken out of the land so that they did not have to face them? No! But God shielded them and preserved them through this terrible time of trouble. So it will be at the end of time, during the worst time of trouble ever to come on the earth. God's people will not be taken away secretly to heaven to avoid the time of trouble. Rather, God will protect them. Notice these reassuring Bible promises in the Psalms on God's protection and presence during the plagues.

God is our refuge and strength,
A very present help in trouble.
Therefore, we will not fear
Though the earth be removed,
and though the mountains carried into the midst of the sea (Psalm 46:1, 2).

He who dwells in the secret place of the Most High
Shall abide under the shadow of the Almighty.
I will say of the LORD, "He is my refuge and my fortress,
My God, in Him I will trust" (Psalm 91:1, 2).

A thousand may fall at your side,
And ten thousand at your right hand;
But it shall not come near you.
Only with your eyes shall you look,
And see the reward of the wicked.

Because you have made the LORD, who is my refuge,
Even the Most High, your dwelling place,
No evil shall befall you,
Nor shall any plague come near your dwelling;
For He shall give His angels charge over you,
To keep you in all your ways (Psalm 91:7–11).

Although we are present on earth during the time of trouble, we are secure in the presence of Jesus. He indeed is our refuge and strength.

This time of trouble is depicted in the book of Revelation as seven terrible plagues that are poured out on the earth—sores, the sea turning into blood, water turning into blood, scorching heat, darkness, demons working miracles, and earthquakes and hail (Revelation 16). In the midst of these plagues, Jesus says, "Behold, I am coming as a thief. Blessed is he who watches, and keeps his garments" (verse 15). Clearly, Jesus returns to earth *after* the plagues have fallen—not before. God does not remove His people from earth before the time of trouble. Through this time, His people look beyond the plagues to fasten their eyes upon their Savior. When every earthly support is cut off, they look to Jesus. The promise of His coming gives them hope. They cling to His promises by faith.

Just as Jesus trusted His loving heavenly Father during the agony of the cross, God's people trust Him during the earth's final conflict. Jesus was surrounded by darkness, condemned as guilty, and consumed with physical and mental agony; yet by faith, He cried out, "Father, 'into Your hands I commit My spirit' " (Luke 23:46). His faith pierced the darkness. He trusted in the relationship He had with His Father from the ceaseless ages of eternity and knew by faith the Father would deliver Him. In earth's last hour, we, too, will have the "faith of Jesus" and, surrounded by darkness during earth's greatest time of trouble, trust God to deliver us. We will hold fast to the promise of His return and trust His Word despite what we see around us. Let your heart be filled with Christ's promises today.

Jesus' return will be glorious

"Then the sign of the Son of Man will appear in heaven, . . . and they will see the Son of Man coming on the clouds of heaven with power and great glory. And He will send His angels with a great sound of a trumpet, and they will gather together His elect from the four winds, from one end of heaven to the other" (Matthew 24:30, 31).

"The Son of Man will come in the glory of His Father with His angels, and then

He will reward each according to his works" (Matthew 16:27).

Notice that Matthew 24 says that Jesus will come with "the clouds of heaven," while Matthew 16 says He will come "with His angels." Those clouds of heaven are clouds of heavenly angels—thousands of thousands and ten thousand times ten thousand. What a glorious sight! The sky from one end of heaven to another is illuminated by their glory! This is what it will be like when Michael stands up to deliver His people!

Only two groups when Jesus returns

Not everyone will welcome this glorious spectacle. Daniel says,

> Many of those who sleep in the dust of the earth shall awake,
> Some to everlasting life,
> Some to shame and everlasting contempt (Daniel 12:2).

The apostle John wrote,

> Then the sky receded as a scroll when it is rolled up, and every mountain and island was moved out of its place. And the kings of the earth, the great men, the rich men, the commanders, the mighty men, every slave and every free man, hid themselves in the caves and in the rocks of the mountains, and said to the mountains and rocks, "Fall on us and hide us from the face of Him who sits on the throne and from the wrath of the Lamb! For the great day of His wrath has come, and who is able to stand?" (Revelation 6:14–17).

The Jesus whom they want to hide from is the Jesus who loved them and wanted to save them. He reached out to them, and they turned their backs on Him. Rather than looking in His face and rejoicing in His presence, they want to hide. Sin runs from God. When Adam and Eve sinned in the Garden of Eden, they ran from God. Isaiah says, "Your iniquities have separated you from your God; and your sins have hidden His face from you" (Isaiah 59:2).

Why does Daniel 12:2 say that "*many* of those who sleep in the dust shall awake"? Jesus said in John 5:28, 29, "The hour is coming in which all who are in the graves will hear His [God's] voice and come forth—those who have done good, to the resurrection of life, and those who have done evil, to the resurrection of condemnation."

The apostle Paul tells us that the righteous dead will be raised to life when Jesus comes (1 Thessalonians 4:16). Revelation tells us that the wicked dead will not be raised to life until a thousand years after Jesus has returned (Revelation 20:5). But what does Daniel mean by saying that "many" of those who sleep in the dust shall awake—some to everlasting life, some to everlasting contempt? Let's look at Revelation 1:7. "Behold, He is coming with clouds, and every eye will see Him, even they who pierced Him." According to this verse, those who crucified Jesus on the cross will be raised to see Him return from heaven in glory. There will be a special resurrection that will include some of those who were most prominent in the death of Jesus when He was here on earth. They last saw Him on the cross. Now they see Him coming in glory with all the angels of heaven!

But let's focus on the glory and majesty of that wonderful day when our Savior appears as He promised. Let's focus on those who are raised to everlasting life. Jesus comes streaming down the corridor of the sky, trailing clouds of shining angels! His faithful people, both the living and those who are raised to life, look up with joy. They cry out,

> "Behold, this is our God;
> We have waited for Him, and He will save us.
> This is the LORD;
> We have waited for Him;
> We will be glad and rejoice in His salvation" (Isaiah 25:9).

Closing the book

There will be only two groups of people when Jesus comes—those who are eternally saved and those who are eternally lost. As Gabriel winds up his explanation of the prophecies God gave to Daniel, he says, "Daniel, shut up the words, and seal the book until the time of the end; many shall run to and fro, and knowledge shall increase" (Daniel 12:4). This text is not speaking so much about scientific knowledge or technical knowledge; it's referring primarily to a knowledge of God's Word. At the time of the end, these prophecies will be understood better and more fully. Those living at the time of the end will have increased knowledge of God's Word. They will be searching to and fro to learn God's will for their lives and His plans for the world. All the light of the ages will shine on the final generation.

Despite Gabriel's explanation of the prophecies, there was much in the visions that Daniel still did not understand. He writes,

> Although I heard, I did not understand. Then I said, "My lord, what shall be the end of these things?"

And he said, "Go your way, Daniel, for the words are closed up and sealed till the time of the end. . . .

". . . For you shall rest, and will arise to your inheritance at the end of the days" (verses 8–13).

You see, Daniel couldn't understand fully because the prophecies were for a time far in the future—the time of the end. So the angel simply told him, "Be content, Daniel, with what God has shown you and what you do understand. Go your way. Close up the book. The generation who will live in the time of the end will have increased knowledge because they will be living in the time to which the prophecies are pointing."

That generation is ours. Time is running out. The sand in the hourglass of time will soon be gone. Soon we are going to look up into the sky and see Jesus! God loves you. He wants you to be saved. He wants you to live with Him forever. He has prepared a place for you.

Why not right now, as you have finished reading this last chapter, open your heart to the moving of the Holy Spirit and pray this simple prayer:

"Dear Jesus, thank You for Your love. Thank You that You want to save me even more than I want to be saved. Thank You that You never have and never will give up on me. I confess my sins to You right now. Forgive me of my rebellion against Your will at times. Forgive my carelessness and neglect of Your Word. Open my heart to be filled with Your grace. I choose to live for You, serve You, and follow You today and forever. I know I have no power to follow through on this commitment, so I ask You to supply me with the strength to do Your will. I praise You that I am Your child. You have redeemed me on the cross and are living as my great High Priest in heaven's sanctuary to encourage me, strengthen me, and empower me to live a godly life. Thank You for all You have done, are doing, and will do for me now and forever. In Your name, *amen*."

> Those living at the time of the end will have increased knowledge of God's Word. They will be searching to and fro to learn God's will for their lives and His plans for the world. All the light of the ages will shine on the final generation.

Understanding Revelation

NOTHING CAN SEPARATE!

Revelation 1

1 The Revelation of Jesus Christ, which God gave Him to show His servants—things which must shortly take place. And He sent and signified it by His angel to His servant John, **2** who bore witness to the word of God, and to the testimony of Jesus Christ, to all things that he saw. **3** Blessed is he who reads and those who hear the words of this prophecy, and keep those things which are written in it; for the time is near.

4 John, to the seven churches which are in Asia:

Grace to you and peace from Him who is and who was and who is to come, and from the seven Spirits who are before His throne, **5** and from Jesus Christ, the faithful witness, the firstborn from the dead, and the ruler over the kings of the earth.

To Him who loved us and washed us from our sins in His own blood, **6** and has made us kings and priests to His God and Father, to Him be glory and dominion forever and ever. Amen.

7 Behold, He is coming with clouds, and every eye will see Him, even they who pierced Him. And all the tribes of the earth will mourn because of Him. Even so, Amen.

8 "I am the Alpha and the Omega, the Beginning and the End," says the Lord, "who is and who was and who is to come, the Almighty."

9 I, John, both your brother and companion in the tribulation and kingdom and patience of Jesus Christ, was on the island that is called Patmos for the word of God and for the testimony of Jesus Christ. **10** I was in the Spirit on the Lord's Day, and I heard behind me a loud voice, as of a trumpet, **11** saying, "I am the Alpha and the Omega, the First and the Last," and, "What you see, write in a book and send it to the seven churches which are in Asia: to Ephesus, to Smyrna, to Pergamos, to Thyatira, to Sardis, to Philadelphia, and to Laodicea."

12 Then I turned to see the voice that spoke with me. And having turned I saw seven golden lampstands, **13** and in the midst of the seven lampstands One like the Son of Man, clothed with a garment down to the feet and girded about the chest with a golden band. **14** His head and hair were white like wool, as white as snow, and His eyes like a flame of fire; **15** His feet were like fine brass, as if refined in a furnace, and His voice as the sound of many waters; **16** He had in His right hand seven stars, out of His mouth went a sharp two-edged sword, and His countenance was like the sun shining in its strength. **17** And when I saw Him, I fell at His feet as dead. But He laid His right hand on me, saying to me, "Do not be afraid; I am the First and the Last. **18** I am He who lives, and was dead, and behold, I am alive forevermore. Amen. And I have the keys of Hades and of Death. **19** Write the things which you have seen, and the things which are, and the things which will take place after this. **20** The mystery of the seven stars which you saw in My right hand, and the seven golden lampstands: The seven stars are the angels of the seven churches, and the seven lampstands which you saw are the seven churches.

Around the world today, men and women are interested in the book of Revelation. There is a sense that our world is moving toward some impending crisis and that the last book of the Bible addresses events that are about to unfold on earth. Multitudes of books, some of them bestsellers, have been written attempting to explain the prophecies of Revelation. Often, they have very different ideas about what these prophecies mean. That's one reason many people feel Revelation is confusing and too filled with strange symbols for anyone to really understand. There are so many interpretations, so many different viewpoints and ideas.

Revelation means "revealed"

Some suggest that we should focus just on the Gospels—Matthew, Mark, Luke, and John—and read about Jesus. Maybe the book of Revelation is so confusing that we shouldn't try to understand it at all. That is an interesting position to take, especially considering the very name of this last book of the Bible. It's titled "Revelation." What does the word *revelation* mean? It means something that is *revealed*. It means the very opposite of "hidden" or "secret." The book of Revelation was originally written in Greek, and the Greek word translated "revelation" is *apokalupsis*, which literally means, "taking away the veil." When we read this book, the veil is taken away from our eyes so that we can clearly see what God is revealing to us.

God gave us this book to reveal something. And the very first words tell us what He is revealing in this book. "The Revelation of Jesus Christ, which God gave Him to show His servants—things which must shortly take place" (Revelation 1:1).

The book of Revelation was given specifically to reveal Jesus Christ and the things that are going to be taking place on this earth. If God wants to reveal Jesus Christ to us and the things that are coming on the earth, do you think He would make it so complicated that we could not possibly understand it? I don't think so. I think He would make His revelation plain.

"But," someone says, "if God wanted to make His revelation plain, why didn't He just tell it like it is. Why use all these symbols—beasts, dragons, seals and trumpets, and women holding cups of wine? If these things are supposed to represent something, why didn't He use plain, simple words?"

That's a good question.

Could one reason be that there is a war going on—a war between good and evil, between God and Satan? When nations are at war, do they share their plans openly with the enemy? During World War II, did Germany tell Great Britain its war plans? Would the United States share its military secrets with the enemy forces?

The book of Revelation identifies key religious and political players in the great controversy down through the ages and at the end of time. Had it exposed those powers plainly, they might have destroyed those portions of the Bible that exposed them. For centuries before the printing press was invented, the Scriptures existed only in handwritten documents. Copies of the Bible were not readily available, and many people could not read in any case. The powers that Revelation exposes might have attempted to change or delete portions of the book that identified them so clearly. An all-wise God protected His Word by putting it in symbolic language.

Another reason for symbols and vivid images is that they stick in our memories. You've heard the saying "A picture is worth a thousand words." God used symbols as word pictures to describe the rise and fall of nations and religious powers as a powerful way to get His message across succinctly. And He has given us explanations to enable us to understand these symbols and know what they represent. Some of them are explained right in the book of Revelation itself. Others are explained in other books of the Bible. Remember also that Jesus used a similar strategy in the first century. He used parables that the religious leaders seeking to destroy Him did not understand and later explained their meaning to His disciples.

It is also important to remember as we study this book that it is a revelation of *Jesus Christ.* We must look for what it tells us about Jesus. It is vital to understand that Jesus is revealed in each chapter and each prophecy of Revelation. The prophecies regarding beasts and dragons and a coming time of trouble all reveal something about Jesus' eternal plan for humanity and His eventual triumph over the forces of evil. The book of Revelation reveals the behind-the-scenes conflict and meaning of these symbols in the light of the final events that are soon to break upon our world.

The first verse of the first chapter of the book tells us that it is a revelation, a revealing, of Jesus Christ. And in the last chapter—almost the last verse—Jesus tells us, "I, Jesus, have sent My angel to testify to you these things in the churches" (Revelation 22:16). He says, "I'm sending my angel to make last-day events plain to you. I'm sending my angel to clear up confusion about what is coming in the future." The book of Revelation reveals Jesus, and it is sent to men and women living in the last days of earth's history.

The theme of Revelation

Since Revelation is the last book of the Bible and a revelation of Jesus, what do you think its major theme might be? The return of Christ to this earth is the closing event involving Jesus as far as this world of sin is concerned. So it seems likely that the theme of the book will be centered on the last days and the return of Jesus. Let's see if that is true.

Revelation 1:7 declares, "He [Jesus Christ] is coming with clouds, and every eye will see Him." Furthermore, three times in Revelation 22, Jesus Himself repeats that He is coming "quickly." He says in verse 7, "I am coming quickly!" In verse 12, He declares, "Behold, I am coming quickly." Finally, in verse 20, he says, "He who testifies to these things says, 'Surely I am coming quickly.' " Jesus wants us to know for certain that He is coming soon. The book of Revelation is a book about the coming of Jesus and the last days of earth's history. That is its theme.

From heaven to John—the steps in the Revelation

The apostle John is the divinely inspired human author of the book of Revelation. He is the one who received visions and wrote down what he saw and what God inspired him to record. At the very beginning, Revelation gives us a detailed progression of where its content comes from and how God passed it on to us.

"The Revelation of Jesus Christ, which God gave Him to show His servants—things which must shortly take place. And He sent and signified it by His angel to His servant John, who bore witness to the word of God, and to the testimony of

Jesus Christ, to all things that he saw" (Revelation 1:1, 2).

These verses tell us that the content of Revelation came from God the Father. He gave it to Jesus Christ. Jesus sent it by "His angel" to the apostle John, and John wrote it down for us. John, you recall, was the disciple who was especially close to Jesus (John 13:23; 19:26; 20:2; 21:7, 20). Jesus loved all His disciples, but there was a special bond between Him and John. John's heart was more receptive to receiving His love. Jesus' love is infinite, and the more we are capable of receiving, the more He will impart to us.

John says that he was on the island of Patmos when he received the visions that make up the book of Revelation. Patmos is a little island in the Aegean Sea between the coasts of Turkey and Greece. It's about nine miles long. In John's time, it was a rocky, barren, Roman penal colony where prisoners were exiled. There was a small mining community there as well—and little else.

Today it has a magnificent harbor and a beautiful, welcoming, idyllic little town called Skala. Tiny chapels dot the island. These chapels are attached to many of the houses as private places of worship.

John was an old man, in his nineties, when he received the visions of Revelation. He had lived a long life in the service of his beloved Master. He had probably been living in Ephesus before his exile to Patmos. Now he was separated from friends and family. He was frail, and it was doubtful he would ever get off this small, isolated island in the midst of the sea. But then, in a blaze of glory, Jesus revealed divine truth to John that would enlighten and encourage God's people for centuries. Our Lord showed him events that are soon to take place in this world and last-day truths to prepare God's people for what will come. Sometimes it's amidst the greatest trials of our lives that God speaks to us most clearly. When we feel lonely and discouraged, Jesus visits us just as He did John and fills us with the warmth of His presence.

You see, the book of Revelation is a book about the Jesus who intervenes. He does not merely sit on His throne in heaven; He enters the affairs of life here on earth. He ministers to us in the trauma, the heartache, and the disappointments we face. When Jesus came down to speak with His beloved disciple, He illuminated rocky, barren Patmos with His glory. There is no place we can find ourselves that is beyond God's reach. He will meet you wherever you are.

A special blessing

The prophecies of the book of Revelation outline events that are soon to come upon our world. Revelation says that God gave us the prophecies in this book "to show His servants—things which must shortly take place" (Revelation 1:1). It goes on to say, "Blessed is he who reads and those who hear the words of this prophecy, and keep those things which are written in it; for the time is near" (verse 3).

The book of Revelation comes from the mind of the all-knowing God. The origin of its message is not earthly; God Himself and Jesus Christ have sent it to us in love and compassion to prepare us for the coming of Jesus. He pronounces a special blessing on us if we do three things: (1) read the prophecies of this book; (2) hear them; that is, pay attention to them; and (3) keep those things which are written in the book. Read, hear, and keep. You see, the purpose of these prophecies is not just to satisfy our curiosity or fill our minds with speculative information. Revelation is a book to be infused into our lives. Its purpose is to reveal Jesus Christ. It will draw us closer to Him. It puts demands on our lives; we are to keep—follow and obey—the things we find in this book.

The Jesus of Revelation

As John begins to write down the revelation Jesus is giving him, he addresses it to "the seven churches which are in Asia" (verse 4). In chapters 2 and 3, we will discover specific messages from Jesus to each of these churches. But, for now, John wants to paint a picture of Jesus—the One who is giving this revelation to His people. John makes several descriptive statements about Jesus in these verses:

- The One "who is and who was and who is to come" (verse 4). Jesus never had a beginning; He will never have an ending. He is eternal.
- "The Alpha and the Omega, the First and the Last" (verse 11). Alpha and omega are the first and last letters of the Greek alphabet. We would say, "He's everything from A to Z." He is "all and in all" (Colossians 3:11).
- "The faithful witness" (verse 5). What does this mean? Jesus is the faithful witness of the Father's love. When we study the life of Jesus, we discover what the Father is like. Jesus also knows all about us. He knows our joys and our sorrows. He understands what we are going through.
- "The firstborn from the dead" (verse 5). Jesus died, but the grave was not able to keep Him. He is the resurrected Redeemer. Because He is the Firstborn from the dead, we do not need to fear death.
- "The ruler over the kings of the earth" (verse 5). As we noted in the book of Daniel, kings rise and fall, but King Jesus reigns over them all—and He reigns forever. There may be chaos in the world and in our lives, but Jesus is still on the throne. He will make things turn out right in the end.
- The One "who loved us and washed us from our sins in His own blood" (verse 5). Jesus is the One who can take away all your sin and guilt. "The blood of Jesus Christ . . . cleanses us from all sin" (1 John 1:7).

This, then, is the Jesus Christ who is revealed to us in the book of Revelation. There is one more thing John wants to point out about Jesus. He is the Jesus who will return to earth as He promised. "Behold, He is coming with clouds, and every eye shall see Him" (Revelation 1:7). Throughout the book of Revelation, we will return to this theme. Again and again, the prophecies of Revelation encourage us with the hope of Jesus' return. Our world will not be reduced to some spinning globe of ash in a thermonuclear war. It will not be destroyed in some cataclysmic natural disaster. Global warming will not eventually wipe out life on planet Earth. Food shortages will not starve planet Earth's population to death, making life extinct. Jesus is coming. There is hope. Revelation's prophecies thunder the message of Christ's return, bringing joy to our hearts.

In the Spirit on the Lord's Day

John says that He "was in the Spirit on the Lord's Day" (verse 10). The phrase "the Lord's Day" is often used to mean "Sunday." Some Christians point to this verse as evidence that the biblical day for worship, the seventh-day Sabbath, has been changed in New Testament times to Sunday. But the text doesn't identify "the Lord's Day" with Sunday or with the seventh-day Sabbath. It only tells us that the Lord has a day that is "His day." It doesn't tell us what that day is. The only texts in the Bible that tell us what day Jesus is Lord of are the three texts connected to the story of Jesus' disciples plucking heads of grain as they walked through a field on the Sabbath. When the religious leaders rebuked them for breaking the Sabbath, Jesus replied, "The Son of Man is also Lord of the Sabbath" (Luke 6:5; see also Matthew 12:8; Mark 2:28). Based on these texts, the seventh-day Sabbath is the Lord's Day. This is only logical. The Sabbath is a memorial of Creation and points us to Jesus as the Creator of the heavens and the earth (see Ephesians 3:8, 9; Colossians 1:13–16). As our Creator and Redeemer, He is Lord over all.

The glorified Jesus

In quiet meditation, John was evidently contemplating the things of eternity. His thoughts focused on heavenly realities. The floodgates of heaven opened, and he received a vision of the glorified Christ. There are striking similarities between Daniel's description of Jesus Christ in Daniel 10:5–9 and this vision of Jesus that John saw.

John says,

> I saw seven golden lampstands, and in the midst of the seven lampstands One like the Son of Man, clothed with a garment down to the feet and girded about

the chest with a golden band. His head and hair were white like wool, as white as snow, and His eyes like a flame of fire; His feet were like fine brass, as if refined in a furnace, and His voice as the sound of many waters; He had in His right hand seven stars, out of His mouth went a sharp two-edged sword, and His countenance was like the sun shining in its strength (Revelation 1:12–16).

This passage describes the glorified Jesus. John knew Jesus when He was on earth, preaching, teaching, healing, and working miracles. He remembered how the children had climbed up in Jesus' lap while He was telling stories. He remembered Jesus reaching out to lepers and curing them of their disease. He recalled the Christ who touched the eyes of the blind, and they were opened, and the ears of the deaf, and they were unstopped. He brought to mind the Christ who broke the bread and fed five thousand and who stooped low to write the sins of the Pharisees in the sand as he forgave an immoral, trembling woman caught in the act of adultery. He remembered the all-powerful, forceful Jesus who drove the money changers from the temple. He remembered the terrible scenes of Jesus hanging on the cross and dying there. He could recall the resurrected Jesus who appeared to the disciples on several occasions before ascending to heaven. But John had never seen Jesus like this—in all of His regal, heavenly splendor yet still clothed in humanity. He is heaven's glorious king yet still our Companion, our Brother, and our Friend.

"When I saw Him, I fell at His feet as dead. But He laid His right hand on me, saying to me, 'Do not be afraid. . . . I am He who lives, and was dead, and behold, I am alive forevermore. Amen. And I have the keys of Hades and of Death. Write the things which you have seen, and the things which are, and the things which will take place after this' " (verses 17–19).

The master key to interpreting the prophecies

Verse 19 gives us a master key to interpreting the entire book of Revelation. Jesus tells John to write (1) "the things which you have seen," (2) "the things which are, and" (3) "the things that will take place after this." You see, prophecies in the Bible always begin where the prophet is, and they take us from that point down to the end of time. We saw that progression in the book of Daniel. In Revelation, Jesus says that some prophecies were fulfilled in John's day. Some are being fulfilled as time progresses. And some are yet to be fulfilled. That is a key principle to keep in mind as we examine the prophecies of Revelation. There is a sequence, a progression. We can't lump all the prophecies of the book into one bag and place them down at the end of time.

For example, in Revelation, we will see several prophetic series—such as seven churches, seven seals, seven trumpets. Some of the truths relating to the seven churches would be applied in John's day. Some would apply to succeeding generations. And some are for the time of the end. Keep in mind also that although there is a historical continuum in these prophecies and there is only one specific fulfillment, there are eternal principles of God's faithfulness and a practical application of universal truths that apply to every generation. The Bible is a living book and relevant to each generation.

Nothing can separate!

Jesus goes on to tell John, "The mystery of the seven stars which you saw in My right hand, and the seven golden lampstands: The seven stars are the angels of the seven churches, and the seven lampstands which you saw are the seven churches" (verse 20).

Chapter 1 prepares the way for chapters 2 and 3—Jesus' messages to the seven churches. John saw Jesus walking among seven golden lampstands. These lampstands, we're told, represent the seven churches. And as we will see, these seven churches represent the Christian church in its entirety from the beginning of Christianity until Jesus comes again.

The picture is one of Jesus, walking about among His people. Jesus is intimately acquainted with each person on earth. He is close to His church, His faithful people. Each church has an "angel" who is held in Jesus' hand. This is another representation of the close union between Jesus and each one of us. He holds us firmly in His grip, and nothing or no one can pluck us out of His protecting hand (John 10:27–29). The apostle Paul asks, "Who shall separate us from the love of Christ?" (Romans 8:35). And he answers his own question by declaring, "I am persuaded that neither death nor life, nor angels nor principalities nor powers, nor things present nor things to come, nor height nor depth, nor any other created thing, shall be able to separate us from the love of God which is in Christ Jesus our Lord" (verses 38, 39).

Nothing can separate! That is the message Jesus was giving John as He walked among the seven golden lampstands, holding seven stars in His right hand. As we study further into the book of Revelation, we will see Satan trying his best to separate us from Jesus and using various powers and forces that will arise in the last days to do his bidding. Nevertheless, Jesus walks among His people, and nothing—"things present nor things to come"—can separate us from His care and His love.

In the next two chapters, Jesus gives messages to each of the seven churches. He is walking among them, observing, encouraging, warning, and rebuking. He presents just the message each church needs because He is the "faithful witness" who knows each church intimately.

FIRST LOVE TURNS TO SPIRITUAL DARKNESS

Revelation 2

1 "To the angel of the church of Ephesus write,

'These things says He who holds the seven stars in His right hand, who walks in the midst of the seven golden lampstands: **2** "I know your works, your labor, your patience, and that you cannot bear those who are evil. And you have tested those who say they are apostles and are not, and have found them liars; **3** and you have persevered and have patience, and have labored for My name's sake and have not become weary. **4** Nevertheless I have this against you, that you have left your first love. **5** Remember therefore from where you have fallen; repent and do the first works, or else I will come to you quickly and remove your lampstand from its place—unless you repent. **6** But this you have, that you hate the deeds of the Nicolaitans, which I also hate.

7 "He who has an ear, let him hear what the Spirit says to the churches. To him who overcomes I will give to eat from the tree of life, which is in the midst of the Paradise of God." '

8 "And to the angel of the church in Smyrna write,

'These things says the First and the Last, who was dead, and came to life: **9** "I know your works, tribulation, and poverty (but you are rich); and I know the blasphemy of those who say they are Jews and are not, but are a synagogue of Satan. **10** Do not fear any of those things which you are about to suffer. Indeed, the devil is about to throw some of you into prison, that you may be tested, and you will have tribulation ten days. Be faithful until death, and I will give you the crown of life.

11 "He who has an ear, let him hear what the Spirit says to the churches. He who overcomes shall not be hurt by the second death." '

12 "And to the angel of the church in Pergamos write,

'These things says He who has the sharp two-edged sword: **13** "I know your works, and where you dwell, where Satan's throne is. And you hold fast to My name, and did not deny My faith even in the days in which Antipas was My faithful martyr, who was killed among you, where Satan dwells. **14** But I have a few things against you, because you have there those who hold the doctrine of Balaam, who taught Balak to put a stumbling block before the children of Israel, to eat things sacrificed to idols, and to commit sexual immorality. **15** Thus you also have those who hold the doctrine of the Nicolaitans, which thing I hate. **16** Repent, or else I will come to you quickly and will fight against them with the sword of My mouth.

17 "He who has an ear, let him hear what the Spirit says to the churches. To him who overcomes I will give some of the hidden manna to eat. And I will give him a white stone, and on the stone a new name written which no one knows except him who receives it." '

18 "And to the angel of the church in Thyatira write,

'These things says the Son of God, who has eyes like a flame of fire, and His feet like fine brass: **19** "I know your works, love, service, faith, and your patience; and as for your works, the last are more than the first. **20** Nevertheless I have a few things against you, because you allow that woman Jezebel, who calls herself a prophetess, to teach and seduce My servants to commit sexual immorality and eat things sacrificed to idols. **21** And I gave her time to repent of her sexual immorality, and she did not repent. **22** Indeed I will cast her into a sickbed, and those who commit adultery with her into great tribulation, unless they repent of their deeds. **23** I will kill her children with death, and all the churches shall know that I am He who searches the minds and hearts. And I will give to each one of you according to your works.

24 "Now to you I say, and to the rest in Thyatira, as many as do not have this doctrine, who have not known the depths of Satan, as they say, I will put on you no other burden. **25** But hold fast what you have till I come. **26** And he who overcomes, and keeps My works until the end, to him I will give power over the nations—

27 'He shall rule them with a rod of iron;
They shall be dashed to pieces like the potter's vessels'—

as I also have received from My Father; **28** and I will give him the morning star. **29** "He who has an ear, let him hear what the Spirit says to the churches." ' "

ু

The purpose of the book of Revelation is to reveal the plans of God and unmask the plans of Satan. It is to demonstrate the faithfulness of God in every age to encourage, strengthen, redeem, and eventually deliver His people. The entire book focuses on the living Christ who overcame the temptations of the devil and how we, too, in His grace and through His power, can overcome. In the messages to the seven churches, our Lord reveals the cunning deceptions of Satan and how we can be overcomers until the day He returns.

Chapter 2 begins the series of messages to the seven churches. In chapter 1, John was given a vision of Jesus walking among seven lampstands, which represent the seven churches. Ephesians 5:25 tells us that Jesus "loved the church and gave Himself for her." At the time John sees Him in vision, Jesus is no longer on earth; He is in heaven. The Jesus that John sees is the glorified Jesus whose appearance causes John to fall at His feet as if dead. But Jesus is still the same loving Shepherd that He was when He was on earth. He still loves and cares for His church. He is still vitally concerned with her well-being.

Chapter 2 contains Jesus' messages to the first four of the seven churches. We will find the messages to the last three churches in chapter 3. Today, when we hear the term *church*, we tend to think of a building—perhaps the church building where we worship each week—as well as the people who worship in that build-

> The seven churches were actual groups of Christian believers located in these seven cities in Asia Minor in John's day. Geographically, the seven were located in a roughly circular pattern, following an established trade route that connected the most populous and influential cities and areas of the province.

ing. Our mental picture is usually a combination of the physical building and the worshipers who gather there. That was not the case in John's day. The early Christian church in New Testament times didn't have buildings at fixed addresses. The Christian believers assembled wherever they could, usually someone's home or some other temporary quarters (see Romans 16:5; 1 Corinthians 16:19; Colossians 4:15). When

Paul wrote his letters to the various churches in Corinth, or Philippi, or Thessalonica, he was thinking of assemblies of *people*, not church buildings. And that is true of the seven "churches" to which Jesus sends messages here in Revelation. These were small groups of Christians, meeting wherever they could.

The seven churches were actual groups of Christian believers located in these seven cities in Asia Minor in John's day. Geographically, the seven were located in a roughly circular pattern, following an established trade route that connected the most populous and influential cities and areas of the province.

We will find, too, that each of the "letters," or messages, Jesus gives to these seven churches follows a similar pattern:

- A salutation: "To the angel of the church at _____, write . . ."
- A description of Jesus that relates to that particular church
- An "I know" statement, in which Jesus points out something about that church that He wants to emphasize
- A reproof or rebuke regarding some shortcoming in that church in all but two of the churches
- An admonition to pay attention to the message
- The promise of a blessing or reward if the church continues to be faithful and become overcomers

There is another aspect of the messages to the seven churches that we need to be aware of before examining each of the messages individually. Each message was intended for the specific group of Christian believers who made up the church in that city. Its content related to their situation and experience as it existed in John's day. When the believers in Ephesus, for example, read Jesus' message to them, they could see that He was speaking directly to them and their experience. However, these messages have a wider significance as well.

Many Bible students have recognized that the seven churches represent the history of the Christian church down through the ages from John's day to the end of time. The characteristics of each of the seven churches correspond to a particular period in the course of the church from the first century to the very end of the earth's history.

So let's take a closer look at the messages Jesus gave to these seven churches. And as we do so, we must think about how they apply to our own lives. Jesus' counsel to these churches applied to those Christian believers in Asia Minor many centuries ago, but they also apply to us today. We face many of the same temptations and attacks of Satan that they faced, even if we live in a greatly different world.

Ephesus—the loveless church (A.D. 31–100)

"To the angel of the church of Ephesus write,

" 'These things says He who holds the seven stars in His right hand, who walks in the midst of the seven golden lampstands: "I know your works, your labor, your patience, and that you cannot bear those who are evil. And you have tested those who say they are apostles and are not, and have found them liars; and you have persevered and have patience, and have labored for My name's sake and have not become weary. Nevertheless I have this against you, that you have left your first love. Remember therefore from where you have fallen; repent and do the first works, or else I will come to you quickly and remove your lampstand from its place—unless you repent. But this you have, that you hate the deeds of the Nicolaitans, which I also hate.

" ' "He who has an ear, let him hear what the Spirit says to the churches. To him who overcomes I will give to eat from the tree of life, which is in the midst of the paradise of God" ' " (Revelation 2:1–7).

In the first century, after Jesus ascended to heaven, the early Christian church was faithful to Jesus Christ. Its doctrine was pure, and the people tested those who claimed to speak for Jesus, rejecting false teachings. The early church was a hard-working church. Jesus commends them for their labors. The early Christians were active in sharing Jesus with the people in the villages and towns around them. The biblical record in the book of Acts states that the members of the early church went everywhere throughout the then known world preaching the gospel, and the church grew. The early church resisted evil and apostasy. They were stalwarts for the truths of the Word. They were faithful to the teachings of Christ.

"Nevertheless," Jesus says, "I have something against you. You have left your first love." Gradually, even in those early years, duty began to take the place of devotion. The Christians in Ephesus were working hard for Jesus, but at the same time, they were losing sight of the Jesus for whom they were working. They were losing their first-love relationship with Him. They began to think that being busy and active was what being a Christian was all about. They were living their Christian lives as a "to do" list. In His message to the church at Ephesus, Jesus was calling them back to loving Him as they had at the beginning.

Are we in danger today of losing our first love for Jesus and His truth? Has prayer become kind of dull and boring? Is studying the Bible not as interesting and exciting as it once was? If you have lost your first love, how do you get it back again? Recently a young man wrote in to our live question-and-answer period on the internet and asked a very similar question: "What do you do when you feel like your spiritual experience is dying?" In other words, how do you break out of spiritual apathy and complacency? What if you still believe, but your soul is barren?

Jesus says that to regain your first love for Him, you need to "remember . . . from where you have fallen; repent and do the first works" (verse 5). Think back to those days when you first became a Christian—how excited you were when Christ transformed your life, the joy you once had in your spiritual life. Remember the peace that came with knowing Jesus and His plan for your life. Think about a time in your life when you felt closest to Christ. What was your prayer life like then? What were your Bible study and devotional life like? How actively were you involved in God's church? The Bible says that by beholding, we become changed (2 Corinthians 3:18). If you want a vibrant spiritual life, turn off the television; reduce your time on the internet and all social media; and spend time with Jesus in prayer, meditation, and His Word. The counsel for recapturing their first love in the church at Ephesus consists of the three Rs—remember, repent, and return. As we recall our early experience, we will realize how far we have fallen away from that first-love encounter with Jesus, and that will lead us to repent and to recapture our first love.

> The Christians in Ephesus were working hard for Jesus, but at the same time, they were losing sight of the Jesus for whom they were working. They were losing their first-love relationship with Him.

The Nicolaitans, mentioned in these verses, claimed to be Christians but believed that it wasn't necessary to obey God's law. Irenaeus, a second-century minister, said the Nicolaitans called themselves Christians, but they considered it "a matter of indifference to practise adultery, and to eat things sacrificed to idols."[1] Evidently, this group believed that so-called love, or sentimental feelings called love, triumphed over obedience to God. Jesus says that He *hates* "the deeds of the Nicolaitans." That's strong language. But the Bible is clear in its stand against those who feel they don't need to obey God's commandments. His Word says, "He who says, 'I know Him [Jesus],' and does not keep His commandments, is a liar, and the truth is not in him" (1 John 2:4). Jesus said, "Not everyone who says to Me, 'Lord, Lord,' shall enter the kingdom of heaven, but he who does the will of My Father in heaven" (Matthew 7:21). As followers of Christ who love Him passionately, we believe His Word is important. We love Him and choose to have a relationship with Him. And that relationship includes obedience to His commands. When we love someone, we *want* to do the things that please him or her.

Jesus closes His message to the Ephesus church with this promise: "To him who overcomes I will give to eat from the tree of life, which is in the midst of the Paradise of God" (Revelation 2:7). Overcomes what? Apathy, spiritual complacency, the form of religion, a lack of true spirituality. The earnest appeal of Christ to the church of the Ephesians is an appeal to know Christ intimately, to love Christ deeply, and to serve Christ faithfully. Our text says that if Christ is our first love, we will one day eat of the tree of life in the paradise of God.

Genesis 2:9 tells us that God planted the tree of life in the center of the Garden of Eden. Revelation 22:1, 2 tells us that it will bear fruit beside the river of life near God's throne in the New Jerusalem. Just imagine what it will be like to eat fruit from that tree! We, like the Christians in Ephesus, will eat from that tree and live forever if we overcome Satan's temptations through the grace of our Savior by relying on His great power.

The description of the church at Ephesus aptly describes the spiritual condition of the early church in the late first century. Although its principles apply to every generation, the historical fulfillment of this prophecy came in the first century.

Smyrna—the persecuted church (A.D. 100–313)

"To the angel of the church in Smyrna write,

" '. . . "I know your works, tribulation, and poverty (but you are rich). . . . Do not fear any of those things which you are about to suffer. Indeed, the devil is about to throw some of you into prison, that you may be tested, and you will have tribulation ten days. Be faithful unto death, and I will give you the crown of life.

"He who has an ear, let him hear what the Spirit says to the churches. He who overcomes shall not be hurt by the second death" ' " (Revelation 2:8–11).

Filled with the Holy Spirit and with hearts overflowing with love for their Savior, the New Testament believers went out to change the world. They shared Christ in villages and cities, by the seashore and in the marketplace, in synagogues and shops and in prisons and palaces. Thousands were converted, and the New Testament church grew rapidly. Converts flocked to the church from all directions. The hosts of hell trembled.

The kingdom of evil was being defeated by the powerful proclamation of the gospel.

The devil decided he needed to do something to stop the progress of the early church. He unleashed a storm of persecution. During the time of the Smyrna church, the Roman government actively began to persecute Christians. *Smyrna* means "sweet-smelling incense." The testimony of the martyrs was as sweet-smelling incense that rose heavenward. Jesus reassured the persecuted church of Smyrna, "I know your tribulation." In other words, I know the trouble you are going through. I know how poor you are, but you are rich in faith. The devil will persecute you, and you will suffer severe tribulation for ten days. Your faith will be tested, but don't be afraid. I will be with you.

We have seen in the book of Daniel that a prophetic "day" equals a literal year of real time in Bible prophecy. Ten prophetic days of severe persecution would mean ten years. Satan inspired some Roman emperors to persecute the church and murder Christians because they would not worship the emperor as a god. One especially cruel emperor was Diocletian, who ruled Rome from 303 to 313—a period of ten years. Diocletian instituted a terrible time of persecution against Christians. Followers of Jesus were burned alive and fed to wild animals in the Colosseum, and some were beheaded. The Smyrna church was truly the persecuted church.

During this time, one of the last of the martyrs to die heroically was Polycarp, the leader of the church at Smyrna. As he faced a bloodthirsty crowd in the city stadium, the Roman governor demanded that he offer incense to the gods of Rome and acknowledge Caesar. Polycarp replied calmly, "Eighty and six years have I served Him, and He did me no wrong. How can I blaspheme my King, who saved me?" Polycarp was burned at the stake in the marketplace of Smyrna for His refusal to burn incense to the gods of Rome in denial of Christ. His faithfulness cost him his life. In every generation, God invites His people to be faithful to Him. The circumstances may be different, but the challenge is the same—commitment to Christ and faithfulness to His Word.[2]

Jesus introduced Himself in unique terms that were especially applicable to that church before giving it His message. Notice how He describes Himself to the suffering, persecuted Smyrna church. He says, "These things says the First and the Last, who was dead, and came to life" (verse 8). The members of the church at Smyrna faced torture, imprisonment, and death for their faith. Smyrna was the church where Christians became martyrs. So Jesus points to His own death and resurrection. He died on the cross, but now He lives. And He is able to give eternal life to the martyrs who gave up their lives in order to remain faithful to Him.

What does this say to you and me today? When the end-time tribulation comes and the beast power issues a death decree against all who refuse to abandon God and worship the beast's image, Jesus is the one who presents Himself as the author of life. The message of Smyrna is that we can anchor our faith in the One who went into the grave and came forth victorious over death.

Notice, too, the promises Jesus makes to the suffering Smyrna church, the church with so many who gave up their lives for Him. He says, "Be faithful unto death, and I will give you the crown of *life*" (verse 10; emphasis added). That's the choice—temporary death for remaining faithful to Jesus versus the crown of eternal life. Jesus ends His message to Smyrna by promising, "He who overcomes shall not be hurt by the second death" (verse 11). The second death is eternal death. Roman persecution meant death for many of the Christians of the Smyrna church, but this was the death that comes to all of us at some point—the first death. These faithful ones—and the faithful in every age—cannot be hurt by the second death. What a promise! Jesus, the Life-Giver, has conquered the grave. He went into the grave and came out alive. He is the resurrection and the life and assures us that in Him, we too have eternal life and one day will live forever in eternity.

Pergamos—the compromising church (A.D. 313–538)

Pergamos was located on a mountain ridge and was known for its many pagan temples and its great library of two hundred thousand scrolls. Pergamos created the first cult worship of a living emperor. That's why it is referred to as the place "where Satan has his throne."

Ephesus, the first of the seven churches, is the church that is doctrinally pure but has left its first love. The second church, Smyrna, is the persecuted church, but it also is the one to which Jesus promises eternal life no matter what it is facing. Pergamos, the third church, is the compromising church. In the Ephesus period (A.D. 31–100), the church grew rapidly. Satan unleashed fierce persecution during the Smyrna period (100–313), trying to stifle the growth of Christianity. However, persecution made the church grow even more rapidly. As Tertullian, an early church leader, wrote, "*The blood of Christians is seed*."[3] Therefore, Satan tried a different tactic. He pursued a new strategy. Rather than trying to destroy the church through persecution, he led the church to compromise its biblical principles by uniting with the state powers. The church was no longer persecuted. It became popular. Through this union of church and state, it was exalted. In the Pergamos period (313–538), Christianity became the recognized religion of the state. To achieve this, the church made compromises. It mixed pagan teachings with biblical principles. It relaxed its standards in order to appeal to non-Christians. Pergamos is the compromising church.

During this period, the church adopted pagan deities and renamed them after

Christian saints. The pagans were used to worshiping idols, so images of the saints were brought into the church for worship. False doctrines were adopted, including the influences of sun worship leading to observance of Sunday—the day of the sun—in place of God's seventh-day Sabbath. The Roman church was being exalted as it united with the Roman government during this time.

That's why Jesus addressed Pergamos in these words: "These things says He who has the sharp two-edged sword" (verse 12). What does the two-edged sword represent? Hebrews 4:12 compares the Word of God to a sharp two-edged sword. The Pergamos church was making compromises and losing sight of God's biblical truth. It was allowing God's Word to be diluted with pagan doctrines and practices. So Jesus reminds them that He is the One who wields the two-edged sword of the Word—the source of true doctrines.

The message to the Pergamos church goes on to say, "I know your works, and where you dwell, where Satan's throne is. And you hold fast to My name, and did not deny My faith. . . . But I have a few things against you, because you have there those who hold the doctrine of Balaam, who taught Balak to put a stumbling block before the children of Israel, to eat things sacrificed to idols, and to commit sexual immorality" (Revelation 2:13, 14).

There were still Christians in Pergamos who didn't deny their faith even in this period of compromise and accommodation with paganism. But Jesus says that some in the Pergamos church were following the example of Balaam. The story of Balaam is found in Numbers 22. Balaam was a false prophet who united with a heathen king, Balak, to lead the children of Israel into apostasy against God through feasting and immorality. Religious power and secular power united in the persons of Balaam and Balak to cause Israel to compromise its faith in God.

> The testimony of the martyrs was as sweet-smelling incense that rose heavenward. Jesus reassured the persecuted church of Smyrna, "I know your tribulation."

The message here is that, in the Pergamos period (313–538), church and state would unite in causing genuine, biblical faith to be compromised. In this period, the world would come into the church, and the church would be exalted. Religious power and political power would come together to support each other and enforce each other's policies and doctrines. Tradition and human doctrines would be accepted into the church in place of Bible truth. That's why Jesus says,

"Repent, or else I will come to you quickly and will fight against them with the sword of My mouth.

"He who has an ear, let him hear what the Spirit says to the churches. To him who overcomes I will give some of the hidden manna to eat" (verses 16, 17).

Jesus says, "I want to give you the hidden manna of my Word. I want you to feast on my Word." Jeremiah wrote, "Your words were found, and I ate them, and Your word was to me the joy and rejoicing of my heart" (Jeremiah 15:16). "Turn from all false doctrines," Jesus urges the Pergamos church, "and feast on My Word."

That's still good advice for us today. Satan is eager to bring compromise and false teachings into the church today. Compromise came into the church during the Pergamos period. It happened then, and Revelation tells us it will happen again in the last days.

It can happen in our personal spiritual experience too. Our only security is to spend time with God's Word, feeding on it and allowing it to nourish us spiritually and inoculate us against Satan's deceptions.

Jesus ends His message to Pergamos with this promise: "I will give him [who overcomes] a white stone, and on the stone a new name written which no one knows except him who receives it" (Revelation 2:17).

In Roman times, if you were on trial in court, when the jury came back, it dropped a white stone in a container if you were acquitted or a black stone if you were found guilty. A white stone represents freedom from guilt.[4] Those who overcome and refuse to be involved in the compromises of this church-state union are free from guilt. Jesus cleanses them from their sins and acquits them with a white stone. All this is an encouragement to us never to compromise our faith but always be faithful to Christ.

Thyatira—the corrupt church (A.D. 538–1500s)

The city of Thyatira lay between two valleys on a principal trading route. It was a flourishing craft center and was famous for its weavers and guilds and its beautiful purple dye used to color cloth. Thyatira was the hometown of Lydia, one of Paul's early converts (Acts 16:14).

Thyatira represents the church in the period known as the Dark Ages (A.D. 538–1500s). Jesus says to this church, "I know your works, love, service, faith, and your patience. . . . Nevertheless I have a few things against you, because you allow that woman Jezebel, who calls herself a prophetess, to teach and seduce my servants to commit sexual immorality. . . . I gave her time to repent of her sexual immorality, and she did not repent. Indeed I will cast her into a sickbed, and those who commit adultery with her into great tribulation, unless they repent of their deeds" (Revelation 2:19–22).

The Thyatira church is guilty of spiritual adultery. Throughout Scripture, we find the relationship between God and His people illustrated by the marriage relationship (Isaiah 54:5; Jeremiah 31:32; Ephesians 5:23; etc.). Christ is often represented as the husband, and the church, as His bride. Just as husband and wife are to be faithful to each other until death, so God and His people are to be faithful to each other. God is always faithful to us, but when we are unfaithful to Him, it is spiritual adultery.

Jezebel was a wicked queen of Israel, wife of King Ahab (1 Kings 21). She withstood the prophet Elijah and fought against his efforts to bring Israel back to God. She appears here in Revelation as a symbol of spiritual adultery—apostasy and unfaithfulness. She is the embodiment of the false church. During this period, the Dark Ages, all kinds of myths and falsehoods flooded into the church. The church combined its authority with that of the political power to coerce men and women into believing and following human traditions rather than the pure teachings of the Bible. Jesus speaks in Revelation 2:22 of the Thyatira church as being sick and calls on her to repent of her sins.

> Satan is eager to bring compromise and false teachings into the church today. Compromise came into the church during the Pergamos period. It happened then, and Revelation tells us it will happen again in the last days.

During the Dark Ages, the light of God's truth flickered. It was nearly snuffed out. But even in these centuries of apostasy, Jesus looked at the church, and He saw some who had remained faithful to Him. They stood against all the temptations and forces of Satan and an apostate church.

Jesus speaks these words of reassurance to those who remained faithful in Thyatira. "Now to you I say, and to the rest in Thyatira, as many as do not have this doctrine, who have not known the depths of Satan, . . . I will put on you no other burden. But hold fast what you have till I come" (verses 24, 25).

Jesus saw some even in Thyatira who had not compromised the truth. God has always had His faithful people. In the last days, when it seems that all the world is following the beast power that opposes God, there will still be those who "keep the commandments of God and the faith of Jesus" (Revelation 14:12). We need to be making the decisions today that will enable us, by God's grace, to be among that faithful group.

The first four churches summarized

The first four of the seven churches represent four periods of church history, reaching from the beginnings of the Christian church in A.D. 31 to the height of the medieval church in the 1500s. We can outline them as follows:

- *Ephesus—the loveless church (A.D. 31–100).* The Ephesus church substituted duty for devotion. It substituted works for a living relationship with Christ. It lost sight of its first love. God calls it back, and if we have lost our first love, He calls us back to a love relationship with Him.
- *Smyrna—the persecuted church (A.D. 100–313).* God encouraged the Smyrna church to be faithful amid persecution. Revelation predicts a time of trouble and persecution in the last days during which we will need Christ's strength to be faithful to God.
- *Pergamos—the compromising church (A.D. 313–538).* The church became popular and exalted—and compromise with the world was the result. By 538, the Christian church had so merged with the Roman government that it assumed both religious and political authority. There is something about human nature that causes us to drift from God when things are going too well. We must resist the tendency to compromise with the world.
- *Thyatira—the corrupt church (A.D. 538–1500s).* The church during this period was in spiritual darkness. But even in spiritual darkness, God looks for those who remain faithful. The further the church moves from God, the more crucial it becomes that we stay close to Him.

Christ's messages to the seven churches in Asia Minor spoke to local churches in the first century, but they especially relate to the church in distinct ages of church history. Still today, relevant and powerful lessons from each of these periods speak with deep meaning for our Christian lives.

Jesus' messages to the last three of the seven churches appear in the next chapter, Revelation 3.

---

1. Irenaeus, *Against Heresies*, 1.6.3, http://www.newadvent.org/fathers/0103126.htm.

2. See Henry Wace, "Dictionary of Christian Biography and Literature to the End of the Sixth Century A.D., With an Account of the Principal Sects and Heresies," *Christian Classics Ethereal Library*, ccel.org, accessed April 2, 2020, https://www.ccel.org/ccel/wace/biodict.html?term=Polycarpus,%20bishop%20of%20Smyrna.

3. Tertullian, *Apologeticus*, 50, http://www.newadvent.org/fathers/0301.htm.

4. Thomas Goodwin, *Moses and Aaron: Civil and Ecclesiastical Rites, Used by the Ancient Hebrews* (R. Scot, T. Basset, J. Wright, R. Chiswel, B. Griffin, G. Connyers, and M. Wotton, 1685), 188.

DEAD, FAITHFUL, AND LUKEWARM

Revelation 3

1 "And to the angel of the church in Sardis write,

'These things says He who has the seven Spirits of God and the seven stars: "I know your works, that you have a name that you are alive, but you are dead. **2** Be watchful, and strengthen the things which remain, that are ready to die, for I have not found your works perfect before God. **3** Remember therefore how you have received and heard; hold fast and repent. Therefore if you will not watch, I will come upon you as a thief, and you will not know what hour I will come upon you. **4** You have a few names even in Sardis who have not defiled their garments; and they shall walk with Me in white, for they are worthy. **5** He who overcomes shall be clothed in white garments, and I will not blot out his name from the Book of Life; but I will confess his name before My Father and before His angels.

6 "He who has an ear, let him hear what the Spirit says to the churches." '

7 "And to the angel of the church in Philadelphia write,

'These things says He who is holy, He who is true, "He who has the key of David, He who opens and no one shuts, and shuts and no one opens": **8** "I know your works. See, I have set before you an open door, and no one can shut it; for you have a little strength, have kept My word, and have not denied My name. **9** Indeed I will make those of the synagogue of Satan, who say they are Jews and are not, but lie—indeed I will make them come and worship before your feet, and to know that I have loved you. **10** Because you have kept My command to persevere, I also will keep you from the hour of trial which shall come upon the whole world, to test those who dwell on the earth. **11** Behold, I am coming quickly! Hold fast what you have, that no one may take your crown. **12** He who overcomes, I will make him a pillar in the temple of My God, and he shall go out no more. I will write on him the name of My God and the name of the city of My God, the New Jerusalem, which comes down out of heaven from My God. And I will write on him My new name.

13 "He who has an ear, let him hear what the Spirit says to the churches." '

14 "And to the angel of the church of the Laodiceans write,

'These things says the Amen, the Faithful and True Witness, the Beginning of the creation of God: **15** "I know your works, that you are neither cold nor hot. I could wish you were cold or hot. **16** So then, because you are lukewarm, and neither cold nor hot, I will vomit you out of My mouth. **17** Because you say, 'I am rich, have become wealthy, and have need of nothing'—and do not know that you are wretched, miserable, poor, blind, and naked— **18** I counsel you to buy from Me gold refined in the fire, that you may be rich; and white garments, that you may be clothed, that the shame of your nakedness may not be revealed; and anoint your eyes with eye salve, that you may see. **19** As many as I love, I rebuke and chasten. Therefore be zealous and repent. **20** Behold, I stand at the door and knock. If anyone hears My voice and opens the door, I will come in to him and dine with him, and he with Me. **21** To him who overcomes I will grant to sit with Me on My throne, as I also overcame and sat down with My Father on His throne.

22 "He who has an ear, let him hear what the Spirit says to the churches." ' "

As I slowly trudged up the narrow, winding Alpine trail in northern Italy, the majesty of the mountains, the pure, fresh mountain air, the flower-filled fields, and the crystal-clear rushing brooks invigorated my spirits. I paused to take in the awe-inspiring views, and my mind drifted back over the centuries. Nearly six hundred years before, a pilgrim band of weary, chilled-to-the-bone, hungry men, women, and children hastily fled from their medieval oppressors over this same trail.

History calls this period the Dark Ages. The thirteenth century was not friendly to those who conscientiously opposed the views of the popular church. They were oppressed, persecuted, and butchered in the name of religion. They found refuge in these mountain meadows, rocky crevices, and dark caves. I felt an attraction to these godly people of such stalwart conviction. In the face of insurmountable odds, they had a death-defying faith. They stood unflinchingly for what they believed and were willing to sacrifice their very lives for it.

MOESIA
THRACIA
MACEDONIA
EPIRUS
ACHAIA
AGEAN SEA
BITHYNIA
ASIA
Pergamum
Thyatira
Sardis
Pliladelphia
Smyrna
Ephesus
Laodicea
Lycia and Pamphylia
Patmos
CRETE
N
NE
E
SE
S
SW
W
NW
MEDITERRANEAN SEA
CYRENAICA
EGYPT

These people had something that the twenty-first century so desperately needs—a purpose to live for. Renowned American psychologist Philip Cushman, in his article "Why the Self Is Empty," discusses people living purposeless lives in a prosperous, self-centered Western individualistic society. He writes of those who have "constructed a self that is, fundamentally, a disappointment to itself."[1] Their beliefs are shallow. Little of real significance matters, and they have nothing worth dying for, so they have little worth living for. The force that drives them is an immediate need for self-gratification that ultimately leaves them empty and unsatisfied.[2]

But the men, women, and children in whose footprints I was walking up this steep, rocky trail were dramatically different. They had an abiding purpose worth living for. What they believed mattered to them, and they were not willing to compromise their integrity. Their core beliefs were part of their spiritual DNA. To deny these beliefs was to deny their identity. In the face of death itself, they had inner peace. Theirs was a serenity of soul deep within that is so absent in our twenty-first-century world of glitz, glamour, and immediate self-gratification. They lived with the certainty that their lives were in the hands of God and He was big enough to handle any problem they might face. In our last chapter, we discovered that there was a faithful "remnant" even in Thyatira, the church of the Middle, or Dark, Ages. In every generation, God has had a faithful remnant of true believers who have been committed to His will and obedient to His Word.

Revelation chapter 3 continues Jesus' messages to the seven churches, specifically to the last three—Sardis, Philadelphia, and Laodicea. Remember: these are *Jesus'* messages to the churches—not John's. Jesus is pictured walking among the golden lampstands that represent the churches (Revelation 1:12, 13, 20). He is closely connected with His church on earth. He is not an absentee landlord with little concern for His church and little care for His people in their trials, tribulations, and challenges. The saga of Revelation's seven churches places Christ in the midst of His people. He is with them in life's trials, strengthening, encouraging, and supporting them. Even in Sardis, He is there to encourage His people to be "watchful and strengthen the things that remain."

Sardis—the dead church (1500s–1790s)

To the church at Sardis, Jesus says, "I know your works, that you have a name that you are alive, but you are dead. Be watchful, and strengthen the things which remain, that are ready to die, for I have not found your works perfect before God" (Revelation 3:1, 2).

Sardis is the "dead church." It purports to be alive, but it is largely dead. It has become an institution and exists primarily to maintain its power and authority. It has a name—a reputation—of being alive spiritually, but Jesus sees Sardis for what it is. There is no evidence in this letter that the church of Sardis was experiencing persecution or heresy or any significant threat. Sardis was at peace, but it was the peace of the dead.

Back in the days of the apostles, when the Christian faith was new, the gospel message gave vitality and an impetus to the mission of the church. The believers were in love with their Lord. They possessed a living faith that caused them to share the good news with their neighbors and friends. The church grew rapidly. But through the centuries, as we have seen, the church began to compromise with the world in order to be accepted and gain popularity. It allowed false doctrines to come in. It substituted ritual for genuine worship and incorporated pagan practices. It became contented, lazy, and weak until it was on its deathbed spiritually even if it was rich and powerful.

> Sardis represents the Christian church at the closing of the medieval period. The gospel had been so distorted and changed that a living faith was hard to find. During this period, the Protestant Reformation arose as a reaction to a church that had the name of being alive but was spiritually dead.

Sardis represents the Christian church at the closing of the medieval period. The gospel had been so distorted and changed that a living faith was hard to find. During this period, the Protestant Reformation arose as a reaction to a church that had the name of being alive but was spiritually dead. Jesus says, "Be watchful, and strengthen the things that remain, that are ready to die" (verse 2).

Although there was little spiritual life left in the church at Sardis, there were those who were still committed to Christ and faithful to His word. "You have a few names even in Sardis who have not defiled their garments; and they shall walk with Me in white, for they are worthy" (verse 4).

In the preceding centuries, the Waldenses, John Huss, and Jerome, and later Ulrich Zwingli, stood firm for biblical truth at the peril of their lives. They were joined and followed by such men as Martin Luther, John Calvin, Philipp Melanchthon, and John Knox. These men of God rose up in various places to blow on the dying embers of those doctrines that remained but were "ready to die." They began to breathe life into the church again. The church was still in spiritual darkness, at the point of death, but Jesus says, "I am going to bring you back to life and shine the light of truth into the world again. Be watchful and strengthen the things that remain."

In our personal spiritual experiences, we can find faith slipping away just as it did in the Christian church through the centuries. A little compromise here, a little neglect there—and we find our connection with God growing weaker. When faith is slipping away in your life, God says to be watchful and strengthen the things that remain.

Jesus continues, "Remember therefore how you have received and heard; hold fast and repent. . . . He who overcomes shall be clothed in white garments, and I will not blot out his name from the Book of Life; but I will confess his name before My Father and before His angels" (verses 3–5).

In other words, Sardis needs to repent by turning back to God and restoring the gospel and the apostolic doctrine. It needs to make the Bible authoritative in the lives of its members. They need to get back to the Word of God. The medieval church relied on human tradition; the Protestant Reformation focused on the Bible. With the living Word, the Reformers opposed the dead teachings of a dead church. When the established church brought Martin Luther to account for his teachings, he defended them from Scripture. "Here I stand," he declared. "I can do no other."

In the last days, Jesus appeals to us to stand on the Word of God when all else is falling around us. At that time, the apostle Paul says, many will have a form of godliness while denying its power (2 Timothy 3:5). Jesus urges us not to have a mere "form of godliness" but to have a living faith—a relationship with him, a love for Him—that nothing can shake. There is no substitute for time in His presence to develop this relationship with Him. In His presence, we are charmed by His presence, amazed at His grace, and overwhelmed with His self-sacrificial love on the cross. Those who overcome will be clothed in the white garments of the righteousness of Jesus. If we are faithful, our names will be written in the Lamb's book of life. And Jesus will stand up in heaven in the judgment before the Father and the angels and confess our names as His faithful followers!

Philadelphia—the faithful church (1790s–1840s)

Philadelphia means "brotherly love." Philadelphia was the church whose members loved one another. To this church Jesus says,

> "These things says He who is holy, He who is true, 'He who has the key of David, He who opens and no one shuts, and shuts and no one opens': 'I know your works. See, I have set before you an open door, and no one can shut it; for you have a little strength, and have kept My word, and have not denied

189

My name. . . . Because you have kept My command to persevere, I also will keep you from the hour of trial which shall come upon the whole world, to test those who dwell on the earth. Behold, I am coming quickly! Hold fast what you have, that no one may take your crown' " (Revelation 3:7–11).

Jesus identifies Himself as the One who has the key of David. He says that He has placed an open door before the Philadelphia church. No one can shut the door He has opened, and no one can open the door He has shut. What is Jesus talking about? The wording of this statement comes from Isaiah 22:22.

Some have seen this "open door" as referring to the door of salvation and the "key of David" as the gospel—the key to eternal life. During the Dark Ages, the medieval church claimed to hold the key to salvation through its priests who could forgive sins. This was the main issue of dispute between the established church and the Protestant Reformers. During the time of the Philadelphia church, the good news of salvation through Jesus was being proclaimed and accepted with joy by many. A door had been opened that had been closed for centuries. Men and women could go through and come directly to Jesus as their Savior without having to come to Him through the mediation of a human priest. The door to salvation had been opened, and no one could shut it.

This open door could also refer to a door of opportunity. During the long centuries of spiritual darkness, the medieval church exercised religious power. Individuals had little opportunity to study the Bible. They had little opportunity to grow spiritually beyond the set traditions and rituals prescribed by the church. Then God began to open a door of opportunity. About 1200, we find the Waldenses copying Scripture by hand and secretly distributing it as they were able. About 1300, you have some individuals, such as John Huss, who were early forerunners of the Reformers. Their motto was obedience to God—not to the church. John Gutenberg invented the printing press, and in 1456, Bibles were some of the first books to be printed. The Scriptures became available in a way they had never been before. Luther preached salvation by grace through faith alone and renounced penances, which were sold by the church as a means of forgiveness. Great preachers such as John Wesley and George Whitefield preached to thousands in the open air. From 1300 to 1800, God prepared the world for a final revelation of the fulness of His truth through men and women who were totally committed to Christ and who fearlessly stood for His Word.

By 1800, mission societies were sending missionaries around the world in fulfillment of Christ's words in Matthew 24:14, "And this gospel of the kingdom will be preached in all the world as a witness to all nations, and then the end will come." Missionaries went to the far-flung corners of the earth, preaching the gospel. Bible societies sprang up, dedicated to translating and distributing the Word of God. Then God raised up the great Advent movement that focused on His soon return. All this happened during the time of the Philadelphia church.

A door was opened that no one could shut. God is saying that even in periods of spiritual darkness, He will open a door into heaven so that His truth can be proclaimed, and nothing or no one can shut it. As the Old Testament prophet Habakkuk predicts, "For the earth will be filled with the knowledge of the glory of the LORD, as the waters cover the sea" (Habakkuk 2:14). Revelation 18 adds, "After these things I saw another angel coming down from heaven, having great authority, and the earth was illuminated with his glory" (verse 1). Christ will triumph at last. His cause will be victorious. His church will rise to its destiny, and His people will proclaim the gospel to the ends of the earth.

There is yet another way of looking at the "open door," which Jesus says He has set before the Philadelphia church. When we come to the next chapter of Revelation, chapter 4, we will find John looking through an "open door" into the throne room of heaven. What he sees through that door is much like the judgment in heaven that Daniel describes in chapter 7 of his book. We saw, too, as we studied the book of Daniel, that the 2,300-day (year) period predicted there ended in 1844. At that time, the sanctuary was to be cleansed, which represents the Day of Atonement—Judgment Day.

In 1844, a door was opened in the sanctuary in heaven. The door to the Most Holy Place was opened, and judgment began. Jesus opened that door, and no one can shut it. When the judgment is completed, Jesus will shut that door, and no one can open it. The eternal destiny of every person is decided. The judgment is over, and Jesus will return as He has promised.

Jesus concludes His letter to the Philadelphia church with these words: "He who overcomes, I will make him a pillar in the temple of My God, and he shall go out no more. I will write on him the name of My God, the New Jerusalem, which comes down out of heaven from My God. And I will write on him My new name" (Revelation 3:12).

The ancient city of Philadelphia was known for its earthquakes. Often during an earthquake, the inhabitants of that city had to flee from their homes. The fear of these natural disasters created uncertainty. Jesus' promise to the church at Philadelphia and to you and me is that all fear is gone. In Christ, there is security, and one day, in that heavenly temple, we will find our permanent home where the sickness, suffering, and sorrows of life will be over forever. The focus is on the sanctuary in heaven and on the New Jerusalem, where God's people will spend eternity with Him. He who overcomes will be secure forever; "he shall go out no more."

Laodicea—the lukewarm church (1840s–the second coming of Jesus)

It is interesting that of the seven churches, Jesus finds something to praise in each one—except for two. He has no words of praise for Sardis or Laodicea. Laodicea is the "lukewarm" church. In fact, many people believe that *Laodicea* means "lukewarm." But that is not so. *Laodicea* means "a people are judged," or "judgment of the people." Laodicea is the last church of the seven. It is the church of the judgment hour, God's last-day church just before Jesus returns. Since Laodicea is the last of the seven churches, it obviously has meaning for the last generation of Christians. What Jesus says to the Laodicean church He is saying to us!

"These things says the Amen, the Faithful and True Witness, the Beginning of the creation of God: 'I know your works, that you are neither cold nor hot. I could wish you were cold or hot. So then, because you are lukewarm, and neither cold nor hot, I will vomit you out of My mouth. Because you say, "I am rich, have become wealthy, and have need of nothing"—and do not know that you are wretched, miserable, poor, blind, and naked—I counsel you to buy from Me gold refined in the fire, that you may be rich; and white garments, that you may be clothed, that the shame of your nakedness may not be revealed; and anoint your eyes with eye salve that you may see' " (verses 14–19).

Jesus identifies Himself to Laodicea as "the Faithful and True Witness." He is going to paint an unflattering picture of this church and its spiritual condition. The Laodicean church members may not want to accept His message; they may disagree with His assessment of them. But He is the "True Witness." They may not like it, but what He says about them is true.

We don't always like to hear what Jesus is saying to us about our spiritual condition. We sometimes want to apply His words to everyone but ourselves. The preacher is delivering God's Word about sin, and we are thinking, *That sure applies to Brother X.* God wants us to understand that He is the "True Witness." He tells us the truth about ourselves, whether we like it or not. He also tells us the truth about God. This is the most important aspect of the expression "the Faithful and True Witness." Jesus is a witness of the Father's love, mercy, grace, and power. He reveals to the members of lukewarm Laodicea, the church of the judgment hour, that He still cares and longs for them to experience the new life He has to offer.

Jesus also says that He is "the Beginning of the creation of God." That doesn't sound quite right. Isn't Jesus eternal as is God the Father? Hasn't He always existed? Is He saying here that He is the first Being that the Father created?

Not at all. The Greek word translated in this verse as "Beginning," is αρχη, which means "beginner" or "first cause." Ephesians 3:9 explains: "God . . . created all things through Jesus Christ." John says, "All things were made through Him, and without Him nothing was made that was made" (John 1:3). Jesus is the One through whom God created. Jesus is telling the Laodiceans, "The One speaking to you and pointing out your sins is the Creator. I can re-create your hearts."

The message to the Laodiceans is a message full of encouragement. It is a message of comfort to our hearts as well. The Almighty Creator, the One who created heaven and earth, longs to re-create our hearts. He longs to make us into His image. If we let Him, if we choose to allow it, He will transform our lives and break through our lukewarm complacency to give us the abundant life He freely offers.

Laodicea was located about six miles across the valley from the town of Hierapolis. Hierapolis was on an elevated plateau with natural hot springs bubbling up from the ground. The water was piped across the valley to Laodicea through a series of ingenious Roman aqueducts and ceramic pipes. By the time it got to Laodicea, it wasn't hot anymore. It was lukewarm. Laodicea had lukewarm water!

Spiritually, too, Laodicea was neither hot nor cold. It was a nauseating, lukewarm church. Jesus says He wishes they were either hot or cold—either is preferable to being lukewarm. A glass of cold water on a steaming-hot day is refreshing, and drinking herbal tea steeped in a cup of hot water can be relaxing. Lukewarm water denotes a spiritual complacency, a careless attitude toward the things of eternity, and a lack of spiritual fervor.

Laodicea was a city of about 150,000 at the time John was writing Revelation. It was a financial center and a place of extreme wealth. In A.D. 61, an earthquake destroyed Laodicea. The Roman government offered financial aid to help rebuild the city, but the Laodiceans replied, "We don't need your help. We have enough money to rebuild our city ourselves." The Roman historian Tacitus wrote, "Laodicea arose from its ruins by the strength of her own resources and with no help from us (Rome)."[3] Laodicea was wealthy and proud. It didn't need help from anyone. This complacent, materialistic church saw itself as rich and in need of nothing.

> Jesus' promise to the church at Philadelphia and to you and me is that all fear is gone. In Christ, there is security, and one day, in that heavenly temple, we will find our permanent home where the sickness, suffering, and sorrows of life will be over forever.

Nevertheless, what does the "True Witness" say of Laodicea? "You are wretched, miserable, poor, blind, and naked" (Revelation 3:17).

The Laodiceans claimed to be rich spiritually. But Jesus counseled them, "Buy from Me gold refined in the fire, that you may be rich" (verse 18). What is the gold that Jesus advises us to "buy" from Him? The apostle Peter writes of our "faith, being much more precious than gold . . . , tested by fire" (1 Peter 1:7). Jesus is telling us that we need a faith that will stand the fiery tests of the last days. The Laodicean message is telling us to develop faith and spiritual strength of character in the days just before Jesus comes that will carry us through to the kingdom.

Laodicea was also known for its garment industry. It was a fashion center as well as a financial powerhouse. There was a certain kind of wool found there that came from specially bred black sheep. It was extremely fine and glossy, and the Laodiceans made it into beautiful garments that were sought after as the height of fashion. Of course, they were very expensive. If you really wanted to be noticed, you wore one of these expensive black garments made from this special wool.

Jesus tells the Laodicean church, "You think you're dressed in the latest fashions? You're naked spiritually, and you don't realize it." His counsel? "Buy from Me . . . white garments, that you may be clothed, that the shame of your nakedness may not be revealed" (Revelation 3:18).

The white garment is a symbol of Jesus' spotless robe of righteousness, which He offers freely to everyone who comes to Him confessing their sins and accepting Him as their Savior (Isaiah 61:10). The prophet Isaiah declares, "But we are all like an unclean thing, and all our righteousnesses are like filthy rags" (Isaiah 64:6). Without Christ, even our good acts are prompted by selfish motives. Laodicea had outward conformity without a heart conversion. Coming to Christ, our glory is laid in the dust, and we depend totally, absolutely, completely on Him. He is our righteousness. He is our sinless Savior. He is the One who bore the guilt, shame, and condemnation of sin on our behalf. He is our forgiving Lord, our all-powerful High Priest, and our coming King. Our salvation is in Him.

Laodicea was also known as a medical center. It was known for developing an eye salve to deal with inflammation and problems of the eye. The Laodicean church thought that it saw itself clearly, and it was pleased with what it saw. But Jesus says, "You are blind. You cannot see at all. You need to buy from Me eye salve that will cure your spiritual blindness. This eye salve will give you clear spiritual vision to see yourself as you really are."

Do you *want* to see yourself as you really are, spiritually? That might not be a pleasing sight. It might be more pleasant to go on thinking you are rich and in need of nothing. The eye salve represents the work of the Holy Spirit, who convicts us of sin and shows us ourselves as we truly are. He convicts us of the reality "of sin, and of righteousness, and of judgment" in our lives (John 16:8). The Spirit reveals our sin. He points us to the righteousness of Jesus that can cover our sins. And He assures us that if we are covered by Jesus' righteousness, we need have no fear of the judgment.

Laodicea is the church that He rebukes most sharply. However, it is also the church to which He makes His most loving, intimate promise. "Behold, I stand at the door and knock. If anyone hears My voice and opens the door, I will come in to him and dine with him, and he with Me. To him who overcomes I will grant to sit with Me on My throne, as I also overcame and sat down with My Father on His throne" (Revelation 3:20, 21).

We sit down to eat with our families. We invite our close friends over for a meal. Mealtimes are times of intimate fellowship. We talk about things important to us as we eat. We share meaningful experiences with each other. Jesus says He would like to fellowship with us by sitting down and eating a meal together. This scripture is saying that He wants to have this close interaction with us, talk to us, and share with us so that we can get to know Him better.

Laodicea is the last church before the coming of Jesus. He wants us to know Him as a close Friend so that when He comes, we can sit down together at the marriage supper of the Lamb (Revelation 19).

He says we will sit with Him on His throne. You remember that is the position that the mother of James and John came asking Jesus to grant to her sons (Matthew 20:20–22). But that privilege is reserved, not for those who ask but for those who overcome (Revelation 3:21). Now is the time to prepare to sit down and eat with Jesus. Now is the time to prepare to sit with Him on His throne. We do that by accepting the gold, the white garments, and the eye salve He offers us so that we are no longer spiritually poor, naked, and blind. Enlightened by the Holy Spirit, we see ourselves as we really are, and we are prompted to seek Jesus with all of our hearts. We enter into an ever-deepening experience of living faith with Him. And we trust Him completely for both pardon from the guilt of sin and power over the grip of sin.

The last three churches summarized

The last three of the seven churches represent the periods of church history from the 1500s to the end of time and the coming of Jesus. We can outline them as follows:

- *Sardis—the dead church (1500s–1790s).* Sardis claims to be alive, but it is mostly dead. The church has become institutionalized and steeped in its traditions. It exists primarily to maintain its authority and power. It resists the efforts to breathe new life into those few doctrines that are still barely alive. The message to Sardis is straightforward. We must have a living faith today. We must spend time with Christ in His Word so we can stand for God's truth when the world around us is full of compromise and confusion.

"Behold, I stand at the door and knock. If anyone hears My voice and opens the door, I will come in to him and dine with him, and he with Me. To him who overcomes I will grant to sit with Me on My throne, as I also overcame and sat down with My Father on His throne" (Revelation 3:20, 21).

- *Philadelphia—the faithful church (1790s–1840s).* Philadelphia is the church that moved through the open door of opportunity that the Lord set before it. There was a renewed focus on the Bible and on evangelism. The good news of salvation went with zeal to the far-flung regions of the world. Judgment began in heaven in preparation for the return of Jesus. The Advent movement arose, emphasizing Jesus' return. We must continue that emphasis, as we wait for the Second Coming, and depend on Jesus to stand for us in the judgment.

- *Laodicea—the lukewarm church (1840s–second coming of Jesus).* The Laodicean church is contented, complacent, and compromised. It believes it needs nothing. It completely fails to understand its true condition. Laodicea is the church of the last generation before Jesus returns. Jesus' message to Laodicea calls us to develop faith and spiritual strength of character in the days just before Jesus comes that will carry us through to the kingdom.

The messages of the seven churches echo their truths to every generation. They speak of faith, courage, commitment, and obedience to God. They call us from compromise and from a faith that exists in name only. They speak of a people who are "overcomers" and who will live with Christ through the ceaseless ages of eternity.

---

1. Philip Cushman, "Why the Self Is Empty: Toward a Historically Situated Psychology," *American Psychologist* 45, no. 5 (May 1990): 608.

2. Cushman, "Why the Self Is Empty," 599–611.

3. Tacitus, *Annals XIV*, 27.

HEAVEN'S THRONE ROOM

Revelation 4

1 After these things I looked, and behold, a door standing open in heaven. And the first voice which I heard was like a trumpet speaking with me, saying, "Come up here, and I will show you things which must take place after this."

2 Immediately I was in the Spirit; and behold, a throne set in heaven, and One sat on the throne. **3** And He who sat there was like a jasper and a sardius stone in appearance; and there was a rainbow around the throne, in appearance like an emerald. **4** Around the throne were twenty-four thrones, and on the thrones I saw twenty-four elders sitting, clothed in white robes; and they had crowns of gold on their heads. **5** And from the throne proceeded lightnings, thunderings, and voices. Seven lamps of fire were burning before the throne, which are the seven Spirits of God.

6 Before the throne there was a sea of glass, like crystal. And in the midst of the throne, and around the throne, were four living creatures full of eyes in front and in back. **7** The first living creature was like a lion, the second living creature like a calf, the third living creature had a face like a man, and the fourth living creature was like a flying eagle. **8** The four living creatures, each having six wings, were full of eyes around and within. And they do not rest day or night, saying:

"Holy, holy, holy,
Lord God Almighty,
Who was and is and is to come!"

9 Whenever the living creatures give glory and honor and thanks to Him who sits on the throne, who lives forever and ever, **10** the twenty-four elders fall down before Him who sits on the throne and worship Him who lives forever and ever, and cast their crowns before the throne, saying:

11 "You are worthy, O Lord,

To receive glory and honor and power; And by Your will they exist and were
For You created all things, created."

※

In November 1998, Charles Colson wrote an article entitled "Astronauts Who Found God."[1] It provided the following insights into the faith of several well-known astronauts.

After John Glenn's return to outer space thirty-six years after his awe-inspiring orbit around the earth, he told reporters, " 'To look out at this kind of creation and not believe in God is to me impossible.'. . . 'It just strengthens my faith.' "[2] You may not realize that many of the early astronaut heroes had a deep religious faith. Their view of infinite space increased their faith. It did not diminish it in any way.

Neil Armstrong and Buzz Aldrin are best known as the first astronauts to land on the moon and take that "giant leap for mankind." But you probably don't know that before they emerged from the spaceship, Aldrin pulled out a Bible, a silver chalice, and sacramental bread and wine. There on the moon, his first act was to celebrate communion.

Frank Borman was commander of the first space crew to travel beyond Earth's orbit. Looking down on the earth from 250,000 miles away, Borman radioed back a message, quoting Genesis 1, "In the beginning, God created the heavens and the earth." As he later explained, "I had an enormous feeling that there had to be a power greater than any of us—that there was a God, that there was indeed a beginning."

The late James Irwin, who walked on the moon in 1971, later became an evangelical minister. He often described the lunar mission as a revelation. In his words, "I felt the power of God as I'd never felt it before."

. . . Guy Gardner is a veteran astronaut who speaks in churches on the reality of God.[3]

There is something about the wonders of creation, the marvels of the universe, the awesome nature of the cosmos, that inspires our hearts and leads us to a sense of the eternal.

Many of this world's greatest thinkers have been so moved by the incredible design, complexity, order, and vastness of the universe that they have developed a bedrock faith in God. Let me give you some examples.

Some people "think science is antagonistic to faith. Yet most of the great figures who shaped the scientific enterprise from the beginning have been devout believers—people like Copernicus, who discovered that the sun, not the earth, is the center of the planets; Isaac Newton, who discovered the law of gravity, Blaise Pascal, who invented the first calculator, and James Maxwell, who formulated the laws of electromagnetism. All were Christians who felt that the study of nature did not challenge their faith but rather strengthened it."[4]

In Revelation 4, John's angelic visitor gives him a view of the throne room of the universe. A door is opened in heaven, and John is given a glimpse of the heavenly scene, a scene of celestial praise. The entire universe sings its adoration to Christ as the Creator. Let's study this amazing theme together.

> I looked, and behold, a door standing open in heaven. And the first voice which I heard was like a trumpet speaking with me, saying, "Come up here, and I will show you things which must take place after this."
>
> Immediately I was in the Spirit; and behold, a throne set in heaven, and One sat on the throne. And He who sat there was like a jasper and a sardius stone in appearance; and there was a rainbow around the throne, in appearance like an emerald. Around the throne were twenty-four thrones, and on the thrones I saw twenty-four elders sitting, clothed in white robes; and they had crowns of gold on their heads. And from the throne proceeded lightnings, thundering, and voices. Seven lamps of fire were burning before the throne, which are the seven Spirits of God (Revelation 4:1–5).

This vision communicates an immense truth. A door is standing open in heaven, not only for John but for each one of us. Heaven's invitation is always, "Come up higher. Enter the realms of glory." This invitation is for you and me. It is an invitation to know Christ more deeply, to experience His love more fully, and to join the heavenly beings in praising Him more completely.

Trying to describe the indescribable

This description of heaven's throne room reminds us of the judgment scene in heaven pictured in Daniel 7:9, 10. John's account contains more details, but both prophets describe the glory, brightness, and grandeur of God and His throne. Yet John seems to struggle, somewhat, to adequately convey what he saw.

Have you ever thought about how difficult it would be to express such a sight accurately? No doubt, much of what John saw was symbolic. But it couldn't have been easy to describe even that which was real. That's why the prophets often try to compare what they saw to something their readers can understand. John says that the appearance of the One who sat on the throne was like the gemstones jasper and sardius. Jasper is an aggregate of quartz and chalcedony and is usually red, yellow, brown, or green in color. The sardius gemstone is what we call today red carnelian. It is blood-red in color.

We can probably best understand John's words here as simply describing the blaze of color and light that he saw when he looked at the throne of God. It was more magnificent than we can imagine. It was more glorious than words can express. It was more awesome than our human minds can comprehend.

Justice mingled with mercy

John goes on to say, "There was a rainbow around the throne, in appearance like an emerald" (Revelation 4:3). Emeralds are green, while rainbows are multicolored. But whatever John saw, the effect was awesome. Ezekiel also reported seeing a rainbow in connection with God's throne (Ezekiel 1:26–28).

We first encounter a rainbow in the Bible at the time of the Flood (Genesis 9:11–17). The rainbow in the sky after the Flood indicated that a just God had to destroy sin, but it also indicated that a merciful God would reach out to His people and that this world would never be destroyed by a flood again. As a sign, the rainbow mixes God's mercy and His justice, just as the rainbow in the sky is a mixture of colors. The rainbow surrounding God's throne in heaven symbolizes this dual aspect of His character—mercy and justice. God invites us to come to Him who never makes a mistake and who will always be just in the way He treats us. Individuals may treat you unjustly at times, but God never will. Furthermore, His justice is always tempered with mercy. The rainbow around God's throne indicates the surety of His Word, the eternal nature of His promises, and the immutability of His commands. We can have the absolute assurance that although His laws never change, His grace is abundant. The rainbow reminds us of His ceaseless mercy and abundant grace.

The twenty-four elders

John says, "Around the throne were twenty-four thrones, and on the thrones I saw twenty-four elders sitting, clothed in white robes; and they had crowns of gold on their heads" (Revelation 4:4). Who are these twenty-four elders that sit around the throne? They are wearing white robes. White robes are a symbol of the righteousness of Jesus (Revelation 7:14). Those who accept Him as their Savior are clothed in His robe of righteousness (Isaiah 61:10). So these twenty-four elders, clothed in white robes, must be human beings who have been saved by accepting the righteousness of Jesus Christ. They must come from the earth. Is there anything in the Bible that would help explain how these persons have arrived in heaven to sit around God's throne?

Matthew tells us that when Jesus died, several miraculous events took place.

Jesus cried out again with a loud voice and yielded up His spirit.

Then, behold, the veil in the temple was torn in two from top to bottom; and the earth quaked, and the rocks were split, and the graves were opened; and many bodies of the saints who had fallen asleep were raised; and coming out of the graves after His resurrection, they went into the holy city and appeared to many (Matthew 27:50–53).

When Jesus died, the graves of certain "saints" were opened, and after His resurrection, these saints were raised to life. They came out of their graves and were witnesses in Jerusalem to the power of God. Now, did these resurrected persons remain on earth only to die again? Paul says in Ephesians, "When He [Jesus] ascended on high, He led captivity captive" (Ephesians 4:8). The Greek wording Paul uses here can more accurately be translated, "When He ascended on high, He led a multitude of captives." Some modern translations of the Bible translate Paul's words this way. For example, the New American Standard Bible says, "When He ascended on high, He led captive a host of captives." The New International Version reads, "When He ascended on high, he took many captives."

When He went back to heaven following His resurrection, Jesus took with Him those who had been raised to life at the time He came forth from the grave. These would have been persons from Old Testament times who had been faithful to Jesus. They formed an honor convoy to escort Jesus back to heaven in triumph. The twenty-four elders dressed in white robes that John saw sitting on thrones surrounding God's throne in heaven were evidently from this select group who were redeemed from the earth at Jesus' resurrection. They represent those who will be resurrected to eternal life in the general resurrection at the end of time.

We don't know the names of these persons, obviously. But when we look up into heaven with John and see them sitting around God's throne, we can imagine what they must have experienced while on earth. They faced temptations. They dealt with discouragement and fear. They were lonely at times and had troubles and problems, as we all do. But they faced all these things in the strength of their faith in the coming Messiah. They gave their lives over to God and let Him lead them. Now they are sitting in heaven with Him. They praise the God who has redeemed them and taken them to be with Him in heaven.

The twenty-four elders fall down before Him who sits on the throne and worship Him who lives forever and ever, and cast their crowns before the throne, saying:

"You are worthy, O Lord,
To receive glory and honor and power;
For You created all things,
And by Your will they exist and were created" (Revelation 4:10, 11).

They are in heaven, praising God, while we are still here in this sinful world. But Jesus is coming soon! Soon, if faithful, we will join them around the throne of God. Meanwhile, there is an "open door" into heaven (verse 1). Like John, we can gaze into heaven through the open door of God's Word and see His throne room. We see the heavenly beings surrounding God's throne, some of whom were redeemed from the earth after enduring the same kinds of trials and temptations we face. We see that justice and mercy are mingled around His throne. We are encouraged to know that if His grace was sufficient to save these faulty, weak, and sometimes disobedient Old Testament men and women, that same grace is sufficient to save us. They were not beyond His grace, and neither are we.

The four living creatures

John continues his description of what he saw when he looked through the open door into heaven's throne room.

Before the throne there was a sea of glass, like crystal. And in the midst of the throne, and around the throne, were four living creatures full of eyes in front and in back. The first living creature was like a lion, the second living creature like a calf, the third living creature had a face like a man, and the fourth living creature was like a flying eagle. The four living creatures, each having six wings, were full of eyes around and within. And they do not rest day or night, saying,

"Holy, holy, holy,
Lord God Almighty,
Who was and is and is to come!" (verses 6–8).

This is symbolic language. John sees four "living creatures" around God's throne; the first was like a lion, the second like a calf, the third like a man, and the fourth like an eagle. Ezekiel saw these same living creatures in vision as well (Ezekiel 1:10). Much of the symbolism in Revelation is drawn from the Old Testament. In fact, the book of Revelation quotes 444 verses from the Old Testament. Is it any wonder that so many people fail to understand this book? If we don't understand what God is telling us in the Old Testament, we'll not be able to understand the book of Revelation.

These "living creatures" are full of eyes. Eyes are a symbol of understanding (Ephesians 1:18). We use a similar expression. We say, "Oh, now I see what you're doing," meaning, "Now I understand." That's why another name in the Bible for a prophet is a "seer." Rather than seeing with human eyes, the prophet sees with the eye of spiritual understanding.

When the nation of Israel wandered in the wilderness, the twelve tribes were organized by groups, each with its own banner (Numbers 1, 2). They camped according to their groups, under their own banner. They marched according to their groups, under their own banner. One banner had on it the figure of a lion; one bore the figure of a calf; one the figure of a man; and one the figure of an eagle. Those banners were a symbol of divine guardianship or divine protection. They were a symbol of Jesus. The lion represents Jesus in all His power and kingly authority. The calf is a beast of burden; it represents Jesus' servanthood and sacrifice. The man represents Jesus in His humanity coming to earth. The eagle represents Jesus as resurrected from the dead and ascended to heaven.

> We are encouraged to know that if His grace was sufficient to save these faulty, weak, and sometimes disobedient Old Testament men and women, that same grace is sufficient to save us.

Around God's throne, the living creatures, representing divine wisdom, cast their crowns before the throne and praise Jesus. One praises Him as the lion of kingly authority over the whole universe. One praises Jesus as the One who became the servant of all and, like a calf, sacrificed His life. Another living creature sings praises to Jesus, who left the glories of heaven, was incarnate in human flesh, dwelt among us, and faced temptations in common with all humanity. He triumphed over the principalities and powers of hell and defeated Satan. And another sings praise to Jesus, the flying eagle, the One who was resurrected from the dead, lives in heaven, and ministers before the throne of God as our great High Priest.

The oratorio of Creation

The twenty-four elders sing a song exalting the Creator, who is worthy to receive glory and honor because He created all things. There are two oratorios in Revelation—one here in chapter 4 (the oratorio of Creation) and one in chapter 5 (the oratorio of Redemption).

"You are worthy, O Lord,
To receive glory and honor and power;
For you created all things,
And by Your will they exist and were created" (Revelation 4:10, 11).

What is the basis of all true worship? Why do we worship God, anyway? Why give Him our allegiance and praise? Verse 11 answers that question. We are not a genetic accident. We are not merely skin covering bones. We are not simply an advanced protein molecule that is more highly developed than other forms of life. We are human beings created in the image of God. We did not evolve. He created us. He fashioned us in His image. We were made to know God, love God, and serve God. There is an inborn desire to know the One who created us.

Did you notice the expression "by Your will they . . . were created?" Before we ever were conceived in the womb of our mothers, we were created in the mind of God. Speaking of Jeremiah the prophet, God says, "Before I formed you in the womb, I knew you; before you were born I sanctified you; I ordained you as a prophet to the nations" (Jeremiah 1:5). God knows us before we are born and has a distinct plan for each of our lives. We worship Him because we are not a cosmic zero accidentally born in a world that we did not choose. We were fashioned by a loving God for a distinct purpose and brought onto the scene of this earth's history at this time to be a shining light of His glory in this world of spiritual darkness.

Revelation 4 reminds us that there is always a door standing open in heaven. God has an eternal plan for our lives. There is a deeper purpose than merely existing. There is something beyond us to live for. Even when we are facing difficulties in life, when every door on earth seems closed to us, God has a door standing open for us in heaven. It is the door of divine revelation. Like John, we can look through that door and see right into the very throne room of God. In His presence, we discover the true meaning of life, and at His throne, we find life's true purpose. God wants to reveal more of His love to us—more of His grace, more of His goodness. There is a door standing open in heaven for us.

The God of Creation, the God who brought the sun, moon, and stars into existence, the God whose awesome power created this planet and filled it with living things, is the God who delivered His people from Egyptian bondage, guided them in their wilderness wanderings, rained manna out of heaven, caused the walls of Jericho to collapse, and defeated Israel's enemies. This God is interested in you and me. He unleashes creation power to defeat the enemy who battles for our soul. And that makes all the difference.

Every single one of us faces battles with temptation every day. Here is the incredible good news—the same God who unleashed His infinite power to create the world unleashes that infinite power to defeat the forces of hell that wage the battle for our souls. Jesus has something much more to offer than frustrated defeat. He has something much more to offer than repeated failure. He has something much more to offer than falling on the same point again and again. Who is it that we serve? The all-powerful Creator who has unlimited, infinite power that is ours when we grasp it by faith. We are transformed, changed, made new by the power of the Creator.

There is an amazing truth in 2 Corinthians 5:17: "If anyone is in Christ, he is a new creation; old things have passed away; behold, all things become new." Let's make this very practical. This week, ask God to give you a deeper and more complete understanding of how His creative power can change your life. Here is a simple prayer to pray: "Dear Lord, You are the Creator of this world and everything in it. You are the God of awesome power. By faith, I believe that You can make of my life a new creation. I surrender to You anything that is not in harmony with Your will and ask You to re-create Your image in me."

Creation speaks of God's infinite power available in the battle between good and evil in each of our lives. That's why Creation matters. Revelation 4 leads us from the lowlands of earth, from its conflict and strife, to the celestial realms of glory, where all is joy and harmony and peace. It takes us from the confusion and conflict on earth to the glories of heaven's eternal realms. There we see the Creator seated upon His throne, guiding the destinies of the nations, overseeing the affairs of earth, and actively involved in each of our lives. As by faith, we enter through the open door of heaven, our hearts are at peace, our souls are at rest, and our minds are fixed on our loving Creator, who does all things right. We join with the beings throughout the entire universe and sing, "Holy, holy, holy." If you have been overwhelmed with the cares of life, and life for you has been a struggle recently, by faith, look through the open door of heaven and be at peace.

1. Chuck Colson, "Astronauts Who Found God," ActsWeb.org, http://www.actsweb.org/articles/article.php?i=17&d=1&c=1&p=1.

2. Julie Zauzmer, "In Space, John Glenn Saw the Face of God: 'It Just Strengthens My Faith,' " *Washington Post*, December 8, 2016, https://www.washingtonpost.com/news/acts-of-faith/wp/2016/12/08/in-outer-space-john-glenn-saw-the-face-of-god/.

3. Colson, "Astronauts Who Found God."

4. "Astronauts Who Found God: A Spiritual View of Space," July 20, 1995, http://www.oocities.org/fcastrocha/glenn.htm.

THE SCROLL AND THE LAMB

Revelation 5

1 And I saw in the right hand of Him who sat on the throne a scroll written inside and on the back, sealed with seven seals. **2** Then I saw a strong angel proclaiming with a loud voice, "Who is worthy to open the scroll and to loose its seals?" **3** And no one in heaven or on the earth or under the earth was able to open the scroll, or to look at it.

4 So I wept much, because no one was found worthy to open and read the scroll, or to look at it. **5** But one of the elders said to me, "Do not weep. Behold, the Lion of the tribe of Judah, the Root of David, has prevailed to open the scroll and to loose its seven seals."

6 And I looked, and behold, in the midst of the throne and of the four living creatures, and in the midst of the elders, stood a Lamb as though it had been slain, having seven horns and seven eyes, which are the seven Spirits of God sent out into all the earth. **7** Then He came and took the scroll out of the right hand of Him who sat on the throne.

8 Now when He had taken the scroll, the four living creatures and the twenty-four elders fell down before the Lamb, each having a harp, and golden bowls full of incense, which are the prayers of the saints. **9** And they sang a new song, saying:

"You are worthy to take the scroll,
And to open its seals;
For You were slain,
And have redeemed us to God by Your blood
Out of every tribe and tongue and people and nation,
10 And have made us kings and priests to our God;
And we shall reign on the earth."

11 Then I looked, and I heard the voice of many angels around the throne, the living creatures, and the elders; and the number of them was ten thousand times ten thousand, and thousands of thousands, **12** saying with a loud voice:

"Worthy is the Lamb who was slain
To receive power and riches and wisdom,
And strength and honor and glory and blessing!"

13 And every creature which is in heaven and on the earth and under the earth and such as are in the sea, and all that are in them, I heard saying:

"Blessing and honor and glory and power
Be to Him who sits on the throne,
And to the Lamb, forever and ever!"

14 Then the four living creatures said, "Amen!" And the twenty-four elders fell down and worshiped Him who lives forever and ever.

On December 17, 1968, Barbara Mackle, a student at Emory University in Atlanta, Georgia, was kidnapped. Imagine Barbara's horror as her kidnappers buried her in a shallow trench inside of a fiberglass-reinforced box. The box was outfitted with an air pump, a battery-powered lamp, water laced with sedatives, and food. Two plastic pipes provided Barbara with outside air. Her kidnappers demanded and received a $500,000 ransom from her father.

On December 20, The FBI received vague directions through a switchboard operator to Barbara's burial place. The FBI set up their base in Lawrenceville, Georgia, and more than one hundred agents spread out through the area to find her, digging the ground with their hands and anything they could find. After hours of searching, Barbara's unmarked, shallow grave was found. The rescuers frantically shoveled the dirt away, and eventually, Barbara was rescued unharmed. She had spent more than three days buried alive.

> Our planet was caught in the grip of sin, condemned to eternal death, kidnapped by a devilish invader. There was no way human beings could free themselves from the bondage and tyranny of the death sentence.

The ransom was paid. The girl was found, and a glorious reunion took place in the Mackle family that holiday season. She was so valuable that her dad paid $500,000 for her. Do you think Barbara woke up one day after her release at home in Florida wondering, *Does my father really love me? Does he really care?* Certainly not! Her dad paid half a million dollars for her. How could she ever doubt his love?

A costly ransom

Are you that valuable? Would anybody pay that much if you were kidnapped? Somebody says, "Oh! Pastor, no one would pay that much for me." Don't underestimate your worth. You are more valuable than you can ever imagine to God. A ransom of infinite price was paid for you. This planet has been kidnapped by a vicious intruder. Every one of us is held hostage in the darkness. There is no hope for any of us unless a ransom is paid, and thank God, it has been paid. The apostle Peter states in plainly, "Knowing that you were not redeemed with corruptible things, like silver or gold, from your aimless conduct received by tradition from your fathers but with the precious blood of Christ, as of a lamb without blemish and without spot." (1 Peter 1:18, 19).

Our planet was caught in the grip of sin, condemned to eternal death, kidnapped by a devilish invader. There was no way human beings could free themselves from the bondage and tyranny of the death sentence, just as Barbara Mackle could not free herself. We needed a deliverer, a redeemer, a Savior.

Heaven provided the costliest ransom imaginable—the divine Son of God. Were you worth the ransom? Are you worth the price Jesus paid for you? Someone says, "No, I am afraid not. I am not worth the price Jesus paid for me." If that is true, then Jesus got cheated. Jesus believes you are worth every drop of blood He shed for you. That's why He paid such a high price. That's what the fifth chapter of Revelation is all about.

Worthy is the Lamb

The bloodstained path through the ancient sanctuary reveals that our heavenly Father would go to any length to save us. The message of the sanctuary is the message of an infinite ransom paid so that there can be a glorious reunion. It is the message of a love beyond comprehension that will never be fully satisfied until His children are safe for eternity.

The plan of salvation, as revealed throughout the Old and New Testaments and especially highlighted in the book of Revelation, describes both Christ's sacrifice for sin and His High Priestly ministry in heaven's sanctuary, which provide for both ransom and reunion. The price of our salvation is far greater than a mere $500,000. It cost the infinite life of the Son of God. First Peter 3:18 declares, "Christ also suffered once for sins, the just for the unjust, that He might bring us to God." The innocent suffered for the guilty. The Sinless One took the sinner's place. From

the day that man fell, God sought to reveal His wonderful plan. In the sacrificial system, He showed that a Substitute would be accepted in the sinner's place. In His wisdom, God gave humanity an opportunity to exercise both faith and choice by participating in the sacrificial ceremonies. The earthly sanctuary that revealed the plan of salvation in miniature has long passed away. Now, God invites us to look to the heavenly sanctuary where Jesus, our great High Priest, ministers on our behalf. This is what Revelation chapter 5 shows us.

Heaven's vision of the slain Lamb

Revelation 5 continues John's vision of heaven's throne room and the things that he saw happening there. It also sets up a series of seven seals, which will occupy our attention in chapters 6 and 8. A pattern is emerging that runs throughout the book of Revelation. Several of the prophecies in this book are presented as a series of sevens. We have already studied the seven churches in chapters 2 and 3. There are seven seals (chapters 6, 8), seven trumpets (chapters 8, 9, 11), and seven last plagues (chapter 16). The number seven in Scripture denotes completion or fullness. In Genesis, God created the world in seven days. In the book of Joshua, Jericho fell after the Israelites marched around the city seven times—and made seven circuits on the seventh day. In 2 Kings, Elisha instructed Naaman to dip himself in the Jordan River seven times to be cleansed of his leprosy. The number seven is a significant number in the Bible. The prophetic series of sevens in Revelation indicates the fullness or the completion of God's plan to accomplish His eternal purposes.

> The issue raised in Revelation 5 is simply this: in the light of the great controversy between good and evil, is there anyone righteous enough who is eternally worthy to save the sinful human race?

A scroll with seven seals

John graphically describes what he saw as he looked through the open door into heaven's throne room:

I saw in the right hand of Him who sat on the throne a scroll written inside and on the back, sealed with seven seals. Then I saw a strong angel proclaiming with a loud voice, "Who is worthy to open the scroll and to loose its seals?"

And no one in heaven or on earth or under the earth was able to open the scroll or to look in it.

So I wept much, because no one was found worthy to open and read the scroll, or to look at it. But one of the elders said to me, "Do not weep. Behold, the Lion of the tribe of Judah, the Root of David, has prevailed to open the scroll and to loose its seven seals" (Revelation 5:1–5).

The first question that comes to mind is, what is the scroll? What is this book that God is holding in His hand? There is a book that frequently appears in Revelation—the book of life. John says in Revelation 20:12, "I saw the dead small and great, standing before God, and books were opened. And another book was opened, which is the Book of Life. And the dead were judged according to their works, by the things which were written in the books."

The book sealed with seven seals, here in Revelation 5, is clearly a book that decides the destiny of all humanity. It is the book that pronounces whether a person is saved or lost. It is a book of judgment. We can identify it as the book of life—or at least one of the "books" in which our lives are recorded and by which we will be judged.

The scene described by John certainly appears to be a judgment scene. It echoes 2 Corinthians 5:10, "For we must all appear before the judgment seat of Christ." Heaven's records contain an accurate account of the thoughts, intents, and deeds of the entire human race. Although we are saved by grace through faith, our works reveal that our faith is genuine. The issue raised in Revelation 5 is simply this: in the light of the great controversy between good and evil, is there anyone righteous enough who is eternally worthy to save the sinful human race?

Who can open the scroll?

John hears an angel ask, "Who is worthy to break open the seals and read the scroll?"

No one on earth has the right to open that book and read its contents. Would you even want to read it? Remember, it contains the record of your life—your good deeds and your sins. Would you want to see all your secrets recorded there? No one on earth can read that book. Furthermore, in response to the angel's question, no one in all of *heaven* steps forward claiming the authority to open the book! No wonder John is distraught and begins to weep.

But there is One who can open the scroll—the Lion of the tribe of Judah. Who is that? Jesus is the Lion of the tribe of Judah. As a human, He was born into the tribe of Judah. And remember in chapter 4, one of the living creatures representing Jesus was like a lion.

John continues, "I looked, and behold, in the midst of the throne and of the four living creatures, and in the midst of the elders, stood a Lamb as though it had been slain, having seven horns and seven eyes, which are the seven Spirits of God sent out into all the earth. Then He came and took the scroll out of the right hand of Him who sat on the throne" (Revelation 5:6, 7).

The Lion has become a Lamb! These are both symbols of Jesus. This symbolic Lamb has seven horns and seven eyes. Seven denotes fullness and completion. Horns represent power and authority. Eyes symbolize understanding and wisdom. So this picture of Jesus as a Lamb with seven horns and seven eyes is emphasizing the fullness of His power and the vastness of His wisdom. He has all the authority and wisdom needed to open the book.

A slain Lamb in heaven's throne room!

There is a key feature John notices about this Lamb. The Lamb appears "as though it had been slain" (verse 6). There is a blood-soaked Lamb in heaven! Moreover, it's not just in heaven but in the very throne room of God! Not only does Jesus have all power and wisdom, but He has also given His life!

That is a significant point. In the throne room, in the midst of the four living creatures and the twenty-four elders that surround God's throne, stands a Lamb that is all bloody. That may seem strange, but it tells us that heaven never tires of honoring the sacrifice that Jesus made to vanquish Satan and redeem us.

Revelation 13:8 speaks of Jesus as "the Lamb slain from the foundation of the world." Didn't Jesus die on the cross in A.D. 31? Why does this text say that He was slain from the foundation of the world? Why did John see a slain Lamb in heaven many decades after the Crucifixion?

You see, Jesus is not simply the Lamb of God who died on the cross. What happened there on Calvary is a revelation to our dull senses of the pain that sin has brought to God's heart from its very inception. This is one of those profound spiritual truths that are so easily overlooked. The cross, terrible as it was, was only a portion of the eternal pain that sin has caused God and His created beings throughout the universe. Jesus is the Lamb slain from the foundation of the world. From the beginning, He has faced the cross, knowing what sin would cost. Moreover, ever since the cross, He still feels the pain sin causes to His people and to His universe. When we see Jesus hanging on the cross, it is a microcosm of the pain that is resident in the universe due to sin. Jesus longs to come put an end to sin and stop the suffering. It is not only this world that suffers due to sin but also the whole universe.

The oratorio of Redemption—the first stanza

Now when He [the Lamb] had taken the scroll, the four living creatures and the twenty-four elders fell down before the Lamb, each having a harp, and golden bowls full of incense, which are the prayers of the saints. And they sang a new song, saying,

> "You are worthy to take the scroll,
> And to open its seals;
> For You were slain,
> And have redeemed us to God by Your blood
> Out of every tribe and tongue and people and nation,
> And have made us kings and priests to our God;
> And we shall reign on the earth" (Revelation 5:8–10).

This is the first stanza of the oratorio of Redemption. It is sung by the living creatures and the elders. They are praising Jesus and rejoicing that He was willing to give His life to redeem them—and us. Heaven never tires of praising the Lamb who was slain. And when we join them in heaven, we will praise Him, too, for all eternity.

Salvation is for all humanity—every tribe, tongue, people, and nation. No matter where you come from, no matter your background, no matter how far you have fallen in sin, the grace of Christ and the salvation He provided by His death is for you.

Notice that in their song, the living creatures and the elders praise the Lamb, because "You . . . have made us kings and priests to our God; and we shall reign on the earth" (verses 9, 10). Salvation has a double quality. Jesus redeems us on the cross from the penalty of sin, but He also redeems us from the power of sin. He not only redeems us from the guilt of the sin of the past but also redeems us by transforming us so that our lives are different today. We are saved not only from sin's penalty but also from sin's power. He redeems us and makes us kings and priests to God. In addition to this verse in chapter 5, the book of Revelation refers several times to the people of God reigning with Him (Revelation 20:4, 6; 22:5) as well as a statement by the apostle Paul, who wrote to Timothy, "If we endure, we shall also reign with Him" (2 Timothy 2:12).

The oratorio of Redemption—the chorus

After the living creatures and the elders finished their stanza of the oratorio of redemption, John heard a great chorus swelling the refrain.

Then . . . I heard the voice of many angels around the throne, the living creatures, and the elders; and the number of them was ten thousand times ten
thousand, and thousands of thousands, saying with a loud voice:

"Worthy is the Lamb who was slain
To receive power and riches and wisdom,
And strength and honor and glory and blessing!"

And every creature which is in heaven and on the earth and under the earth
and such as are in the sea, and all that are in them, I heard saying,

"Blessing and honor and glory and power
Be to Him who sits on the throne,
And to the Lamb, forever and ever!" (verses 11–13).

John is careful to include every possible "creature" in every possible location
throughout the universe in the great chorus that praises the Lamb. He says that the
number of angels in the chorus was "ten thousand times ten thousand and thousands
of thousands." This is not an exact number, of course. It's like saying, "Millions of
millions and thousands of thousands"—an innumerable company of angels.

The Lamb restores all that is lost through sin

This oratorio of redemption proclaims that the Lamb is worthy to receive seven
things—power, riches, wisdom, strength, honor, glory, and blessing (verse 12).
Interestingly, those are seven things we lost through sin, and they are seven basic
needs of the human heart. We either find them in Jesus or search for them in the
world. These seven qualities God built into every man and woman at Creation.

Power. When God created Adam and Eve, He gave them dominion over the earth.
They had power over God's creation. When they sinned, they lost that dominion,
authority, or power. At times, all of us feel subject to forces over which we have little
or no control. Natural disasters burst upon us suddenly with unexpected frequency.
War, conflict, strife, and terrorism thrust millions into circumstances over which they
have no choice. Every one of us, since our natures are fallen, must deal with genetic
predispositions inherited from our parents. There is something deep within the fabric
of our beings that longs to be in control of our destiny. We also seek power—power
over the things that hold us back from being all we can be and from being what
God wants us to be. Jesus promises to give us power over temptation and sin in our

lives. He will restore us to our true dominion over this planet that has fallen by sin and been caught in the grip of the evil one. (See Micah 4:8.)

Riches. At the end of Creation week, God saw that everything He had made was very good. Humanity had everything it needed for a rich, abundant life. As a result of sin, we lost the richness of life God originally gave us. Millions search in vain for material riches and things that simply perish. Today's best-selling commodities are tomorrow's broken items ready for the trash bin. Somehow, the things money can buy never satisfy the hidden hunger of our souls. In Christ, we find riches beyond anything we can ever imagine. Paul says, "In Him [Jesus] we have redemption through His blood, the forgiveness of sins, according to the riches of His grace" (Ephesians 1:7).

Wisdom. Eve lost true wisdom, trying to be like God and eating fruit from the tree of knowledge of good and evil. Wisdom is understanding the true purpose of life. We find the essence of genuine wisdom in Jesus. The wisdom that comes from heaven is pure, peaceable, gentle, and full of mercy and good works (James 3:17).

Strength. Because of sin, we have no strength in ourselves to withstand Satan's temptations. Today, we look in all kinds of places for strength to overcome the weaknesses we see in ourselves, but the only real source of spiritual strength is in the power of Jesus (Ephesians 6:10).

Honor. John 5:44 tells us that the only honor that counts comes from God. In the sinful world in which we live, people want to have a name; they want to be somebody. But the honor of humans is nothing compared to the honor that comes from being a child of God.

> Every one of us, since our natures are fallen, must deal with genetic predispositions inherited from our parents. There is something deep within the fabric of our beings that longs to be in control of our destiny.

Glory. In sinless Eden, Adam and Eve reflected the glory of God before the entire universe. God's glory is His character. Through Jesus, His glory, or character, so defiled in us by sin, will be restored to His faithful followers. John puts it this way, "Beloved, now are we children of God; and it has not yet been revealed what we shall be, but we know that when He is revealed, we shall be like Him, for we shall see Him as He is. And everyone who has this hope in Him purifies himself, just as He is pure" (1 John 3:2, 3). The only way we can be purified is to come to the One who is the essence of purity and appear in the spotless robes of His righteousness—appear before the Father transformed by His love and changed by His grace.

Blessing. God's richest blessing is His divine benediction upon all our lives. His blessing is His divine favor upon all we do. We are immensely blessed as He restores all that was lost through sin.

The center of heaven's praise

Looking through the open door into heaven's throne room in Revelation 5, we see Jesus at the center of a rapturous chorus of praise for the Lamb who was slain from the foundation of the world. He is the only Being in heaven or earth who can open the seven seals on the scroll. He is the only one worthy to deliver us from the condemnation of sin. He is the only one worthy to stand in our place in the judgment. He is the only one worthy to open the seals. His death on the cross is His supreme qualification to be our Savior.

As the Savior hung upon the cross, He listened for some word or token from humanity that would indicate that His sacrifice was appreciated; but only jeers, taunts, and curses were borne to His ears from the surging mass below. Even one of the thieves by His side joined in the railing, but the other thief, turning to Jesus, said, "Lord, remember me when You come into Your kingdom." The reply of Jesus, "Assuredly, I say to you, today," contained the assurance of pardon. Jesus left no question; "You *will* be with Me in Paradise" (Luke 23:42, 43). Even while the cleansing blood of Christ was flowing from His veins, the thief rejoiced in its power to cleanse from sin. And He who was thought by His enemies to be conquered died a mighty Conqueror. The thief experienced the fulfilment of the promise, "Though your sins are like scarlet, they shall be as white as snow" (Isaiah 1:18).

In the earthly sanctuary, the wool of the lamb was stained with its blood. There is great significance in this blood-soaked wool. It is almost impossible to remove scarlet stains, but "though your sins are like scarlet," the blood of Christ can make them "white as snow." You may be condemned and counted as an outcast by everyone on earth, but if you look to the Savior and claim His cleansing power, He will wash away your sins and put joy and rejoicing in your heart. He is the Christ who is worthy to open the seals and the Jesus who triumphed over the principalities of hell. The opening of these seals and His eternal victory are the subject of chapter 7. The judgments of God eventually fall upon the unrighteous and the oppressors of God's kingdom. His purposes prevail. His plan triumphs. And because He has triumphed, we can be victorious with Him.

THE LAMB OPENS THE FIRST SIX SEALS

Revelation 6

1 Now I saw when the Lamb opened one of the seals; and I heard one of the four living creatures saying with a voice like thunder, "Come and see." **2** And I looked, and behold, a white horse. He who sat on it had a bow; and a crown was given to him, and he went out conquering and to conquer.

3 When He opened the second seal, I heard the second living creature saying, "Come and see." **4** Another horse, fiery red, went out. And it was granted to the one who sat on it to take peace from the earth, and that people should kill one another; and there was given to him a great sword.

5 When He opened the third seal, I heard the third living creature say, "Come and see." So I looked, and behold, a black horse, and he who sat on it had a pair of scales in his hand. **6** And I heard a voice in the midst of the four living creatures saying, "A quart of wheat for a denarius, and three quarts of barley for a denarius; and do not harm the oil and the wine."

7 When He opened the fourth seal, I heard the voice of the fourth living creature saying, "Come and see." **8** So I looked, and behold, a pale horse. And the name of him who sat on it was Death, and Hades followed with him. And power was given to them over a fourth of the earth, to kill with sword, with hunger, with death, and by the beasts of the earth.

9 When He opened the fifth seal, I saw under the altar the souls of those who had been slain for the word of God and for the testimony which they held. **10** And they cried with a loud voice, saying, "How long, O Lord, holy and true, until You judge and avenge our blood on those who dwell on the earth?" **11** Then a white robe was given to each of them; and it was said to them that they should rest a little while longer, until both the number of their fellow servants and their brethren, who would be killed as they were, was completed.

12 I looked when He opened the sixth seal, and behold, there was a great earthquake; and the sun became black as sackcloth of hair, and the moon became like blood. **13** And the stars of heaven fell to the earth, as a fig tree drops its late figs when it is shaken by a mighty wind. **14** Then the sky receded as a scroll when it is rolled up, and every mountain and island was moved out of its place. **15** And the kings of the earth, the great men, the rich men, the commanders, the mighty men, every slave and every free man, hid themselves in the caves and in the rocks of the mountains, **16** and said to the mountains and rocks, "Fall on us and hide us from the face of Him who sits on the throne and from the wrath of the Lamb! **17** For the great day of His wrath has come, and who is able to stand?"

The battle between good and evil began in heaven when Lucifer, an angelic being of dazzling brightness who was created with free will, rebelled against God. This conflict has waged on earth throughout the centuries. At times, it has appeared that evil will triumph, and righteousness will be defeated. God's truth has been compromised, cast down, and trampled upon. God's people have been oppressed, imprisoned, and slaughtered, and the enemy has poured out his vicious wrath against God's church. Revelation, chapter 6, is the story of God's church and Satan's attempts to destroy it through any means possible. Down through the ages, he has used persecution, compromise, heresy, and popular favor to negate the influence of the church. This chapter is one of the most thrilling in the entire Bible. It reveals how Christ has been with His people in every generation. He is there protecting, guiding, strengthening, and empowering His church. As Jesus declared, "I will build My church, and the gates of Hades shall not prevail against it" (Matthew 16:18). Christ's church will ultimately triumph over the powers of Hades—or hell. It will be victorious over the forces of evil. It will weather every storm and come through every attack even stronger.

Opening the seals

Revelation 6 begins unfolding the series of the seven seals that were first introduced in the previous chapter. Before we examine each of the seven, let's notice some things about the seals in general.

First, these seven seals secure a scroll, or book, that John saw in God's right hand (Revelation 5:1). What is this book? In the previous chapter, we identified that scroll as either the book of life containing the names of those who are saved or, at least, one of the books by which each person will be judged. It is God's comprehensive record of the conflict between good and evil, and it reveals how the entire human race played a part in that conflict (Revelation 20:12). Second, what is the significance of the fact that the book is sealed? A sealed book would indicate that its contents (the amazing record of this great controversy) were not yet ready to be released. The judgment is not yet finished, and its results are still sealed up. Loosing the seals, then, would mean that the records contained in that book are being released—that the results of the judgment are taking place as the book is progressively "unsealed."

Finally, who is the only One on earth or in heaven who is able to loose the seals and open the book? Jesus Christ, the Lamb who was slain from the foundation of the world (Revelation 13:8). Jesus is opening the seals of history, the seals of the lives of every person who has ever lived on earth, the seals that reveal how this cosmic drama—this intergalactic battle that began in heaven—played out on earth, and Christ's complete victory over the forces of evil. The course of His people down through the centuries is progressively revealed as we see what happens when each seal is removed from the scroll. When the last seal, the seventh seal, is removed, the scroll is open, and the final decisions of the judgment are made plain. Time ends, and each person's eternal destiny is revealed.

Let's turn now to each of the seven seals and examine it more closely.

The first seal—a white horse

"Now I saw when the Lamb opened one of the seals; and I heard one of the four living creatures saying with a voice like thunder, 'Come and see.' And I looked, and behold, a white horse. He who sat on it had a bow; and a crown was given to him, and he went out conquering and to conquer" (Revelation 6:1, 2).

One of the living creatures invites John to "come and see" as the Lamb opens the first seal. It is important to notice who is opening the seals. It is the Lamb of God, Jesus Christ. This is significant: Jesus, our triumphant Lord, opens the seals to give us a behind-the-scenes look at salvation history. Given how upset John was when no one could be found to open the seals (Revelation 5:4), I'm sure he was eager to see what would take place when the first seal was opened. He saw a rider on a white horse. The rider was holding a bow and wore a crown. He was going forth to conquer. Throughout the New Testament, white is a symbol of apostolic-era purity, and a rider on a horse symbolizes conquest.

Although at times these symbols may seem strange to us, first-century believers easily understood them. When a Roman general conquered his foes and defeated an enemy army, he often entered Rome riding a white horse. His armies, with the prisoners of war and wagons loaded with the spoils of conquest, trailed behind him. Revelation 19 pictures the return of our Lord as a warrior riding a white horse with the angelic armies of heaven behind him. The rider on this white horse is the symbol of victory. White throughout Revelation represents a pure, uncompromised faith. The lukewarm church in Revelation 3:18 is counseled to clothe their spiritual nakedness with the white garments of Christ's righteousness. In Revelation 19:8, 9, the bride of Christ, His church, is clothed in the white garments of Christ's righteousness. What a marvelous picture. Biblical faith triumphs over the powers of hell.

Remember, we have noted earlier that prophetic sequences in the Bible always begin in the time and at the place where the prophet himself is. John is living in the first century after Jesus' return to heaven. The white horse galloping across the sky represents the apostolic church of the first century going forth to conquer the world for the gospel of Jesus. The church is like a horseman on a white horse, shooting the sharp, convicting arrows of God's Word into the hearts of pagans across the empire. Many of those struck by these arrows die to their old life of sin and come alive to a new life of grace and salvation in Jesus.

The first seal thus symbolizes the powerful, pure apostolic faith that invaded marketplaces, homes, and even Caesar's household (Philippians 4:22). The apostle Paul writes that the gospel was "preached to every creature under heaven." "Believers were increasingly added to the Lord, multitudes of both men and women" (Colossians 1:23; Acts 5:14).

The white-horse period covered the years from approximately A.D. 31, the days of Jesus' ministry, on through the time of the apostles in the first century.

The church historian Eusebius put it like this:

We beheld the most wonderful ardor, and the truly divine energy and zeal of those who believed in the Christ of God. For as soon as sentence was pronounced against the first, one after another rushed to the judgment seat, and confessed themselves Christians. And regarding with indifference the terrible things and the multiform tortures, they declared themselves boldly and undauntedly for the religion of the God of the universe. And they received the final sentence of death with joy and laughter and cheerfulness; so that they sang and offered up hymns and thanksgivings to the God of the universe till their very last breath.[1]

The gospel was so powerful in the first century that it went under the unction of the Holy Spirit to the entire then-known world (Acts 17:6; 24:5). Faithful to Christ, the New Testament believers cherished His Word, were filled with His grace, and were totally committed to sharing the gospel with their communities and beyond (Acts 1:8). The devil was furious. He had to do something about the rapid spread of Christianity, so he unleashed all his fury on the growing church. When Jesus opened the first seal, all of heaven was amazed at the faithfulness of the New Testament church. When God's people are totally dedicated to Christ and are faithful to His Word, transformed by His love, and proclaim His message of saving grace, it changes the world.

The second seal—a red horse

"When He [the Lamb] opened the second seal, I heard the second living creature saying, 'Come and see.' Another horse, fiery red, went out. And it was granted to the one who sat on it to take peace from the earth, and that people should kill one another; and there was given to him a great sword" (Revelation 6:3, 4).

The fiery red horse symbolizes the period of fiery persecution Satan unleashed on the church in an attempt to stop its growth. John saw a rider with a sword taking peace from the earth. The violent persecutions that believers suffered at the hands of Roman magistrates are well documented in the history of the early church. Christians were thrown to the lions; they were burned at the stake; they were massacred with the sword. Yet they died praising God.

Christians were not necessarily persecuted because they were followers of Christ. There were many pagan religions in the Roman Empire that blended into Roman society quite well. Rome was tolerant of varying religions as long as the followers of these religions gave allegiance to the empire and worshiped Caesar. The imperial Roman cult deified the emperors, so the emperors became the people's gods.

In the middle of the third century, the emperors Decius and Valerian passed edicts commanding all Roman subjects to sacrifice to the Roman gods or face either imprisonment or persecution.[2] The persecution of the Roman emperor Diocletian, or the Great Persecution, began in 303. A series of edicts revoked the legal rights of Christians, demanding they obey the mandates of the state and comply with the decrees to worship the emperor and the Roman gods. All Roman citizens were commanded to offer sacrifices to the Roman gods. Christians, of course, refused to obey the laws of the Roman state regarding worship. As the apostle Peter stated in the first century, "We ought to obey God rather than men" (Acts 5:29). The early church father Tertullian defended the Christian faith before the Roman magistrates and demanded that Christians be afforded legal rights in the empire. In his treatise, he declared, "*The blood of Christians is seed.*"[3] The blood-stained faith carried the banner of truth high. The gospel impacted all of Roman society and beyond. Persecution could not stop the proclamation of the gospel by these stalwart believers.

The red-horse period of persecution extended from about 100 to 313 without Satan accomplishing his purposes. Satan knew that he must change his strategy. What he could not accomplish by persecution, he would attempt to do by compromise. Remember that the opening of the seals is a revelation of the unfolding of the Christian history in the light of the eternal judgment. The opening of the seals reveals how each living human being responds to the gospel in either acceptance or rejection, in obedience or disobedience, in loving submission or conscious rebellion.

The third seal—a black horse

Though it was a terrible time for the Christian church, the devil's persecution under the second seal failed to destroy the church or keep it from growing. Satan turned to a different tactic. John says, "When He [the Lamb] opened the third seal, I heard the third living creature say, 'Come and see.' So I looked, and behold, a black horse, and he who sat on it had a pair of scales in his hand. And I heard a voice in the midst of the four living creatures saying, 'A quart of wheat for a denarius, and three quarts of barley for a denarius; and do not harm the oil and the wine' " (Revelation 6:5, 6).

If a white horse represented the purity of the apostolic church, what do you think a black horse would symbolize? A black horse represents the opposite. It represents a falling away from the truth. It represents the church's compromise with paganism that brought false doctrines into the church.

What does the pair of scales represent? Scales represent judgment. Daniel told Belshazzar, "You have been weighed in the balances, and found wanting" (Daniel 5:27). In this black-horse period (313–538), the church is judged and found to be lacking in faithfulness. Satan tried to destroy the church's effectiveness through compromise with the world. The apostle Paul warned the church in his day of this very thing. "I know this, that after my departure savage wolves will come in among you, not sparing the flock. Also from among yourselves men will rise up, speaking perverse things, to draw away the disciples after themselves" (Acts 20:29, 30).

The savage-wolf period was the period of Roman persecution during the blood-stained time under the red horse. But Paul warns that in the period of the black horse, individuals would arise from within the church itself, "speaking perverse things." They would be teaching doctrines not in harmony with the Word of God, but in harmony with the world and its pagan religions.

Large church edifices would take the place of the simplicity of God's Word.

Outward ornaments of religion would be substituted for the inner power of the gospel. Unconverted persons would be baptized and brought into the church. These new "converts" were accustomed to worshiping a number of different gods all at the same time. So when these pagans were brought into the Christian church, in an attempt to make them feel comfortable, the church renamed their gods after Christian saints and introduced their images into Christian worship. The pagans were used to worshiping the sun god on *deis solis*, Sunday, the day of the sun. John Eadie gives us this insight: "Sunday was a name given by the heathens to the first day of the week, because it was the day on which they worshipped the sun."[4] It was a popular pagan holiday. For a more detailed account, please see the chapter on Daniel 7, pages 99, 100.

The church brought Sunday into Christianity as the day of worship in honor of Christ's resurrection. Salvation through faith in Jesus Christ was replaced by salvation through the sacraments of the church and its ritual. Biblical truth was compromised during this time, and false teachings and practices became the norm. The simple faith of the Bible was replaced by the elaborate pomp and complex ritual of the church.

As the third seal was opened, John heard a voice saying, "A quart of wheat for a denarius, and three quarts of barley for a denarius; and do not harm the oil and the wine" (Revelation 6:6). These prices are about twelve times higher than the normal price for wheat and barley in John's day. It is describing a time of scarcity. There was a scarcity of Bible truth in the church during the time of the third seal. There was a scarcity of genuine faith. There was a famine in the land for the Word of God.

The heavenly messenger then speaks. "Do not harm the oil and the wine" urges the voice John heard. Oil in Scripture represents the Holy Spirit. The Holy Spirit inspired the Scriptures and still speaks to us through the Word (2 Peter 1:21). Wine represents the grace of Christ revealed in the gospel (Matthew 26:27, 28). At a time of compromise, religious apostasy, and heresy, the truths of God's Word and the preciousness of the gospel would be faithfully preserved and proclaimed by God's people. We can understand this as a plea to preserve the apostolic gospel that was being threatened by the compromise invading the church.

Let's summarize what we have learned about the seals so far. Under the first seal, the white horse, the church is powerful in its apostolic purity. It goes out to conquer, witnessing to the world, and winning men and women to Christ. During the time of the second seal, the red horse, Satan unleashes severe, bloody persecution against the church. But the church continues to grow. Under the third seal, the black horse, Satan brings pagans and compromises into the church to water down the Christian faith. Images come in. Earthly priests come in. Sunday comes in and replaces God's seventh-day Sabbath. God's truth becomes scarce.

The fourth seal—a pale horse

"When He opened the fourth seal, I heard the voice of the fourth living creature saying, 'Come and see.' So I looked, and behold, a pale horse. And the name of him who sat on it was Death, and Hades followed with him. And power was given to them over a fourth of the earth, to kill with sword, with hunger, with death, and by the beasts of the earth" (Revelation 6:7, 8).

This pale horse is the color of nausea and death. The Greek word translated "pale" is *chlōros*, which means a greenish-yellow color. The Greek writer Thucydides used this word to describe the skin color of those suffering from the plague. The color of this pale horse reminded John of the sickly, greenish-gray color of a corpse with decaying flesh. The rider sitting on this gruesome animal is named "Death." None of the horsemen in the previous seals were given a name. "Hades" rides with Death. Hades—called hell in some translations—refers to the grave. John's description is of a sickly, decaying horse ridden by Death, with Hades following behind, gathering up the dead in the grave.

The church that should have been pointing the way to eternal life was instead spreading spiritual disease and death. During the time of the fourth seal (538–1500s), moral and intellectual paralysis set in across Christendom. The Bible was forbidden to ordinary Christians, most of whom couldn't read, anyway—certainly not Latin, and the Bible was not available in the common languages. Nobles and commoners alike were ignorant of the Scriptures and the great truths they contain. The church had united with the political power to exercise both secular and spiritual authority.

Notice an interesting comparison between the church of the first seal and that of the fourth. Spiritually, the apostolic church was pure in doctrine and practice. It went forth conquering the world for Christ in the power of the gospel. At the same time, it was outwardly weak and without influence or authority in secular political society. By the time of the fourth seal, however, the situation was reversed. Spiritually, the church had become a pale, decaying corpse. Its doctrines were laced with pagan influences and were based more on human traditions than on the Word of God. Outwardly, though, the church loomed large in the secular world. It had united with the state to exercise nearly universal power. It had large, costly churches and cathedrals. Its bishops and cardinals were dressed in finery and lived in luxury.

John says that the riders on this pale horse were given the power to kill by the sword, hunger, death, and wild beasts. Those who did not go along with the authority of the church were persecuted, and thousands were killed. Describing this period, historian James Wharey makes this amazing statement: "When Christianity became the established religion of the Roman Empire, and took the place of paganism, it assumed, in a great degree, the forms and rites of paganism, and participated in no small measure of its spirit also. Christianity as it existed in the dark ages, might be termed, without much impropriety of language, *baptized paganism.*"[5]

These centuries are called the Dark Ages for a good reason. The darkness of biblical ignorance and apostasy descended on the church. The persecution of anyone who resisted the church's authority or questioned its doctrines cast darkness across the religious landscape.

The fifth seal—the cry of the martyrs

"When He opened the fifth seal, I saw under the altar the souls of those who had been slain for the word of God and for the testimony which they held. And they cried with a loud voice, saying, 'How long O Lord, holy and true, until You judge and avenge our blood on those who dwell upon the earth?' Then a white robe was given to each of them; and it was said to them that they should rest a little while longer, until both the number of their fellow servants and their brethren, who would be killed as they were, was completed" (verses 9–11).

What is the altar, and who are the souls under the altar? Is there really an altar in heaven with the souls of those faithful ones who have died for the Lord crying out beneath it for vengeance?

So far, the descriptions of these seals have been highly symbolic. We don't understand that there is a white horse or a red horse riding in heaven. Yet many of those studying Revelation point to these souls under the altar as evidence that the righteous dead go to heaven when they die. "There they are," they declare. "The Bible says they are in heaven crying out for vengeance."

In the first place, if the souls of the martyrs really are in heaven, under an altar, crying out for their death to be avenged—that's a rather grim picture of what their existence in heaven is like! If that's the case, would you want to go to a heaven like that? How could heaven be heaven if we hear the haunting cries of the martyrs crying out for justice in a sad lament? The language used here is clearly symbolic.

What does the symbolism mean? What does it mean that their "souls" are crying out? In the Bible, a "soul" often refers to a living person, not to some immortal entity within us that leaves the body at death. Genesis 2:7 (KJV) says, "And the LORD God formed man of the dust of the ground, and breathed into his nostrils the breath of life; and man became a living soul." The NKJV says that "man became a

225

living being." The Bible does not say that God put a soul into the man at Creation; it says that He created a living being. The souls under the altar are those who were martyred here on earth. They are in their graves, but their voices still symbolically cry out for God's justice to be done. They are not literally under the altar crying out. This is symbolic language, like when God told Cain, "The voice of your brother's blood cries out to Me from the ground" (Genesis 4:10).

When we looked at the Old Testament sanctuary and its ceremonies, we saw that a sinner in Israel brought a lamb to the sanctuary as a sacrifice on the altar. So the altar represents the place where the sacrifice is killed. When the fifth seal was opened, John saw those who have been killed for their faithfulness to God and His Word—especially those who were killed during the time of the fourth seal, when so many lost their lives for Jesus. He saw them "under the altar." So the altar here symbolizes the earth. Just like a lamb was sacrificed on the altar, so these martyrs were sacrificed on earth. Through the centuries since their deaths, the testimony of their faithful lives continues to cry out, saying, "Lord, avenge our death." The blood of the martyrs cries out for God's justice to set things right.

When this fifth seal is opened, we see all those who were persecuted down through the ages. It's drawing near the time for God's judgment to sit. It's coming time for accounts to be settled and their deaths to be avenged. God's judgment hour is about to strike on the celestial clock. Revelation 11:18, 19 expands on this:

> "Your wrath [God's wrath against sin] has come,
> And the time of the dead, that they should be judged,
> And that you should reward Your servants the prophets and the saints,
> And those who fear Your name, small and great,
> And should destroy those who destroy the earth."

> Then the temple of God was opened in heaven, and the ark of His covenant was seen in His temple.

Notice that last sentence: "Then the temple of God was opened in heaven, and the ark of His covenant was seen in His temple." That is very significant.

When we looked at the judgment in Daniel, we saw that the annual Day of Atonement in the earthly sanctuary symbolized the judgment at the end of time in heaven. On that day, and only on that day, the way into the Most Holy Place was opened. The high priest went into the Most Holy Place with sacrificial blood to cleanse the sanctuary of its accumulation of sin. The Most Holy Place was where the ark of the covenant was located. This represented God's throne.

So Revelation 11:18 is telling us that the time has come for judgment to begin in the sanctuary in heaven. The time that the souls of the martyrs under the altar, described in Revelation 6:9, have been calling for—the time when God will set things right.

When we looked at Daniel's prophecy of the 2,300 days (years), at the end of which the sanctuary in heaven was to be cleansed, we saw that that prophetic period ended in 1844. That is when "the temple of God was opened in heaven, and the ark of His covenant was seen" (Revelation 11:19). That is when the time of judgment began, and the symbolism of the sanctuary moved from the Holy Place to the Most Holy Place.

The fifth seal covers the period from the 1500s to 1844 when God begins to answer the cry of the martyrs to avenge their blood. The Reformation began the process of the restoration of God's truth. The Word was translated into multiple languages. The gospel was proclaimed with new power. Truths long lost sight of down through the centuries and covered in the rubbish of error were rediscovered. The setting was right for the rise of God's prophetic last-day movement to prepare a world for the coming of Jesus. The cry of the martyrs in the fifth seal is their cry that Jesus will come and resurrect them from their graves, and righteousness will reign throughout the universe for all eternity.

But the end is not quite yet. "It was said to them that they should rest a little while longer, until both the number of their fellow servants and their brethren, who would be killed as they were, was completed" (Revelation 6:11).

The end is near, but there is a little time yet to pass before the judgment is completed and Jesus returns. The gospel must be preached to all the world, and every human being must make their eternal, irrevocable decision for or against Christ and His truth (Revelation 22:11, 12).

The sixth seal—cosmic disturbances on earth and in the heavens

"I looked when He opened the sixth seal, and behold, there was a great earthquake; and the sun became black as sackcloth of hair, and the moon became like blood. And the stars of heaven fell to the earth, as a fig tree drops its late figs when it is shaken by a mighty wind" (Revelation 6:12, 13).

At the opening of the judgment, just before the court sits in heaven, just before all human destinies are settled, God says He is going to set out some signs so that we can know where we are in the stream of time. He says that when we see a great earthquake and we see the sun becoming dark and the moon turning red like blood and the stars falling from the sky—then we can know that we are in the time of the sixth seal and that judgment is beginning in heaven.

And these four signs have to come in that order. The stars are not to fall from the sky before the sun turns dark. The moon cannot become red as blood before the great earthquake. Each sign appears in order, one after another. These signs would prepare a generation for the judgment hour that is coming. God's judgment hour would take place in heaven over a period of time before Jesus returns.

Did these signs happen as God predicted they would? Yes, they did.

At the end of the fifth seal and the beginning of the sixth, a great earthquake struck Europe with its center in Lisbon, Portugal, on November 1, 1755. It was one of the largest and most deadly earthquakes ever to hit this world. It shook most of Europe as far north as Finland and as far south as northern Africa. Some sources say shocks were felt in Greenland and the Caribbean. Deaths in Lisbon alone were estimated to be as high as 100,000.

As terrible as this earthquake was, we might not see it as that significant prophetically unless it was followed by the other signs under the sixth seal. Was the sun darkened following the earthquake?

On May 19, 1780, some twenty-five years after the earthquake, people all up and down the east coast of North America woke up to a new morning. For some, the daylight seemed normal. In other areas, the sun seemed unnaturally hazy and obscured. Around ten or eleven o'clock, extraordinary darkness took place. The sun turned dark. Chickens went to roost, and tree frogs began peeping as if night had fallen. Darkness covered the land, and it remained dark until that evening.

The *Boston Gazette,* May 29, 1780, reported on this unusual event, saying, "There was the appearance of midnight at noonday. . . . Perhaps it was never darker since the children of Israel left the house of bondage."

Thomas Gage recalled, "By ten o'clock, A.M., the darkness was such as to occasion farmers to leave their work in the field, and retire to their dwellings; fowls went to their roosts; and, before noon, lights became necessary to the transaction of business within doors; the darkness continued through the day; and the night, till near morning, was as unusually dark as the day."[6]

That evening the moon rose red in color like blood. Milo Bostick is quoted as saying, "The moon which was at its full, had the appearance of blood."[7]

What about the stars falling from the sky like ripe figs from a tree? The *American Journal of Science* in 1834 contained this account: "The morning of Nov. 13, 1833, was rendered memorable by an exhibition of the phenomenon called shooting stars, which was probably more extensive and magnificent than any similar one hitherto recorded. . . . Probably no celestial phenomena has ever occurred in this country, since its first settlement, which was viewed with so much admiration and delight by one class of spectators, or with so much astonishment and fear by another class."[8] Years later, it was reported, "For nearly four hours the sky was literally ablaze. More than a billion shooting stars appeared over the United States and Canada alone."[9]

What were these heavenly signs for? They were signals for the generation then living that the next phase in God's plan for earth would be the dawning of the judgment hour, followed by the return of Jesus. The sixth seal closes with a dramatic picture of the Second Coming and the effect this event would have on those who were not ready.

> The sky receded as a scroll when it is rolled up, and every mountain and island was moved out of its place. And the kings of the earth, the great men, the rich men, the commanders, the mighty men, every slave and every free man, hid themselves in the caves and in the rocks of the mountains, and said to the mountains and rocks, "Fall on us and hide us from the face of Him who sits on the throne and from the wrath of the Lamb! For the great day of His wrath has come, and who is able to stand?" (verses 14–17).

Is there a more heartrending picture given anywhere else in the Bible? Those who are not ready to meet Jesus when He returns would rather be crushed to death by the rocks and mountains than to look on His face! He wanted to save them. He called to them throughout their lives, but they refused to listen. Now they hide in terror.

Verses 14–17 are often considered to be describing the return of Jesus and the terror and dismay of those who are lost. Yet we are still in the time of the sixth seal; the seventh seal has yet to be opened. Those hiding in the rocks and mountains cry out to be hidden from whom and what? From "the face of Him who sits on the throne and from the wrath of the Lamb." This could refer to Jesus at His coming. But it also can refer back to what John saw through the open door into heaven—God sitting on his throne and the Lamb who was slain from the foundation of the world (Revelation 5). This may be a description of the wicked at the Second Coming. Or it may be symbolically describing the panic and despair of those who are condemned in the judgment going on in the sanctuary in heaven. The verdict is announced, and they are eternally lost! Either way, it is a solemn appeal to surrender our lives to Christ, to love Him supremely, and to worship Him completely. It is an appeal to place Him first in our lives and daily rejoice in the salvation He has provided.

Revelation 6 ends with the question, "Who is able to stand?" Who is going to be able to stand in the judgment? Revelation 7 will answer that question. Chapter 7 is a parenthetical account placed between the sixth and the seventh seals. The seventh seal is not opened until chapter 8 because John pauses in chapter 7 to answer the question, "Who is able to stand?"

1. Eusebius, *Church History* 9.5, https://www.ccel.org/ccel/schaff/npnf201.iii.xiii.x.html.

2. David Potter, *Imagining Emperors in the Later Roman Empire* (Leiden, NL: Brill, 2018), 19.

3. Tertullian, *Apologeticus* 50, http://www.newadvent.org/fathers/0301.htm.

4. John Eadie, *A Biblical Cyclopædia; or Dictionary of Eastern Antiquities, Geography, Natural History, Sacred Annals and Biography, Theology, and Biblical Literature, Illustrative of the Old and New Testaments* (London: Religious Tract Society, 1883), s.v. "Sabbath," https://babel.hathitrust.org/cgi/pt?id=nnc1.cr60168021&view=1up&seq=587.

5. Gibbons, *Faith of Our Fathers*, 112.

6. James Wharey, *Sketches of Church History. Comprising a Regular Series of the Most Important and Interesting Events in the History of the Church, From the Birth of Christ to the Nineteenth Century*, rev. and cor. ed. (Philadelphia: Presbyterian Board of Publication, 1840), 24, https://babel.hathitrust.org/cgi/pt?id=umn.31951001493336b&view=1up&seq=30.

7. Thomas Gage, *The History of Rowley, Anciently Including Bradford, Boxford, and Georgetown, From the Year 1639 to the Present Time* (Boston, 1840), 423, https://books.google.com/books?id=gNUWAAAAYAAJ&printsec=frontcover#v=onepage&q&f=false.

8. *Facts for the Times, Containing Historical Extracts, Candid Admissions, and Important Testimony From Eminent Authors, Ancient and Modern, on the Leading Topics of the Scriptures and Signs of the Times*, 4th ed. (Battle Creek, MI: Review and Herald®, 1893), 69, https://books.google.com/books?id=IkxJAAAAYAAJ.

9. William Ambrose Spicer, *Our Day in the Light of Prophecy* (Washington, DC: Review and Herald®, 1918), 95.

10. Austin Cooke, *An Enduring Vision: Revelation Revealed*, rev. ed. (n.p.: TEACH Services, 2017), https://books.google.com/books?id=cSCYBgAAQBAJ.

THE SEAL OF GOD AND THE 144,000

Revelation 7

1 After these things I saw four angels standing at the four corners of the earth, holding the four winds of the earth, that the wind should not blow on the earth, on the sea, or on any tree. **2** Then I saw another angel ascending from the east, having the seal of the living God. And he cried with a loud voice to the four angels to whom it was granted to harm the earth and the sea, **3** saying, "Do not harm the earth, the sea, or the trees till we have sealed the servants of our God on their foreheads." **4** And I heard the number of those who were sealed. One hundred and forty-four thousand of all the tribes of the children of Israel were sealed:

5 of the tribe of Judah twelve thousand were sealed;
of the tribe of Reuben twelve thousand were sealed;
of the tribe of Gad twelve thousand were sealed;
6 of the tribe of Asher twelve thousand were sealed;

of the tribe of Naphtali twelve thousand were sealed;
of the tribe of Manasseh twelve thousand were sealed;
7 of the tribe of Simeon twelve thousand were sealed;
of the tribe of Levi twelve thousand were sealed;
of the tribe of Issachar twelve thousand were sealed;
8 of the tribe of Zebulun twelve thousand were sealed;
of the tribe of Joseph twelve thousand were sealed;
of the tribe of Benjamin twelve thousand were sealed.

9 After these things I looked, and behold, a great multitude which no one could number, of all nations, tribes, peoples, and tongues, standing before the throne and before the Lamb, clothed with white robes, with palm branches in their hands, **10** and crying out with a loud voice, saying, "Salvation belongs to our God who sits on the throne, and to the Lamb!" **11** All the angels stood around the throne and the elders and the four living creatures, and fell on their faces before the throne and worshiped God, **12** saying:

> "Amen! Blessing and glory and wisdom,
> Thanksgiving and honor and power and might,
> Be to our God forever and ever. Amen."

13 Then one of the elders answered, saying to me, "Who are these arrayed in white robes, and where did they come from?"

14 And I said to him, "Sir, you know."

So he said to me, "These are the ones who come out of the great tribulation, and washed their robes and made them white in the blood of the Lamb. **15** Therefore they are before the throne of God, and serve Him day and night in His temple. And He who sits on the throne will dwell among them. **16** They shall neither hunger anymore nor thirst anymore; the sun shall not strike them, nor any heat; **17** for the Lamb who is in the midst of the throne will shepherd them and lead them to living fountains of waters. And God will wipe away every tear from their eyes."

The book of Revelation is the "Revelation of Jesus Christ" (Revelation 1:1). It is both the revelation Jesus *gives* and the revelation *about* Jesus. So every chapter comes from Jesus and tells us something about Him. We need to look for Jesus in every part of the book.

For many people, chapter 7 is one of the most confusing chapters in Revelation. But it is confusing only if we approach it through the viewpoint of our own understanding and perspective. However, if you come to chapter 7 through the eyes of biblical symbolism, it becomes rich in meaning and significance. The chapter deals with the seal of God and the 144,000.

Chapter 6 closed with the question: Who shall be able to stand? That is, who shall be able to stand in the judgment and be vindicated and acquitted of Satan's charges? Chapter 7 answers that question before picking back up with the seventh seal in chapter 8.

Four angels, four winds

John says, "After these things I saw four angels standing at the four comers of the earth, holding the four winds of the earth, that the wind should not blow on the earth, on the sea, or on any tree" (Revelation 7:1).

Let's look at the symbols in this verse. What number is repeated several times in this verse? The number four. *Four* angels are standing on the *four* corners of the earth, holding *four* winds. Numbers in Revelation are significant. For example, there is a parallelism in Revelation with the number three. Three is the number of the Godhead—Father, Son, and Holy Spirit. And there is a counterfeit trinity—the dragon, the beast, and the false prophet (Revelation 16:13). There is a threefold blessing connected with Revelation—a blessing on those who hear, read, and keep the things written in this book. There are three angels proclaiming God's last messages to the whole world (Revelation 14). The number three is associated with divinity. In the three angels' messages of Revelation 14, it is associated with heaven's divinely inspired message for all humanity just before the coming of Jesus. There are also times the number three is linked to the triumph of error or apostasy. There are three unclean spirits who go to the kings of the earth to gather them to the world's last great battle (Revelation 16:13, 14). Seven, of course, represents perfection or completeness. There are seven churches, seven seals, seven trumpets, and seven lamps of fire.

What is the significance of the number four? Four symbolizes "universality" in the book of Revelation. When Revelation 7:1 talks about four angels standing on the four corners of the earth, it is emphasizing universality, or totality. We, too, use the phrase "the four corners of the earth" to indicate all the earth—north, south, east, and west. There is a universal ring of angels encircling the totality of the world. It is not that there are simply four angels standing at four spots around the earth. They are everywhere. Occasionally a gust of wind may get through their fingers when God allows a judgment upon the earth. But He does not allow the full force of satanic fury to come upon us or our world.

What about the four winds that the angels are holding back so that they do not blow on the earth, the sea, or the trees? The four winds represent calamity, destruction, strife, and war, threatening the earth from every direction. In the Old Testament, the prophet Jeremiah predicted the destruction of Israel's enemies with the symbolism of the catastrophic power of the wind:

"Against Elam I will bring the four winds
From the four quarters of heaven,
And scatter them toward all those winds. . . .

233

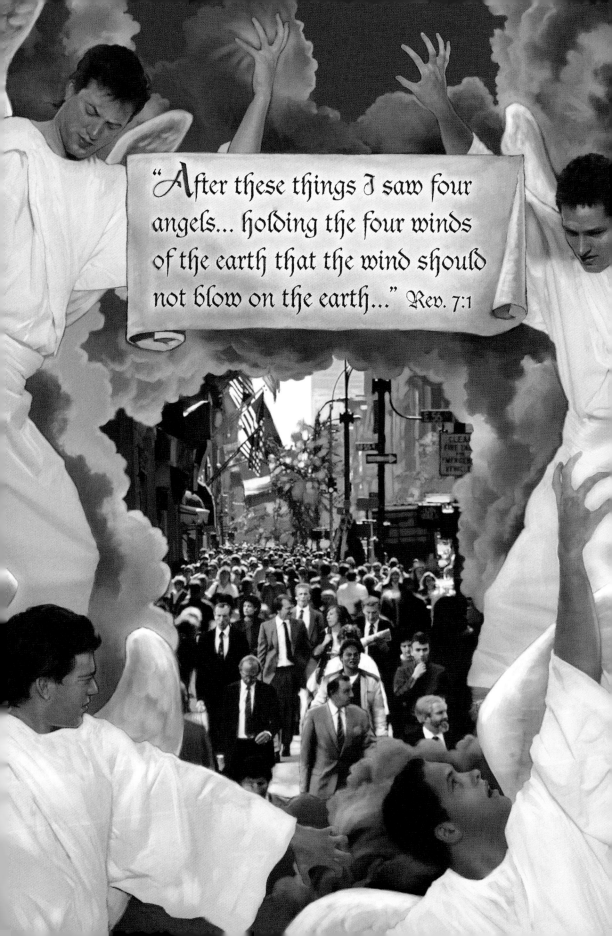

For I will cause Elam to be dismayed before their enemies
And before those who seek their life.
I will bring disaster upon them" (Jeremiah 49:36, 37).

In this passage, the blowing of the winds signifies disaster or destruction. In Daniel 7:2, 3, four beasts arise out of a windy, turbulent sea, indicating the rise of nations amid the conflict of war, strife, and disaster. Angelic beings hold back the winds of destruction on this planet until every person has had the opportunity to decide for or against Christ.

The seal of the living God

John continues, "Then I saw another angel ascending from the east, having the seal of the living God. And he cried with a loud voice to the four angels to whom it was granted to harm the earth and the sea, saying, 'Do not harm the earth, the sea, or the trees till we have sealed the servants of our God on their foreheads.' And I heard the number of those who were sealed. One hundred and forty-four thousand of all the tribes of the children of Israel were sealed" (Revelation 7:2–4).

This "seal of the living God" is *not* one of the seven seals closing the scroll that we have been studying in chapter 6. This seal belongs to God. It is His seal. A seal attests to the authority of a document. It says that a document has legal authority. It attests that the document is genuine. If you have ever had a document notarized, you know that a notary public attaches his or her seal to the document, thus guaranteeing its authenticity. Your high school or college diploma, your marriage license, the title to your automobile, all bear a seal that authenticates them as genuine. This seal of the living God is placed on the foreheads of His people, identifying and authenticating them as His genuine followers. Paul writes, "Nevertheless the solid foundation of God stands, having this seal: 'The Lord knows those who are His' " (2 Timothy 2:19). Jesus makes an urgent end-time appeal to those living in the last days of earth's history to be totally consecrated to Him and to stand for His truth at whatever cost to themselves. The apostle Paul appeals to us, "Do not grieve the Holy Spirit of God, by whom you were sealed unto the day of redemption" (Ephesians 4:30). Those who "seek first the kingdom of God and His righteousness" (Matthew 6:33) and set their affections on things above (Colossian 3:2) will be sealed by the Holy Spirit. This sealing is a settling into the truth of God's Word both spiritually and intellectually so they cannot be moved. It is the working of the Holy Spirit in our lives that seals us for the day of judgment. We will be studying this seal much more in later chapters of Revelation. God's seal stands in contrast to the mark of the beast introduced in Revelation 13. God's seal identifies His people; the mark of the beast identifies those who follow Satan. God will have a seal in the last days, a sign of His creative power and authority that will distinguish His people and identify them as His. Just as the Hebrew worthies in Daniel 3 refused to bow down to Nebuchadnezzar's counterfeit image, God's last-day people will not bow to the counterfeit that the beast power commands. They "keep the commandments of God and the faith of Jesus" (Revelation 14:12).

Here in chapter 7, Jesus is telling His angels, "Don't allow the last great time of tribulation to come until each one of My people has had the opportunity to accept My grace, respond to My love, and receive My seal." The angels "hold back," or restrain, the winds of destruction, strife, conflict, war, natural disasters, and total chaos until every person on planet Earth has had the opportunity to accept Jesus and His last-day message fully.

Sealed on the forehead versus sealed on the hand

Notice where God's seal is placed on His people. They are sealed "on their foreheads" (Revelation 7:3). When we study the counterfeit to God's seal—the mark of the beast—we will see that it is placed on either the forehead or the hand of those who receive it (Revelation 13:15–17). Why the difference?

> Jesus makes an urgent end-time appeal to those living in the last days of earth's history to be totally consecrated to Him and to stand for His truth at whatever cost to themselves.

The forehead, or better stated the forebrain, indicates the mind. It is the seat of intelligence where conscience, reason, and judgment are located. The frontal lobe of the brain is where we exercise our God-given power of choice. Of all the faculties that God has given us, the freedom of choice is the most significant. This power makes us fully human. God presents His truth to us and allows us to choose whether to accept it or reject it. Those who are sealed with God's seal on their forehead have willingly accepted His truth and have chosen to be identified as one of His followers.

The beast, however, marks his followers either on the forehead or the hand. Those who receive the mark of the beast on the forehead are those who believe his deceptive lies. Jesus stated it plainly when He stated that the devil was the father of lies (John 8:44). He has deceived multitudes into thinking that truth is error, and error is truth. They accept his false teachings. But there are others who accept the mark of the beast because of the pressure to conform or the consequence of refusing to bear his mark. They accept the beast's mark because they fear fines, persecution, torture, imprisonment, or even death. We will study much more about this later in Revelation 13. These people don't really believe in the beast, but they go along to get along. They receive the mark of the beast because they feel pressured or coerced. In Revelation 13, the hand is a symbol of the pressure to conform. God never forces His will on us. He wants us to respond to Him freely out of love. The beast will accept even a grudging, forced commitment.

So God tells His angels, "Don't allow the final time of tribulation to come—the winds of strife to blow—until My people have had the opportunity to settle truth in their minds and make a free choice to belong to Me."

Of course, neither God's seal nor the mark of the beast is literally stamped or affixed to the forehead or the hand. We are dealing here with symbols, not literal seals or marks. They symbolize allegiance and loyalty in the last days—either to God or to His opponent.

Who are the 144,000?

John says that the number of those who were sealed with the seal of the living God was 144,000. Who are these? Is this a literal number? Let's look, first, at who makes up the 144,000, and then we will consider whether this is a literal or symbolic number.

There are seven identifying characteristics of the 144,000. Let's look at them briefly.

1. They stand through the final crisis. Here is the answer to the question posed at the close of chapter 6—"Who is able to stand?" The answer is that the 144,000 can stand.

2. They stand with the Lamb (Jesus Christ) on Mount Zion (Revelation 14:1). They are anchored in Jesus. Their lives are totally committed to Him. They are redeemed by His grace, strengthened by His Word, and empowered by His Spirit.

3. They have the Father's name written on their foreheads (Revelation 14:1). The Father's name is His character. They are honest in a dishonest world, pure in an impure world, faithful in a faithless world, unselfish in a selfish world, giving in a taking world, and loving in a world of hate.

4. They sing a new song that only they can sing. It is the song of Moses and the Lamb (Revelation 14:3; 15:3). After the plagues were poured out on Egypt and God's people miraculously escaped through the Red Sea, Moses and the children of Israel sang a song of deliverance (Exodus 15). In the last days of earth's history, God will deliver His people, and they will sing a song of mighty deliverance like Moses and the children of Israel. It is the song of God's faithfulness and their unique experience of trust in the greatest time of trouble for God's people in this planet's history.

5. They are virgins (Revelation 14:4). They have not committed spiritual adultery against God. They hold to the pure, true doctrines of God's truth. The apostle James speaks of those who have compromised their faith as having committed spiritual adultery. He says, "Adulterers and adulteresses! Do you not know that friendship with the world is enmity with God?" (James 4:4). As a bride is faithful to only one husband and gives her affection only to him, God's people give their affection to Jesus. He is their loving Savior, living Lord, and coming King.

6. They are redeemed from the earth (Revelation 14:3). They are alive when Jesus comes, and they greet Him with joy. They are translated without seeing death like Enoch and Elijah. They have the "faith of Jesus" in earth's greatest time of trouble and live for the honor of His name.

7. They are without fault before God's throne (Revelation 14:5). The righteousness of Christ covers them, their sins are forgiven, their lives are transformed by His grace, and they reflect His character.

Revelation 7:4 says that the 144,000 come from "all the tribes of the children of Israel." From this, some of those studying Revelation believe that the 144,000 are Jews who, at the end of time, will be converted to Christianity and go out after the tribulation to preach the gospel. Is this a valid conclusion to draw from Revelation 7?

There are several reasons to reject this idea. First, the entire book of Revelation is written in highly symbolic language, as we have seen. Also, Revelation 7:5–8 breaks down the 144,000 as 12,000 from each of the twelve tribes of Israel. This artificial structure suggests a symbolic number. In addition, the Jewish people today no longer trace their lineage from any particular tribe as listed in the Old Testament. It would be difficult, if not impossible, to identify at the end of time 12,000 Jews from each tribe of Israel.

Second, the New Testament is clear that distinctions between Jew and Gentile have been swept away by the gospel of Jesus Christ. Paul says, "You are all sons of God through faith in Christ Jesus. For as many of you as were baptized into Christ have put on Christ. There is neither Jew nor Greek, there is neither slave nor free, there is neither male nor female; for you are all one in Christ Jesus. And if you are Christ's, then you are Abraham's seed, and heirs according to the promise" (Galatians 3:26–29).

In the New Testament era, all who accept Christ and become His disciples are spiritual Israelites. So who are the 144,000? They are not converted Jews. They are spiritual Israelites. They are Christian believers who live through the final tribulation at the end time and are redeemed from the earth. They are the redeemed who are alive on the earth when Jesus comes.

144,000—literal or symbolic?

What about the number 144,000? Are we to understand this literally? Will there be exactly 144,000 individuals redeemed at the end of time who meet the seven characteristics listed above?

If so, it seems rather strange that out of a planet with an estimated population of almost 8 billion persons, only 144,000 will be redeemed from among those living when Jesus comes. As mentioned previously, symbolic language is the norm in the book of Revelation. The twelve tribes of Israel represent all of Israel, God's chosen people in the Old Testament. The twelve disciples represent the entire New Testament Christian church, His chosen people in the Christian era. The twelve gates in the walls of the New Jerusalem on the north, south, east, and west represent the complete number of the redeemed entering the Holy City from all corners of the earth when Jesus returns to take us home.

The fact that the 144,000 number comprises 12,000 from each of the twelve tribes of Israel strongly suggests that this is a symbolic number, not a literal one. The twelve tribes formed the totality of God's chosen people in the Old Testament. Twelve thousand from each of these twelve tribes indicates completeness. It's a symbolic representation of the complete number of the redeemed that live through the final tribulation and see Jesus come. These are people who are fully committed to Jesus Christ in the end time of church history.

Revelation 7 is a call to you and to me to be faithful to Christ. It is a call to be a part of God's chosen people, or in the biblical sense, true spiritual Israelites. It is a call to be a part of this complete number of the redeemed in the last days of earth's history.

The great multitude

John describes what he saw next. "After these things, I looked, and behold, a great multitude which no one could number, of all nations, tribes, peoples, and tongues, standing before the throne and before the Lamb, clothed with white robes, with palm branches in their hands, and crying out with a loud voice, saying, 'Salvation belongs to our God who sits on the throne, and to the Lamb!'" (Revelation 7:9, 10).

The 144,000 are those faithful followers of Jesus who will be living on the earth when He comes. However, they are not the only ones who will be saved to live with Him forever. John sees a great multitude beyond counting, made up of people from every age, speaking every language, and from every ethnic group that has ever existed on earth. These have "come out of the great tribulation, and washed their robes and made them white in the blood of the Lamb" (verse 14). These are the saved who have died in Christ through the ages and who will be raised to life again at the second coming of Jesus.

Who shall be able to stand?

Notice that verse 9 says of this great multitude that they were *standing* before the throne and before the Lamb. Revelation 14:1 says that the 144,000 are *standing* with the Lamb on Mount Zion. This answers the question raised at the close of Revelation 6— "Who shall be able to stand?"

The 144,000 shall be able to stand. The great multitude shall be able to stand. And why are they able to stand? They all can stand because they have "washed their robes and made them white in the blood of the Lamb." They have been charmed by His love, saved by His grace, and transformed by His power. They stand in the presence of the Holy God in Christ. His righteousness pardons their guilty past. The life-changing faith of Jesus dwells in their hearts as an active force and changes their lives. His righteousness is their righteousness received by faith and accepted by a conscious choice of their will. They are complete in Him.

The 144,000 have also accepted everything Jesus offers. His grace is theirs. His righteousness is theirs. His power is theirs. They have been sealed in their foreheads with the seal of the living God. They have settled it for all eternity. His grace is enough, and all they want is to please Him, obey Him, and serve Him through all eternity. Together, the redeemed of all ages stand in the righteousness of Jesus.

Chapter 7 ends with this glorious promise: "They [all God's redeemed people] shall neither hunger anymore nor thirst anymore; the sun shall not strike them, nor any heat; for the Lamb who is in the midst of the throne will shepherd them and lead them to living fountains of waters. And God will wipe away every tear from their eyes" (verses 16, 17).

Notice that the Lamb becomes our Shepherd! We become His sheep, and He leads us to "living fountains of waters." In Christ, we are fully satisfied. In Him, we have everything we need. In Him, our thirst for eternity is fully quenched. He invites us to commit our lives fully to Him today so that we can one day stand on the sea of glass and live with Him through all eternity.

TRUMPETS OF JUDGMENT

Revelation 8

1 When He opened the seventh seal, there was silence in heaven for about half an hour. **2** And I saw the seven angels who stand before God, and to them were given seven trumpets. **3** Then another angel, having a golden censer, came and stood at the altar. He was given much incense, that he should offer it with the prayers of all the saints upon the golden altar which was before the throne. **4** And the smoke of the incense, with the prayers of the saints, ascended before God from the angel's hand. **5** Then the angel took the censer, filled it with fire from the altar, and threw it to the earth. And there were noises, thunderings, lightnings, and an earthquake.

6 So the seven angels who had the seven trumpets prepared themselves to sound.

7 The first angel sounded: And hail and fire followed, mingled with blood, and they were thrown to the earth. And a third of the trees were burned up, and all green grass was burned up.

8 Then the second angel sounded: And something like a great mountain burning with fire was thrown into the sea, and a third of the sea became blood. **9** And a third of the living creatures in the sea died, and a third of the ships were destroyed.

10 Then the third angel sounded: And a great star fell from heaven, burning like a torch, and it fell on a third of the rivers and on the springs of water. **11** The name of the star is Wormwood. A third of the waters became wormwood, and many men died from the water, because it was made bitter.

12 Then the fourth angel sounded: And a third of the sun was struck, a third of the moon, and a third of the stars, so that a third of them were darkened. A third of the day did not shine, and likewise the night.

13 And I looked, and I heard an angel flying through the midst of heaven, saying with a loud voice, "Woe, woe, woe to the inhabitants of the earth, because of the remaining blasts of the trumpet of the three angels who are about to sound!"

The major theme of Revelation is the great controversy between good and evil. This fascinating Bible book unfolds the cosmic conflict from the opening of the battle with Satan's rebellion in heaven to its close with the creation of new heavens and new earth. The first part of Revelation describes the conflict between Christ and Satan from the first century until the second coming of Christ in three sequences of sevens—the seven churches, the seven seals, and the seven trumpets.

In Revelation chapters 2 and 3, the seven churches reveal the spiritual condition of Christ's church in each generation and Satan's attacks upon it. In chapter 6, John sees the Lamb open the first six seals. The seventh seal isn't opened until chapter 8. That is because chapter 7 interrupts the sequence of the seals to answer a question raised in connection with the sixth seal: "Who shall be able to stand in the judgment?" We saw the answer to that question in our study of chapter 7. Now chapter 8 picks back up with the seventh seal, and it begins a new sequence—the series of seven trumpets. Let's see what Jesus is telling us in this chapter.

The seventh seal—silence in heaven

John sees the Lamb open the seventh seal. "When He [the Lamb] opened the seventh seal, there was silence in heaven for about half an hour" (Revelation 8:1).

That's it! That is all that John has to say about the seventh seal. When each of the first six seals was opened, he described horses and horsemen and the souls of the martyrs in heaven under an altar. John described persecution and conquering the world for the gospel. He described earthquakes and the stars falling from the sky. You might think that the seventh seal would be the climax of the series and that it would have the most details of all. But John says only, "There was silence in heaven for about half an hour."

What does this mean?

We are dealing here with time. Is it literal time or symbolic time? We aren't told. But given the fact that so much of Revelation is couched in symbolic language, it is likely that this is symbolic time. The details connected to the previous six seals have been mostly symbolic. So we can reason that this language is symbolic as well.

We've seen throughout Daniel and Revelation that, in Bible prophecy, one prophetic day equals one literal year of actual time. So how long would a symbolic half hour be in literal time? Let's do the math. There are 24 hours in a day, so a prophetic half hour is 1/48 of a prophetic day. In biblical times, a month was usually considered to be 30 days, so the year had 360 days—not 365. If we divide 360 days by 48 (the number of half hours in a day), we get an answer of 7 1/2. If our conclusion is correct, a prophetic half hour would equal 7 1/2 days of actual, literal time.

Why would there be silence in heaven for 7 1/2 days? Heaven is a busy place. There are ten thousand times ten thousand and thousands and thousands of angels. Although heaven is a place of peace and heavenly joy, I'm sure it isn't silent! It is a place of constant activity. All of heaven is focused on our salvation. From heaven, angels wing their way earthward to impress our hearts with divine truth. They beat back the dark angelic forces of hell that seek to influence our minds. They protect us from the clutches of the evil one and guide us in making the best possible life decisions.

> We are dealing here with time. Is it literal time or symbolic time? We aren't told. But given the fact that so much of Revelation is couched in symbolic language, it is likely that this is symbolic time.

In his vision of a ladder that stretched from earth to heaven, the Old Testament patriarch Jacob saw angels descending and ascending that ladder. These heavenly beings were continually traveling from earth to heaven on God's missions. The book of Hebrews describes the angels as "sent forth to minister for those who will inherit salvation" (Hebrews 1:14).

The expression "silence in heaven" could very well be describing Christ, saying to the angels, "It's time. Let's go gather My children home." Heaven empties, and ten thousand times ten thousand angels accompany Christ on His glorious return. There is silence in heaven. And Matthew tells us that this is just what will happen when Jesus returns to earth. Matthew says, "The Son of Man will come in the glory of His Father *with His angels*" (Matthew 16:27; emphasis added).

How many angels is Jesus going to bring with Him when He comes? All of them! Heaven empties itself when Jesus leaves to return to earth! All the angels want to go with Him. Not one wants to be left behind. They are all coming because the graves are going to open, and the righteous dead will be resurrected. All the angels accompany Christ on this mission to deliver His people from the clutches of death. They celebrate with Him, as the righteous dead and the righteous living are clothed with immortality and ascend to their heavenly home. The angels are participants in this grand day of rejoicing for the entire universe. Heaven is empty as we journey through the illimitable, vastness of space with Jesus and the angels, enjoying the wonders of the universe on our way home for just over seven days.

This is an interesting insight into how long it will take for Jesus and all the angels to leave heaven, come to earth, and then go back to heaven with the redeemed. I'm sure Jesus could do this using any amount of time He might choose. But if our interpretation of Revelation 8:1 is correct, the journey from heaven to earth and back again will take 7½ days. Heaven is silent during that time because the entire attention of the universe is focused on the redemption of planet Earth. But it won't be silent when we all get there—Jesus, the Father, the Holy Spirit, the angels, and the redeemed. What a homecoming that will be! The entire universe with all the unfallen worlds will rejoice with us as the Father, Son, and Holy Spirit welcome us home.

The seven trumpets

John's vision moves immediately from the series of seven seals to a series of seven trumpets.

> I saw the seven angels who stand before God, and to them were given seven trumpets. Then another angel, having a golden censer, came and stood at the altar. He was given much incense, that he should offer it with the prayers of all the saints upon the golden altar which was before the throne. And the smoke of the incense, with the prayers of the saints, ascended before God from the angel's hand. Then the angel took the censer, filled it with fire from the altar, and threw it to the earth. And there were noises, thunderings, lightnings, and an earthquake.
>
> So the seven angels who had the seven trumpets prepared themselves to sound (Revelation 8:2–6).

Before the trumpets sound, bringing judgments on the earth, we have this beautiful picture of our prayers ascending to heaven as incense, where they are received at the very throne of God! Sometimes it seems to us that our prayers go no higher than the ceiling. Sometimes we don't really know what we should be praying for. We don't know how to express the desires of our hearts. But here, John sees our prayers ascending from the angel's hand to the presence of God Himself like sweet-smelling incense. That should encourage us as we pray. Our prayers do reach heaven; God does listen. Our prayers are important to Him. Every prayer offered in sincere faith lodges in the heart of God and will be answered in the way, and at the time, He knows best.

Next, John sees the angel throw the censer of incense to the earth, causing thunder and lightning and an earthquake. This is the language of judgment. The seven trumpets symbolize God's sevenfold judgment down through the seven major ages of history—judgments upon those who have flagrantly rebelled against His gracious invitations for salvation, oppressed His people, and persecuted His faithful followers.

In Bible times, trumpets heralded two things. They heralded great political or religious gatherings, and they heralded the approach of war or disaster. Trumpets in the Bible are often associated with judgment.

These trumpets follow much the same outline as we have seen with the seven churches and the seven seals. They have some different details, but the sequence is similar. The seven churches depict the inner spiritual life of the church in every age from the beginning of Christianity to the end of time. There were seven literal churches, but those seven churches represented seven periods of time. The seven seals describe how Christianity made an impact on society and the world during these same periods and culminate in God's ultimate deliverance of His people. The seven trumpets reveal God's judgments through the centuries on those who reject the plan of salvation that He so freely offered, rebel against His will, and live in opposition to His plans. As we study these trumpets, we will see the following sequence:

First trumpet—judgment on Jerusalem
Second trumpet—judgment on the Western Roman Empire
Third trumpet—judgment on apostate Christianity
Fourth trumpet—judgment on apostate Christianity intensifies
Fifth trumpet—judgment on the Eastern Roman Empire
Sixth trumpet—judgment on the Eastern Roman Empire intensifies
Seventh trumpet—judgment on all humanity

Chapter 8 deals with the first four of these trumpets. Trumpets five and six are found in chapter 9. And the seventh trumpet doesn't appear until chapter 11.

The first trumpet—judgment on Jerusalem

"The first angel sounded: And hail and fire followed, mingled with blood, and they were thrown to the earth. And a third of the trees were burned up, and all green grass was burned up" (verse 7).

Immediately, we realize that these trumpets are about destruction. Hail and fire, mingled with blood, are rained down upon the earth. Trees and grass are destroyed. But what does this mean? What is being destroyed? When does this take place? Can we determine when this first trumpet in the series begins?

Remember a principle we first discovered in the book of Daniel: time prophecies in the Bible always begin at the time of the prophet receiving the prophecy. In Daniel 2, the golden head of the image represented Babylon—the kingdom in which Daniel himself was living. The same with the lion in the sequence of Daniel 7. The lion represented Babylon, the time in which Daniel was living. Here in Revelation, the seven churches begin with Ephesus, the church of the first century in which John was living. So biblical time prophecies start where the prophet is and then proceed to the next generation, followed by the succeeding generations. That is a principle of biblical prophetic interpretation.

The Bible gives us another interesting clue about when this first trumpet begins. We find it in Luke's Gospel. As Luke is describing Jesus being led to Calvary, where He would die on the cross, he writes: "A great multitude of the people followed Him, and women who also mourned and lamented Him. But Jesus, turning to them, said, 'Daughters of Jerusalem, do not weep for Me, but weep for yourselves and for your children. For indeed the days are coming in which they will say, "Blessed are the barren, wombs that never bore, and breasts which never nursed!" . . . For if they do these things in the green wood, what will be done in the dry?' " (Luke 23:27–31).

What is Jesus talking about? What was going to come upon Jerusalem? The whole city was going to be destroyed. The Romans were going to burn up Jerusalem and not leave one green tree. Blood would run in the streets. They were going to destroy that city! "Weep for yourselves," Jesus told them. "Don't weep for Me. If they crucify Me, the tree of righteousness, a green and living tree, what will they do when the trees are dry? The Romans will come and destroy you and your city." That happened in A.D. 70. Here is Christ's point: if the leaders of the Jewish nation failed to recognize and accept Him as the Messiah while He was present in their midst—experiencing the spring of God's favor when the trees were green—then there would be no hope for the nation once He was crucified. As a judgment, when His blessings were withdrawn, Jerusalem would be destroyed and burned as dry trees in a great conflagration. In fulfillment of this "green tree" prophecy, the Roman armies destroyed Jerusalem just as this first trumpet describes.

The first trumpet sounds and although tens of thousands of Jews believed that Jesus was the Messiah in the first century, the majority of Israel's leadership did not, and the judgments of God fell on those who rejected Jesus and their capital city in A.D. 70 by way of the attacks led by the Roman General Titus.

Who destroyed Jerusalem and persecuted Christians in those early centuries? Rome. So Rome, too, faces judgment from God. It was imperial Rome that crucified Christ, persecuted Christians, and martyred the people of God in the first, second, and third centuries.

The second trumpet—judgment on the Western Roman Empire

"Then the second angel sounded: And something like a great mountain burning with fire was thrown into the sea, and a third of the sea became blood. And a third of the living creatures in the sea died, and a third of the ships were destroyed" (Revelation 8:8).

Often in the Bible, a mountain represents a kingdom. So the kingdom, or mountain, that overthrew Jerusalem would itself be destroyed in this period of the second trumpet. The judgments of God would fall on the Western Roman Empire that persecuted Christians so cruelly in those early centuries of the church. The Visigoths, under the fierce warrior Alaric, invaded Thrace, Macedonia, and Greece about A.D. 396. This was the first of a continuing series of invasions by the barbarian tribes from the north. In 410, the Visigoths crossed the Alps and conquered Rome. These northern invaders divided up the empire. The Franks occupied the area we now know as France. The Anglo-Saxons invaded Britain. The Ostrogoths, Heruli, Vandals, Alemanni, and other tribal peoples carved up the empire. The Huns, under the leadership of Attila, conducted a fierce military campaign of devastation and slaughter throughout central Europe. Rome was crushed as it crumbled from within and lost its strength to resist the foreign invaders. The empire was broken up between 351 and 476 into the ten divisions predicted in Daniel 2 and Daniel 7. Just as Jerusalem, the Jewish leaders, and their nation were judged, so the Western Roman Empire was judged because it persecuted God's people and openly rejected scriptural truth.

The third trumpet—judgment on apostate Christianity

"Then the third angel sounded: And a great star fell from heaven, burning like a torch, and it fell on a third of the rivers and on the springs of water. The name of this star is Wormwood. A third of the waters became wormwood, and many men died from the water, because it was made bitter" (verses 10, 11).

The trumpets are following parallels to the sequence of the seven churches and seven seals. After the total collapse and destruction of the Roman Empire, the period we now know as the Dark, or Middle, Ages began in the sixth century.

According to Revelation 8:10, when the third trumpet sounded, a great star fell from heaven. What does a star represent? In Revelation 1, John saw Jesus holding seven stars in His hand. Jesus told him that the stars represented the angels of the seven churches. So a star represents an angel. What great angel fell from heaven?

Jesus said, "I saw Satan fall like lightning from heaven" (Luke 10:18). Satan was one of the stars of heaven, a mighty angel called Lucifer. Revelation 12 tells us that there was war in heaven, and Satan was cast out of heaven along with the angels who followed him in rebellion against God. The great star that falls from heaven when the third trumpet sounds is Satan being cast out of heaven. Now, Satan was cast out long before the Dark Ages. But during the time of the third trumpet, this angelic being who was once a bright and shining star in the heavenly courts deceived men and women on earth with great intensity and success (Isaiah 14:12–14). Satan caused the Christian church itself to fall into apostasy and turn away from God's truth. Christianity itself became corrupt. The being of dazzling brightness became the prince of darkness (Ephesians 2:2; 6:12).

The star fell on the rivers and springs of water. What do these represent?

Isaiah says, "With joy you will draw water from the wells of salvation" (Isaiah 12:3). Proverbs 13:14 says, "The law of the wise is a fountain of life, to turn one away from the snares of death." God says in Jeremiah, "My people have committed two evils: they have forsaken Me, the fountain of living waters, and hewn themselves cisterns—broken cisterns that can hold no water" (Jeremiah 2:13). The springs of water represent God's salvation—His grace, His Word, His truth, and His law. During the Dark Ages, the time of the third trumpet, Satan falls upon the earth introducing poison—wormwood—into God's fountain of life.

What does *wormwood* mean? The name of the angel that falls from heaven is Wormwood, and he introduces wormwood into the streams of water—the fountain of God's Word. *Wormwood* means "punishment for apostasy." That is the root of the word. Wormwood is a bitter-tasting plant that is also a symbol of idolatry (Deuteronomy 29:17, 18). Satan came into the church itself and poisoned the pure teachings of the gospel. He introduced false doctrines and apostasy into the church.

> Before the trumpets sound, bringing judgments on the earth, we have this beautiful picture of our prayers ascending to heaven as incense, where they are received at the very throne of God!

"And many men died from the water, because it was made bitter" (Revelation 8:11). During the Dark Ages, the time of the third trumpet, many men and women did indeed die. They died spiritually because of the apostasy in the church. And they died physically, resisting that apostasy, as the church put to death those who disagreed with its authority and false doctrines. God's judgments fell upon apostate Christianity—the medieval church itself—under the third trumpet. Yet that apostasy only grew greater as the church united with the state to exert its authority more and more. Truth was compromised even further.

The fourth trumpet—judgment on apostate Christianity intensifies

"Then the fourth angel sounded: And a third of the sun was struck, a third of the moon, and a third of the stars, so that a third of them were darkened. A third of the day did not shine, and likewise the night" (Revelation 8:12).

In the Bible, darkness is contrasted with the light that comes from God. Jesus said, "I am the light of the world. He who follows Me shall not walk in darkness but have the light of life" (John 8:12). The apostle John wrote of Jesus that He is "the true Light which gives light to every man coming into the world" (John 1:9). God's Word is a light to illuminate our path (Psalm 119:105).

> During the Dark Ages, the time of the third trumpet, many men and women did indeed die. They died spiritually because of the apostasy in the church. And they died physically, resisting that apostasy, as the church put to death those who disagreed with its authority and false doctrines.

In contrast, Isaiah says, "Behold, the darkness shall cover the earth, and deep darkness the people" (Isaiah 60:2). The apostle Paul warns the New Testament believers against spiritual powers and "against the rulers of the darkness of this age" (Ephesians 6:12). He encourages them to trust God, who "has delivered us from the power of darkness" (Colossians 1:13). Under the fourth trumpet, the sun, moon, and stars are struck so that their light is greatly diminished. As Isaiah predicted, darkness increases on the earth—deep spiritual darkness covers the people. As the church consolidated its power—both religious and secular—over the people, the darkness of apostasy grew ever greater. It was as if the sun, moon, and stars were going out!

The first four trumpets summarized

What is the message of the first four trumpets in Revelation 8? The message is that God's mercy is always blended with His justice. A loving God forgives our sins, but His judgments fall upon those who willingly, knowingly persist in sin. There is an eternal truth recorded in Galatians 6:7: "Do not be deceived. God is not mocked; for whatever a man sows, that he will also reap." If we reject truth like Israel's leaders, God's judgments will fall on us. If we fight against God's truth as the pagan Roman Empire did, God's judgments will fall on us. If we compromise truth as the Christian church did, through apostasy and union with secular power, God's judgments will fall on us. God still sits upon the throne. He is a God of mercy, but also a God of justice. God reaches out to sinners in love, but He cannot compromise with sin. Justice is an essential aspect of His character, as is love and mercy.

The security of the universe for the ceaseless ages of eternity depends on our understanding the depth of God's love, the wonders of His grace, and the immense cost of sin. Sin cost heaven everything. There can be no greater sacrifice than Jesus hanging on the cross, suspended between earth and heaven, bearing the guilt, shame, and condemnation of our sins. When we understand how good God is and how bad sin is, we will turn to Him and away from sin forever.

A trumpet of salvation and a trumpet of judgment

Revelation 8 tells us that the trumpets are sounding. Trumpets in the Bible do two things. They announce a gathering, and they announce judgment. In these days just before Jesus returns, the trumpets of God are gathering His people from the north to the south and from the east to the west. He is calling His people to come to Him and be ready for the second coming of Jesus. The Bible says that a trumpet will sound when Jesus returns. That trumpet blast will raise the righteous dead to life! That trumpet is God's trumpet of salvation.

But in these days before the return of Jesus, the trumpets of judgment are sounding as well. God's judgments fall on those who insist on rejecting Him, who resist Him and embrace error in the place of truth. Revelation chapter 8 is a heaven-sent appeal for each of us to live godly, committed, uncompromising lives in the light of the coming of Jesus. In Revelation 9, Jesus continues His appeal for us to be ready for His soon return. The trumpet of judgment sounds, calling each one of us to faithfulness to Christ in these critical hours of earth's history.

THE TRUMPETS CONTINUE TO SOUND

Revelation 9

1 Then the fifth angel sounded: And I saw a star fallen from heaven to the earth. To him was given the key to the bottomless pit. **2** And he opened the bottomless pit, and smoke arose out of the pit like the smoke of a great furnace. So the sun and the air were darkened because of the smoke of the pit. **3** Then out of the smoke locusts came upon the earth. And to them was given power, as the scorpions of the earth have power. **4** They were commanded not to harm the grass of the earth, or any green thing, or any tree, but only those men who do not have the seal of God on their foreheads. **5** And they were not given authority to kill them, but to torment them for five months. Their torment was like the torment of a scorpion when it strikes a man. **6** In those days men will seek death and will not find it; they will desire to die, and death will flee from them.

7 The shape of the locusts was like horses prepared for battle. On their heads were crowns of something like gold, and their faces were like the faces of men. **8** They had hair like women's hair, and their teeth were like lions' teeth. **9** And they had breastplates like breastplates of iron, and the sound of their wings was like the sound of chariots with many horses running into battle. **10** They had tails like scorpions, and there were stings in their tails. Their power was to hurt men five months. **11** And they had as king over them the angel of the bottomless pit, whose name in Hebrew is Abaddon, but in Greek he has the name Apollyon.

12 One woe is past. Behold, still two more woes are coming after these things.

13 Then the sixth angel sounded: And I heard a voice from the four horns of the golden altar which is before God, **14** saying to the sixth angel who had the trumpet, "Release the four angels who are bound at the great river Euphrates." **15** So the four angels, who had been prepared for the hour and day and month and year, were released to kill a third of mankind. **16** Now the number of the army of the horsemen was two hundred million; I heard the number of them. **17** And thus I saw the horses in the vision: those who sat on them had breastplates of fiery red, hyacinth blue, and sulfur yellow; and the heads of the horses were like the heads of lions; and out of their mouths came fire, smoke, and brimstone. **18** By these three plagues a third of mankind was killed—by the fire and the smoke and the brimstone which came out of their mouths. **19** For their power is in their mouth and in their tails; for their tails are like serpents, having heads; and with them they do harm.

20 But the rest of mankind, who were not killed by these plagues, did not repent of the works of their hands, that they should not worship demons, and idols of gold, silver, brass, stone, and wood, which can neither see nor hear nor walk. **21** And they did not repent of their murders or their sorceries or their sexual immorality or their thefts.

❧

The famed English preacher Charles Spurgeon is said to have declared, "The roaring thunder of the law and the fear of the terror of judgment are both used to bring us to Christ, but the final victory culminating in our salvation is won through God's loving-kindness." The book of Revelation is the revelation of Jesus Christ. Although it reveals God's judgments, it does so in the light of God's grace. One of the prominent titles of Jesus in the book is the "Lamb." It is Jesus, the sacrificial Lamb, who is worthy to open the seven seals. It is Jesus, the sacrificial Lamb, who was slain for the sins of all humanity. It is Jesus, the sacrificial Lamb, who defeated Satan on the cross and will one day vanquish him forever. The seven trumpets in chapters 8 and 9 describe both Christ's judgments on the wicked and His trumpet blast of victory over sin and Satan. They are trumpets of doom and trumpets of triumph. They are trumpets of judgment and trumpets of victory. They are trumpets of warning and trumpets of celebration. They reveal that the triumphant Christ will not allow rebellion to go on forever.

Perhaps you noticed that John's descriptions of the first four trumpets in chapter 8 are quite brief—just one or two verses each. In chapter 9, he describes the fifth and sixth trumpets. His descriptions of these two are much longer and contain more details. The first four trumpets take us down through the centuries from the beginning of the Christian church to the end of the Dark Ages. They denote God's judgments during those centuries on those who spurn His loving entreaties, despise His grace, disregard His law,

253

and oppress His people. Likewise, the fifth and sixth trumpets are trumpets of judgment.

The fifth trumpet—judgment on the Eastern Roman Empire

"Then the fifth angel sounded: And I saw a star fallen from heaven to the earth. To him was given the key to the bottomless pit. And he opened the bottomless pit, and smoke arose out of the pit like the smoke of a great furnace. So, the sun and the air were darkened because of the smoke of the pit" (Revelation 9:1, 2).

We saw a star fall from heaven in chapter 8 when the third angel sounded his trumpet. We learned that this represented Satan bringing his rebellious activity against God to earth in a powerful way. Jesus is the Light of the world. He declares, "He who follows Me shall not walk in darkness, but have the light of life" (John 8:12). In contrast to Jesus as the Light of the world, Satan is the prince of darkness. He obscures the truth of the gospel and clothes humanity in darkness. We saw in the fourth trumpet that darkness symbolizes spiritual darkness and turning away from God. Satan uses every available means to bring spiritual darkness on the earth and blind the minds of men and women to God's truth.

Whenever the Scriptures describe a star falling from heaven, we know Satan is active. The text says that he was given the key to the bottomless pit. When we study Revelation 20, we will find Satan himself is bound and thrown into the bottomless pit, where he will remain for a thousand years. But for now, he has the key to the pit. He can unlock it and let loose a great cloud of smoke that darkens the air.

John continues: "Then out of the smoke locusts came upon the earth. And to them was given power, as the scorpions of the earth have power. They were commanded not to harm the grass of the earth, or any green thing, or any tree, but only those men who do not have the seal of God on their foreheads" (verses 3, 4).

Every time we encounter locusts in the Old Testament, one of two things is happening. Either literal locusts or enemy armies that invade like a swarm of locusts are bringing devastation, destruction, disaster, and death. Jeremiah puts it this way. "The LORD of hosts has sworn by Himself: 'Surely I will fill you with men, as with locusts, and they shall lift up a shout against you' " (Jeremiah 51:14). The locusts are the invading armies that sweep across the land, destroying everything in their path.

At times in the Old Testament, literal locusts were the instruments that brought God's judgments on those who rebelled against Him. One of the plagues that fell upon Egypt, as recorded in the book of Exodus, was locusts. A locust plague also fell upon Israel as a judgment for rebellion against God's law. Joel prophesies of the coming locust plague this way: "What the chewing locust left, the swarming locust has eaten; what the swarming locust left, the crawling locust has eaten; and what the crawling locust has left, the consuming locust has eaten" (Joel 1:4). In other words, the crops are utterly destroyed. There is nothing left. Locusts are a symbol of absolute destruction. In Revelation, as in the Old Testament, the coming of locusts is never good news; it is always bad news.

The first four trumpets deal with judgments of God on Israel, the pagan Western Roman Empire, and apostate Christianity. But what about the Eastern Roman Empire? You see, after the time of Constantine, the Roman Empire gradually separated into western and eastern spheres of influence, with two capitals—Rome in the west, and Constantinople in the east. Christianity in these two areas developed somewhat differently. That is why today we have the Roman Catholic Church, which developed in the west, and the Greek Orthodox Church, which developed in the east.

After the Western Roman Empire was destroyed by barbarian tribes and broken up into what would become the nations of Europe, what was taking place in the eastern part of the empire? The eastern part of the empire was geographically connected to the part of the world where Islam originated. Out of that part of the world, Islam swept across the eastern empire and into Europe like locusts bringing destruction as they attempted to conquer and spread the Muslim faith. That devastation is what the fifth trumpet brings to view. The Muslim invasion, like a judgment of God, shook Europe tremendously. Like smoke, it swept from the east across eastern Europe and then into western Europe. To the Christians in Europe, it was like being attacked by scorpions with poison in their tails. When nations rebel against God's revealed will, in mercy, He withdraws His protective hand so they can learn in sorrow what they failed to learn in a time of peace. God is not the author of war; Satan is. God is not the author of suffering and death; Satan is. God is not the author of natural disasters, political strife, or social chaos; Satan is. But God will use these calamities sometimes, bringing whole societies to their knees so they can see His will for their lives more clearly.

Here is something very fascinating. These scorpions were commanded not to harm anyone who had the seal of God on his or her forehead. Faithful followers of God are symbolized by the grass and green, living things that the scorpion invasion was not to harm. The psalmist describes those who are faithful to Christ and refuse to compromise their integrity:

Blessed is the man
Who walks not in the counsel of the ungodly,
Nor stands in the path of sinners,
Nor sits in the seat of the scornful;
But his delight is in the law of the LORD,

255

And in His law he meditates day and night.
He shall be like a tree
Planted by the rivers of water,
That brings forth its fruit in its season,
Whose leaf also shall not wither;
And whatever he does shall prosper (Psalm 1:1–3).

The righteous are like a flourishing green tree. Even in the midst of apostasy, during all these years of spiritual darkness, God would still have faithful people holding the banner of truth high while judgments from God swept across Europe.

The invasions that swept across Europe would not last forever. When God allows calamity to come, it is always for a limited time and for a specific purpose. God allows natural forces to play out. He does not always intervene, but His eternal purpose is to draw us close to him through all of life's circumstances. Notice how Revelation 9:5–10 carefully details the duration of these invasions from the east:

They [the locusts] were not given authority to kill them [those on whom God's judgments were falling], but to torment them for five months. Their torment was like the torment of a scorpion when it strikes a man. In those days men will seek death and will not find it; they will desire to die, and death will flee from them.

The shape of the locusts was like horses prepared for battle. On their heads were crowns of something like gold, and their faces were like the faces of men. They had hair like women's hair, and their teeth were like lions' teeth. And they had breast-plates like breastplates of iron, and the sound of their wings was like the sound of chariots with many horses running into battle. They had tails like scorpions, and there were stings in their tails. Their power was to hurt men five months.

What are these five months during which the judgments of God would fall upon the Eastern Roman Empire? Again, let's look at the math. In Bible times, months were 30 days. So five prophetic months are 150 prophetic days. And since a day in Bible prophecy symbolizes a year of literal time, these five months (150 days) represent 150 literal years. The Muslim invaders were to have the power to "hurt men" for 150 years. Do we find anything in history that corresponds to this 150-year period of judgment?

The Muslim Turks attacked the Byzantine Empire (another name for the Eastern Roman Empire) at the Battle of Bapheus on July 27, 1299.[1] Exactly 150 years later, on July 27, 1449, the Byzantine Empire collapsed! At that point, the Byzantine emperor had to get the permission of the Muslim sultan to occupy the throne.[2]

Again, we see Bible prophecy fulfilled precisely. The Bible predicts a judgment that would come from the east, like an invasion of locusts. It predicts they would bring destruction for 150 years. And history tells us that is exactly what happened!

The sixth trumpet—judgment on the Eastern Roman Empire intensifies

"Then the sixth angel sounded: And I heard a voice from the four horns of the golden altar which is before God, saying to the sixth angel who had the trumpet, 'Release the four angels who are bound at the great river Euphrates.' So, the four angels, who had been prepared for the hour and day and month and year, were released to kill a third of mankind" (verses 13–15).

It is fascinating that the prophecy in verses 5 and 9 accurately predicted 150 years of judgment due to the Muslim invasion of the Eastern Roman Empire and Europe. But it is even more fascinating and exciting to see the fulfillment of the prophecy in the sixth trumpet. John says that four angels had been prepared for an hour, day, month, and year, and now they are released to kill a third of mankind.

What does this time prophecy mean? How long is an hour, day, month, and year of prophetic time? We will have to do some calculations. Remember that in Bible times, a month was made up of 30 days and a year was 360 days. We can add up this time prophecy as follows:

1 prophetic year = 360 prophetic days = *360 literal years*
1 prophetic month = 30 prophetic days = *30 literal years*
1 prophetic day = *1 literal year*
1 prophetic hour = 1/24 of a prophetic day [1 literal year or 360 days] = *15 literal days*

Adding these together, we find that a prophetic hour, day, month, and year equal 391 years and 15 days of literal time. This prophecy says that under the sixth trumpet, the Muslim invaders would have 391 years and 15 days to bring judgment by invading the Eastern Roman Empire. If we take July 27, 1449 (the date the Muslim invaders established the zenith of their power under the fifth trumpet), as the starting point, and extend that by 391 years and 15 days, we arrive at the date August 11, 1840.

Here is something amazing. Josiah Litch was a preacher of the Advent movement that began with William Miller's studies in Daniel. In the 1800s, Litch began to predict that the Ottoman Empire (the Muslim's Turkish Empire) would fall on August 11, 1840. He based this on Revelation 9 and the time prophecy in the sixth trumpet. Litch's precise prediction was popularized in many newspapers across the United States. Many people thought he was crazy. They didn't believe him. Litch went over the prophecy again and again. He believed the biblical year-day principle applied to this prophecy. Despite the ridicule, he kept preaching his belief that the Ottoman Empire would end on August 11, 1840.

It happened exactly as predicted in Scripture. On August 11, 1840, the Treaty of London was signed by Britain, Prussia, Austria, and Russia, taking away the power of the Ottoman Empire! Josiah Litch didn't look so foolish. His interpretation and its fulfillment were widely reported in the press of the day. The fulfillment of that prophecy awakened the interest of thousands in the Scriptures and the Advent movement. It led to the great Second Advent revival that swept the United States and other countries in the 1840s. People saw that Christianity is based on solid biblical evidence.

The sixth trumpet goes on to describe a variety of judgments from God that would fall as a result of a rejection of God and His truth during the time of this trumpet. It concludes on an extremely negative note.

"The rest of mankind, who were not killed by these plagues, did not repent of the works of their hands, that they should not worship demons, and idols of gold, silver, brass, stone, and wood, which can neither see nor hear nor walk. And they did not repent of their murders or their sorceries or their sexual immorality or their thefts" (verses 20, 21).

These passages reveal an eternal truth stated by Jesus to the religious leaders in His day. In the Gospel of John, He says, "A little while longer the light is with you. Walk while you have the light, lest darkness overtake you; he who walks in darkness does not know where he is going. While you have the light, believe in the light, that you may become sons of light" (John 12:35, 36). Jesus, the Light of the world, shines in the heart of every person born in this world. He is the true Light that gives light to every person born into this world (John 1:9). His light shines in our hearts through His Holy Spirit. His light illuminates our minds through His Word. If we walk in that light, it will lead us to the kingdom of God. The devil attempts to obscure that light and shroud our minds in darkness. When individuals, churches, or nations fail to walk in the light that God graciously gives them, they are chained in the darkness of error and will eventually experience the judgments of God.

Summary of the first six trumpets

As we have seen, the trumpets herald God's judgments on those who persist in rejecting Him and His truth. The first trumpet announced His judgments on Jerusalem and the nation of Israel. Jerusalem was destroyed in A.D. 70. The second trumpet announced judgments upon the pagan Western Roman Empire for its rejection of Christianity and its persecution of Christians. The third trumpet announced judgments upon apostate Christianity. Under the fourth trumpet, those judgments intensified as the Christian church slipped deeper into apostasy and spiritual darkness, The fifth trumpet announced God's judgments on apostate Christianity in the Eastern Roman Empire. Muslim invaders swept in to conquer and convert. Those judgments intensified under the sixth trumpet until the prophecy was fulfilled in the 1840s.

The trumpets have taken us all the way from A.D. 70 to the 1840s when the Ottoman Empire crumbled. What is next on the horizon? There is an interlude here in Revelation before the seventh angel sounds his trumpet. But the sixth trumpet ends with a picture of continued rebellion against God. They "did not repent of the works of their hands" (verse 20). What are those works? Murders, sorceries, sexual immorality, and theft. Verses 20 and 21 aptly describe our twenty-first-century, end-time generation that continues in rebellion against God. We live in a materialistic, secular, godless society that worships anything and everything except God and righteousness. It's a generation filled with crime and unrestrained sexual immorality. Revelation 9 makes it plain that just as every generation in the past down through centuries has experienced God's judgments because of its sins and its rejection of His grace, so too will this society at the end of time.

Revelation chapters 8 and 9 span the centuries. Revelation's descriptions of the historical, political, social, and religious events have unfolded as prophecy predicted. These chapters are solemn appeals to be faithful to God. They are messages of love inviting us to respond to His grace. They contain urgent last-day truths for this generation.

In Revelation 9, God appeals to our hearts. He yearns for us to be among His faithful people who are ready to meet Jesus when He comes. He is urging us to repent of our waywardness and rebellion. He invites us to accept His righteousness in place of our unrighteousness, His strength in place of our weakness, His wisdom in the place of our folly, and His truth in place of our own self-styled ignorance. In Him, through Him, and because of Him, we can live victoriously through the final scenes of earth's history. We can thrive in the days ahead because He is the One who has never lost a battle with Satan. We need not fear the future because He is with us always, even to the end of the world (Matthew 28:20). His promise is sure. "I will never leave you nor forsake you" (Hebrews 13:5).

---

1. Alberto R. Treiyer, "The Chronology of Events in the History of Pachymeres Related to the Battle of Bapheus and the Beginning of the Ottoman Empire," *International Journal of Humanities and Social Science* 7, no. 8 (August 2017): 23, http://www.ijhssnet.com/journals/Vol_7_No_8_August_2017/4.pdf.

2. Josiah Litch, *The Probability of the Second Coming of Christ About A.D. 1843* (Boston, MA: David H. Ela, 1838), 146–158.

THE BITTERSWEET LITTLE BOOK

Revelation 10

1 I saw still another mighty angel coming down from heaven, clothed with a cloud. And a rainbow was on his head, his face was like the sun, and his feet like pillars of fire. **2** He had a little book open in his hand. And he set his right foot on the sea and his left foot on the land, **3** and cried with a loud voice, as when a lion roars. When he cried out, seven thunders uttered their voices. **4** Now when the seven thunders uttered their voices, I was about to write; but I heard a voice from heaven saying to me, "Seal up the things which the seven thunders uttered, and do not write them."

5 The angel whom I saw standing on the sea and on the land raised up his hand to heaven **6** and swore by Him who lives forever and ever, who created heaven and the things that are in it, the earth and the things that are in it, and the sea and the things that are in it, that there should be delay no longer,

7 but in the days of the sounding of the seventh angel, when he is about to sound, the mystery of God would be finished, as He declared to His servants the prophets.

8 Then the voice which I heard from heaven spoke to me again and said, "Go, take the little book which is open in the hand of the angel who stands on the sea and on the earth."

9 So I went to the angel and said to him, "Give me the little book."

And he said to me, "Take and eat it; and it will make your stomach bitter, but it will be as sweet as honey in your mouth."

10 Then I took the little book out of the angel's hand and ate it, and it was as sweet as honey in my mouth. But when I had eaten it, my stomach became bitter. **11** And he said to me, "You must prophesy again about many peoples, nations, tongues, and kings."

⁂

God is never caught by surprise. He is the ruler of the universe and guides the destinies of all humanity. At times, we face sorrow, tragedy, and disappointment, but He is there to lift us up, inspire us with hope, and place a new joy in our hearts. We are never left alone to face life's disappointments. Joseph was not left alone when his jealous brothers sold him into Egypt as a slave. Moses was not left alone when he was placed in a basket made of reeds by a fearful mother. Daniel was not left alone in the lions' den. The three Hebrews were not left alone in the fiery furnace. And we can be certain Jesus will never leave us alone in the trials, tragedies, and disappointments of life. The theme of Revelation 10 is the Christ who brings joy out of our sorrow, meaning out of our disappointments, and triumph out of apparent defeat. This is one of the most fascinating studies in the entire book of Revelation.

Just as there was a break between the sixth and seventh seals—with an entire chapter (chapter 7) intervening between them, so there is a break between the sixth and seventh trumpets. The sixth trumpet sounds at the end of Revelation 9, but the seventh angel doesn't sound his trumpet until Revelation 11:15.

The vision recorded in chapter 10 describes the historical development of God's true church. It reveals that in the last days, His people, like the early disciples, would experience deep disappointment. However, they would then rise to become a worldwide force for God, revealing His grace and truth to the world.

An angel with a little book

With chapters 8 and 9 as a background, let's see what Jesus is telling us in Revelation 10. John says,

> I saw still another mighty angel coming down from heaven, clothed with a cloud. And a rainbow was on his head, his face was like the sun, and his feet like pillars of fire. He had a little book open in his hand. And he set his right foot on the sea and his left foot on the land, and cried with a loud voice, as when a lion roars. When he cried out, seven thunders uttered their voices. Now when the seven thunders uttered their voices, I was about to write; but I heard a voice from heaven saying to me, "Seal up the things which the seven thunders uttered, and do not write them" (Revelation 10:1–4).

John records that this angel comes from heaven, clothed with a cloud. What does that mean? What is the significance of being clothed with a cloud?

As the children of Israel were journeying from Egypt to the Promised Land, God instructed Moses to build a portable sanctuary that could be set up and taken down to accompany them on their travels. When the sanctuary was finished, the Bible says that a "cloud covered the tabernacle of meeting, and the glory of the LORD filled the tabernacle. And Moses was not able to enter the tabernacle of meeting, because the cloud rested above it, and the glory of the LORD filled the tabernacle. Whenever the cloud was taken up from above the tabernacle, the children of Israel would go onward in all their journeys. But if the cloud was not taken up, then they did not journey till the day that it was taken up" (Exodus 40:34–37).

> In prophetic vision, John saw an angel come down from heaven. He was clothed with the glory of God. He had a book in his hand, and he stood with one foot on the land and the other on the sea. Standing on both the land and sea denotes that this angel has a message that is universal in nature.

Notice that twice in these verses, the cloud signifies "the glory of the LORD" filling the tabernacle. During the wilderness wanderings of the children of Israel, God led them in a cloud by day and a pillar of fire by night (Numbers 9:15–23). God's presence was in the cloud. Several times later in Israel's history, a cloud filled the sanctuary, and it was understood that this was the glory of God filling the temple (2 Chronicles 5:14; Ezekiel 10:4).

So when John sees an angel coming down from heaven clothed with a cloud, he understands that this angel is clothed with the glory of God. He comes from heaven bearing a message from God and clothed in the glory of God. He is speaking for God. Since this is a message directly from God's throne, it is of the utmost importance for everyone living on earth.

This angel also has a rainbow on his head. We saw previously that a rainbow encircles God's throne in heaven (Revelation 4:3). That rainbow, like the original one after the Flood, is a sign of God's promise to Noah and his descendants—that God would never again destroy the entire earth with a flood. The rainbow symbolizes God's justice against sin, combined with His mercy toward the sinner. God's justice is always tempered with mercy.

The angel has a "little book" open in his hand (Revelation 10:2). He says something in a "loud voice." John doesn't tell us what the angel said. But when the angel spoke, "the seven thunders uttered their voices" (verse 3).

We've seen that the number seven denotes perfection or completion in the Bible. So this is complete thunder, pure thunder speaking. Can we understand the meaning of this symbol?

Shortly before His crucifixion, Jesus prayed,

"Father, glorify Your name."

Then a voice came from heaven, saying, "I have both glorified it and will glorify it again."

Therefore, the people who stood by and heard it said that it had thundered. Others said, "An angel has spoken to Him" (John 12:28, 29).

God's voice sounded like thunder to those standing nearby.

Describing how God had delivered Him from His enemies, the psalmist uses these words: "The LORD thundered from heaven, and the Most High uttered His voice" (Psalm 18:13). When God came down on Mount Sinai to give the Ten Commandments, it sounded to the people like thunder (Exodus 19:16; 20:18). When we read about thunder in the Bible, we are reading about the voice of God. Thus, *seven* thunders emphasize the perfection and completeness of God's declarations to humankind.

John was on the verge of writing down what the seven thunders said, but he was instructed not to do so (Revelation 10:4). Wouldn't you like to know what these seven thunders said? We could speculate on what John heard the seven thunders say, but apparently, it was something that God decided it would be better for humanity not to know at that time. The Bible says, "The secret things belong to the LORD our God, but those things which are revealed belong to us and to our children forever" (Deuteronomy 29:29). God told John not to write because there are some things in this message that are not for you and me to understand. But He has revealed the things that He wants us to know, the things that are most important for us to understand.

The little book identified

What is the little book in the angel's hand? Verse 2 makes a point of the fact that the book in the angel's hand is open, suggesting a contrast to a closed book. It suggests that this book was once sealed or closed. Is there any book mentioned in Scripture that was once closed or sealed?

Yes, there is! At the close of the Old Testament book of Daniel, the angel Gabriel tells the prophet to "shut up the words, and seal the book until the time of the end"

(Daniel 12:4; see also verse 9). The book of Daniel was sealed until *the time of the end.* Now the book is *open* in the hand of the angel. This tells us that Revelation 10 relates to the end time. The book that was sealed in Daniel 12:4 is now unsealed for God's people to understand it.

What specific aspect of Daniel would be unsealed at the end time? Daniel understood the prophecy of the great metallic image (Daniel 2). He understood the prophecy of chapter 7 and the sequence of beasts representing kingdoms. He even understood something of the symbolism of the little horn power that would arise out of the Roman Empire. But the prophecy that begins in Daniel 8:14—the prophecy of the cleansing of the sanctuary and the 2,300 days—Daniel admits, "I was astonished by the vision, but no one understood it" (verse 27). The long time prophecy of 2,300 years and all the implications of the cleansing of the sanctuary were things that Daniel never fully understood even though Gabriel came to try to help him understand. So the angel told Daniel, "Seal up the vision, for it refers to many days in the future" (verse 26). It was this portion of Daniel's book—the prophetic portion having to do with time far down in the future—that would be sealed right down to the time of the end.

Now this glorious angel descends from the throne of God with a little book open in his hand and declares that "there should be delay no longer, but . . . the mystery of God would be finished" (Revelation 10:6, 7).

At the end of time, Daniel's sealed book would be unsealed. God's people would study the time prophecies having to do with the judgment and the final cleansing of His sanctuary. They would be thrilled with what they found in the little open book and go out to proclaim God's last-day message with great power.

No more delay

In prophetic vision, John saw an angel come down from heaven. He was clothed with the glory of God. He had a book in his hand, and he stood with one foot on the land and the other on the sea. Standing on both the land and sea denotes that this angel has a message that is universal in nature. It is for all humanity everywhere. He has a message of the greatest importance from God. Through him, God's voice thunders through the earth with a message for all humankind at the end of time.

John records the words of this angel. "The angel whom I saw standing on the sea and on the land raised up his hand to heaven and swore by Him who lives forever and ever, who created heaven and the things that are in it, the earth and the things that are in it, and the sea and things that are in it, that there should be delay no longer, but in the days of the sounding of the seventh angel, when he is about to

sound, the mystery of God would be finished, as He declared to His servants the prophets" (Revelation 10:5–7).

When the Bible pictures an angel with one foot on the earth and one foot on the sea, denoting a universal message, and when that angel lifts his hand to heaven in a solemn oath, that message must be one of utmost importance. When the Bible pictures an angel coming from the very presence of God accompanied by His thundering voice, it must be a message we should pay attention to. The angel swears by Him who lives forever and who created all things in heaven, earth, and sea. In other words, he is bringing a message from the Creator that Daniel's time prophecy of the 2,300 days (years) is unsealed—that there shall be no more delay. It is time for God's judgment hour to begin and for His last-day message to go to the ends of the earth.

In the King James Version, the angel says, "There shall be time no longer" (verse 6). In the New Testament, there are two words for "time." One word has to do with an event that happens, for example, July 4 or December 25. These are dates on a calendar; they are specific points of time. The word for a point of time in the Greek language is χαιρος (*chairos*). If something happens at a point in time, you use that word. However, that is not the word used in Revelation 10:6 when it says, "There should be time no longer." The word used here is χρονος (*chronos*). That's the Greek word from which we get the English words *chronology* and *chronometer. Chronos* is not a specific point in time but a "length of time" or a "period of time."

The angel in Revelation 10 is saying, "There should be a *period of time* or a *length of time* no longer." The time prophecies of Daniel take us down the sequence of the ages—Babylon, Media-Persia, Greece, Rome, and onward to the breakup of the pagan Roman Empire, the rise of the little horn (papal Rome), the judgment, and the coming of Jesus. The longest time prophecy in the Bible is the 2,300-year prophecy relating to the judgment. That chronology, that time period, would run out in 1844. There would be delay no longer. The clock had struck the hour. God's great judgment hour had come, and God's people would go out preaching the soon return of Jesus to the whole world in light of the special time they lived in.

The mystery of God is finished

At the close of the 2,300 years, God would raise up a divine movement of destiny to proclaim His last-day message in the power of the Holy Spirit to the ends of the earth. As a result of this mighty spiritual revival, the mystery of God would be finished. The completion of God's plan would be accomplished. God's purposes would be fulfilled, and the gospel commission completed.

What is the *mystery* of God? Paul wrote, "To them [the saints] God willed to make known what are the riches of the glory of this mystery among the Gentiles: which is Christ in you, the hope of glory" (Colossians 1:27). According to the apostle Paul, the mystery of God to be finished in the last days is "Christ in you, the hope of glory." Yes, it is the gospel, the good news, of salvation in Jesus, the truths of His Word, and the glory of His second coming. But this mystery is not only something to be *proclaimed*. It is something to be *lived*! It is something we show in our daily lives. It is Christ in us, revealing His compassion, kindness, and forgiveness. In the last days of earth's history, Jesus sends out His people into a world of selfishness, greed, bitterness, and anger, not simply to proclaim with their lips but to demonstrate with their lives. We are to internalize the gospel message of the little book that is open in the hand of the angel. That is what John's vision in Revelation 10 turns to next.

Eating the little book

Then the voice which I heard from heaven spoke to me again and said, "Go, take the little book which is open in the hand of the angel who stands on the sea and on the earth."

So I went to the angel and said to him, "Give me the little book."

And he said to me, "Take and eat it; and it will make your stomach bitter, but it will be as sweet as honey in your mouth."

Then I took the little book out of the angel's hand and ate it, and it was as sweet as honey in my mouth. But when I had eaten it, my stomach became bitter. And he said to me, "You must prophesy again about many peoples, nations, tongues, and kings" (verses 8–11).

What does it mean to take the prophecies of Daniel and eat them? It means to internalize them, live in the joy that comes from following God, and rejoice in Christ—the One who holds this world in His hands and is coming soon to take us home. The psalmist wrote,

How sweet are Your words to my taste,
Sweeter than honey to my mouth! (Psalm 119:103).

The prophet Jeremiah testified,

Your words were found, and I ate them,
And Your word was to me the joy and rejoicing of my heart (Jeremiah 15:16).

This group of end-time people were to take the prophecies of Daniel, the words of God, and eat them—take them into their life. They would find these prophecies sweet as honey in their mouth but bitter in their stomach.

Sweetness turns to bitterness

These early believers in the advent, or coming, of Jesus were so excited when they saw the prophecies of Daniel coming to a close in the early 1800s. "Jesus is coming!" they told each other. "Jesus is coming!" they told the world. But they were bitterly disappointed when His coming was delayed and He didn't return as soon as they expected.

In the early 1800s, God raised up faithful men and women around the world who fervently believed Jesus was coming soon. These early Adventists studied Revelation 10. They studied Daniel. As they did so, they concluded that the sanctuary that was to be cleansed at the end of the 2,300-year prophecy was the earth and that it would be cleansed by fire at the second coming of Jesus. They learned that the 2,300 years were to end in 1844. They traced and retraced Daniel's prophecy and became convinced that Jesus would return in 1844, at the close of the prophecy. As they studied the prophecy further and refined their understanding, these early Adventist believers settled on the date of October 22, 1844. They were sure Jesus would come on that day.

Advent preachers arose to warn the world of what they had learned in the prophecies of Daniel. William Miller in the United States; Manuel Lacunza, a Jesuit priest, in South America; Edward Irving in Great Britain; Johann Bengel in Germany; Joseph Wolff in Asia; and many others spread the message—Jesus is coming! They didn't all preach the date of October 22, 1844, but they all looked for Jesus to come soon. In the United States, many followed the belief that October 22, 1844, was the date.

There was a worldwide spiritual revival and anticipation of Jesus' return in the 1840s. It was so sweet in their mouths! It was like honey to think that soon they would be with their Savior. Then October 22, 1844, arrived—and Jesus didn't return!

They had been so certain that He was coming. Many had sold their possessions, believing they wouldn't need them anymore. They had settled all their earthly affairs. But now He hadn't come! They were bitterly disappointed. They wept and wept. As Revelation predicted, the little book was sweet as honey in their mouths but bitter in their stomachs.

The great disappointment at the cross

Shouldn't they have known better? Didn't Jesus say that no one knew the hour of His coming—not even the angels in heaven (Matthew 24:36)?

We shouldn't judge them too harshly. Their disappointment in 1844 wasn't the only one that has taken place in connection with the followers of Christ. They weren't the only ones to be mistaken. Christ's disciples in the first century made a similar mistake. They overlooked the prophecies in the Old Testament that predicted the Messiah's suffering and death. Right up until the Crucifixion, they were looking for Jesus to set up His kingdom on earth. He tried to prepare them for His death, but they didn't listen because they were so certain He would soon usher in His kingdom. There are two kinds of prophecies in the Old Testament that describe the coming of Jesus as the Messiah. One group focuses on His first coming as a suffering servant—the Lamb of God bearing our sins, and on His role as the Messiah, ushering in the kingdom of grace. These prophecies foretell the birth, life, and death of Christ. The second group of Old Testament prophecies predicts Christ's coming as a King to restore the Messianic kingdom of glory. They describe the majesty of His second coming. The disciples misunderstood the prophecies. They thought He was coming to earth to set up His glorious kingdom, and when He went to the cross, they were bitterly disappointed. When Christ died on the cross, His followers were devastated. Their hopes were crushed. Their dreams were smashed like a bottle thrown against a brick wall and shattered in pieces.

> Out of the disciples' bitter disappointment came a deeper understanding of God's Word and a clearer purpose for their lives. The darkness that engulfed the cross that Friday, filling their lives with sorrow, gave way to the light of a new day on Resurrection morning.

Beginning in disappointment, ending in joy

Out of the disciples' bitter disappointment came a deeper understanding of God's Word and a clearer purpose for their lives. The darkness that engulfed the cross that Friday, filling their lives with sorrow, gave way to the light of a new day on Resurrection morning. Hope once again dawned in their hearts. Christ had risen! And the world must know of His saving grace. God poured out His Spirit powerfully on these disciples, and they went out preaching the gospel to the world. The New Testament Church was raised up after the disappointment of the cross in A.D. 31. The Advent movement was raised up after the disappointment of A.D. 1844. Both movements were born out of disappointment to preach the gospel to the world. What happened in the first century to launch the Christian church would happen in a similar way in the end. Christ's last-day disciples would study the prophecies anew and discover their mistake. The sanctuary to be cleansed at the end of the 2,300 years was not the earth at Jesus' second coming. It was the sanctuary in heaven—the beginning of a special work of judgment. Like the first-century disciples, these early Adventists went out to preach the gospel message. Additionally, they especially emphasized the judgment going on in heaven. Notice the parallels between the disappointment at the cross and the disappointment in 1844.

The early church
1. Students of prophecy
2. Believed Christ would set up an earthly kingdom
3. Bitterly disappointed
4. Directed attention to the ministry of Christ in the sanctuary
5. Preached a message of Christ's grace and Bible truth to the world

The last-day church
1. Students of prophecy
2. Believed Christ would set up an earthly kingdom
3. Bitterly disappointed
4. Directed attention to the ministry of Christ in the sanctuary
5. Preached a message of Christ's grace and Bible truth to the world

God brings joy out of disappointment. Out of the disappointment of the cross, God brought joy and a movement that went to the then-known world with the good news of salvation in Jesus. Out of the disappointment of 1844, God raised up an end-time movement to prepare men and women for the return of Jesus.

To those disappointed people in the time of the end, the angel says, "You must prophesy again about many peoples, nations, tongues, and kings" (Revelation 10:11). God says, "I have a message for you to take to the ends of the earth to every nation and language." We will be looking at that threefold message in Revelation 14. Just as He sent out those disappointed early Christians, God would take this bitterly disappointed small group of people at the time of the end and commission them to go to the entire world with a message to prepare men and women for the return of Jesus.

Revelation 10 portrays a group of people raised up, through a bittersweet experience, to go to the ends of the earth proclaiming the message of Jesus until He comes again. Revelation 10 speaks of our day. It speaks not only of a task begun but a task that is to be finished. It speaks of a task that begins in disappointment but ends in glory and in power.

THE TWO WITNESSES

Revelation 11

1 Then I was given a reed like a measuring rod. And the angel stood, saying, "Rise and measure the temple of God, the altar, and those who worship there. **2** But leave out the court which is outside the temple, and do not measure it, for it has been given to the Gentiles. And they will tread the holy city underfoot for forty-two months. **3** And I will give power to my two witnesses, and they will prophesy one thousand two hundred and sixty days, clothed in sackcloth."

4 These are the two olive trees and the two lampstands standing before the God of the earth. **5** And if anyone wants to harm them, fire proceeds from their mouth and devours their enemies. And if anyone wants to harm them, he must be killed in this manner. **6** These have power to shut heaven, so that no rain falls in the days of their prophecy; and they have power over waters to turn them to blood, and to strike the earth with all plagues, as often as they desire.

7 When they finish their testimony, the beast that ascends out of the bottomless pit will make war against them, overcome them, and kill them. **8** And their dead bodies will lie in the street of the great city which spiritually is called Sodom and Egypt, where also our Lord was crucified. **9** Then those from the peoples, tribes, tongues, and nations will see their dead bodies three-and-a-half days, and not allow their dead bodies to be put into graves. **10** And those who dwell on the earth will rejoice over them, make merry, and send gifts to one another, because these two prophets tormented those who dwell on the earth.

11 Now after the three-and-a-half days the breath of life from God entered them, and they stood on their feet, and great fear fell on those who saw them. **12** And they heard a loud voice from heaven saying to them, "Come up here." And they ascended to heaven in a cloud, and their enemies saw them. **13** In the same hour there was a great earthquake, and a tenth of the city fell. In the earthquake seven thousand people were killed, and the rest were afraid and gave glory to the God of heaven.

14 The second woe is past. Behold, the third woe is coming quickly.

15 Then the seventh angel sounded: And there were loud voices in heaven, saying, "The kingdoms of this world have become the kingdoms of our Lord and of His Christ, and He shall reign forever and ever!" **16** And the twenty-four elders who sat before God on their thrones fell on their faces and worshiped God, **17** saying:

"We give You thanks, O Lord God Almighty,

The One who is and who was and who is to come,
Because You have taken Your great power and reigned.
18 The nations were angry, and Your wrath has come,
And the time of the dead, that they should be judged,
And that You should reward Your servants the prophets and the saints,
And those who fear Your name, small and great,
And should destroy those who destroy the earth."

19 Then the temple of God was opened in heaven, and the ark of His covenant was seen in His temple. And there were lightnings, noises, thunderings, an earthquake, and great hail.

In Revelation 10, we left God's people experiencing the sweet joy of expecting Jesus to come on October 22, 1844, followed by the bitter disappointment when that expectation proved wrong. They had been so certain. They had gone over the prophecy of Daniel 8:14 again and again—"For two thousand three hundred days; then the sanctuary shall be cleansed." They interpreted this to mean that the earth would be cleansed by fire at the Second Coming. They were correct on the date but wrong on the meaning of the sanctuary. In time, they came to understand that the sanctuary to be cleansed at the end of the 2,300 years was not the earth but the sanctuary in heaven. The subject of the sanctuary was the key that unlocked their bitter disappointment. And the sanctuary—or temple—is the focus of the opening verses of Revelation chapter 11.

Measuring the temple

John writes, "Then I was given a reed like a measuring rod. And the angel stood saying, 'Rise and measure the temple of God, the altar, and those who worship there. But leave out the court which is outside the temple, and do not measure it; for it has been given to the Gentiles. And they will tread the holy city underfoot for forty-two months' " (Revelation 11:1, 2).

Those preaching that Jesus would return in 1844 thought the sanctuary was the earth. They were looking to earth rather than heaven. Chapter 11 points them to the solution for their mistake. God is saying, "Get your eyes off of earth and focus on the heavenly temple and measure it."

What does it mean to measure the temple?

In Scripture, measuring is always associated with some form of judgment. For example, Jesus said, "With what judgment you judge, you will be judged; and with the measure you use, it will be measured back to you" (Matthew 7:2). So when the angel tells John to measure the temple, he is talking about judgment in the temple. In the Old Testament, judgment has to do with restoration, setting things right, and vindication. In Zechariah chapter 2, the prophet pictures someone measuring the temple and worshipers coming to preserve and restore it. In Ezekiel, measuring the temple included a restoration of the temple (Ezekiel 43:4–9). Additionally, the judgment scene Daniel saw in vision in Daniel 7:9–14 portrays God's restoration of His eternal kingdom as God's cosmic judgment sits before the whole universe.

What happens in the judgment? First, the judgment vindicates God. Satan claimed that God was unfair, unjust, and arbitrary. The judgment proves that God is just and fair in His dealing with sin during the great controversy between good and evil. It proves that Satan's accusations are false. The judgment shows that those who are lost eternally are lost because of their own choices and not because of God's arbitrary selection. He has done everything He could to save every human being.

The cosmic judgment in heaven's celestial sanctuary reveals God's justice and mercy before the universe. It establishes forever in the light of Christ's sacrifice on the cross that He is worthy to receive the kingdom and reign forever and ever. In Revelation 11, the attention of men and women is directed from earth to heaven, where God sits in judgment, finishing His work on earth. In the blazing light of heaven's sanctuary, the truth about Jesus as our dying Lamb, our living Priest, and our coming King is restored. Truths long lost sight of in the rubbish of error are brought to light. Tradition gives way to Bible truth, and the message of Christ is powerfully proclaimed.

Remember the angel's statement to Daniel? "For two thousand three hundred days; then the sanctuary shall be cleansed" (Daniel 8:14). This cleansing of the sanctuary in heaven was illustrated in Israel's earthly sanctuary by the yearly Day of Atonement. Notice that the angel tells John to measure "the temple of God, the altar, and those who worship there" (Revelation 11:1). This is a reference to Day of Atonement symbolism. The only place in the Bible where we find this same exact sequence—temple of God, altar, and those that worship there—is Leviticus 16:33. Chapters 16 and 23 of Leviticus describe the Day of Atonement in the Old Testament sanctuary ritual. It symbolized God's final judgment and the end of sin. On that day, every Israelite was to fast, or afflict his or her soul. That means that they were to search their hearts and repent of their sins. Revelation 11:1, 2 is talking about a final judgment, a final call to all humanity to repent—a final call to accept God's grace and live in harmony with His will. John points us beyond the persecution of the Dark Ages and the disappointment of God's people in Revelation 10 to the final triumph of the kingdom of God in the judgment.

> The cosmic judgment in heaven's celestial sanctuary reveals God's justice and mercy before the universe. It establishes forever in the light of Christ's sacrifice on the cross that He is worthy to receive the kingdom and reign forever and ever.

The court of the Gentiles

The angel tells John not to measure the court, for it has been given to the Gentiles (Revelation 11:2). What does this mean?

In the Old Testament sanctuary, there was an outer court often called "the court of the Gentiles." Gentiles were not allowed to enter the temple; they could go no further than this outer court. In the judgment now taking place in the sanctuary in heaven, God's people enter into that sanctuary by faith. They are secure in the judgment covered by the righteousness of Jesus. If you don't enter the sanctuary by faith, you are not secure in Jesus. You are outside, in the court with the Gentiles. Inside the sanctuary, there is no way you can be lost. Outside the sanctuary, there is no salvation.

The angel tells John to leave out the court of the Gentiles when he measures the temple. The Gentiles symbolize those who oppose God and His truth. They have rebelled against God. They are trying to destroy God's people and stamp out God's truth. They are treading the holy city underfoot.

These opponents of God will continue to tread down the truth for forty-two months. Remember, a month in Bible times consisted of 30 days. Forty-two prophetic months equal 1,260 prophetic days. We find this same time period—1,260 days—in the next verse in connection with the "two witnesses," and we will consider it in detail at that point.

The Gentiles were excluded from the Jewish sanctuary, but did that mean no Gentile could be saved? Not at all. You see, there were Gentiles who converted to the Jewish religion. They worshiped the God of heaven. Beyond that, when Jesus died on the cross, He died for every person on earth—Jew or Gentile, male or female. The apostle Paul stressed the fact that in Jesus Christ, all these distinctions were abolished. He wrote to the Christians at Galatia: "For as many of you as were baptized into Christ have put on Christ. There is neither Jew nor Greek, there is neither slave nor free, there is neither male nor female; for you are all one in Christ Jesus. And if you are Christ's, then you are Abraham's seed, and heirs according to the promise" (Galatians 3:27–29).

The Gentiles mentioned in Revelation 11:2 symbolize those who oppose God and His truth. God is saying, "Throughout history, unbelievers have tried to stamp out My truth, but by faith, you will be safe with Me in the sanctuary in heaven. You will stand justified in the judgment by the blood of Jesus."

The two witnesses

"I will give power to my two witnesses, and they will prophesy one thousand two hundred and sixty days, clothed in sackcloth."

These are the two olive trees and the two lampstands standing before the God of the earth. And if anyone wants to harm them, fire proceeds from their mouth and destroys their enemies. And if anyone wants to harm them, he must be killed in this manner. These have power to shut heaven, so that no rain falls in the days of their prophecy; and they have power over waters to turn them to blood, and to strike the earth with all plagues, as often as they desire (Revelation 11:3–6).

There have been many attempts to identify these two witnesses. Some have suggested Moses and Elijah—two individuals in the Bible who were taken to heaven. Let's look at what the angel says about these two witnesses and see whether we can determine who or what they are.

• They prophesy for 1,260 days clothed in sackcloth.

- They are symbolized by two olive trees and two lampstands.
- They can destroy their enemies by fire that proceeds from their mouths.
- They can shut heaven so that no rain falls.
- They can turn water to blood and strike the earth with all kinds of plagues.

In Zechariah 4, the prophet saw two olive trees on either side of a golden lampstand—the same imagery that we find here in Revelation 11. Zechariah is told that this represents "the two anointed ones, who stand beside the Lord of the whole earth" (Zechariah 4:14). The olive trees are feeding their oil into the lampstand so that it continues to burn and give light. We are reminded of what the psalmist wrote: "Your word is a lamp to my feet and a light to my path" (Psalm 119:105). Trees and lampstands are also a symbol of God's people in the book of Revelation (Revelation 9:4 and 1:20). Oil represents the Holy Spirit (Zechariah 4:6). John's vision in Revelation 11 is describing God's people proclaiming His Word in the power of the Holy Spirit to lighten the world with the glory of God.

God's two witnesses can prophesy and keep rain from falling for as long as they predict. They can turn water to blood and smite the earth with plagues. Can the Word of God do those things? Elijah, by the Word of God, predicted three years in which no rain would fall on Israel, and it happened just as he said. He prayed to God, and the rain returned after the false prophets of Baal failed to end the drought (1 Kings 17; 18). Moses, by the Word of God, brought plagues of all kinds on the Egyptians, including turning water to blood, because Pharaoh refused to let God's people go free (Exodus 7).

The Word of God says that those who resist His Word and remain His enemies will die. "The wages of sin is death" (Romans 6:23). Those who seek to harm the Scriptures will be consumed by the fire that comes from their mouth. God says, "Because you speak this word, behold, I will make My words in your mouth fire, and this people wood, and it shall devour them" (Jeremiah 5:14). God's Word pronounces judgment upon all those who reject it. His Word is like fire in the mouth.

Who are these two witnesses? Based on the characteristics given in Revelation 11, we can identify them as God's Word—the Old and New Testaments. Here is further evidence of this identification.

Jesus told the religious leaders of His day, "You search the Scriptures, for in them you think you have eternal life; and these are they which testify of Me" (John 5:39). The Greek word translated "testify" in this verse is μαρτυρέω (*martureō*). And the very same root word (μάρτυς) is used in Revelation 11:3 for the two witnesses. The two witnesses are the Scriptures that Jesus is talking about in John's Gospel. They are the Old and New Testaments, communicating God's light and truth to the world. Jesus says, "The Scriptures are My witnesses; they testify of Me."

One thousand two hundred and sixty days (42 months)

These two witnesses, the Old and New Testaments, "will prophesy one thousand two hundred and sixty days, clothed in sackcloth" (Revelation 11:3). This is the same time period as the forty-two months during which the Gentiles (those who oppose God's truth) will tread the holy city underfoot (verse 2). So we have the enemies of God treading underfoot His truth for 1,260 days (42 × 30 = 1,260), and we have God's two witnesses, the Old and New Testaments, prophesying against them during this same time.

> The two witnesses, the Old and New Testaments, had testified against the opponents of God all during the 1,260 years. The voices of the biblical prophets spoke through God's Word as men and women of faith taught it.

By now, we know that 1,260 prophetic days represent 1,260 actual years. What does it mean that the Old and New Testaments will prophesy in sackcloth for 1,260 years?

For 1,260 years God's Scriptural witnesses would be clothed in sackcloth as they spoke judgment against the Gentile world, against those who were treading down God's truth. We've seen this period before in the seals and the trumpets. It is presented in several different ways in the prophecies of Daniel and Revelation.

Daniel 7:25 says that the little-horn power that would arise out of the breakup of the Roman Empire would persecute God's people "for a time and times (the literal meaning is two times) and half a time." A "time" is one year (360 days). "Times" is two years (720 days). And "half a time" is a half year (180 days). Added together, they equal 1,260 days.

Revelation 12:6 talks about 1,260 days of persecution for the people of God. Revelation 12:14 talks of a time, times, and half a time. Revelation 13:5 talks about 42 months. We find both 42 months and 1,260 days mentioned in Revelation 11. All of these prophecies are speaking of the same thing.

What is this period? It is the Dark Ages, the centuries from roughly 538 to 1798. During this time, the church descended into deep spiritual darkness. The teachings of the church often replaced the Scriptures. The decrees of priests and prelates were substituted for the commandments of God. The traditions of human religious leaders overshadowed the simplicity of the gospel. The Roman Church united with the secular power to exercise its authority over all of Europe. It persecuted those who remained faithful to God and resisted its false doctrines.

During these 1,260 years, the Word of God was obscured—His two witnesses were clothed in sackcloth. They were kept from the people and chained in monasteries. Their truths were hidden under a vast pile of tradition and ritual. Nevertheless, they still prophesied; they were still God's two witnesses. Even amid this spiritual darkness, God's Word was preserved, and there were those who cherished it and lived by its precepts.

There were those who stood faithful for God's truth, as the Bible testifies. But in comparison to the masses living in Europe, they were few. The Waldenses, John Huss, Jerome of Prague, Martin Luther, Ulrich Zwingli, John Calvin, John and Charles Wesley, and a host of other reformers were faithful to God's Word as they understood it. They did not comprehend the fullness of truth, but of this, they were certain: Christ was their Savior and the Bible was their guide. The two witnesses testified in sackcloth.

The two witnesses are killed

Revelation 11 goes on to say this about the two witnesses,

> When they finish their testimony, the beast that ascends out of the bottomless pit will make war against them, overcome them, and kill them. And their dead bodies will lie in the street of the great city which spiritually is called Sodom and Egypt, where also our Lord was crucified. Then those from the peoples, tribes, tongues, and nations will see their dead bodies three-and-a-half days, and not allow their dead bodies to be put into graves. And those who dwell on the earth will rejoice over them, make merry, and send gifts to one another, because these two prophets tormented those who dwell on the earth (verses 7–10).

The two witnesses will witness for 1,260 years, and at the end of that time, the beast from the bottomless pit will overcome them and kill them. Can we understand what is happening here?

Most Bible commentators place the beginning of the 1,260 days at A.D. 538. Why then? By that date, the Roman Empire had collapsed. Justinian, the pagan Roman emperor, handed over civil, political, and religious authority to Pope Vigilius II. Thus, the long period of the Roman Church's domination began.[1]

The two witnesses testified for 1,260 years—or until 1798. On February 10 of that year, the French general Berthier, on orders from Napoleon, marched into Rome unopposed and demanded the restoration of the Roman Republic under Napoleon. Pope Pius VI was taken captive and brought to France, where he died. This date marks the end of the Roman Church's secular authority.

The two witnesses, the Old and New Testaments, had testified against the opponents of God all during the 1,260 years. The voices of the biblical prophets spoke through God's Word as men and women of faith taught it. The witness of the Word kept the truth of the gospel alive during the long period of the Dark Ages, but a time of trouble was coming far greater than anyone might recognize.

Revelation 11:7 tells us that the beast that ascends from the bottomless pit would make war against the Scriptures and attempt to annihilate them. The beast is Satan, who has the key to the bottomless pit, as we saw in chapter 9. But Satan always works through his agents on earth. How would Satan, the beast from the bottomless pit, attack and attempt to destroy the Bible, the Word of God, around 1798 at the close of the 1,260 days?

Can you recall what significant event was taking place in world history at this time? The French Revolution began in 1789 and lasted for almost ten years. It was taking place right at the time that the 1,260 days of prophecy were coming to a close.

The French Revolution was known for its repudiation of Christianity and the church. Sir Walter Scott wrote the following referring to the atheistic stance taken by the leaders of the revolution: "The world for the first time heard an assembly of men, born and educated in civilization, and assuming the right to govern one of the finest of the European nations, uplift their united voice to deny the most solemn truth which man's soul receives, and renounce unanimously the belief and worship of a Deity."[2]

In the French Revolution, the government officially established the Cult of Reason as a state-sponsored atheistic religion intended to replace Christianity. A Festival of Reason was held nationwide on November 10, 1793. Churches across France were turned into Temples of Reason, and a living woman was enthroned as the Goddess of Reason. Bibles were burned in the streets. God, it was declared, did not exist, and death was pronounced to be an endless sleep. Satan worked through godless men to kill God's two witnesses. Their influence was destroyed. Their power was destroyed in the atheism that reigned. The Bible says that their dead bodies would "lie in the street of the great city which spiritually is called Sodom and Egypt, where also our Lord was crucified" (Revelation 11:8).

What city is spiritually like Sodom and Egypt?

Egypt enslaved God's people and refused to let them go. Pharaoh said, "Who is the LORD, that I should obey His voice to let Israel go? I do not know the LORD, nor will I let Israel go" (Exodus 5:2). When you think about Egypt, you think about a society with many gods but a society that denies the true God. What about Sodom? What do we think of in connection with Sodom? Gross immorality. Perversion. In the French Revolution at the end of the 1790s, when the 1,260 years were coming to a close, God's two witnesses—the Old and New Testaments—lay dead due to the atheism and immorality that ran rampant as normal restraints were loosed in revolution and bloodshed. In the French Revolution, a power arose that, like Egypt, said, "I don't know the Lord." A power arose that, like Sodom, glorified immorality.

Revelation 11:9 says that the bodies of God's two witnesses would lie unburied for three and a half days. Atheism was at its height in the French Revolution for approximately three and a half years. This period may be reckoned from November 26, 1793, when a decree issued in Paris abolished religion, to June 17, 1797, when the French government removed its restrictive religious laws. The prophecies of Scripture have been fulfilled with uncanny accuracy.

Today, we are still reaping the results of the philosophies undergirding the French Revolution in a secular, materialistic, godless, atheistic, sex-centered, morally twisted society. Any time the influence of God's Word is ignored, marginalized, or ridiculed, society will descend into social and moral chaos. As the NIV puts it, "Righteousness exalts a nation, but sin condemns any people" (Proverbs 14:34).

The two witnesses resurrected

Although the truth of God's Word was crushed and cast aside by the popular church, it would rise again in God's last-day movement. During the French Revolution, the two witnesses lay dead in the streets. However, the prophecy continues, "Now after the three-and-a-half days the breath of life from God entered them, and they stood on their feet, and great fear fell on those who saw them" (Revelation 11:11).

God's Word would come to life. There would be a mighty revival. Great fear would fall on those who saw God's Word once more become the living power of God unto salvation.

As the eighteenth century came to an end, God raised up men and women who were committed to taking the gospel to the ends of the earth. The 1790s were an era that launched missions around the world. One of the earliest of these was the Baptist Missionary Society, founded in 1792 by William Carey. Carey traveled to India and translated the Bible into dozens of Indian dialects. He believed Christ's command to take the gospel to the world was still relevant.

The London Missionary Society was founded in 1795, the Scottish Mission

Society in 1796, and the Netherlands Mission Society in 1797. The British Mission Society was founded in 1799, one year after the end of the Dark Ages in 1798. Since its inception, it has sent more than 9,000 missionaries around the world, to Africa, India, the West Indies, and the Middle East. It is not by accident that these worldwide mission endeavors arose at the end of the French Revolution. God's Word is a living Word, and although apparently "dead," it was still living in the hearts of believers and would rise to full life as Revelation's prophecies predicted.

> When the seventh angel sounds his trumpet, the mystery of God is finished! The kingdoms of this world have become the kingdoms of our Lord. Christ is victorious. Jesus wins, and Satan loses.

There is another remarkable aspect of this prophecy. Remember the angel's words to God's people at the end of Revelation 10, "You must prophesy again about many peoples, nations, tongues, and kings" (verse 11)? Following their bitter disappointment when Jesus did not return as they expected, these early Adventists discovered their mistaken understanding of the sanctuary. You will recall from our previous studies that they had understood the cleansing of the sanctuary to be the cleansing of the earth by fire. As they studied the prophecies of our Lord's return more carefully, they saw that the sanctuary of Daniel 8:14 referred to the heavenly sanctuary. The cleansing of the sanctuary described the Day of Atonement, or the judgment. This new understanding gave impetus to their preaching. They now proclaimed the message of God's grace, obedience to His law, and His soon return with a new power and urgency. They exalted the Word of God. It was the very heart and foundation of their faith.

God's two witnesses had been attacked, trampled down, and oppressed, but now they rose again to their rightful place as prophecy had predicted. They breathed new life into believers everywhere. The living Word of God is still alive today, and it is still speaking to human hearts, breathing new life into those who are willing to listen and follow its teachings.

The seventh trumpet—judgment on all humanity

Then the seventh angel sounded: And there were loud voices in heaven, saying, "The kingdoms of this world have become the kingdoms of our Lord and of His Christ, and He shall reign forever and ever!" And the twenty-four elders who sat before God on their thrones fell on their faces and worshiped God, saying:

"We give You thanks, O Lord God Almighty,
The One who is and who was and who is to come,
Because You have taken Your great power and reigned.
The nations were angry, and Your wrath has come,
And the time of the dead, that they should be judged,
And that You should reward Your servants the prophets and the saints,
And those who fear Your name, small and great,
And should destroy those who destroy the earth."

Then the temple of God was opened in heaven, and the ark of His covenant was seen in His temple. And there were lightnings, noises, thunderings, an earthquake, and great hail (Revelation 11:15–19).

Revelation 10:7 previews the sounding of the seventh trumpet in these words: "In the days of the sounding of the seventh angel, when he is about to sound, the mystery of God would be finished." The "mystery of God" is the gospel message of salvation in Jesus (Colossians 1:27). God's work of salvation is finished in the time of the seventh trumpet. The great controversy comes to a close. God's grace and salvation triumph over evil, and sin is eradicated from the universe.

Notice the specific items that are listed in Revelation 11:15–19 as taking place when the seventh trumpet sounds:

- The kingdoms of the world become the kingdoms of God and Jesus (verse 15).
- God reigns forever (verse 15).
- The dead are judged (verse 18).
- God rewards His people who serve Him (verse 18).
- God destroys those who destroy the earth (verse 18).
- The temple of God is opened in heaven (verse 19).
- There are cataclysmic eruptions of nature on earth—earthquakes, hail, and lightning (verse 19).

This is a picture of the end of time and of the events taking place in connection with the return of Jesus. The dead are judged. Judgment is pronounced on all humanity. Some are judged righteous because they have accepted Jesus' robe of righteousness empowering them to do good. Others are judged as unrighteous because they have refused to accept that robe. Jesus said, "The hour is coming in which all who are in the graves will hear His voice and come forth—those who have done good, to the resurrection of life, and those who have done evil, to the resurrection of condemnation" (John 5:28, 29). The angel told Daniel, "Those who sleep in the dust of the earth shall awake, some to everlasting life, some to shame and everlasting contempt" (Daniel 12:2).

When the seventh angel sounds his trumpet, the mystery of God is finished! The kingdoms of this world have become the kingdoms of our Lord. Christ is victorious. Jesus wins, and Satan loses. Righteousness triumphs. Truth reigns. Evil is defeated.

At this final trumpet, the temple of God is opened in heaven. The heart of the sanctuary is the Most Holy Place with the ark of the covenant. In the Old Testament sanctuary, which was a type, or pattern, of the great original in heaven, the glorious presence of God shone between the two angelic figures on the cover of the ark of the covenant. Within the ark was the law of God. No Jew would ever think of the Most Holy Place and the ark of the covenant without thinking about the law of God. Although we are saved by grace alone through faith, obedience to God's law reveals whether our faith is genuine. Genuine faith results in good works. The law of God is the basis, or the standard, of judgment.

Revelation 11:15–19 is an urgent, end-time appeal, in the light of God's eternal judgment, to live grace-filled, godly lives. It is heaven's final appeal to live obedient lives through His grace and by His power, in the light of the judgment hour. In Revelation chapter 12, we will discover how God has always had a people who were His loyal followers in every generation. Satan has attacked them viciously, but they have remained faithful. Come with me as we journey through the centuries and survey the cosmic conflict between good and evil.

---

1. Keum Young Ahn, et. al. "538 A.D. and the Transition from Pagan Roman Empire to Holy Roman Empire," *International Journal of Humanities and Social Science* 7, no. 1 (January, 2017), accessed April 5, 2020, https://www.ijhssnet.com/journals/Vol_7_No_1_January_2017/7.pdf.

2. Ellen G. White, *The Great Controversy Between Christ and Satan* (Mountain View, CA: Pacific Press®, 1911), 269, 270.

THE WOMAN, THE DRAGON, AND THE MALE CHILD

Revelation 12

1 Now a great sign appeared in heaven: a woman clothed with the sun, with the moon under her feet, and on her head a garland of twelve stars. **2** Then being with child, she cried out in labor and in pain to give birth.

3 And another sign appeared in heaven: behold, a great, fiery red dragon having seven heads and ten horns, and seven diadems on his heads. **4** His tail drew a third of the stars of heaven and threw them to the earth. And the dragon stood before the woman who was ready to give birth, to devour her Child as soon as it was born. **5** She bore a male Child who was to rule all nations with a rod of iron. And her Child was caught up to God and His throne. **6** Then the woman fled into the wilderness, where she has a place prepared by God, that they should feed her there one thousand two hundred and sixty days.

7 And war broke out in heaven: Michael and his angels fought with the dragon; and the dragon and his angels fought, **8** but they did not prevail, nor was a place found for them in heaven any longer. **9** So the great dragon was cast out, that serpent of old, called the Devil and Satan, who deceives the whole world; he was cast to the earth, and his angels were cast out with him.

10 Then I heard a loud voice saying in heaven, "Now salvation, and strength, and the kingdom of our God, and the power of His Christ have come, for the accuser of our brethren, who accused them before our God day and night, has been cast down. **11** And they overcame him by the blood of the Lamb and by the word of their testimony, and they did not love their lives to the death. **12** Therefore rejoice, O heavens, and you who dwell in them! Woe to the inhabitants of the earth and the sea! For the devil has come down to you, having great wrath, because he knows that he has a short time."

13 Now when the dragon saw that he had been cast to the earth, he persecuted the woman who gave birth to the male Child. **14** But the woman was given two wings of a great eagle, that she might fly into the wilderness to her place, where she is nourished for a time and times and half a time, from the presence of the serpent. **15** So the serpent spewed water out of his mouth like a flood after the woman, that he might cause her to be carried away by the flood. **16** But the earth helped the woman, and the earth opened its mouth and swallowed up the flood which the dragon had spewed out of his mouth. **17** And the dragon was enraged with the woman, and he went to make war with the rest of her offspring, who keep the commandments of God and have the testimony of Jesus Christ.

⁂

Revelation chapter 12 is the hinge upon which the whole book turns. Up until chapter 12, history is being revealed. Chapters 1–11 cover three sequences of sevens—the seven churches, the seven seals, and the seven trumpets—outlining events from the beginning of Christianity to the end of time from different perspectives. The second half of the book focuses on final events.

Chapter 12 deals with three characters—a woman, a dragon, and a male Child. These three are the main players in the great controversy—that centuries-long battle between good and evil that began in heaven and was transferred to earth. This chapter takes up four episodes in the great controversy:

- Episode 1: Satan attempts to kill Jesus. That doesn't work. God wins; Satan loses.
- Episode 2: Satan attempts to take over God's throne in heaven. That doesn't work. God wins; Satan loses.
- Episode 3: Satan attempts to destroy God's followers in every age. That doesn't work. God wins; Satan loses.
- Episode 4: Satan attempts to destroy Jesus' end-time church. That doesn't work. God wins; Satan loses.

This list of episodes is numbered in the order in which they are presented here in chapter 12. But you will note that they are somewhat out of order chronologically. Chronologically, Episode 2 took place before Episode 1. Satan tried to take over

God's throne in heaven before he tried to kill Jesus when He came to earth. However, we will take up these episodes in the order in which they appear in chapter 12. The important message is that God is always going to win, and Satan is always going to lose.

Episode 1—Satan attempts to kill Jesus

Now a great sign appeared in heaven: a woman clothed with the sun, with the moon under her feet, and on her head a garland of twelve stars. Then being with child, she cried out in labor and in pain to give birth.

And another sign appeared in heaven: behold, a great, fiery red dragon having seven heads and ten horns, and seven diadems on his heads. His tail drew a third of the stars of heaven and threw them to the earth. And the dragon stood before the woman who was ready to give birth, to devour her Child as soon as it was born. She bore a male Child who was to rule all nations with a rod of iron. And her Child was caught up to God and His throne (Revelation 12:1–5).

Let's look at the symbols being used here. What does the woman represent? In Scripture, a pure woman represents God's church, His faithful people. In the Old Testament, the faithful people of God, His true church, is often presented as a woman or the bride of Christ (Isaiah 54:5, 6; Jeremiah 6:2). The New Testament also follows this theme of the church as a woman, or the bride of Christ. Paul wrote to the Christians at Corinth, "For I am jealous for you with godly jealousy. For I have betrothed you to one husband, that I may present you as a chaste virgin to Christ" (2 Corinthians 11:2; see also Ephesians 5:25). In contrast, as we will see later in Revelation 17, an impure woman, a harlot, represents apostate Christianity. However, here in chapter 12, this woman represents the true church. Christ is born and establishes the Christian church.

Who does the dragon represent? We don't have to guess. Verse 9 tells us plainly that the dragon is "that serpent of old, called the Devil and Satan."

Whom does the male Child represent? Clearly, this is a reference to Jesus, who left heaven and came to earth to be the Child of Mary.

These three—the woman, the dragon, and the Child—are the main characters in this chapter. But we have seen this same trio before in Scripture. They are first introduced in the Garden of Eden at the beginning of the world. There in Eden, we have the woman, Eve. We have the dragon, the serpent who deceived her into sin. And we have the woman's "Seed," her Child, the promised Messiah. Do you recall what happened in Eden after Adam and Eve disobeyed God? The Bible records that God said to the serpent,

"I will put enmity
Between you and the woman,
And between your seed and her Seed;
He shall bruise your head,
And you shall bruise His heel" (Genesis 3:15).

God tells Satan that the Child, the promised Messiah, the Seed of Eve, will "bruise your head." Bitter conflict would take place between the serpent and the woman, between his followers and her seed. The "Seed" of the woman, the Messiah, would gain victory by crushing the head of the serpent while suffering a wound to His heel. Satan heard God's words and took them seriously. He knew Jesus would someday come to earth to inflict on him a mortal blow. Is it any wonder that he tried to kill Jesus as soon as He was born?

The woman John saw stands on the moon, is clothed with the sun, and has a garland of twelve stars encircling her head. As a symbol of God's true church, she is clothed with the glory of God. The birth of Christ brought in a new era. The types and shadows of the Old Testament, as symbolized by the moon, pointed forward to the coming of the Messiah. The lesser light would be surpassed by the glorious light of the gospel. Some have suggested that the twelve stars adorning the woman's head represent the twelve apostles of the early church. The woman is pregnant. In fact, she is in labor, and on the verge of giving birth (Revelation 12:2). The New Testament church, at the time of Christ's birth, is presented in this context. As Isaiah prophesied, "Unto us a Child is born, unto us a Son is given" (Isaiah 9:6).

Standing before the woman is a great fiery red dragon. He is waiting, prepared to "devour her Child as soon as it was born" (Revelation 12:4).

This is clearly a picture of what happened at the birth of Jesus in Bethlehem. Using King Herod as his agent, Satan tried to kill the Baby Jesus as soon as He was born. "Then Herod, when he saw that he was deceived by the wise men, was exceedingly angry; and he sent forth and put to death all the male children who were in Bethlehem and in all its districts, from two years old and under, according to the time which he had determined from the wise men" (Matthew 2:16). Satan remembered God's words in Eden. He knew Jesus had come to gain the promised victory and destroy his power.

Satan tried to kill Jesus, but the "Child was caught up to God and His throne"

(Revelation 12:5). Of course, Satan did manage to kill Jesus on the cross. Although it might have seemed like a victory for the dragon, Jesus' death on the cross dealt a mortal wound to the dragon's head. Satan was defeated. Christ's death on the cross proclaimed the immense love of God in the conflict between good and evil. It answered Satan's charges that God was unfair and unjust. It revealed that heaven was willing to do whatever necessary to save all humanity. In His life and in His death, Jesus revealed God's love to our sinful planet. Jesus was resurrected and returned to heaven. His death was a temporary blow to His heel. God won, and Satan lost this episode in the great controversy.

The "Seed" of the woman, the Messiah, would gain victory by crushing the head of the serpent while suffering a wound to His heel. Satan heard God's words and took them seriously. He knew Jesus would someday come to earth to inflict on him a mortal blow.

You may wonder why the events of chapter 12 are not listed in chronological order. Why does John describe Lucifer's rebellion in heaven after the rise of the Christian church and the devil's attempt to destroy Jesus? The thought patterns of people in Bible times were quite different from the thought patterns of the modern Western mind-set. At times in Revelation, the conclusion comes first, and then the events that lead up to the conclusion follow. The main purpose of chapter 12 is to introduce Christ's victory in the great controversy between good and evil. John begins there and then proceeds to Satan's rebellion in heaven that would eventually lead up to his vicious attack upon Christ and His church.

Episode 2—Satan attempts to take over God's throne in heaven

War broke out in heaven: Michael and his angels fought with the dragon; and the dragon and his angels fought, but they did not prevail, nor was a place found for them in heaven any longer. So the great dragon was cast out, that serpent of old, called the Devil and Satan, who deceives the whole world; he was cast to the earth, and his angels were cast out with him. Then I heard a loud voice saying in heaven, "Now salvation, and strength, and the kingdom of our God, and the power of His Christ have come, for the accuser of our brethren, who accused them before our God day and night, has been cast down" (verses 7–10).

289

Episode 2 brings us back to the very beginning of the great controversy in heaven. Sin originated with Satan in heaven itself. There was no reason for Satan's disobedience. There is no logical explanation for why Lucifer, this perfect angel, should have allowed pride and jealousy to take root in his heart and grow into rebellion against his Creator. The prophet Isaiah reveals what went on in Lucifer's mind that led to his all-out rebellion in the heavenly courts:

"How you are fallen from heaven,
O Lucifer, son of the morning!
How you are cut down to the ground,
You who weakened the nations!
For you have said in your heart:
'I will ascend into heaven,
I will exalt my throne above the stars of God;
I will also sit on the mount of the congregation
On the farthest sides of the north;
I will ascend above the heights of the clouds,
I will be like the Most High' " (Isaiah 14:12–14).

Satan's pride ripened into open revolt. He accused God of being unjust and unfair. He infected the angels with his doubts and accusations. Revelation 12:4 says, "His tail drew a third of the stars of heaven and threw them to the earth." A third of heaven's angels sided with Satan and joined him in rebellion.

The rebellion came to the point of open warfare. When God could no longer allow Satan to continue his rebellion, "war broke out in heaven: Michael and his angels fought with the dragon, and the dragon and his angels fought, but they did not prevail, nor was a place found for them in heaven any longer. So the great dragon was cast out, that serpent of old, called the Devil and Satan, who deceives the whole world; he was cast to the earth, and his angels were cast out with him" (verses 7–9).

We learned in Daniel 10 that Michael is one of the names in the Bible for Jesus Christ. It is the name used for the eternal, all-powerful Christ in direct conflict with Satan. It is the name of our victorious, everlasting Lord. When war broke out in heaven, the angels had to decide—would they follow Lucifer or Michael? Satan or Jesus? It's interesting that Michael is the leader of the loyal forces arrayed against Lucifer. We might have expected that God the Father would have been the One taking command of the forces resisting Satan in heaven. This suggests that Jesus may have been a major focus of Satan's jealousy and dissatisfaction with his role in heaven.

What was the nature of this war that broke out in heaven? Was it a physical war like those on earth that use weapons to kill the enemy? Or was it a war of ideas like those on earth against poverty or drugs? Or did it include elements of both kinds of war? We don't know. But at any rate, the conflict was physical enough that Satan and his angels were "cast out," "nor was a place was found for them in heaven any longer" (Revelation 12:9, 8). Here is one thing that we know for certain. Every angel had to make a decision for or against Christ. Whom would they follow? To whose voice would they listen? The loyal angels chose to be obedient to Christ's loving commands, while one-third of the angels listened to the voice of Lucifer, disobeyed God, and lost heaven. We, too, in this critical time of earth's history, are called to make a decision for or against Christ. We, too, are to declare whose side we are really on: Christ's or Satan's.

The dragon lost this opening episode in the great controversy. The theme of Revelation 12 is Jesus wins; Satan loses. "The accuser of our brethren, who accused them before our God day and night, has been cast down" (verse 10).

Episode 3—Satan attempts to destroy God's followers in every age

> Woe to the inhabitants of the earth and the sea! For the devil has come down to you, having great wrath, because he knows that he has a short time.
>
> Now when the dragon saw that he had been cast to the earth, he persecuted the woman who gave birth to the male Child. But the woman was given two wings of a great eagle, that she might fly into the wilderness to her place, where she is nourished for a time and times and half a time, from the presence of the serpent. So, the serpent spewed water out of his mouth like a flood after the woman, that he might cause her to be carried away by the flood. But the earth helped the woman, and the earth opened its mouth and swallowed up the flood which the dragon had spewed out of his mouth (verses 12–16).

Where did Satan and his angel followers go when they were cast out of heaven? They were cast down to this earth. Verse 12 says, "Woe to the inhabitants of the earth and the sea! For the devil has come down to you, having great wrath, because he knows that he has a short time." The apostle Peter puts it like this: "Be sober, be vigilant; because your adversary the devil walks about like a roaring lion, seeking whom he may devour" (1 Peter 5:8).

When the dragon lost the battle in heaven, he transferred his rebellion to earth. He successfully deceived Eve, who tempted Adam to join her in disobeying God and surrendering allegiance to Satan. As a result, Satan claims this world as his own.

Ever since Eden, he has continued the great controversy and tried to destroy God's followers in every age. We have seen in both Daniel and Revelation how his attacks against God and against God's faithful people intensified during the great spiritual darkness and apostasy of the Dark Ages. Satan's attempts to destroy the followers of God during this time are described in these verses as spewing out a flood of water in an attempt to carry away the woman, God's church (Revelation 12:15).

Whenever God's people remain faithful to Him, Satan is enraged, and he brings persecution upon them. Verse 14 says that the woman was forced to fly into the wilderness, "where she is nourished for a time and times and half a time." Revelation 12:6 says, "The woman fled into the wilderness, where she has a place prepared by God." God's people would be nourished in the wilderness. His Word would strengthen and sustain them. In the darkest times of their lives and amid their fiercest trials, they would find a "place prepared" for them by God.

In life's greatest challenges, God always prepares a place for His faithful followers. Possibly, as you are reading these pages, you are going through some of the greatest challenges of your life. These may be financial challenges, marital problems, family conflict, a life-threatening disease, or overwhelming discouragement. God has a place prepared for you. He is the One who says, "Come to Me, all you who labor and are heavy laden, and I will give you rest" (Matthew 11:28). There are rest and peace in His presence for weary and worn people. He has a place prepared in His heart just for you. There you will find comfort and strength. During the time of their greatest trial, God's people found refuge in the place He prepared for them.

We have seen this time period of the 1,260 days, or years, before. In chapter 11, we learned that the 1,260 days, the 42 months, and the time, times, and half time are all referring to the same period—538 to 1798—the Dark Ages, when church and state united. Spiritual darkness covered the earth. God's people had to "fly into the wilderness" in order to worship God. Millions of Christians were martyred during that time because they obeyed God and His Word instead of human traditions and rituals. Revelation 12:11 declares, "They overcame him [Satan] by the blood of the Lamb and by the word of their testimony, and they did not love their lives to the death."

Believers overcome the wiles of the evil one through faith in Christ's atoning sacrifice for their sins. In Christ, they are set free from the guilt and grip of sin. They are no longer in bondage to their sinful natures. His grace has set them free. They overcome "through the blood of the Lamb." Christ's victory over Satan on the cross becomes their victory. Their lives are a living testimony of His grace, and day by day, they testify of His love. He has overcome the grave, so all fear of death is gone. Their testimony is fearless because they serve the Christ who has conquered death itself.

At times, the flood that Satan sent to destroy God's people seemed about to overwhelm them. But God protected His people. "The earth opened its mouth and swallowed up the flood which the dragon had spewed out of his mouth" (verse 16). Toward the end of the 1,260 years in the wilderness, a new world was discovered. America became a place where those who were persecuted for their faith could find relief. There the devil's flood was swallowed up. God won, and Satan lost. But the dragon was still intent on continuing the great controversy.

Episode 4—Satan attempts to destroy Jesus' end-time church

As we look at the history of Satan's attacks down through the centuries since Eden, it often seems that he was successful in drawing men and women away from God. In every age, only a small number remained faithful to the God of heaven, compared to the great majority who followed the dragon. Although it may seem that Satan was winning the great controversy, there were always those who "overcame him by the blood of the Lamb and by the word of their testimony" (verse 11). They "washed their robes and made them white in the blood of the Lamb" (Revelation 7:14).

You see, it's not a matter of numbers. Truth is not determined by a majority vote. Satan continues to lose, and God continues to win in the great controversy. But this only makes the devil more determined never to stop attacking God's people. "The dragon was enraged with the woman, and he went to make war with the rest of her offspring, who keep the commandments of God and have the testimony of Jesus Christ" (Revelation 12:17).

The dragon made war against God in heaven. He made war with Jesus on earth and tried to destroy Him. He has made war with God's followers down through the ages. And now, enraged and desperate, he goes "to make war with the rest of her offspring" (verse 17). Who are they?

Throughout salvation history in the great controversy between good and evil, God has always had a people who have remained loyal to Him. He has always had a remnant—those who remained true to His Word while the majority departed from the faith. God's faithful remnant people living in the last days are the offspring of all those generations who have gone before—the apostles, the martyrs, the Reformers, the faithful men and women who stood for truth during all those long, dark centuries.

Can we identify this end-time remnant?

Verse 17 gives two identifying characteristics of this last-day group with whom the dragon is enraged and with whom he makes war. First, they keep the commandments of God. In the last days before Jesus returns, God is going to have a people who keep His commandments—not because they believe that obeying the commandments will save them. Not because they are trying to earn salvation. They are keeping God's commandments because they love Him—because they want to please Him and show their loyalty to Him. Jesus said, "If you love Me, keep My commandments" (John 14:15). Love is the most powerful motive for obedience. When we grasp even a glimpse of His love at the cross, our hearts are broken. We long to serve Him. As the apostle John states, "We love Him because He first loved us" (1 John 4:19). Jesus also said, through the psalmist, "I delight to do Your will, O my God, and Your law is within my heart" (Psalm 40:8). Love is the motive. Obedience is the response. You can't really love and be disobedient. So that is the first identifying characteristic of God's remnant people: they keep His commandments. All of His commandments.

The second characteristic of God's last-day remnant is that they will "have the testimony of Jesus Christ" (Revelation 12:17). What does this mean?

Revelation 19:10 says, "The testimony of Jesus is the spirit of prophecy." Just as God guided Israel with the gift of prophecy in the days of Moses; just as He guided Israel throughout the Old Testament with the gift of prophecy; just as God brought the gifts of prophecy to the New Testament church, likewise in the last days of earth's history, God will have a remnant church guided by the gift of prophecy. His remnant will take the testimony of Jesus through His prophetic voice seriously.

Just before He returned to heaven, Jesus gave His church their marching orders. We call this the Great Commission: "Go therefore and make disciples of all the nations, baptizing them in the name of the Father and of the Son and of the Holy Spirit, teaching them to observe all things that I have commanded you; and lo, I am with you always, even to the end of the age" (Matthew 28:19, 20).

At the end of time, God's remnant will proclaim the gospel message of salvation to the ends of the earth, teaching people to observe all those things that Jesus has commanded. He will be with His people to the very end. The dragon is enraged against them. He will make war against them with every hellish power at his command. But Jesus says, "Lo, I am with you always, even to the end" (verse 20). Down through the ages, Jesus has never lost a battle with Satan. He is our all-powerful, conquering, triumphant Lord. In this last battle, once again, God wins; Satan loses!

THE BEAST AND ITS MARK

Revelation 13

1 Then I stood on the sand of the sea. And I saw a beast rising up out of the sea, having seven heads and ten horns, and on his horns ten crowns, and on his heads a blasphemous name. **2** Now the beast which I saw was like a leopard, his feet were like the feet of a bear, and his mouth like the mouth of a lion. The dragon gave him his power, his throne, and great authority. **3** And I saw one of his heads as if it had been mortally wounded, and his deadly wound was healed. And all the world marveled and followed the beast. **4** So they worshiped the dragon who gave authority to the beast; and they worshiped the beast, saying, "Who is like the beast? Who is able to make war with him?"

5 And he was given a mouth speaking great things and blasphemies, and he was given authority to continue for forty-two months. **6** Then he opened his mouth in blasphemy against God, to blaspheme His name, His tabernacle, and those who dwell in heaven.

7 It was granted to him to make war with the saints and to overcome them. And authority was given him over every tribe, tongue, and nation. **8** All who dwell on the earth will worship him, whose names have not been written in the Book of Life of the Lamb slain from the foundation of the world.

9 If anyone has an ear, let him hear. **10** He who leads into captivity shall go into captivity; he who kills with the sword must be killed with the sword. Here is the patience and the faith of the saints.

11 Then I saw another beast coming up out of the earth, and he had two horns like a lamb and spoke like a dragon. **12** And he exercises all the authority of the first beast in his presence, and causes the earth and those who dwell in it to worship the first beast, whose deadly wound was healed. **13** He performs great signs, so that he even makes fire come down from heaven on the earth in the sight of men.

14 And he deceives those who dwell on the earth by those signs which he was granted to do in the sight of the beast, telling those who dwell on the earth to make an image to the beast who was wounded by the sword and lived. **15** He was granted power to give breath to the image of the beast, that the image of the beast should both speak and cause as many as would not worship the image of the beast to be killed. **16** He causes all, both small and great, rich and poor, free and slave, to receive a mark on their right hand or on their foreheads, **17** and that no one may buy or sell except one who has the mark or the name of the beast, or the number of his name.

18 Here is wisdom. Let him who has understanding calculate the number of the beast, for it is the number of a man: His number is 666.

The book of Revelation is a book of contrasts. There are two leaders: the lamb and the dragon. There are two harvests: the harvest of golden grain and the harvest of gory grapes. There are two women: the woman in white and the woman dressed in scarlet. Both women represent the church. The woman in white represents the true church undefiled with error and human tradition. The woman in scarlet represents the false church defiled with a distorted gospel and corrupt doctrines. She has committed spiritual adultery with the world. There are two cities: the New Jerusalem, the city of God; and Babylon, the dwelling of demons. There are two signs, the seal of God and the mark of the beast. Every man, woman, and child that lives to see Jesus come will receive either God's seal or Satan's mark. It is vital to understand what the mark of the beast is and how to avoid it and what the seal of God is and how to receive it. Revelation chapters 13 and 14 clearly identify who the beast is and what his mark is. Moreover, they tell us how to keep from receiving the mark of the beast. In this chapter, we will concentrate especially on Revelation 13.

Two beasts and a mark

Revelation 13 deals with two beasts that John sees in vision and a mark that one of the beasts imposes. This chapter has raised multiple questions in people's minds: What is the mark of the beast? Is the mark a type of government identification number like one's Social Security number? Is the mark of the beast similar to the bar code on a product in the grocery store that can be scanned? Is it like a credit card?

How does one receive this mark, and how can we avoid receiving it?

Who or what is the beast? Is it a person—some sinister dictator or mafia boss? Is the beast a person, a religious organization, or some political ideology? Is the beast a worldwide financial organization or some governmental power?

These questions have resulted in a lot of speculation. Many different answers have been given. As we study Scripture, we will discover exactly what Revelation 13 says. Let's allow God's Word to answer these questions and help us understand what God is trying to tell us in this chapter.

Identifying the sea beast

John writes, "Then I stood on the sand of the sea. And I saw a beast rising up out of the sea, having seven heads and ten horns, and on his horns ten crowns, and on his heads a blasphemous name. Now the beast which I saw was like a leopard, his feet were like the feet of a bear, and his mouth was like the mouth of a lion. The dragon gave him his power, his throne, and great authority" (Revelation 13:1, 2).

Does this sound familiar? Where have we seen something like this before?

Remember, in Daniel 7, the prophet had a vision in which he saw four beasts rising out of the sea. The first three were like a lion, a bear, and a leopard (verses 1–6), respectively. When we studied Daniel 7, we also discovered that the lion represented Babylon; the bear represented Media-Persia, and the leopard represented Greece. Daniel saw a fourth beast as well—"dreadful and terrible, exceedingly strong" (verse 7). We saw that this fourth beast symbolized the pagan Roman Empire. Daniel 7 also brings to view a little horn that grew out of the breakup of the Roman Empire (verse 8). According to Daniel's prophecy, the little horn represented a religio-political power that would rise out of the Roman Empire and attempt to change the very law of God (Daniel 7:25). The beast pictured in Revelation 13 is a composite beast having the features of Babylon, Media-Persia, Greece, and Rome and arises out of the ruins of the old Roman Empire.

What does the sea represent? Revelation 17:15 tells us. "The waters which you saw . . . are peoples, multitudes, nations, and tongues." So the fact that this first beast of

> What is the mark of the beast? Is the mark a type of government identification number like one's Social Security number? Is the mark of the beast similar to the bar code on a product in the grocery store that can be scanned?

Revelation 13 rises out of the sea indicates that it will appear from among established nations and populated areas of the world. In contrast, as we will see, the second beast of Revelation 13 rises from the earth (verse 11). This would indicate the opposite of the sea—those portions of the world without established nations and populations.

Parallels to the vision of Daniel 7

It's clear that the beast John saw rising out of the sea has parallels to the vision Daniel saw of four beasts rising out of the sea as recorded in his book. It is as if Revelation 13 is pointing us back to Daniel 7 to help us identify this first beast. John goes on to give us several details about this beast and its activities:

> And I saw one of his heads as if it had been mortally wounded, and his deadly wound was healed. And all the world marveled and followed the beast. So, they worshiped the dragon who gave authority to the beast; and they worshiped the beast, saying, "Who is like the beast? Who is able to make war with him?"
>
> And he was given a mouth speaking great things and blasphemies, and he was given authority to continue for forty-two months. Then he opened his mouth in blasphemy against God, to blaspheme His name, His tabernacle, and those who dwell in heaven. It was granted to him to make war with the saints and to overcome them. And authority was given him over every tribe, tongue, and nation. All who dwell on the earth will worship him, whose names have not been written in the Book of Life of the Lamb slain from the foundation of the world (Revelation 13:3–8).

Note the identifying characteristics of this first beast from the sea:

- The dragon gives the beast its power, throne, and authority (verse 2).
- All the world worships the beast (verses 3, 4, 8).
- It speaks "great things," and blasphemies (verse 5).
- It exercises authority for forty-two months (verse 5).
- It blasphemes God, His temple, and the inhabitants of heaven (verse 6).
- It makes war against God's saints and overcomes them (verse 7).
- It exercises authority over every nation and group of people (verse 7).

Does any of this sound familiar? Going back to the parallels with Daniel 7, we note that this list mirrors the description Daniel gives of the little-horn power brought to view in his vision.

- The beast speaks "great things and blasphemies" (Revelation 13:5).
  The little horn "speak[s] pompous words against the Most High" (Daniel 7:25).
- The beast makes war with the saints (Revelation 13:7).
  The little horn "persecute[s] the saints of the Most High" (Daniel 7:25).
- The beast is "given authority to continue for forty-two months" (Revelation 13:5).
  The little horn has authority "for a time and times and half a time" (Daniel 7:25).

Clearly, the beast John saw rising from the sea in Revelation 13 is the same power Daniel saw as a little horn growing out of the ten horns of the fourth beast—the pagan Roman Empire. The descriptions of the two are the same. They both exercise authority for the same 1,260-year time period from 538 to 1798. As we have seen, the prophetic periods of "forty-two months" and "time, times, and half a time" both equal 1,260 prophetic days, or 1,260 actual years.

Identifying the beast from the sea

What is this power symbolized by a little horn in Daniel and a beast from the sea in Revelation? As we saw in Daniel 7, the power that exercised authority during this period and made war against God's faithful people was the medieval church of Rome, the papacy, fallen into apostasy and gross spiritual darkness. The clues to identify the beast power of Revelation 13 are extremely specific. Let's look at five of these clues in some detail. The first clue we find has to do with the origin of this power.

Clue no. 1. "The dragon gave him [the beast] his power, his throne, and great authority" (verse 2). Who is this dragon that gives the beast power of Revelation 13 its power, throne, and authority?

We read about the dragon in Revelation 12. Revelation 12:3–5 says this "dragon"— the devil—attempted to destroy "as soon as it was born" the "male Child" who was later "caught up to God and to His throne"—referring to Christ. The dragon is identified clearly in these verses. In simple language stripped of all symbolism, God's Word tells us that the dragon is the devil, or Satan (verses 8, 9).

None other than the archenemy of God and man is behind the human instrumentality called the beast power. But the devil works through *human* agents. Just as God works through His church, the devil works through fallen religious institutions who have rejected God's truth and turned their back on His law. Although the dragon is *primarily* Satan, as we've just learned, the dragon in a secondary sense was the pagan Roman Empire. Let me demonstrate this fact: Satan used pagan Rome in his attempt to destroy the "male Child," for Matthew 2:1–20 tells us that King Herod, Rome's agent, tried to destroy the Babe.

Later, Satan used pagan Rome to crucify Christ:

- A *Roman* governor, Pilate, condemned Christ to die (Matthew 27:2, 17–26).
- A *Roman* executioner nailed Him to the cruel cross (verses 27, 35).
- A *Roman* soldier pierced His heart with a spear (John 19:34).
- A *Roman* seal was affixed to His tomb (Matthew 27:66).
- A *Roman* squad of soldiers guarded His tomb (verses 62–65).

Still later, the dragon, through pagan Rome, gave the beast his seat, or throne (the original language of Revelation 13:2 uses the Greek word *thronos*). This happened when the Roman emperor Constantine decided to move the capital from Rome to what came to be called Constantinople, in modern-day Turkey. This left a power vacuum at the former throne, or seat, of the Caesars, the imperial city of Rome. Therefore, careful Bible students expect to find the beast power located in Rome.

It was the dragon, or the devil, working through pagan Rome, who tried to destroy Christ. And it was that same power that gave the beast its seat, or capital city, power, and authority. Nations don't do that very often! To whom did pagan Rome give its seat of government? How did it take place? History is clear. Baldassare Labanca, who was a history professor at the University of Rome, has been translated as saying, "To the succession of the Caesars came the succession of the pontiffs in Rome."

"By retiring to the East he [Constantine] left the field clear for the Bishops of Rome. . . . The Papacy is but 'the ghost' of the deceased Roman Empire, sitting crowned upon the 'grave thereof' "[1] The papal system of religion is the one described in Revelation 13. We must remember here that we are talking about a system, not about individual members of that system. The beast is not a person; it is a false religious organization.

Clue no. 2. The second clue closely parallels the first clue. The power that rises out of Rome is a power that commands worship. It is a religious power. Revelation 13:3 declares that "all the world marveled and followed the beast." Verse 4 says, "They worshiped the beast." The organization described here is a religious power that grows into a universal system of worship.

This leads us to the third clue in identifying the beast.

Clue no. 3. "I [John] stood on the sand of the sea. And I saw a beast rising up out of the sea, having seven heads and ten horns, and on his horns ten crowns, and on his heads a *blasphemous* name" (verse 1; emphasis added). "Then he opened his mouth in *blasphemy* against God, to *blaspheme* His name, His tabernacle, and those who dwell in heaven" (verse 6; emphasis added).

According to the Bible, what is blasphemy? You will recall that the religious leaders of Jesus' day charged Him with blasphemy. Their charges, of course, were blatantly false, but they provide a definition of blasphemy from the Gospels. Here is their charge: "The Jews answered Him, saying, 'For a good work we do not stone You, but for blasphemy, and because You, being a Man, make Yourself God' " (John 10:33). "And the scribes and the Pharisees began to reason, saying, 'Who is this who speaks blasphemies? Who can forgive sins but God alone?' " (Luke 5:21).

There were two occasions when the Lord Jesus was unjustly accused of blasphemy, thus giving us two examples from the Bible what is meant by that sin: (1) if any human pretends to be or claims to be God or have the privileges and prerogatives of God, and (2) if any human claims the power to forgive sins. In Jesus' case, the accusations were unjust because He truly was and is God and holds all the powers and prerogatives of God—including the right to forgive us of our sins.

Now that we understand specifically what the Word of God calls blasphemy, let's discover how blasphemy was revealed in the apostate church of the Middle Ages. The Roman Church has two distinctive doctrines that fit the biblical description of blasphemy. One is its claim to have the power to forgive sins. The other is attributing to the pope the office of God on earth. We'll examine each of these in turn. First, the Roman Church claims that the power of forgiveness, or absolution, is vested in her human priests:

> Seek where you will, throughout heaven and earth, and you will find but one created being who can forgive the sinner, who can free him from the chains of sin and hell; and that extraordinary being is the priest, the Catholic priest. "Who can forgive sins except God?" was the question which the Pharisees sneeringly asked. "Who can forgive sins?" is the question which the Pharisees of the present day also ask, and I answer, there is a man on earth that can forgive sins, and that man is the Catholic priest.
>
> Yes, beloved brethren, the priest not only declares that the sinner is forgiven, but he really forgives him. The priest raises his hand, he pronounces the word of absolution, and in an instant, quick as a flash of light, the chains of hell are burst asunder, and the sinner becomes a child of God. So great is the power of the priest, that the judgments of heaven itself are subject to his decision.[2]

Jesus is our true Priest, and only He can forgive our sins. We are not righteous enough to appear before God. We need a mediator. And the incredibly good news is we have a Mediator, Jesus Christ, and Scripture teaches that there is only "one Mediator between God and men" (1 Timothy 2:5).

The Vatican not only intends to keep its priestly army of mediators interposed between the repentant sinner and the forgiving God but also insists that sinners cannot approach God for forgiveness but *must* go through a Roman Catholic priest! Proof of this fact is seen in a news item announcing "an authoritative Papal statement" under the headline "No Forgiveness 'Directly from God,' Pope Says."[3]

Now, turning to our second Bible example of blasphemy, let's deal with the claim of any human to be God or to stand in the place of God. Here are just a few statements from authoritative Catholic sources:

> The Pope is of so great dignity and so exalted that he is not a mere man, but as it were God, and the vicar of God. . . .
>
> Hence the Pope is crowned with a triple crown, as king of heaven and of earth and of the lower regions.
>
> The Pope is as it were God on earth . . . chief king of kings, . . . entrusted by the omnipotent God to govern the earthly and heavenly kingdoms.[4]

Pope Leo XIII urged "complete submission and obedience of will to the Church and to the Roman Pontiff, as to God himself"![5] The same proud pontiff also boasted: "We [the popes] hold upon this earth the place of God Almighty."[6]

Clue no. 4. As we explore the identity of the beast power, it becomes obvious that the identification points to the Roman Church in the Middle Ages. Here is the fourth clue: "He [the beast power] was given a mouth speaking great things and blasphemies, and *he was given authority to continue for forty-two months*" (Revelation 13:5; emphasis added).

The beast would continue for a specific period of time. Keep in mind, as we study this clue, the important scriptural principle that in symbolic time prophecies, one prophetic day equals one literal year. We have studied this in detail previously. Forty-two months with thirty days in a biblical month are equivalent to 1,260 prophetic days or literal years. In 538, Justinian, the pagan Roman emperor, officially granted the Roman bishop the role of defender of the empire, the definer of heretics, and defender of the faith. The papacy exercised great influence from 538 to 1798.[7] In 1798 the French general Berthier, under orders from Napoleon, took Pope Pius VI captive. The act of General Berthier taking the pope captive—wittingly or unwittingly—fulfilled God's prophecy: "He who *leads into captivity* shall *go into captivity*" (verse 10; emphasis added). It was the sword of Berthier and his military might that *captured* Pope Pius VI and unceremoniously *removed* him from the papal throne. He was moved from prison to prison and at length imprisoned in a fortress high in the Alps. He was later removed to Valence, France, where he died in 1799, alone and in exile.

Satan himself worked through the medieval church to distort the pure gospel of Jesus Christ and lead men and women away from the truth about salvation. The church taught that salvation comes through the church and its priesthood. It blasphemed by claiming the privileges and prerogatives of God. It claimed that it could forgive sins through the sacraments and the mass. It elevated its traditions and rituals above the Bible. It even attempted to change God's law—specifically the commandment dealing with time—the seventh-day Sabbath of the Bible. Instead, it instituted worship on Sunday, the first day of the week.

Clue no. 5. The fifth and final clue to the identity of the beast from the sea is found in Revelation 13:18: "Let him who has understanding calculate the number of the beast, for it is the number of a man: His number is 666." We have noted that in the Bible, seven is the number representing perfection. So the number six (one less than seven) would represent imperfection. The beast and his image decreed "that no one may buy or sell except one who has the mark or the name of the beast, or the number of his name." And Scripture goes on to say, "Here is wisdom. Let him who has understanding calculate the number of the beast, for it is the number of a man: His number is six hundred and sixty-six" (verses 17, 18).

The number 666, then, would apply to the official title of the leader of the Roman Church. Individual popes over the years have had many names, such as John, Paul, John Paul, Gregory, and so on. But what is the *official* title used by the papacy, which, like an umbrella, covers the whole dynasty of popes? Several general titles are used, such as "Holy Father" and "Roman Pontiff," but the main one—the one on which the other titles are based—is "Vicar of the Son of God," along with its variations, "Vicar of Christ," "Vicar of Jesus Christ," and "Vicar of God." That official title in Latin is *Vicarius Filii Dei.* The pope claims to stand in the place of Jesus as His substitute since the latter has returned to heaven.

This exalted title, *Vicarius Filii Dei,* or some equivalent form of it, has appeared frequently in Roman Catholic literature and rituals for centuries. In the earliest collection of Roman Catholic canon law, we read:

"*Beatus Petrus in terris vicarius Filii Dei videtur esse constitutes.*" The English translation reads: "Blessed Peter is seen to have been constituted vicar of the Son of God on the earth."[8]

This title is in Latin—not only the language of the Roman Empire but also the official language of the Roman Catholic Church itself. Consequently, the Latin language would naturally be used in computing the number 666. Latin's alphabet letters have numeric values in Roman numerals. Revelation 13:17, 18 says quite plainly that "the number of the *beast* . . . is the number of a *man*." More specifically, it's "the number of his *name*" (emphasis added). So let's investigate the possibility that the pope's name, his official title, fits this clue. Let's count the Roman numeral letters of his name, *Vicarius Filii Dei*:

V	5
I	1
C	100
A	0 (not used as a numeral)
R	0 (not used as a numeral)
I	1
U	5 (formerly the same as V)
S	0 (not used as a numeral)
F	0 (not used as a numeral)
I	1
L	50
I	1
I	1
D	500
E	0 (not used as a numeral)
I	1
Total = 666	

As you can see, this convincing computation totals 666 exactly—no more, no less. In the early centuries, the letter U was always calculated as a V.

Putting together all these identifying characteristics of this first beast in Revelation 13 and comparing them with Daniel's vision of the little horn in Daniel 7 leads to the conclusion that the beast John saw rising from the sea represents the Roman Church itself, mired in apostasy during the spiritual darkness of the medieval period. John now proceeds to the second beast rising from the land and the mark of the beast.

The beast from the earth

John writes,

Then I saw another beast coming up out of the earth, and he had two horns like a lamb and spoke like a dragon. And he exercises all the authority of the first beast in his presence and causes the earth and those who dwell in it to worship the first beast, whose deadly wound was healed. He performs great signs, so that he even makes fire come down from heaven on the earth in the sight of men. And he deceives those who dwell on the earth by those signs which he was granted to do in the sight of the beast, telling those who dwell on the earth to make an image to the beast who was wounded by the sword and lived. He was granted power to give breath to the image of the beast, that the image of the beast should both speak and cause as many as would not worship the image of the beast to be killed. He causes all, both small and great, rich and poor, free and slave, to receive a mark on their right hand or on their foreheads, and that no one might buy or sell except one who has the mark or the name of the beast, or the number of his name (Revelation 13:11–18).

The first beast rose out of the sea; the second beast comes "up out of the earth" (verse 11). We discovered earlier that seas represent peoples and nations and multitudes (Revelation 17:15). The earth, in contrast, would represent those portions of the world where there are not multitudes and nations—a sparsely populated, undeveloped part of the world. This second beast arises at the close of the forty-two months, during which the first beast exercises authority (Revelation 13:5). That is, it rises around 1798. It emerges in a part of the world that is sparsely populated—one that is not part of the crowded, struggling nations of the Old World. What power fits those two criteria?

The United States of America declared its independence in 1776. It adopted its constitution in 1789 and was being recognized as a world power by the end of the 1700s. It arose in a part of the world that was sparsely populated and not part of the Old World of people, nations, and multitudes.

John goes on to say, "He had two horns like a lamb and spoke like a dragon" (verse 11). Horns in Bible prophecy symbolize power—the power of the kingdom or nation being depicted. Notice this beast has no crowns on its horns, indicating that this beast power is not a monarchy or a kingdom. "It had two horns like a lamb." This signifies a young, peaceful nation. The two horns represent the two primary governing principles of the United States—civil liberty and religious liberty. In the Old World, there were established religions that were connected to the government. Citizens were taxed to support those churches. There were religious tests for political office. Religious dissidents were often oppressed and marginalized, if not directly persecuted. In this new, lamblike nation of the United States, religious liberty became one of its founding principles. Church and state were separated. Freedom of worship was guaranteed in its Constitution.

A lamb that speaks like a dragon

"It had two horns like a lamb." Unfortunately, the prophecy does not end at this point. John says, "It had two horns like a lamb and spoke like a dragon" (verse 11). What does this mean?

The dragon, as we have seen, is none other than Satan himself—that old serpent called the devil (Revelation 12:9). Despite its beginnings in religious liberty and freedom of worship, this lamblike power, the Bible says, will end up speaking like the dragon. Revelation 13 says that this second beast, the United States of America, will speak like the dragon in five ways:

1. It will exercise "all the authority of the first beast" (verse 12). It will abandon its principles of religious liberty and, like the first beast, will become a persecuting power that forces the conscience.

2. It will cause "the earth and those who dwell in it to worship the first beast" (verse 12). The United States will take the lead in enforcing the authority of the first beast and in requiring everyone on earth to worship it by recognizing its spiritual and secular authority.

3. It will work signs and wonders to deceive the world into making an image to the first beast. What would constitute an "image" to the first beast? The first beast represents apostate Christianity, the medieval church that combined religious and secular power—the church that persecuted those who disagreed with her doctrines and practices. The church that exalted human traditions and false doctrines above the Word of God. An image to that power would be a copy, a likeness, of it. According to this prophecy, the United States will combine the powers of the civil government with those of the religious authority of apostate Christianity to form an image to the beast—a union of church and state. It will require everyone to "worship" this image.

4. It will "cause as many as would not worship the image of the beast to be killed" (verse 15). According to this prophecy, laws will be passed restricting our religious liberty, and those who are faithful to God and His commands will be oppressed, persecuted, and eventually, face a death decree. The persecution of the medieval period in the Dark Ages will return. In a time of chaos, economic crisis, natural disasters, and international conflict, these decrees will be enforced globally to unite the world.

5. Finally, it will cause "all . . . to receive a mark on their right hand or on their foreheads" (verse 16). We must now ask, what is this mark of the beast?

The mark of the beast and the seal of God

One of the most significant contrasts in Revelation is the one between the mark of the beast (Revelation 13) and the seal of God (Revelation 7). A "seal" and a "mark" are the same thing, according to Romans 4:11. In order to understand the mark of the beast, we must first understand what the seal of God is. The Bible clearly identifies God's seal, mark, or sign. God says, "I also gave them [His people] My Sabbaths, to be a *sign* between them and Me, that they might know that I am the LORD who sanctifies them." . . . "Hallow My Sabbaths, and they will be a *sign* between Me and you, that you may know that I am the LORD your God" (Ezekiel 20:12, 20; emphasis added). "It [the Sabbath] is a *sign* between Me and the children of Israel forever; for in six days the LORD made the heavens and the earth, and on the seventh day He rested" (Exodus 31:17; emphasis added).

Isaiah 8:16 says, "*Seal* the law among my disciples" (emphasis added). So God's seal is found in connection with His law. What does a seal do? A seal authenticates a document; a seal testifies that a document is legal. A seal consists of three elements—the name of the one issuing the seal, his or her title, and the location or area of the seal's jurisdiction. For example, your high school diploma probably has a seal on it, which contains the name of the school superintendent or principal, the name of the school, and the city in which the school is located. God says that His seventh-day Sabbath is a sign, or seal, between Him and His people, testifying that He is the One who sanctifies them. Isaiah says the seal is connected to God's law. Can we find God's seal in His law?

The fourth commandment of God's law reads: "Remember the Sabbath day, to keep it holy. Six days you shall labor and do all your work, but the seventh day is the Sabbath of the LORD your God. In it you shall do no work. . . . For in six days the LORD made the heavens and the earth, the sea, and all that is in them, and rested the seventh day. Therefore, the LORD blessed the Sabbath day and hallowed it" (Exodus 20:8–11).

Here in the Sabbath commandment, we find the seal of the living God. It contains His name—"the LORD your God." It contains His title—"Creator." And it contains His jurisdiction—"the heavens and the earth." God says the seventh-day Sabbath is a "sign" between Him and His people forever (Exodus 31:17). The Sabbath represents loyalty to God. It represents obedience to God. The Lord blessed the Sabbath day and hallowed it. Why? Because it is the seal of His authority.

Even secular people accept most of the commandments as common-sense principles that are good for society in general. But the Sabbath places us in a special position of worship and loyalty to the Creator. That is why it is singled out as the keystone commandment, the "sign," or seal, of the covenant. By observing the Sabbath, God's last-day people are placing their seal, giving their assent and agreement to the covenant. It is their pledge of loyalty and obedience to the whole law, an acknowledgment of their position as subjects of the divine King.

The prophecy of Revelation 13 tells us that in the last days, during the time of universal crisis, God's people step forward and place their stamp, their seal, on the covenant by keeping the Sabbath. When they do this, it will be God's turn. Then He will step forward and place His seal of approval on them. This is His guarantee, His ratification given in the sight of the universe, showing that these are, indeed, His true followers.

Every Sabbath, as we worship the Creator, we praise Him and acknowledge that He created us. We show that we want to be His loyal servants by obeying His law. The central issue regarding the mark of the beast is worship. It is a matter of worshiping the Creator or worshiping the beast (Revelation 13:15).

Identifying the mark of the beast

What then, is the mark of the beast?

The mark of the beast is the opposite of God's seal. It has to do with worship. It is an issue of worship. It concerns the law—God's commandment to worship on the Sabbath (Exodus 20:8–11) versus the decree of the beast to worship its image (Revelation 13:15). So the mark of the beast involves a counterfeit to God's day of worship.

The Roman Church claims to have changed the observance of God's seventh-day Sabbath to worship on Sunday, the first day of the week. It points to this change as a sign of its authority in spiritual matters, saying Sunday is its mark of authority.[9] God says, "The Sabbath is the seal of My authority." The Roman Church says that Sunday is its mark of authority.

Revelation 13 predicts that the United States of America will link hands with Rome to create a church-state union at a time of spiritual crisis. The historic freedoms of religious liberty will be eroded and abandoned. Church and state will unite to enforce Sunday worship in disobedience to God's commandment. The "mark" of the beast is the establishment of a counterfeit to God's day of worship that is set up by a union of church and state and enforced by law under the penalty of death.

The beast demands that everyone receive this mark—accept its counterfeit to

God's day of worship—either on the forehead or the hand. The forehead represents the mind (Hebrews 10:16). Some will accept the mark of the beast with their minds. They believe it is necessary in order to regain God's favor. Others will accept the mark in their hand—not believing in the mind but going along to get along and avoid the penalty of the law.

This does *not* mean that sincere Christians today who worship on Sunday have received the mark of the beast. The mark of the beast comes into being only when Sunday worship is enforced by law. When that happens, each person will have to make a choice. Worship God or worship the beast. Receive God's seal or receive the mark of the beast. That is why Revelation 13:10 says, "Here is the patience and the faith of the saints." God's last-day people are patiently waiting for the coming of Jesus. His love fills their hearts and leads them to keep His commandments (Revelation 12:17).

The issue at the end of time will be one of worship—worship of God or worship of the beast power. That is why in the next chapter of Revelation, God sends angels bearing a threefold message to the whole world, calling on men and women everywhere to worship Him and prepare for the final harvest of the earth.

---

1. Arthur Penrhyn Stanley, *Lectures on the History of the Eastern Church* (New York: Charles Scribner's Sons, 1884), 197.

2. Michael Muller, *The Catholic Priest* (Baltimore: Kreuzer Bros., 1876), 78, 79.

3. Don A. Schanche, "No Forgiveness 'Directly From God,' Pope Says," *Los Angeles Times*, December 12, 1984, 11.

4. Lucius Ferraris, "Papa," *Prompta Bibliotheca* (Handy library), vol. 5, art. 2 (Rome: Press of the Propaganda, 1899), 26–29. A summary of 82 points—a rough English translation, http://biblelight.net/prompta.htm.

5. Pope Leo XIII, "On the Chief Duties of Christians as Citizens: Encyclical Letter *Sapientiæ Christianæ*, January 10, 1890," in *The Great Encyclical Letters of Pope Leo XIII: Translations From Approved Sources* (New York: Benziger Brothers, 1903), 193.

6. Pope Leo XIII, "The Reunion of Christendom: Encyclical Letter *Præclara Gratulationis Puvlicæ*, June 20, 1894," in *Great Encyclical Letters of Pope Leo XIII*, 304.

7. Keum Young Ahn, et. al. "538 A.D. and the Transition from Pagan Roman Empire to Holy Roman Empire" *International Journal of Humanities and Social Science* 7, no. 1 (January, 2017), accessed April 5, 2020, https://www.ijhssnet.com/journals/Vol_7_No_1_January_2017/7.pdf.

8. *Decretum of Gratian*, part 1, div. 96.

9. " 'Sabbath Observance' " *Catholic Record*, September 1, 1923, 4, https://www.canadiana.ca/view/oocihm.8_06663_2342/4?r=0&s=4.

GOD'S FINAL MESSAGE
AND EARTH'S FINAL HARVEST

Revelation 14

1 Then I looked, and behold, a Lamb standing on Mount Zion, and with Him one hundred and forty-four thousand, having His Father's name written on their foreheads. **2** And I heard a voice from heaven, like the voice of many waters, and like the voice of loud thunder. And I heard the sound of harpists playing their harps. **3** They sang as it were a new song before the throne, before the four living creatures, and the elders; and no one could learn that song except the hundred and forty-four thousand who were redeemed from the earth. **4** These are the ones who were not defiled with women, for they are virgins. These are the ones who follow the Lamb wherever He goes. These were redeemed from among men, being firstfruits to God and to the Lamb. **5** And in their mouth was found no deceit, for they are without fault before the throne of God.

6 Then I saw another angel flying in the midst of heaven, having the everlasting gospel to preach to those who dwell on the earth—to every nation, tribe, tongue, and people— **7** saying with a loud voice, "Fear God and give glory to Him, for the hour of His judgment has come; and worship Him who made heaven and earth, the sea and springs of water."

8 And another angel followed, saying, "Babylon is fallen, is fallen, that great city, because she has made all nations drink of the wine of the wrath of her fornication."

9 Then a third angel followed them, saying with a loud voice, "If anyone worships the beast and his image, and receives his mark on his forehead or on his hand, **10** he himself shall also drink of the wine of the wrath of God, which is poured out full strength into the cup of His indignation. He shall be tormented with fire and brimstone in the presence of the holy angels and in the presence of the Lamb. **11** And the smoke of their

torment ascends forever and ever; and they have no rest day or night, who worship the beast and his image, and whoever receives the mark of his name."

12 Here is the patience of the saints; here are those who keep the commandments of God and the faith of Jesus.

13 Then I heard a voice from heaven saying to me, "Write: 'Blessed are the dead who die in the Lord from now on.' "

"Yes," says the Spirit, "that they may rest from their labors, and their works follow them."

14 Then I looked, and behold, a white cloud, and on the cloud sat One like the Son of Man, having on His head a golden crown, and in His hand a sharp sickle. **15** And another angel came out of the temple, crying with a loud voice to Him who sat on the cloud, "Thrust in Your sickle and reap, for the time has come for You to reap, for the harvest of the earth is ripe." **16** So He who sat on the cloud thrust in His sickle on the earth, and the earth was reaped.

17 Then another angel came out of the temple which is in heaven, he also having a sharp sickle.

18 And another angel came out from the altar, who had power over fire, and he cried with a loud cry to him who had the sharp sickle, saying, "Thrust in your sharp sickle and gather the clusters of the vine of the earth, for her grapes are fully ripe." **19** So the angel thrust his sickle into the earth and gathered the vine of the earth, and threw it into the great winepress of the wrath of God. **20** And the winepress was trampled outside the city, and blood came out of the winepress, up to the horses' bridles, for one thousand six hundred furlongs.

※

In Revelation, one chapter leads into the next. Revelation 12 ends with Satan enraged against God's last-day church and going forth to make war on God's people. Chapter 13 tells us that worship is the main issue in this war. The war will occur when church and state unite to enforce worship of the beast under the penalty of death. In chapter 14, God sends angels with a threefold message to the entire world, calling their attention to the issue of worship and calling them to worship the Creator rather than the beast.

Revelation 14 is divided into three parts—a people who stand on Mount Zion in heaven with Jesus (verses 1–5), the threefold message that prepares them to stand there (verses 6–13), and the event for which they must prepare—earth's final harvest (verses 14–20).

The 144,000 standing on Mount Zion

John writes,

> I looked, and behold, a Lamb standing on Mount Zion, and with Him one hundred and forty-four thousand, having His Father's name written on their foreheads. And I heard a voice from heaven, like the voice of many waters, and like the voice of loud thunder. And I heard the sound of harpists playing their harps. They sang as it were a new song before the throne, before the four living creatures, and the elders; and no one could learn that song except the hundred and forty-four thousand who were redeemed from the earth. These are the ones who were not defiled with women, for they are virgins. These are the ones who follow the Lamb wherever He goes. These were redeemed from among men, being firstfruits to God and to the Lamb. And in their mouth was found no deceit, for they are without fault before the throne of God (Revelation 14:1–5).

We looked at these verses previously in connection with chapter 7, where the 144,000 are first brought to view. There, we discovered that 144,000 is a symbolic number representing God's faithful, loyal people—those who receive His seal at the end of time because their minds are committed to Him. They are the saved who are alive on earth when Jesus returns.

Now we can see that verses 1–5 make a bridge between the solemn predictions about false worship, death decrees, the beast, and its mark, in chapter 13, and the threefold message God sends to prepare the 144,000 to stand with the Lamb on Mount Zion. The triumph of those who have gained the victory over the beast and his image forms a glorious contrast to the distressing scenes of the previous chapter. They followed Jesus faithfully against great odds while on earth. In heaven, they "follow the Lamb wherever He goes" (verse 4).

So let's turn to the threefold message God sends to every man, woman, and child on earth.

Three angels, three messages

God has always sent messages to prepare people for significant events that affect their eternal destiny. When the world was going to be destroyed by water, God sent Noah to warn the people and urge them to enter the ark of safety. When Jesus was about to take up His ministry on earth as the promised Messiah, God sent John the Baptist with a message of repentance to prepare the way. God sent Jonah with a message to the people of Nineveh—"Your city will be destroyed in forty days!" And the people repented. They repented in response to Jonah's message, and their city was spared. (See Jonah 3.) Every time there has been a major event affecting people's spiritual destiny, God sent a message to prepare them to meet it by His grace. It would be strange, then, if God did not have a special message for the people of earth's last generation uniquely designed to help them meet the challenges they face.

The three angels here in Revelation 14 proclaim messages of the greatest significance. They are God's final appeal to the inhabitants of the earth. The beast is demanding worship; all must decide whether they will conform. In that context, God speaks to earth through the three angels.

Just before His crucifixion, Jesus cried out with tears in His voice, "O Jerusalem, Jerusalem, the one who kills the prophets and stones those who are sent to her! How often I wanted to gather your children together, as a hen gathers her chicks under her wings, but you were not willing!" (Matthew 23:37).

God is feeling that same emotion as He sends these urgent messages to earth. Many times, His Spirit has pled with men and women to turn to Him and be saved. As the end rapidly approaches, Satan is enraged against God's people. The beast power is demanding worship. People must decide where they stand. And God does everything He can to encourage them to come to Him. He has promised to be with them to the very end (Matthew 28:20). He looks ahead to the time when the 144,000 will stand with the Lamb on Mount Zion. He wants as many as possible to be among that group.

Throughout history, God allowed sin to continue for only so long before His judgments fall. Although He has created us with the freedom of choice, He is sovereign. Our choices can never supersede His overall plan for this world. Sin and rebellion have their limits.

Let's look at each of these three messages.

The message of the first angel

"I saw another angel flying in the midst of heaven, having the everlasting gospel to preach to those who dwell on the earth—to every nation, tribe, tongue, and people—saying with a loud voice, 'Fear God and give glory to Him, for the hour of His judgment has come; and worship Him who made heaven and earth, the sea and springs of water' " (Revelation 14:6, 7).

Here is an urgent message—the angel is flying in midheaven, speaking with a loud voice. It is an eternal, or everlasting, message—the angel has the everlasting gospel. And it is universal—it is to be proclaimed to every person on earth. A message that is urgent, eternal, and universal must be incredibly relevant and important for an end-time generation.

Notice what this first angel is preaching. This angel has the everlasting gospel to preach to those living on earth. He is not preaching some new gospel. The angel doesn't try to shape the gospel to meet the current whims or fads of society. The angel preaches a gospel that is everlasting. It is the same gospel that Paul and the other apostles preached in the first century. It is the same gospel that Luther preached in the Reformation. It is the same gospel that the Bible has been teaching since the beginning. The beauty of the gospel is that it appeals to the hearts and minds of every generation. Society may change, but the deepest needs of our fundamental lives remain essentially the same.

At the end of time, the fundamental need of people everywhere is to hear the good news of salvation through faith in Jesus Christ. There is no path to salvation except through the Cross. So the foundation of God's threefold appeal to earth in the last days is the everlasting gospel.

The angel fleshes out the meaning of the gospel, emphasizing four points for the end time.

1. Fear God. Fear is used in verse 7, not in the sense of being afraid of God but in the sense of reverence, awe, and respect. It conveys the thought of absolute loyalty to God and full surrender to His will. It is an attitude of mind that is God-centered rather than self-centered. It is the opposite of Lucifer's attitude in Isaiah 14:13, 14, when he says in his heart,

> "I will ascend into heaven,
> I will exalt my throne above the stars of God;
> I will also sit on the mount of the congregation
> On the farthest sides of the north;
> I will ascend above the heights of the clouds,
> I will be like the Most High."

The essence of the great controversy revolves around submission to God. Lucifer was self-centered. He refused to submit to any authority except his own. Rather than submit to the One upon the throne, Lucifer desired to rule from the throne.

We discover the depth of the meaning of this expression "fear God" by observing its usage in other parts of the Bible. In Scripture, the fear, or reverence, of God leads to obedience to His commands. Let's consider two passages that make this point crystal clear.

Speaking to Israel, God instructed the people to "fear the LORD your God, to keep all His statutes and His commandments which I command you" (Deuteronomy 6:2).

The book of Ecclesiastes states it in language too plain to be misunderstood. "Let us hear the conclusion of the whole matter: Fear God and keep his commandments: for this is the whole duty of man. For God shall bring every work into judgment, with every secret thing, whether it be good, or whether it be evil" (Ecclesiastes 12:13, 14, KJV).

Heaven's urgent appeal is for those saved by grace to live godly lives. Grace does not free us from obeying the commands of God. However, if we fail, we can come in humble repentance, confessing our sins, and He graciously pardons us. That's why the apostle Paul states so emphatically in Romans 8:1, "There is . . . no condemnation to those who are in Christ Jesus." The gospel not only delivers us from the guilt of our past but also empowers us to live godly, obedient lives in the present. The apostle Paul declares of believers, "We have received grace and apostleship for obedience to the faith among all nations" (Romans 1:5). We fear God when we stand in awe of His goodness, marvel at His grace, and are overwhelmed with His love.

2. Give glory to Him. How can we possibly give glory to God? He is the King of the universe. How can we do anything to add to His glory? We can give glory to Him by living for Him. We glorify God by allowing Him to demonstrate His grace and power in our lives.

Notice this contrast. Fearing God speaks of an attitude of God-centered obedience. Giving glory to God speaks of our actions—how we live. Fearing God has to do with what we think. Giving glory to God is about what we do. Fearing God is the inner commitment to make God the center of our lives. Giving glory to God is translating our inner convictions into a lifestyle that honors God in all we do.

Many people have the idea that how they treat their bodies is unrelated to their faith. They believe that their bodies are theirs to do with what they please. The apostle Paul declares, "I beseech [urge] you therefore, brethren, by the mercies of God, that you present your bodies a living sacrifice, holy, acceptable to God, which is your reasonable service" (Romans 12:1). The New Testament Greek word for bodies is *sumata*, which is better translated as the collective sum of who you are—body, mind, emotions. The Phillips translation of the Bible translates "reasonable service" as "an act of intelligent worship." In other words, when you make a total commitment to "fear God and give glory to Him"—give your mind, body, and emotions to Him in all you do—it is an act of intelligent worship.

According to the apostle Paul, our bodies are a sanctuary, the dwelling place of the Spirit of God, a temple made holy by the presence of God. And he is emphatic: "If anyone defiles the temple of God, God will destroy him. For the temple of God is holy, which temple you are" (1 Corinthians 3:17). The Scriptures give us a clarion call to glorify God in every aspect of our lives. At a time when multitudes are abusing their bodies and damaging their brains with drugs, alcohol, and other destructive habits, God says, "I'm calling you back to a life of faithful obedience. Place your body on the altar as a living sacrifice; open your heart and mind to My Spirit so that I can live in you. Then your body will truly be My temple."

When God is the center of our lives, our one desire is to give glory to Him in every aspect of our lives, whether that has to do with our diet and the things we eat, our dress and the things we wear, our entertainment and the things we view, or our music and the things we listen to. We give glory to God as we reveal His character of love to the world through lives committed to doing His will. This becomes even more important in the light of the earth's end-time judgment.

3. Worship Him who made heaven and earth. Here we get to the issue that is paramount at the end of time—worship. Revelation 13 has set up the crisis facing this last generation—worship the beast or worship God. Be marked by the beast or sealed by God. That is the choice. God deserves our worship because He made us. He is the Creator.

Creation speaks of our value in God's sight. It speaks of our worth to Him. We are not alone in the universe—some speck of cosmic dust. He created us. He fashioned us. He made us. We did not evolve. We are not a genetic accident. Jesus is worthy of our worship because He not only created us but also redeemed us. Creation and Redemption are at the heart of all true worship. This is why the Sabbath is so significant. The Sabbath speaks of a Creator's care and a Redeemer's love.

Speaking of the conclusion of Creation week, Genesis 2:1–3 declares, "Thus the heavens and the earth, and all the host of them, were finished. And on the seventh day God ended His work which He had done, and He rested on the seventh day from all His work which He had done. Then God blessed the seventh day and sanctified it, because in it He rested from all His work which God had created and made." God did not rest because He was tired. He rested refreshed in the beauty and majesty of the world He had made. He rested as an example to us. The Sabbath is a weekly pause to praise the One who made us. As we worship on the Sabbath, we open our hearts to receive the special blessing He placed on that day—a blessing that was placed on no other day.

The Sabbath reminds us that we are not cosmic orphans on some spinning globe of rock. It points us to a Creator who created us with a purpose and loved us too much to abandon us when we drifted from that purpose. The Sabbath reminds us of the One who has provided all the good things of life for us.

Sabbath is an eternal symbol of our rest in Him. It is a special sign of loyalty to the Creator (Ezekiel 20:12, 20). Rather than an arbitrary, legalistic requirement, it reveals that true rest from righteousness by works is found in Him. The Sabbath speaks of a God who has achieved so that we can rest in His achievements. True Sabbath rest is the rest of grace in the loving arms of the One who created us, the One who redeemed us, and the One who is coming again for us. Do you remember that unique phrase in Genesis 2:3, "In it [the Sabbath] *He rested* from all His work which God had created and made"? The Sabbath is God's rest. He rested on the seventh day in a divine acknowledgment that His work was completed. Hebrews 4:9, 10 liken God's rest when He ceased from His works at the end of the Creation week to our Sabbath rest today. Hebrews puts it this way, "There remains therefore a rest for the people of God. For he who has entered His rest has himself also ceased from his works as God did from His." According to Scripture, our Sabbath rest is an act of supreme worship in which we rest totally in Him for our salvation.

The message of Revelation 14, God's end-time message, calls us to remember the One who created us and rest in His love and care each Sabbath. Sabbath is a symbol of rest, not works; of grace, not legalism; of assurance, not condemnation; of depending upon Him and not ourselves. Each Sabbath, we rejoice in His goodness and praise Him for the salvation that can be found only in Christ.

The Sabbath is also the eternal link between the perfection of Eden in the past and the glory of the new heavens and the new earth in the future. One day the splendors of Eden will be restored. One day God will create a new heaven and a new earth. One day sickness, suffering, and sorrow will be no more. One day disease, disaster, and death will be over. One day joy, gladness, and peace will reign forever and ever and ever. Until that day, as we worship Him with all our hearts as the Creator of heavens and earth, we rest in His everlasting love, praise Him for His grace, and long for the day that He will soon return and make all things right.

4. The hour of God's judgment has come. We have seen that judgment began in heaven at the end of Daniel's 2,300-day (year) prophecy, which closed in 1844. God's last-day message includes a focus on this judgment that is determining the eternal destiny of every person on earth. When the judgment is finished, Jesus will come.

In the judgment, all wrongs will be made right. Righteousness will triumph over evil. The powers of hell will be defeated, and God's name will be vindicated. Injustice will not have the last word; our just and loving God will. The entire universe will then worship the One who loves them with an unfathomable love.

The message of the second angel

"And another angel followed, saying, 'Babylon is fallen, is fallen, that great city,

because she has made all nations drink of the wine of the wrath of her fornication' "
(verse 8).

John wrote the book of Revelation at the end of the first century. By this time, the ancient city of Babylon was a dust heap on the landscape of history. Babylon ruled from 605 B.C. to 539 B.C. In 539 B.C., the Medes and Persians conquered Babylon. The city was attacked on multiple occasions and ultimately laid waste. Revelation's prediction on the fall of Babylon cannot possibly be referring to the ruins of the ancient city of Babylon that stood on the Tigris River in modern-day Iraq. When John penned the messages in the book of Revelation, the literal city of Babylon had been destroyed for over five hundred years. We must remember, however, that Revelation is a book of vivid symbolism.

In these prophecies of Revelation, Babylon represents a false religious system. Because Babylon took God's people captive in Old Testament times, it became a symbol of the enemies of God and His truth. In Revelation, Babylon is a symbol of false religion in the last days (Revelation 17:1–6). Babylon epitomizes self-centered arrogance and human pride. In Daniel 4:30, the king of Babylon arrogantly boasts, "Is not this great Babylon, that I have built?" Babylon represents the proud achievements of humanity. It is a symbol of human works in contrast to God's grace—a symbol of human traditions in defiance of God's commandments. It has mingled truth and error, distorted the gospel, changed God's law, and substituted man-made decrees for Bible truth.

Revelation 14 describes two religious streams flowing from entirely different fountains—the fountain of truth and the fountain of error. Revelation's everlasting gospel presents the powerful truths of God's Word to a world desperately seeking for meaning. The devil's counterfeit system, termed "Babylon," is a distortion of truth and originates with the father of lies (see John 8:44).

At the time of the second angel's message, apostate Christianity seems ascendant. All the world will wonder after the beast and worship it—except for those whose names are written in the Lamb's book of life (Revelation 13:3, 8). The beast has power to kill those who refuse to worship its image. But at the height of its power, Babylon's fall is announced by the angel. It falls specifically because it attempts to make men and women "drink of the wine of the wrath of her fornication" (Revelation 14:8). Spiritual fornication is unfaithfulness to God.

Two whole chapters (chapters 17 and 18) deal with the fall of Babylon, and we will examine the details when we come to those chapters. However, we should note one verse of chapter 18. John says, "I heard another voice from heaven saying, 'Come out of her [Babylon], my people, lest you share in her sins, and lest you receive of her plagues' " (Revelation 18:4). God is calling His people to come out of Babylon before she falls. God is calling His people to leave false religions behind and stand for truth.

The message of the third angel

> Then a third angel followed them, saying with a loud voice, "If anyone worships the beast and his image, and receives his mark on his forehead or on his hand, he himself shall also drink of the wine of the wrath of God, which is poured out full strength into the cup of His indignation. He shall be tormented with fire and brimstone in the presence of the holy angels and in the presence of the Lamb. And the smoke of their torment ascends forever and ever; and they have no rest day or night, who worship the beast and his image, and whoever receives the mark of his name" (Revelation 14:9–11).

These verses are among the most severe and fearful found in God's Word. God is merciful, but He is also just. He is a God of truth. He can save to the uttermost, but those who refuse to accept His salvation will suffer the results of their choice. On the one hand is the wine of the wrath of Babylon's fornication. On the other hand is the wine of the wrath of God's indignation against sin. Again, it comes down to an issue of worship. The first angel urges us to worship the Creator. The third angel warns of the terrible consequences of worshiping the beast.

At its very heart, the mark of the beast exalts the human above the divine. It places humanity's word above God's Word. It attempts to replace the commandments of God with human decrees. It promotes giving glory to humans rather than to God.

In the third angel's message, drinking the "wine of the wrath of God" is defined as being "tormented with fire and brimstone" forever and ever (verses 10, 11). Does this mean that sinners will burn eternally in hellfire? Many sincere Christians would answer, "Yes." They believe the Bible teaches that sinners will be tormented in the fires of hell for all eternity. They point to texts such as this one in Revelation 14.

Other sincere Christians believe that the fires of hell will go out once sinners have been burned up and destroyed forever. They point out that if sinners continue to suffer throughout eternity, sin will never be eradicated from the universe. Yet the Bible says God will make an utter end to sin, and it will never rise again (Nahum 1:9). They point to Revelation 21:3, 4, which declares there will be no more pain, sorrow, or crying after Jesus returns, which certainly could not be the case should sinners continue to be tormented eternally.

How, then, are we to explain Revelation 14:10, 11, which says the smoke of the torment of the lost ascends "forever and ever"?

The Bible often uses the term *forever* to refer to things that have an end. See, for example, Exodus 21:6 and Deuteronomy 15:17, where a slave who chose to remain with his master rather than going free could go through a procedure after which the slave would serve his master "forever." The meaning, of course, is that the slave would serve his master as long as he lived. We use the word *forever* in the same way. Sometimes we may say, "I'll remember that day forever," meaning *as long as we live.* (Many texts in the Bible teach that hell will have an end and that sinners will be destroyed. Here are just a few: Malachi 4:1–3; Psalm 37:10, 20; Proverbs 10:25; Obadiah 16; Isaiah 47:14; and Hebrews 12:29.) We must understand texts such as Revelation 14:10, 11 to mean that sinners will be burned in hellfire until they are burned up—not throughout the unending ages of eternity.

God's last-day, threefold message to the world comes to a climax in Revelation 14:12. "Here is the patience of the saints; here are those who keep the commandments of God and the faith of Jesus." Here, John describes a group of grace-filled, end-time believers who "keep the commandments of God and the faith of Jesus." Rather than worship the beast, God's faith-filled people are obedient to His will.

Those who heed the messages of these three angels and turn away from Babylon and its false teachings are commended for two things—their obedience and their faith. They keep the commandments of God, and they have the faith of Jesus. They are patiently waiting for Jesus to return. By His grace and through His power, they are keeping His commandments. They have the faith of Jesus—both faith in Jesus and the quality of faith from Jesus that enables them to be overcomers. A faith that results in obedience enables them to stand when most in this world are bowing to the beast power.

Looking at those who overcome, John says, "Here is the patience of the saints." Most modern translations translate the word *patience* as "endurance." God's people have been patiently enduring the trials and heartaches of this world, watching and waiting for Jesus to come ever since He went back to heaven. The apostle Paul wrote words of encouragement to Christian believers in Rome in the first century. Those words have increasing relevance to this generation waiting for Christ's return: "Do this, knowing the time, that now it is high time to awake out of sleep; for now, our salvation is nearer than when we first believed. The night is far spent, the day is at hand. Therefore, let us cast off the works of darkness, and let us put on the armor of light" (Romans 13:11, 12).

Earth's final harvest

The third section of Revelation 14 deals with the earth's final harvest. The chapter began with the 144,000 standing on Mount Zion in heaven (verses 1–5). The next section presented the threefold message that prepares them to stand there (verses 6–13). And this final section deals with the event for which the 144,000 have been preparing—Earth's final harvest (verses 14–20).

The harvest depicts the conclusion of the great controversy. Two harvests are brought to view in these verses: the harvest of golden grain and the harvest of gory grapes—the harvest of the saved (verses 14–16) and the harvest of the lost (verses 17–20).

"Then I looked, and behold, a white cloud, and on the cloud sat One like the Son of Man, having on His head a golden crown, and in His hand a sharp sickle. And another angel came out of the temple, crying with a loud voice to Him who sat on the cloud, 'Thrust in Your sickle and reap, for the time has come for You to reap, for the harvest of the earth is ripe.' So He who sat on the cloud thrust in His sickle on the earth, and the earth was reaped" (Revelation 14:14–16).

The harvest symbolizes the end of the world, when the final destiny of every person on earth is made manifest. Jesus told a parable about the harvest: "Another parable He put forth to them, saying: 'The kingdom of heaven is like a man who sowed good seed in his field; but while men slept, his enemy came and sowed tares among the wheat and went his way' " (Matthew 13:24, 25).

When the wheat and the weeds both began to spring up, his servants asked if they should uproot the weeds. The master replied, "Let both grow together until the harvest, and at the time of the harvest I will say to the reapers, 'First gather together the tares and bind them in bundles to burn them, but gather the wheat into my barn' " (verse 30).

Jesus explained to His disciples the symbolism of the parable. The man who sowed good seed in his field represents Jesus Himself. The wheat represents the saved; the tares represent the lost. The reapers are the angels, and the harvest is the end of the world (verses 37–40). Much of the symbolism in this parable is the same that John uses to depict the final harvest of the earth. Revelation 14 uses golden grain to portray the harvest of the saved and gory grapes to describe the lost.

At the end of time, the righteous will be gathered into God's kingdom in a joyous harvest. Matthew pictures that harvest in these words: "Then all the tribes of the earth . . . will see the Son of Man coming on the clouds of heaven with power and great glory. And He will send His angels with a great sound of a trumpet, and they will gather together His elect from the four winds, from one end of heaven to the other" (Matthew 24:30, 31).

The apostle Paul describes it like this: "The Lord Himself will descend from heaven with a shout, with the voice of an archangel, and with the trumpet of God. And the dead in Christ will rise first. Then we who are alive and remain shall be caught up together with them in the clouds to meet the Lord in the air. And thus we shall always be with the Lord" (1 Thessalonians 4:16, 17).

How different is the harvest of the lost! Revelation pictures that harvest as a harvest of grapes. "So the angel thrust his sickle into the earth and gathered the vine of the earth, and threw it into the great winepress of the wrath of God. And the winepress was trampled outside the city, and blood came out of the winepress" (Revelation 14:19, 20).

When grapes are harvested for their juice, they are put in a press. In Bible times, the grapes were trampled by human feet to extract the juice. Revelation pictures the grape juice as blood coming out of the winepress in a graphic illustration of the truth that "the wages of sin is death" (Romans 6:23).

Notice that in both the harvest of the saved and the harvest of the lost, it is specifically stated that the harvest is "ripe" (verses 15, 18). God has borne long with sin on the earth. He has given every man and woman ample opportunity to accept His salvation. Each person has made his or her irrevocable choice. Not until the harvest is "fully ripe" does God thrust in His sickle and reap. Those who are in the harvest of the saved stand with the Lamb on Mount Zion. Those who are lost are thrown into "the great winepress of the wrath of God" (Revelation 14:19).

The book of Revelation presents us with two destinies, two choices, two masters, and all of heaven is appealing to us to make the right choice. Jesus has done, and is now doing, everything possible to save us. Now the choice is up to us. Will we respond to the wooing of His Spirit? Will we respond to His loving appeals? How can we possibly resist or reject such love? The decision is ours! Will you just now bow your head and commit your life anew to this almighty, all-knowing, all-powerful Creator God of the universe?

REDEMPTION AND THE SEVEN LAST PLAGUES: PART 1

Revelation 15

1 Then I saw another sign in heaven, great and marvelous: seven angels having the seven last plagues, for in them the wrath of God is complete.

2 And I saw something like a sea of glass mingled with fire, and those who have the victory over the beast, over his image and over his mark and over the number of his name, standing on the sea of glass, having harps of God. **3** They sing the song of Moses, the servant of God, and the song of the Lamb, saying:

"Great and marvelous are Your works,
Lord God Almighty!
Just and true are Your ways,
O King of the saints!
4 Who shall not fear You, O Lord,
   and glorify Your name?
For You alone are holy.

For all nations shall come and worship
   before You,
For Your judgments have been
   manifested."

5 After these things I looked, and behold, the temple of the tabernacle of the testimony in heaven was opened. **6** And out of the temple came the seven angels having the seven plagues, clothed in pure bright linen, and having their chests girded with golden bands. **7** Then one of the four living creatures gave to the seven angels seven golden bowls full of the wrath of God who lives forever and ever. **8** The temple was filled with smoke from the glory of God and from His power, and no one was able to enter the temple till the seven plagues of the seven angels were completed.

In the previous chapter, we studied God's last-day message to this dying, sin-polluted planet. Jesus sends His grace-filled message of salvation, the everlasting gospel, to the ends of the earth to prepare a people for His soon return. Millions will respond to that message and one day rejoice with Him forever throughout all eternity. Revelation 15 is a prophetic picture of the redeemed who have accepted Christ's last-day message and stood victoriously with Him in His victory over the beast and its mark. It provides a transition from Revelation 14 to the seven last plagues presented in chapter 16. The seven last plagues reveal God's judgments on those who have spurned His love, rejected His grace, persecuted His people, and rebelled against His law.

As we have noted previously, the prophecies of Daniel and Revelation often retrace the same periods of time from different perspectives. In addition, there is not a strict chronological progression from chapter to chapter in Revelation. For example, chapter 14 ends with the final harvest of the earth, when the saved and the lost meet their eternal destiny at the end of time. But chapter 15 goes back to introduce the seven last plagues that will be poured out on the earth just prior to the return of Jesus. The individual plagues are the subject of chapter 16.

Standing on the sea of glass

In the middle of introducing the seven last plagues, John breaks in with a description of the saved in heaven—those who make up the harvest of the saved. "I saw something like a sea of glass mingled with fire, and those who have the victory over the beast, over his image and over his mark and over the number of his name, standing on the sea of glass, having harps of God. They sing the song of Moses, the servant of God, and the song of the Lamb" (Revelation 15:2, 3).

John had seen this sea of glass earlier (Revelation 4:6) when he looked through the open door into the throne room of God in heaven. He described it as being clear "like crystal." Now he sees the redeemed standing on it—those who have been victorious over the beast and his image and his mark—and the glassy sea looks

> The seven last plagues reveal God's judgments on those who have spurned His love, rejected His grace, persecuted His people, and rebelled against His law.

like it is "mingled with fire." This may be symbolic imagery referring to the fiery trials through which the redeemed have come, or perhaps it is a description of the glory surrounding them in heaven. Whatever John saw in vision must have been impressive—a vast "sea" looking like crystal mixed with fire!

The song of Moses and the Lamb

The redeemed sing "the song of Moses, the servant of God, and the song of the Lamb." Some commentators have understood this to mean two different songs, while others see it as a single song with two titles. The reference clearly looks back to the song Moses and the Israelites sang praising God following their miraculous deliverance from the Egyptians at the Red Sea (Exodus 15). One of the verses of that song says,

"You in Your mercy have led forth
The people whom You have redeemed;
You have guided them in Your strength
To Your holy habitation" (verse 13).

This was sung originally in reference to the exodus from Egypt and what happened at the Red Sea, but it aptly describes the experience of the redeemed who stand on the sea of glass in heaven. The song of Moses commemorated the greatest act of God's deliverance in Israel's history. Now those whom God has delivered from the persecutions of the beast have been saved from the greatest time of trouble in the history of the world and sing this song as their own.

If we see the song of Moses and the song of the Lamb as a single song, it illustrates the perfect harmony between God's plan of redeeming sinners both before the Cross and afterward. Deliverance from sin in Old Testament times came through faith in the Lamb who *would* die on the cross, and deliverance from sin in New Testament times comes from the Lamb who *has* died on the cross. The song of Moses is a hymn of deliverance from almost certain death at the hands of the armies of an oppressive Egyptian pharaoh. The song of the Lamb is a hymn of deliverance from an oppressive beast power who has passed a death decree to destroy them. The parallels are exact. In both instances, Jesus miraculously delivers them.

The song of the redeemed

The redeemed add their own verses to the song.

"Great and marvelous are Your works,
Lord God Almighty!
Just and true are Your ways,
O King of the saints!
Who shall not fear You, O Lord, and glorify Your name?
For You alone are holy.
For all nations shall come and worship before You,
For Your judgments have been manifested" (Revelation 15:3, 4).

The first angel's message in the previous chapter calls on men and women to "fear God and give glory to Him" (Revelation 14:7). And the song of the redeemed in chapter 15 says, "Who shall not fear You, O Lord, and glorify Your name?" Those who stand on the sea of glass are the ones who have heeded the angel's counsel.

We should note one more thing about the song of the redeemed. It contains not one word about what they have done to overcome the beast and his mark; it is all about what God has done. No one who stands on the sea of glass will be looking to self; all the attention and praise is focused on the One who has delivered them. They have come through a trying, dangerous time. They have successfully resisted the beast and its demand for worship. They have overcome. Nevertheless, they know that none of this has happened in their own strength, but only by the grace of God and in His power.

Seven angels, seven plagues

John writes,

> Then I saw another sign in heaven, great and marvelous: seven angels having the seven last plagues, for in them the wrath of God is complete. . . .
> . . . Out of the temple came the seven angels, having the seven plagues, clothed in pure bright linen, and having their chests girded with golden bands. Then one of the four living creatures gave to the seven angels seven golden bowls full of the wrath of God who lives forever and ever. The temple was filled with smoke from the glory of God and from His power, and no one was able to enter the temple till the seven plagues of the seven angels were completed (Revelation 15:1, 6–8).

The transition is abrupt. From the redeemed standing on the sea of glass praising God in song, the scene swings completely around to focus on seven plagues ready to be poured out upon the earth. These plagues complete God's wrath against sin.

These plagues remind us of the plagues God poured out on Egypt when Pharaoh refused to obey God and let the Israelites go free. At least four of the ten plagues inflicted on Egypt have counterparts in the seven last plagues that fall on earth at the end of time—water turning to blood, painful sores, darkness, and hail.

John says that "the temple was filled with smoke from the glory of God and from His power, and no one was able to enter the temple till the seven plagues of the seven angels were completed" (verse 8). On occasion, the presence and glory of God filled the Old Testament sanctuary like a cloud so that no one could enter (Exodus 40:34, 35; 1 Kings 8:10, 11; 2 Chronicles 5:13, 14; Ezekiel 10:4). At this point, the intercession of Christ in the heavenly sanctuary ceases. All persons on planet Earth have made their final, irrevocable decision for or against Christ. Their wills are set. Their choices are made. Their characters are fixed for eternity. The smoke that fills the temple, preventing anyone from entering during the time of the plagues, indicates that the decisions of the judgment are fixed and irrevocable at this point.

There is another vital truth in verse 8, when the angel emphatically states, "No one was able to enter the temple till the seven plagues of the seven angels were completed." Just as the Israelites were in Egypt protected by God during the plagues, God's end-time people will remain in this world, protected by God during the last plagues, and will be delivered to enter His glorious temple after the plagues. As Jesus declares in Matthew 24:13, "He who endures to the end shall be saved." During the plagues, God demonstrates before the entire universe that His grace can sustain and strengthen His people in the worst of circumstances. Even during the plagues, His love is revealed.

> The song of Moses commemorated the greatest act of God's deliverance in Israel's history. Now those whom God has delivered from the persecutions of the beast have been saved from the greatest time of trouble in the history of the world and sing this song as their own.

The angels' glory, the plagues' horror

The appealing description of the seven angels' clothing and appearance forms a distinct contrast to the loathsome plagues they pour out upon the earth. John describes them as "clothed in pure bright linen, and having their chests girded with

331

golden bands" (Revelation 15:6). God's judgments against sin, although severe, are just. The psalmist wrote: "The judgments of the LORD are true and righteous altogether" (Psalm 19:9). "Righteous are You, O LORD, and upright are Your judgments" (Psalm 119:137). God must punish sin and sinners, but He does so only as a last resort. " 'As I live,' says the Lord GOD, 'I have no pleasure in the death of the wicked, but that the wicked turn from his way and live' " (Ezekiel 33:11).

Revelation 15 introduces the seven angels and their seven bowls filled with the seven last plagues. The description of what happens when each angel pours out his bowl upon the earth is reserved for chapter 16.

Plagues and promises

In the prophecies of the book of Revelation, God reveals an outline of end-time events to inform His people of what is coming so they can be prepared in advance. As Jesus said to His disciples, "I have told you before it comes, that when it does come to pass, you may believe" (John 14:29). Revelation 16 outlines the completion of God's wrath against sin—the seven last plagues (Revelation 15:1). These are the final scenes on earth before the coming of Jesus.

> In the prophecies of the book of Revelation, God reveals an outline of end-time events to inform His people of what is coming so they can be prepared in advance.

There are similarities between the seven last plagues of Revelation 16 and the seven trumpets (Revelation 8; 9). However, the intensity increases under the plagues. The first four trumpets result in a third of the trees being burned up, a third of the sea becoming blood, and a third of the living things in the sea dying, a third of the freshwater becoming bitter, and the light from the sun, moon, and stars being reduced by a third (Revelation 8:7–12). The seven last plagues cause *all* water—the oceans and the rivers and streams—to turn to blood, *all* living things in the sea to die, and *great* darkness (Revelation 16:3, 4, 10). The trumpets reveal God's judgments through the centuries on those who have oppressed His people and rejected His grace-filled initiative to save them. The seven last plagues reveal God's final judgment over the entire planet on those who have oppressed His people and rejected the fullest revelation of His love and truth that has been proclaimed through the power of the Holy Spirit at the time of the end.

REDEMPTION AND THE SEVEN LAST PLAGUES: PART 2

Revelation 16

1 Then I heard a loud voice from the temple saying to the seven angels, "Go and pour out the bowls of the wrath of God on the earth."

2 So the first went and poured out his bowl upon the earth, and a foul and loathsome sore came upon the men who had the mark of the beast and those who worshiped his image.

3 Then the second angel poured out his bowl on the sea, and it became blood as of a dead man; and every living creature in the sea died.

4 Then the third angel poured out his bowl on the rivers and springs of water, and they became blood. **5** And I heard the angel of the waters saying:

"You are righteous, O Lord,
The One who is and who was and who is to be,
Because You have judged these things.
6 For they have shed the blood of saints and prophets,
And You have given them blood to drink.
For it is their just due."

7 And I heard another from the altar saying, "Even so, Lord God Almighty, true and righteous are Your judgments."

8 Then the fourth angel poured out his bowl on the sun, and power was given to him to scorch men with fire. **9** And men were scorched with great heat, and they blasphemed the name of God who has power over these plagues; and they did not repent and give Him glory.

10 Then the fifth angel poured out his bowl on the throne of the beast, and his kingdom became full of darkness; and they gnawed their tongues because of the pain. **11** They blasphemed the God of heaven because of their pains and their sores, and did not repent of their deeds.

12 Then the sixth angel poured out his bowl on the great river Euphrates, and its water was dried up, so that the way of the kings from the east might be prepared. **13** And I saw three unclean spirits like frogs coming out of the mouth of the dragon, out of the mouth of the beast, and out of the mouth of the false prophet. **14** For they are spirits of demons, performing signs, which go out to the kings of the earth and of the whole world, to gather them to the battle of that great day of God Almighty.

15 "Behold, I am coming as a thief. Blessed is he who watches, and keeps his garments, lest he walk naked and they see his shame."

16 And they gathered them together to the place called in Hebrew, Armageddon.

17 Then the seventh angel poured out his bowl into the air, and a loud voice came out of the temple of heaven, from the throne, saying, "It is done!" **18** And there were noises and thunderings and lightnings; and there was a great earthquake, such a mighty and great earthquake as had not occurred since men were on the earth. **19** Now the great city was divided into three parts, and the cities of the nations fell. And great Babylon was remembered before God, to give her the cup of the wine of the fierceness of His wrath. **20** Then every island fled away, and the mountains were not found. **21** And great hail from heaven fell upon men, each hailstone about the weight of a talent. Men blasphemed God because of the plague of the hail, since that plague was exceedingly great.

Before looking at each of the seven plagues in detail, let's consider the Old Testament context from which they are drawn. The exodus from Egypt was the event that created Israel as a people with a shared history. They saw God's deliverance of them from Egypt as the greatest example of His redemptive power. When Pharaoh refused God's demand to let His people go free, God sent ten plagues upon the land of Egypt (Exodus 7–11). These plagues parallel the seven last plagues to fall on sinners at the end of time:

- Plagues fell on Egypt; Israel was freed from slavery, and as a result, God led them to the Promised Land.
- Likewise, plagues will fall on the beast power and its followers at the end of time; God's people will be delivered, and as a result, God will lead them to the Promised Land of heaven.

With that background, let's proceed to a detailed look at these plagues.

First plague—loathsome sores

"So the first [angel] went and poured out his bowl upon the earth, and a foul and loathsome sore came upon the men who had the mark of the beast and those who worshiped his image" (Revelation 16:2).

Notice that this plague fell on those "who had the mark of the beast and those who worshiped his image." From this, we can draw two conclusions. First, the plagues fall only on the wicked, not on the righteous. Second, humanity has been divided into two groups—the wicked and the righteous—when the plagues begin. Let's break these conclusions down further.

Only the first plague specifically states that it falls on the wicked. Can we conclude that the same is true of all seven? Although the specific statement is made only in connection with the first plague, mention is made repeatedly throughout the seven that the recipients of the plagues blaspheme God and do not repent of their sins. Deceived by Satan through the beast, an end-time religious and political power, unrepentant humans will continue to defy and blaspheme God even as the seven last plagues fall on them.

There is no mention of the righteous suffering from the plagues. The implication is that the plagues fall only on the wicked. If that is so, then clearly, every person on earth has been determined to be in either one group or the other—wicked or righteous—at the time the plagues begin to fall. Everyone on earth has made a final choice—to worship God and keep His commandments or to worship the beast power opposed to God. Probation has closed at this time, and those who have knowingly chosen to give their allegiance to the beast will be recipients of the seven last plagues.

> Everyone on earth has made a final choice—to worship God and keep His commandments or to worship the beast power opposed to God.

The first plague consists of a "loathsome sore." Revelation doesn't elaborate further. In the ten plagues that fell on Egypt, the sixth plague was boils and sores. In the Egyptian plagues, the first three fell on the Israelites and the Egyptians alike. The last seven, however, afflicted only the Egyptians. The Israelites did not suffer the boils and sores of the sixth plague.

Are the seven last plagues literal calamities that afflict human beings, or are they symbolic? Some have seen symbolic imagery in these plagues, but Revelation 16

gives no indication that these are symbolic rather than literal. Certainly, the plagues that fell on Egypt were real, literal calamities. The evidence indicates that although there may be some symbolic significance to these plagues, they also are real events that befall those who have rejected God.

Each plague carries with it a deep spiritual lesson. The plagues are not arbitrary judgments by a vindictive God. Since all of Scripture testifies of Jesus (John 5:39), where is Jesus in the seven last plagues? You will notice that, according to Revelation 16:2, "a loathsome sore came upon the men who had the mark of the beast and those who worshiped his image." A loathsome sore afflicts the body. It brings painful physical suffering. Those who received the mark of the beast did so to escape physical suffering. They were looking for physical security. The first plague reveals that the only physical security now and forever is in Christ. The righteous can proclaim with the psalmist, "God is our refuge and strength, a very present help in trouble" (Psalm 46:1).

Second plague—the sea turns to blood

"Then the second angel poured out his bowl on the sea, and it became blood as of a dead man; and every living creature in the sea died" (Revelation 16:3).

Rather than speculate about what this passage might mean, let's take it just as it reads. The plagues are supernatural judgments. They are God's divine decree against a planet that has largely rebelled against Him and persecuted His people. What would happen to international commerce, world trade, and an interrelated global economy if anything like what this verse predicts happened? If the sea turned blood red and through the excessive pollution of our oceans, every living thing died in the sea, global trade and commerce would be interrupted immediately. The sea is the primary highway to transport goods globally. Any interruption of sea travel would create an immediate economic collapse. Those who received the mark of the beast were looking for economic security. They wanted to be able to buy and sell. The second plague speaks in trumpet tones that there is no real economic security outside of Christ. His promises are sure. Just as He has provided for His people in every age, He will also provide for us. Our bread and water will be sure (see Isaiah 33:16). He is the Christ who provides for our every need now and forevermore.

Third plague—rivers turn to blood

Then the third angel poured out his bowl on the rivers and springs of water, and they became blood. And I heard the angel of the waters saying:

"You are righteous, O Lord,
The One who is and who was and who is to be,
Because You have judged these things.
For they have shed the blood of saints and prophets,
And You have given them blood to drink.
For it is their just due."

And I heard another from the altar saying, "Even so, Lord God Almighty, true and righteous are Your judgments" (Revelation 16:4–7).

There is no reason to believe that these plagues are not literal environmental catastrophes brought about by the divine judgments of God just as the passage reads. Water turning to blood was also one of the plagues that God sent on the Egyptians (Exodus 7:17). A literal interpretation would see rivers and streams becoming infected by the environmental pollution that has wreaked havoc with the oceans as the result of two things: first, God withdrawing His Spirit from a world that has rejected the eternal principles of His way of life, and second, the wanton selfishness of an industrial society that indiscriminately pollutes our waterways.

In reference to this third plague, John heard an angel saying, "You are righteous, O Lord . . . for they have shed the blood of saints and prophets, and You have given them blood to drink" (Revelation 16:6). This verse is the key to understanding the spiritual meaning behind each one of the plagues. God gives them blood-red water to drink because "they have shed the blood of saints and prophets." The beast power has enforced a death decree. Revelation 13 points out that anyone who did not worship the beast and his image would be killed (verse 15). The deeper meaning of this plague is that Christ is the Creator, Sustainer, and Protector of our life. Our life is hidden with Christ in God, and we can trust Him through the plagues falling on the wicked. The psalmist assures us,

A thousand may fall at your side,
And ten thousand at your right hand;
But it shall not come near you.
Only with your eyes shall you look
And see the reward of the wicked (Psalm 91:7, 8).

The first plague states that all physical security is in Christ. The second plague speaks of our economic well-being in Christ. The third plague reveals that Christ is the author of all life and sustains our lives as our Creator and Redeemer.

Giving the wicked blood to drink is a just retribution for those who have persecuted God's people to the death and shed their blood. The words of this angel (and the one in Revelation 16:7) vindicate the justice and righteousness of God's judgments in the plagues that fall on the wicked.

There are similarities here with the experience of Elijah during the three-year drought God brought on Israel for its sins. As the waters dried up, God preserved Elijah's life at the brook Cherith, with water from the brook and food delivered by ravens (1 Kings 17:1–6). During the third plague, the wicked have no water to drink, but God promises His people bread to eat and water to drink (Isaiah 33:16). Just as God took care of Elijah during the calamity in his day, so God will care for His people during the plagues. Elijah was taken to heaven without dying. Likewise, those who have the seal of the living God (Revelation 7:1–4) will be taken to heaven without dying when Jesus returns.

> The first plague states that all physical security is in Christ. The second plague speaks of our economic well-being in Christ. The third plague reveals that Christ is the author of all life and sustains our lives as our Creator and Redeemer.

Fourth plague—scorching heat from the sun

"Then the fourth angel poured out his bowl on the sun, and power was given to him to scorch men with fire. And men were scorched with great heat, and they blasphemed the name of God who has power over these plagues; and they did not repent and give Him glory" (Revelation 16:8, 9).

Some point to the effects of climate change as present-day indicators of how this plague could affect humanity as the earth's temperatures rise. Ultraviolet radiation has increased significantly in recent years as the ozone layer of the earth's atmosphere has degraded. These phenomena, however, are more gradual. The fourth plague comes from God as a judgment upon sin and sinners. Those scorched by the unnatural heat from the sun "blasphemed the name of God . . . ; and they did not repent and give Him glory." The plagues come as judgments against sin and sinners who have made an irreversible choice—not as a chastisement designed to bring them back to God.

God's people are spared the scorching heat that torments the wicked. The psalmist wrote:

He who dwells in the secret place of the Most High
Shall abide under the shadow of the Almighty.
I will say of the LORD, "He is my refuge and my fortress;
My God, in Him I will trust." . . .

He shall cover you with His feathers
And under His wings you shall take refuge (Psalm 91:1–4).

The final conflict between Christ and Satan is over worship. God's people worship Him as the Creator (Revelation 4:11; 14:7). However, pagan cultures, for centuries, have worshiped the sun. The chief, or most important, god in Egyptian worship was Ra, the sun god. The Mesopotamian and Babylonian god of the sun was Shamash. He was part of a triad of false gods worshiped by the Babylonians. The Persians and early Romans worshiped the sun god Mithra. The Roman worship of Mithra was a sign of loyalty to the emperor. Sol Invictus, the unconquered sun, was the official sun god of the later Roman Empire. The Israelites and God's loyal followers through the ages have worshiped the Creator on the Bible Sabbath. The seventh-day Sabbath was a sign of loyalty to the true God (Ezekiel 20:12, 20). In the last days of earth's history, laws will be passed enforcing worship on Sunday, the day of the sun. The fourth plague reveals that our Lord is the center of all true worship.

Fifth plague—darkness and pain

"Then the fifth angel poured out his bowl on the throne of the beast, and his kingdom became full of darkness; and they gnawed their tongues because of the pain. They blasphemed the God of heaven because of their pains and their sores, and did not repent of their deeds" (Revelation 16:10, 11).

Darkness was the ninth of the ten plagues that fell on the Egyptians for Pharaoh's refusal to recognize God and obey Him (Exodus 10:21–29). This plague strikes directly at the "throne of the beast." The beast power has kept people in spiritual darkness, and now darkness descends on it. Light comes from God; there is no darkness in Him (1 John 1:5). Jesus is the Light of the world, so spiritual darkness falls upon those who reject Him. John wrote in his Gospel,

In Him [Jesus Christ] was life, and the life was the light of men. And the light shines in darkness, and the darkness did not comprehend it . . .

. . . That was the true Light [Jesus Christ] which gives light to every man coming into the world.

He was in the world, . . . and the world did not know Him (John 1:4–10).

God's Word could have brought light to those in spiritual darkness under the reign of the beast. "The entrance of Your words gives light" (Psalm 119:130). But instead of searching for light, the apostate church tampered with God's law and kept the light of the Word from the people. Darkness and pain are the result.

The fifth plague reveals that the light of truth is found in Jesus Christ. Christ and His Word are inseparable, and as the psalmist puts it, "Your Word is a lamp to my feet and a light to my path" (Psalm 119:105). The light of God's Word shines forth from Jesus, but darkness engulfs the domain of the beast.

Sixth plague—Euphrates River dried up

Then the sixth angel poured out his bowl on the great river Euphrates, and its water was dried up, so that the way of the kings from the east might be prepared. And I saw three unclean spirits like frogs coming out of the mouth of the dragon, out of the mouth of the beast, and out of the mouth of the false prophet. For they are the spirits of demons, performing signs, which go out to the kings of the earth and of the whole world, to gather them together to the battle of that great day of God Almighty. . . .

And they gathered them together to the place called in Hebrew, Armageddon (Revelation 16:12–16).

The sixth plague dries up the river Euphrates to prepare the way for the kings from the east. This is reminiscent of the sixth trumpet, where that angel is told to " 'release the four angels who are bound at the great river Euphrates.' So the four angels . . . were released to kill a third of mankind" (Revelation 9:14, 15). Several times in the Old Testament, drying up waters is associated with the power of God. It was so for the Exodus crossing at the Red Sea (Exodus 14:21). God also miraculously parted the Jordan River so that the Israelites could cross over into Canaan "on dry ground" (Joshua 3:17; see also Isaiah 11:15; 44:27; Jeremiah 51:36; Zechariah 10:11).

But the sixth plague reminds us most strikingly of Babylon's fall to the Medes and Persians on the night of Belshazzar's feast (Daniel 5). You recall that Cyrus diverted the waters of the Euphrates River, drying them up where they flowed through the city of Babylon so that his armies could march underneath the gates of the city and overthrow it. The Medes and Persians came from the east to overthrow Babylon. John is drawing on this imagery in describing the sixth plague.

The second angel of Revelation 14 cries out, "Babylon is fallen, is fallen" (verse 8). Spiritual Babylon—the beast power—is being overthrown by God in the closing hours of earth's history. God is calling His people to come out of her so as not to be a part of her sins and her destruction. The waters of literal Babylon dried up when it was overthrown by Cyrus. According to Revelation 17:15, the waters of spiritual Babylon are the nations and peoples that support it. This support will dry up as Babylon falls and the seven last plagues bring down the curtain on sin and sinners.

The battle of Armageddon

Under the sixth plague, John saw "three unclean spirits like frogs coming out of the mouth of the dragon, out of the mouth of the beast, and out of the mouth of the false prophet" (Revelation 16:13). These unclean spirits are the spirits of demons gathering the kings of the earth to the battle of Armageddon.

There is a sort of play on words here in the Greek language in which John wrote. The Greek word for "spirit" is *pneuma*, which means "breath." So to say that an evil "spirit" (*pneuma*) came out of the mouth of the dragon is the same as saying an evil "breath" (*pneuma*) came out of the mouth of the dragon. It's a way of saying that the dragon, the beast, and the false prophet breathed out evil influences.

We have previously identified the dragon as Satan and the beast as the apostate Roman Church. But who is the false prophet?

Revelation 19:20 says, "The beast was captured, and with him the false prophet who worked signs in his presence, by which he deceived those who received the mark of the beast and those who worshiped his image." Speaking of the beast that arose from the earth, Revelation 13:13, 14 says, "He performs great signs, so that he even makes fire come down from heaven on the earth in the sight of men. And he deceives those who dwell on the earth by those signs which he was granted to do in the sight of the beast." When we put the two texts together, it appears that the false prophet is the second beast of Revelation 13, which we have identified as the United States of America—the lamblike beast that speaks like a dragon.

The evil spirits, or influences, coming from the dragon, the beast, and the false prophet gather the kings of the earth to a great battle at a "place called in Hebrew, Armageddon" (Revelation 16:16). This name has been associated with Megiddo, a city in Israel on the Plain of Esdraelon, on the ancient highway from Egypt to Damascus. This plain was a great battleground of the ancient world. It was where Barak and Deborah defeated Sisera and his chariots (Judges 4). King Ahaziah died there in battle (2 Kings 9:27). Good king Josiah lost his life there, in a battle with Pharaoh Necho (2 Kings 23:29). It was a battleground famous in Hebrew history.

The word *Armageddon* has come to stand for a final showdown or a climactic struggle that ends in total defeat for one side and total victory for the other. There has been much speculation regarding who would be the antagonists in the battle of Armageddon at the end of time. Various national match-ups have been suggested. But it is important to keep the main theme of Revelation in mind. Revelation is revealing Christ's ultimate victory in the ages-long battle with evil.

Revelation says that the dragon, the beast, and the false prophet gather the kings of the earth to this battle. Given this imagery, it seems that the battle that Armageddon refers to is not a literal military battle between the nations of the earth, but rather, it is the final battle in the spiritual struggle that has been the focus of the book of Revelation from the beginning. Certainly, there will be military conflicts and international wars before Jesus returns. Jesus details these events as signs of the last days in Matthew 24, Luke 21, and Mark 13. However, the climax of the ages occurs when church and state unite to enforce the mark of the beast. Every person on earth makes their final choice, the plagues are poured out, and Jesus descends from the sky to deliver His people. Armageddon is the final showdown in the great controversy between God and Satan. It is the final matchup between good and evil before Jesus comes.

> Revelation says that the dragon, the beast, and the false prophet gather the kings of the earth to this battle. Given this imagery, it seems that the battle that Armageddon refers to is not a literal military battle between the nations of the earth, but rather, it is the final battle in the spiritual struggle that has been the focus of the book of Revelation from the beginning.

Seventh plague—hail and cosmic destruction

Then the seventh angel poured out his bowl into the air, and a loud voice came out of the temple of heaven, from the throne, saying, "It is done!" And there were noises and thundering and lightnings; and there was a great earthquake, such a mighty and great earthquake as had not occurred since men were on the earth. Now the great city was divided into three parts, and the cities of the nations fell. And great Babylon was remembered before God, to give her the cup of the wine of the fierceness of His wrath. Then every island fled away, and the mountains were not found. And great hail from heaven fell upon men, each hailstone about the weight of a talent. Men blasphemed God because of the plague of the hail, since that plague was exceedingly great (Revelation 16:17–21).

Each of the seven angels has poured out his plague on a different target—(1) the earth; (2) the sea; (3) rivers and springs; (4) the sun; (5) the throne of the beast; (6) the river Euphrates; and (7) the air. When the seventh angel pours out his plague into the air, cosmic calamities of unimaginable destruction take place in the atmosphere as well as on the earth—hail, lightning, thunder, a great earthquake, mountains collapsing, and islands disappearing. Hail was also one of the plagues poured out upon Egypt at the time of the Exodus (Exodus 9:24). A voice from heaven declares, "It is done!" This reminds us of Jesus' cry as He died on the cross, "It is finished!" (John 19:30).

The battle of Armageddon—the final act in the great controversy—ends with the cataclysmic events that precede the appearance of Jesus on the clouds of heaven in power and great glory (Matthew 24:30).

Babylon thought that it could do as it pleased. It thought it could defy God successfully. Now it falls into pieces and is "remembered before God, to give her the cup of the wine of the fierceness of His wrath" (Revelation 16:19). Truly, the wrath of God against sin is completed in the seven last plagues (Revelation 15:1).

In the final moments of earth's history, when spiritual darkness covers the earth, and God's people face certain death, Christ returns in a blaze of glory to deliver them. The devil and the forces of hell are defeated, the righteous dead are resurrected, and together with the righteous living, they are transformed into immortal bodies and ascend in the clouds to be with Christ forever.

A SCARLET WOMAN SITS ON A SCARLET BEAST

Revelation 17

1 Then one of the seven angels who had the seven bowls came and talked with me, saying to me, "Come, I will show you the judgment of the great harlot who sits on many waters, **2** with whom the kings of the earth committed fornication, and the inhabitants of the earth were made drunk with the wine of her fornication."

3 So he carried me away in the Spirit into the wilderness. And I saw a woman sitting on a scarlet beast which was full of names of blasphemy, having seven heads and ten horns. **4** The woman was arrayed in purple and scarlet, and adorned with gold and precious stones and pearls, having in her hand a golden cup full of abominations and the filthiness of her fornication. **5** And on her forehead a name was written:

MYSTERY, BABYLON THE
GREAT,
THE MOTHER OF HARLOTS
AND OF THE ABOMINATIONS
OF THE EARTH.

6 I saw the woman, drunk with the blood of the saints and with the blood of the martyrs of Jesus. And when I saw her, I marveled with great amazement.

7 But the angel said to me, "Why did you marvel? I will tell you the mystery of the woman and of the beast that carries her, which has the seven heads and the ten horns. **8** The beast that you saw was, and is not, and will ascend out of the bottomless pit and go to perdition. And those who dwell on the earth will marvel, whose names are not written in the Book of Life from the foundation of the world, when they see the beast that was, and is not, and yet is.

9 "Here is the mind which has wisdom: The seven heads are seven mountains on which the woman sits. **10** There are also seven kings. Five have fallen, one is, and the other has not yet come. And when he comes, he must continue a short time. **11** The beast that was, and is not, is himself also the eighth, and is of the seven, and is going to perdition.

12 "The ten horns which you saw are ten kings who have received no kingdom as yet, but they receive authority for one hour as kings with the beast. **13** These are of one mind, and they will give their power and authority to the beast. **14** These will make war with the Lamb, and the Lamb will overcome them, for He is Lord of lords and King of kings; and those who are with Him are called, chosen, and faithful."

15 Then he said to me, "The waters which you saw, where the harlot sits, are peoples, multitudes, nations, and tongues. **16** And the ten horns which you saw on the beast, these will hate the harlot, make her desolate and naked, eat her flesh and burn her with fire. **17** For God has put it into their hearts to fulfill His purpose, to be of one mind, and to give their kingdom to the beast, until the words of God are fulfilled. **18** And the woman whom you saw is that great city which reigns over the kings of the earth."

❦

One of the things happening amid the chaos of the seventh plague is the punishment of Babylon. "Great Babylon was remembered before God, to give her the cup of the wine of the fierceness of His wrath" (Revelation 16:19). Chapter 17 follows up with an account of Babylon's illicit relationship with the political powers of earth in their combined opposition to God.

Babylon, the great oppressor of God's people

Throughout Scripture, Babylon represents the oppressor of God's people. It is the citadel of error and the center of apostasy. It prompts rebellion against God and disobedience to the divine commands. God's judgments on Old Testament Babylon represent His final judgments upon the world. The story of Babylon's fall is instructive to the end-time people. You will recall that Babylon attacked Jerusalem and forced many of the leading young Israelite men into captivity, including Daniel. Cyrus, the Persian king from the east, eventually conquered Babylon, freed the Jewish captives, and allowed them to return to Jerusalem and worship the true God.

Once again, at the time of the end, God's people will be oppressed and persecuted by a religious oppressor called Babylon the Great (Revelation 17:5). The book of Revelation predicts that at a time of social chaos, political crisis, natural disasters, and economic collapse, Jesus will return to triumph over the oppressive powers of the world and liberate His people. He will reign eternally. He will establish His throne securely in the universe forever. In the battle for the throne, He will be the victor. His people will journey with Him through the corridors of time and limitless space to worship in the New Jerusalem.

A scarlet woman on a scarlet beast

Then one of the seven angels who had the seven bowls came and talked with me, saying to me, "Come, I will show you the judgment of the great harlot who sits on many waters, with whom the kings of the earth committed fornication, and the inhabitants of the earth were made drunk with the wine of her fornication."

So he carried me away in the Spirit into the wilderness. And I saw a woman sitting on a scarlet beast which was full of names of blasphemy, having seven heads and ten horns. The woman was arrayed in purple and scarlet, and adorned with gold and precious stones and pearls, having in her hand a golden cup full of abominations and the filthiness of her fornication. And on her forehead a name was written:

MYSTERY,
BABYLON THE GREAT,
THE MOTHER OF HARLOTS
AND OF THE ABOMINATIONS
OF THE EARTH.

I saw the woman, drunk with the blood of the saints and with the blood of the martyrs of Jesus. And when I saw her, I marveled with great amazement (verses 1–6).

The descriptions given in these verses point us back to chapter 12, where John saw another woman and a fiery red dragon. Notice the marked contrast between this woman and the woman John saw in chapter 12:

- The pure woman in chapter 12 is clothed with the sun. She is adorned with the glory of Christ's righteousness.
  This woman is dressed in purple and scarlet garments. She is adorned with human falsehood and tradition.
- The pure woman has a garland of stars on her head. She is guided by the teachings of the apostles in her mission.

This woman is adorned with gold, precious stones, and pearls. She depends on her lavish wealth and outward adorning to impress and attract her followers.

- The pure woman stands on the moon. She derives her power from the prophetic Word.

This woman sits on a scarlet beast. She derives her power from the state, or political, powers of the earth.

The scarlet woman is identified as Babylon by the name written on her forehead. Her followers also have a mark on their foreheads—the mark of the beast on which she sits, while the followers of God bear His seal on their foreheads. The contrast between the pure woman of Revelation 12 (God's true church) and the scarlet woman of Revelation 17 (Babylon, the oppressor of God's church) could not be more distinct.

The scarlet woman sits on a scarlet-colored beast that has seven heads and ten horns (verse 3). In Revelation 12, the fiery red dragon that stands before the pure woman also has seven heads and ten horns. That dragon represents Satan. The beast that rises from the sea in Revelation 13 has seven heads and ten horns also. That beast represents the medieval church of apostate Christianity. So what does this scarlet beast in Revelation 17 represent?

The fact that Satan, the apostate church, and this scarlet beast all share similar characteristics suggests that this is a composite symbol of the forces arrayed against God at the end of time. The emphasis here in Revelation 17 is on the combined aspects of the religious and political components of that power, all intertwined with Satan himself. The scarlet woman symbolizes the religious component; the scarlet beast represents the political component, and the whole is motivated and empowered by Satan and his hatred of God and God's people.

> The scarlet woman is identified as Babylon by the name written on her forehead. Her followers also have a mark on their foreheads—the mark of the beast on which she sits, while the followers of God bear His seal on their foreheads.

The woman is drunk with the blood of the saints. This is a vivid picture of Babylon's persecution of God's people. She has shed so much blood that she is drunk with slaughter and revels in it as a drunkard revels in his drink.

Let's study these verses more closely. Revelation 17:1, 2 states, "Then one of the seven angels who had the seven bowls came and talked with me, saying to me, 'Come, I will show you the judgment of the great harlot who sits on many waters, with whom the kings of the earth committed fornication, and the inhabitants of the earth were made drunk with the wine of her fornication.' " This harlot woman has left her true husband, Jesus Christ. Here is a picture, not of the true church but of the fallen church. She departed from her true love, Jesus.

The Bible says that this woman "sits on many waters." The angel continues, "The waters which you saw, where the harlot sits, are peoples, multitudes, nations, and tongues" (verse 15). Just as ancient Babylon sat on the waters of the Euphrates River, spiritual Babylon sits on and is supported by the multitudes of the earth who have given their allegiance to the beast and have received its mark. The waters supporting ancient Babylon dried up, and the city was overthrown. Likewise, at the end time, spiritual Babylon's support will dry up, and she will fall. That fall is the subject of chapter 18.

The Bible goes on, "With whom the kings of the earth committed fornication" (verse 2). What is fornication? It's an illicit union. In the fallen church system, the church is united with the state. In the true church system, the church is united with Jesus Christ. The fallen church looks to the kings and the political leaders of the earth for power. When the church leaves its true lover, Jesus Christ, and rejects His power, it must look for power from a secular source. It looks for power from the kings of the earth or the state authorities. The fallen church system, the harlot woman, has committed spiritual adultery. She has united with the state powers to dominate multitudes. John continues his description of spiritual Babylon in verse 3: "So he carried me away in the Spirit into the wilderness. And I saw a woman sitting on a scarlet beast which was full of names of blasphemy, having seven heads and ten horns." The harlot woman represents a false system of religion, while the beast represents a king or a kingdom.

So it's the woman that's behind the power of the state. She derives power from the state, but she also influences the state. What a powerful symbol of an illicit union between church and state! The woman represents the apostate church, and the beast represents state or political powers. When a nation turns its back on the principles of God's kingdom, it becomes beastlike. When the church leaves her true husband and looks to the state for power and support, it compromises biblical principles and becomes the harlot. The fallen church gets her power from the state, but she also influences the state to support her falsehoods.

Revelation declares, "And the inhabitants of the earth were made drunk with the wine of her fornication" (verse 2). She passes around her wine cup of erroneous doctrine. The world becomes intoxicated with falsehoods. Millions drink of the wine of Babylon and are deceived. Verse 4 adds this fascinating little detail: "The woman was arrayed in purple and scarlet, and adorned with precious stones and pearls."

What are the colors that God uses to describe this fallen system of religion that appeals to the state? The colors are purple and scarlet. Do you know of a religious system whose priests wear purple and scarlet? In other words, in the hand of this fallen system of religion whose colors are purple and scarlet, there is a wine cup, and all the world drinks and becomes confused by these false doctrines.

The scarlet beast

The angel told John, "The beast that you saw was, and is not, and will ascend out of the bottomless pit and go to perdition. And those who dwell on the earth will marvel, whose names are not written in the Book of Life from the foundation of the world, when they see the beast that was, and is not, and yet is" (verse 8).

Earlier, we concluded that the scarlet beast on which the woman sits represents the political or secular component of the religious-political power that is Babylon in the last days. The main thrust of this chapter is clear. An apostate religious power will unite with the state to achieve absolute control over the world. Let's look at some of the details the angel points out about the scarlet beast:

- The beast ascends "out of the bottomless pit." When we looked at Revelation 9 and 11, we identified Satan as the beast that ascends from the bottomless pit. So the beast here in Revelation 17 is a confederacy of the apostate church and state powers in union with Satan.
- Everyone whose name is not written in the Lamb's book of life will marvel at the scarlet beast. The same is said of the beast that rises out of the sea in Revelation 13 (verses 3–8). The peoples of this world will be deceived by the church-state confederacy.
- The scarlet beast has seven heads and ten horns. So does the first beast of Revelation 13. We have already identified the first beast of Revelation 13 as the papacy.

The prophetic key to Revelation 17 is found in verse 5:

And on her forehead a name was written:

MYSTERY,
BABYLON THE GREAT,
THE MOTHER OF HARLOTS
AND OF THE ABOMINATIONS
OF THE EARTH.

Now, if you can solve the "mystery [of] Babylon the Great," you can then understand the crucial significance of the symbolism of Revelation 17.

What does the Bible mean when it says, "Mystery, Babylon the Great"? By the first century, literal Babylon, the mighty empire that had dominated the Middle East, had already been destroyed. Once the Persian armies under Cyrus attacked and defeated Belshazzar, Babylon never rose to prominence again. Our passage cannot possibly be talking about literal Babylon, which had been destroyed for more than five hundred years by the time John wrote Revelation. Revelation 17 is talking about spiritual Babylon, an apostate religious system that would depart from the pure teaching of God's Word and reintroduce into Christianity many of the teachings of Old Testament Babylon. This may sound amazing, but it is true. Let's take a closer look at what the Bible says.

Babylon's falsehoods

Let's turn to the book of Genesis and learn something about Old Testament Babylon so that we can understand why God calls the woman in Revelation "Mystery, Babylon the Great." If you understand the mystery of Babylon the great, you can understand what God is calling us *from* and what He is calling us *to*. In the Old Testament, not long after the Flood, there was a group of men and women who rebelled against God. They built a tower, which came to be known as the Tower of Babel. The Genesis account puts it this way: "Therefore its name is called Babel, because there the LORD confused the language of all the earth" (Genesis 11:9).

The Tower of Babel was built in direct defiance of the Word of God. They did not accept God's Word that the world would never again be destroyed by a flood. Lacking faith, they substituted a man-made idea. Refusing to hear what God said, they rebelled and began building a tower called the Tower of Babel. To protect themselves, they turned from God's promise to a human plan.

Babylon: Confused values

It was at this point that God confused their languages. The city of Babylon was built on the site of the Tower of Babel (compare Genesis 11:2; Daniel 1:2). When you think of Babylon, think "confusion." What are the first four letters in the word *Babylon*? *B-A-B-Y*. What does that spell? Baby. Why do you call a baby a baby? You call a baby a baby because it babbles. A baby has confused speech, so it is a babbler. In the religious world, when religion becomes confused, truth becomes distorted, and human opinions are elevated above God's Word, it is nothing more than babbling, or Babylon. When a church babbles in confusion, it loses its power. However, when a church clearly preaches God's truth, it is not babbling, it is proclaiming, and there is a difference between proclaiming truth and babbling tradition.

The book of Daniel is a companion book to Revelation. The prophet Daniel, describing the fundamental attitude of Babylonian philosophy, records the king's arrogance in these words, "The king spoke, saying, 'Is not this great Babylon, that I have built for a royal dwelling by my mighty power and for the honor of my majesty?' " (Daniel 4:30). Catch the significance of this. Babylon is a man-made system. Spiritual Babylon represents a religion based on human teachings, established on human ideas, and supported by human traditions. There is a form of man-made religion, built by brilliant, human religious leaders, that stands in opposition to the power of the gospel and the church that Jesus built.

Jesus Himself said, "I will build My church, and the gates of Hades shall not prevail against it" (Matthew 16:18). There are two systems of religion: one man-made and one God-made. Christ's church has a solid foundation, Jesus Christ Himself. It is built on the truth of God's Word—guided by the authority of the Scriptures. On the other hand, Babylon is a man-made system of religion. Christ is the only true Head of the church. In fact, someone once put it this way: Christ's church is the only organization so big that its body is upon the earth, but its Head is in heaven.

A human leader or a divine Head

When King Nebuchadnezzar sat in his temple on his royal throne, he spoke as a god. His commands were, supposedly, the voice of a god. Once again, in the last days, a church-state system will arise called spiritual Babylon. It will have a spiritual leader claiming to speak as God. There would be one whose word would be declared to be the very word of God. The apostle Paul adds these words exposing this power, "Who opposes and exalts himself above all that is called God or that is worshiped, so that he sits as God in the temple of God, showing himself that he is God" (2 Thessalonians 2:4). Spiritual Babylon's leader would claim that his word had the authority of the very God of heaven.

Babylon was the center of idolatry

Babylon was the center of image worship, but Christ invites us to come directly to Him. Images limit the ability of the Holy Spirit to impress upon our minds the things of eternity. They are often given the sacredness and homage that belongs to God alone. We do not need to come to Jesus through the image of a saint. Jesus is our Intercessor, our great High Priest. Jesus, our Savior and Redeemer, invites us to worship Him directly, not through the medium of a wooden image or one carved of stone. The Ten Commandment law makes this plain: "You shall not make for yourself a carved image—any likeness of anything that is in heaven above, or that is in the earth beneath, or that is in the water under the earth; you shall not bow down to them nor serve them. For I, the LORD your God, am a jealous God" (Exodus 20:4, 5).

Babylon used images prolifically in its worship service, and many of those images found their way from paganism to Rome and into the Christian church. These images are considered sacred today. Many of them represent so-called "saints" who supposedly intercede for us before God. The Bible says there is only one Mediator between God and humanity—Jesus Christ, our Lord. There is salvation in no other (1 Timothy 2:5; Acts 4:12).

Tragically, millions of Christians revere images as objects of so-called worship. This is one of Satan's deceptions to cloud minds from the truth of God's Word.

Babylon and immortality

Babylon, in the Old Testament, was the center of false teachings about death. It was the center of the doctrine of the immortality of the soul. The idea that when you die, there is an immortal soul that continues eternally did not come from Christianity. Now here is one of the most incredible texts in the Bible showing what can happen when God's people depart from the clear teachings of His Word. "And He said to me, 'Turn again, and you will see greater abominations that they are doing.' So He brought me to the door of the north gate of the LORD's house; and to my dismay, women were sitting there weeping for Tammuz" (Ezekiel 8:13, 14). Now, who was Tammuz? Tammuz was the god of fertility who embodied new life in the spring.

The Babylonians believed that when winter darkened the sky, and there were long nights, Tammuz had died. But in the spring, there would be a resurrection. Some of God's people, the Jews, accepted this false idea directly from Babylonian paganism. That's why Ezekiel describes them as worshiping Tammuz. They are worshiping the dead.

This false idea that the dead live on and the soul is immortal slipped into the Old Testament church directly from paganism. Here's what the Bible has to say about the truth of death:

For the living know that they will die;
But the dead know nothing,
And they have no more reward,
For the memory of them is forgotten (Ecclesiastes 9:5).

The living know that they shall die, but the dead don't know anything. The Bible teaching on death could not be any clearer. The doctrine of the immortal soul is not in the Bible. This whole idea of the immortal soul comes from paganism.

Here is an excerpt from a sermon by a biblical preacher, Amos Phelps, who wrote these powerful words over one hundred years ago, in his sermon "Is Man, by Nature, Immortal?" He discusses the question of the immortality of the soul and concludes, "This doctrine can be traced through the muddy channels of a corrupted Christianity, a perverted Judaism, a pagan philosophy, a superstitious idolatry, to the great instigator of mischief in the Garden of Eden. The Protestants borrowed it from the Catholics, the Catholics from the Pharisees, the Pharisees from the pagans, and the pagans from the old Serpent, who first preached the doctrine amid the lowly bowels of Paradise to an audience all too willing to hear and heed the new and fascinating theology—'You shall not surely die.' "[1]

> Tragically, millions of Christians revere images as objects of so-called worship. This is one of Satan's deceptions to cloud minds from the truth of God's Word.

What did Satan say to Eve in the Garden of Eden? "You will not surely die" (Genesis 3:4). He said, "Eve, you are immortal."

The idea of the immortality of the soul, of worshiping the dead, bowing before images supposedly representing the saints, led to the pagan doctrine of bringing offerings for the dead. It opened the door of praying to the saints who supposedly are hovering around us, desiring to communicate with us.

You see, the idea of the immortality of the soul greatly diminishes the doctrine of the second coming of Christ. It cuts at the very heart of the church. If you believe in the immortality of the soul, you believe that when you die, you will immediately go to heaven. Why would Jesus come to resurrect the dead if they were already in heaven?

It was God's intent that the church in every age would long for the second coming of Christ. According to the Bible, our loved ones rest in Jesus until the second coming of Christ. Together, with them, we will be caught up to meet Jesus in the air (see

1 Thessalonians 4:16, 17). Our hearts can beat with the eager anticipation that our dead loved ones who died longing for the return of their Lord will be resurrected to meet Christ in the sky.

Why is it that so many churches today are spiritually dead? Why do so many churches lack spiritual power? It is because they have lost the urgency of the second coming of Christ. It is because they have lost their passion for Jesus' return.

Babylon was also the center of sun worship

Sun worship was prominent in Egypt, Assyria, Persia, and certainly Babylon. In his book *The Worship of Nature*, Dr. James G. Frazer makes this observation: "In ancient Babylonia the sun was worshipped from immemorial antiquity."[2] Babylonian sun-worship, at one time, had an influence on the people of God.

As we have discovered, some Jews accepted the Babylonian idea that the soul was immortal, so they were praying to Tammuz. But they were doing something else in the inner court of the Lord's house. What was it? Ezekiel, a contemporary of Daniel, wrote about the influence of Babylonian sun worship on some worshipers in Judea. "So He brought me into the inner court of the LORD's house; and there, at the door of the temple of the LORD, between the porch and the altar, were about twenty-five men with their backs toward the temple of the LORD and their faces toward the east, and they were worshiping the sun toward the east" (Ezekiel 8:16). When these worshipers came to the temple, they did not turn their backs to the east as was customary but faced the east to worship the sun. This, of course, was a pagan practice directly from Babylon.

Here is a fascinating bit of history that helps clarify the origin of Sunday worship. In every generation, Satan has attempted to exalt the creation above the Creator. He is the master deceiver. His attempt is to get people worshiping the objects of creation rather than the One who created those objects. He has attempted to counterfeit the truth of Scripture with falsehoods.

In Revelation 17, John describes a time when the principles of Babylon, including sun worship, would, during an age of compromise, slip into the Christian church. In his book *The Two Babylons*, Dr. Alexander Hislop helps us understand what happened in the early centuries of the church. "To conciliate the Pagans to nominal Christianity, Rome, pursuing its usual policy, took measures to get the Christian and Pagan festivals [of Sunday] amalgamated [united], and . . . to get Paganism and Christianity—now far sunk in idolatry—in this as in so many other things, to shake hands."[3]

So Christianity and paganism "shook hands." Sunday became a vehicle to unite the two religions—paganism and Christianity. At its very heart, Revelation 17 warns all committed believers that falsehoods would enter the Christian church. It is an appeal from Jesus Himself to be on guard that the purity of the Christian faith is not compromised. The culture of Babylon is a religious system based on the idea of human merit for salvation—what we can do rather than what Christ has done—images in worship as representations of the divine, false teachings about death and immortality, and the adoptation of Sunday rather than the biblical Sabbath.

Now, here is a remarkable statement by Dr. Edward T. Hiscox, the author of the *Baptist Manual*. In 1893, he addressed a group of hundreds of Baptist ministers and shocked them as he explained how Sunday came into the Christian church. "What a pity that it [Sunday] comes branded with the mark of paganism, and christened with the name of the sun god, then adopted and sanctioned by the papal apostasy, and bequeathed as a sacred legacy to Protestantism!"[4]

Ezekiel, the prophet, would also say what a pity because God gave us the seventh-day Sabbath as a sign. "Moreover I also gave them My Sabbaths, to be a sign between them and Me, that they might know that I am the LORD who sanctifies them" (Ezekiel 20:12).

As noted earlier, the prophetic key to Revelation 17 is in verse 5: "And on her forehead a name was written." Now, what name is on her forehead? "The mother of harlots and of the abominations of the earth."

Even to the casual observer of church history, it is obvious that pagan practices have crept into the Christian church. Teachings from ancient Babylon have influenced most Christian churches. When the Protestant churches protested against some of these abuses, they did not protest enough. They escaped the mother church of Rome, but they did not go far enough. This mother church has multiple daughters who have retained many of her false teachings and unbiblical doctrines.

God raised up the Reformers, but unfortunately, they retained some of the errors from the mother church. The immortality of the soul and Sunday worship are just two examples of the falsehoods the great deceiver has led multitudes to accept.

The good news is that God has millions of honest-hearted men and women who love Him and long to know His truth. As they study God's Word and learn new truths, their hearts respond. All they want is what God wants. They are amazed that more of their religious leaders are not teaching the fullness of God's truth from His Word.

In the days of Ezekiel, when error slipped in among the people of God, He cried out, "Her priests have violated My law and profaned My holy things; they have not distinguished between the holy and unholy, nor have they made known the difference between the unclean and the clean; and they have hidden their eyes from My Sabbaths, so that I am profaned among them" (Ezekiel 22:26). John the revelator echoes these same thoughts in Revelation chapters 17 and 18. He makes an urgent appeal for honest-hearted people in Babylon—in apostate churches teaching contrary to biblical teachings—to leave. If he were alive today, he would cry out for people to flee from the errors that have become part of a fallen church system called spiritual Babylon.

God is calling an end-time people back to faithfulness to His Word. Jesus prayed, "Sanctify them by Your truth. Your word is truth" (John 17:17). The truth of God's Word, not human opinion or tradition, is the North Star to guide God's people in this critical hour of earth's history.

God's appeal is for a group of people who believe that you can come directly to Jesus without a lifeless image as an intermediary. He is looking for a group of people whose hearts long for the Christ who came once to come again, the second time, and take us home. They do not accept the unbiblical idea of the immortal soul. They long to see their saved loved ones again on that glorious resurrection morning. Jesus Christ's bride will adore Him as the Creator of heaven and earth and worship Him on the Bible Sabbath.

The woman in scarlet and purple, riding on the scarlet beast, has passed around her wine cup, and the world is drunk with Babylon's false doctrines. These erroneous teachings have influenced millions.

Christ's victory in earth's final battle

The scarlet beast exhibits characteristics representing all of the components of the powers fighting against God and His people at the end of time. Again, the main thrust of the picture of Babylon, given in Revelation 17, is that it is an all-inclusive combination of religious and secular authority, motivated by Satan, teaming up to fight against God and His people. The woman sitting on a scarlet beast combines all of the end-time activities of Satan, apostate religion, and the secular, political authority of the nations. All these will "make war with the Lamb" (verse 14).

The angel says that "those who dwell on the earth will marvel . . . when they see the beast that was, and is not, and yet is" (verse 8). This seems to be a reference to the beast from the sea in Revelation 13:3. "I saw one of his heads as if it had been mortally wounded, and his deadly wound was healed. And all the world marveled and followed the beast." Again, the scarlet beast is associated with the first beast of Revelation 13.

The vision of the beast that God gave to John is from the perspective of emerging from the wilderness at the end of the Dark Ages. Our text says that the beast "was, is not, and yet is." The French general, Berthier, on orders from Napoleon, took the pope of Rome captive in 1798. At that time, prophecy declared that the beast power "was, [but] is not." Yet the Roman Church would not come to an end, so Scripture says it "yet is." Once again, it would rise to the zenith of power, unite with the state, pass around the wine cup of false doctrines, and become a major world force.

The great city

The angel concludes his explanation to John. "The woman whom you saw is that great city which reigns over the kings of the earth" (verse 18). Note that Babylon "reigns over the kings of the earth." The secular, political authority of the nations at the end of time will be subservient to the agenda of the religious oppressor of God's people. The kings of the earth will enforce her religious decrees regarding worship.

We should not leave Revelation 17, however, without taking note of verse 14: "These will make war with the Lamb, and the Lamb will overcome them, for He is Lord of lords and King of kings, and those who are with Him are called, chosen, and faithful." Christ wins, and Satan loses.

One of the reasons you are reading this book is because you long to know God's will for your life. You have a desire to understand Revelation's prophecies better, and deep within your heart, you long to know the truth of God's Word so you can follow it. The great combination of forces arrayed against the truth at the end of time may seem unstoppable. Babylon may be drunk on the blood of the saints, but "the Lamb will overcome them, for He is Lord of lords and King of kings." God's purposes will triumph, His plans will triumph, and His people will triumph. He has never ever lost a battle with Satan and will once again be victorious in the final battle between good and evil.

---

1. Amos Phelps, quoted in John H. Pettengell, *The Life Everlasting: What is it?* (Philadelphia, PA: J. D. Brown, 1883), 640, 641.

2. James Frazer, *The Worship of Nature*, vol. 1 (London: Macmillan, 1926), 529.

3. Alexander Hislop, *The Two Babylons* (Camridge, England: Ravenio Books, 1956), 105.

4. Edward T. Hiscox, reported in the *New York Examiner*, November 16, 1893, quoted in Allen Walker, *The Law and the Sabbath* (Roseville, CA: Amazing Facts, 1985), 91, 92.

"BABYLON IS FALLEN, IS FALLEN!"

Revelation 18

1 After these things I saw another angel coming down from heaven, having great authority, and the earth was illuminated with his glory. **2** And he cried mightily with a loud voice, saying, "Babylon the great is fallen, is fallen, and has become a dwelling place of demons, a prison for every foul spirit, and a cage for every unclean and hated bird! **3** For all the nations have drunk of the wine of the wrath of her fornication, the kings of the earth have committed fornication with her, and the merchants of the earth have become rich through the abundance of her luxury."

4 And I heard another voice from heaven saying, "Come out of her, my people, lest you share in her sins, and lest you receive of her plagues. **5** For her sins have reached to heaven, and God has remembered her iniquities. **6** Render to her just as she rendered to you, and repay her double according to her works; in the cup which she has mixed, mix double for her. **7** In the measure that she glorified herself and lived luxuriously, in the same measure give her torment and sorrow; for she says in her heart, 'I sit as queen, and am no widow, and will not see sorrow.' **8** Therefore her plagues will come in one day—death and mourning and famine. And she will be utterly burned with fire, for strong is the Lord God who judges her.

9 "The kings of the earth who committed fornication and lived luxuriously with her will weep and lament for her, when they see the smoke of her burning, **10** standing at a distance for fear of her torment, saying, 'Alas, alas, that great city Babylon, that mighty city! For in one hour your judgment has come.'

11 "And the merchants of the earth will weep and mourn over her, for no one buys their merchandise anymore: **12** merchandise of gold and silver, precious stones and pearls, fine linen and purple, silk and scarlet, every kind of citron wood, every kind of object of ivory, every kind of object of most precious wood, bronze, iron, and marble; **13** and cinnamon and incense, fragrant oil and frankincense, wine and oil, fine flour and wheat, cattle and sheep, horses and chariots, and bodies and souls of men. **14** The fruit that your soul longed for has gone from you, and all the things which are rich and splendid have gone from you, and you shall find them no more at all. **15** The merchants of these things, who became rich by her, will stand at a distance for fear of her torment, weeping and wailing, **16** and saying, 'Alas, alas, that great city that was clothed in fine linen, purple, and scarlet, and adorned with gold and precious stones and pearls! **17** For in one hour such great riches came to nothing.' Every shipmaster, all who travel by ship, sailors, and as many as trade on the sea, stood at a distance **18** and cried out when they saw the smoke of her burning, saying, 'What is like this great city?'

19 "They threw dust on their heads and cried out, weeping and wailing, and saying, 'Alas, alas, that great city, in which all who had ships on the sea became rich by her wealth! For in one hour she is made desolate.'

20 "Rejoice over her, O heaven, and you holy apostles and prophets, for God has avenged you on her!"

21 Then a mighty angel took up a stone like a great millstone and threw it into the sea, saying, "Thus with violence the great city Babylon shall be thrown down, and shall not be found anymore. **22** The sound of harpists, musicians, flutists, and trumpeters shall not be heard in you anymore. No craftsman of any craft shall be found in you anymore, and the sound of a millstone shall not be heard in you anymore. **23** The light of a lamp shall not shine in you anymore, and the voice of bridegroom and bride shall not be heard in you anymore. For your merchants were the great men of the earth, for by your sorcery all the nations were deceived. **24** And in her was found the blood of prophets and saints, and of all who were slain on the earth."

❧

Revelation's prophecies reveal a God of incredible love who will go to any length to save lost humanity. They present Christ at the very center of the conflict of the ages, battling on behalf of His children. In Revelation 17, the Lamb does battle with the dragon. The logical outcome of a battle between a lamb and a dragon, of course, is that the dragon would completely destroy the lamb. However, Revelation

17 reverses that outcome. "These will make war with the Lamb, and the Lamb will overcome them, for He is Lord of lords and King of kings; and those who are with Him are called, chosen, and faithful" (verse 14). Jesus wins, so we win too! In Him, our victory over the powers of evil is certain. He has taken the initiative. He has called us to salvation, chosen us to be His witnesses, and strengthened us to remain faithful.

Revelation 18 is heaven's final appeal to His people who are still deceived by the bewitching power of Babylon's deceptions. In this chapter, the combined forces of evil at the end of time reach the point of no return. Babylon has filled to overflowing her cup of "abominations and the filthiness of her fornication," and she falls. But before Babylon's final collapse, God sends an urgent message of salvation to His honest-hearted people still in this apostate religious system. Multitudes respond to heaven's final appeal, and the earth is illuminated with the glory of God.

The glory of God and the fall of Babylon

John writes,

> After these things I saw another angel coming down from heaven, having great authority, and the earth was illuminated with his glory. And he cried mightily with a loud voice, saying, "Babylon the great is fallen, is fallen, and has become a dwelling place of demons, a prison for every foul spirit, and a cage for every unclean and hated bird! For all the nations have drunk of the wine of the wrath of her fornication, the kings of the earth have committed fornication with her, and the merchants of the earth have become rich through the abundance of her luxury."
>
> And I heard another voice from heaven saying, "Come out of her, my people, lest you share in her sins, and lest you receive of her plagues. For her sins have reached to heaven, and God has remembered her iniquities" (Revelation 18:1–5).

The angel that announces the fall of Babylon has "great authority." He comes directly from heaven and still bears the glory of God so strongly that it illuminates the entire earth! The original word that is translated "authority" or "power" from the Greek text of the New Testament is *exousia*. It has to do with triumphing over the principalities and powers of hell by the authority of Jesus Christ. Jesus uses this word in the Gospel of Matthew in harmony with the sending out of His disciples. In Matthew 10:1, Jesus gives His disciples "power" over the principalities and powers of hell. He sends them out with divine power to be victorious in the battle between good and evil. In Matthew 28:18, 19, He once again sends them out, but this time with "all authority . . . in heaven and earth" to "go therefore and make disciples of all the nations."

Filled with the power of the Holy Spirit and going forth with the authority of the living Christ, who in His life and death triumphed over the principalities and powers of hell, the New Testament church lightened the earth with the glory of God. In a few short years, the disciples proclaimed the gospel to the then-known world (see Colossians 1:23). At the end time, the Holy Spirit will be poured out in unprecedented power, and the gospel will be rapidly spread to the ends of the earth. Thousands will be converted in a day, and God's grace and truth will impact the entire planet.

If this is true, and it is, is it not wise for us to open our hearts to receive this mighty outpouring of the Spirit?

Is it not wise to ask Jesus to take anything out of our lives that would hinder this mighty outpouring of the Spirit?

Is it not wise to seek God for the heart cleansing necessary to receive the latter rain of the Spirit in all His fullness?

Let us consider the next phrase in verse 1: "and the earth was illuminated with his glory." Throughout Revelation, there are three words linked with God: God's glory, God's honor, and God's power. Revelation 4:11 states, "You are worthy, O Lord, to receive glory and honor and power." In Revelation 5:12, John once again says that Jesus is worthy to receive, among other things, "power . . . honor and glory." And again in Revelation 19:1, we discover this same thought: "Salvation and glory and honor and power belong to the Lord our God."

Notice how Revelation closes: "And they shall bring the glory and the honor of the nations into it" (Revelation 21:26). The great controversy between good and evil in the universe is about God's honor, His reputation. Satan, a rebel angel, has declared that God is unjust, that He demands worship but gives little in return. The evil one declares that God's law is arbitrary, restricts our freedom, and limits our joy.

Jesus' life, death, and resurrection exploded that myth. The One who created us plunged into this snake pit of a world to redeem us. On the cross, He answered

> Filled with the power of the Holy Spirit and going forth with the authority of the living Christ, who in His life and death triumphed over the principalities and powers of hell, the New Testament church lightened the earth with the glory of God.

Satan's charges and demonstrated that God is both loving and just.

What is God's glory? How will His glory be revealed in the last moments of time on a darkened, sin-polluted planet?

Do you remember when Moses asked God to show him His glory? What did God reveal? "Then He said, 'I will make all My goodness pass before you, and I will proclaim the name of the LORD before you. I will be gracious to whom I will be gracious, and I will have compassion on whom I will have compassion' " (Exodus 33:19). God's glory is His character. The glory of God fills the earth at a time of spiritual darkness as His people, overwhelmed with His love, transformed by His grace, and committed to His mission, reveal—in their lives and witness—His loving character to the world. The witness of their unselfish lives and the proclamation of the message of His goodness, grace, and truth are in stark contrast to the selfishness, pride, and falsehoods of this world's system.

> Babylon has filled the cup of her iniquity. God keeps an accurate record of the sins of individuals and earthly powers, and when the figures reach a certain amount, God says, "enough."

Charmed by His love and concerned about His honor, His end-time people reveal His glory—His loving, self-sacrificing character—to a self-centered, godless world. Thus, the character of God will illuminate the earth.

The Holy Spirit will be poured out in the fullness of His power just before the coming of Jesus, and the earth will be lightened with the glory of God. Revelation 18:1 is a fulfillment of the words of the Old Testament book of the prophet Habakkuk in chapter 2, verse 14: "For the earth will be filled with the knowledge of the glory of the LORD, as the waters cover the sea."

God's final appeal

An angel descends from heaven with a message directly from the throne of God that calls His people out of an apostate religious-political confederacy named Babylon. His appeal is "Babylon the great is fallen, is fallen, and has become a dwelling place of demons" (Revelation 18:2). This proclamation mirrors that of the second angel of Revelation 14, who also announced the fall of Babylon (verse 8).

Babylon has hardened her heart in rebellion. Demonic forces have control of Babylon. She is "a dwelling place of demons, a prison for every foul spirit." God's people are filled with the Holy Spirit, but the spirits of demons fill Babylon. When any individual or religious organization knowingly turns from Bible truth and scriptural teachings, they become open to spiritual delusions. The only way not to be controlled by unholy spirits is to be controlled by the Holy Spirit.

Carefully notice the wording in Revelation 18:3: "For all the nations have drunk of the wine of the wrath of her fornication, the kings of the earth have committed fornication with her, and the merchants of the earth have become rich through the abundance of her luxury." Babylon's deceptions become universal, for *all nations* drink the wine of her fornications.

Wine represents false doctrines. Those who drink the wine of Babylon become confused in their thinking and mistake error for truth and conclude that truth is error. Fornication is an illicit union. Three groups unite in this end-time confederacy: Babylon (apostate religion), the kings of the earth (political or state powers), and the merchants of the earth (economic forces).

Revelation 18:4 is God's last call to all humanity. He urgently appeals, "Come out of her [Babylon], my people, lest you share in her sins, and lest you receive of her plagues." Why is God calling His people out of Babylon at this point? Verse 5 tells us, "For her sins have reached to heaven, and God has remembered her iniquities." Sin is the transgression of God's law (1 John 3:4). God is calling His people to come out of every lawbreaking church.

Babylon has filled the cup of her iniquity. God keeps an accurate record of the sins of individuals and earthly powers, and when the figures reach a certain amount, God says, "enough." In the days of Noah, God sent a message of redemption, but after the number of sins reached a certain amount and every person on earth had a chance to repent, the rains came. In the days of Sodom and Gomorrah, Lot made a solemn appeal to his family to leave Sodom. When the iniquity reached a certain amount, the fire fell. In ancient Babylon, God sent message after message of repentance, but when those messages were rejected, the Medes and Persians invaded. God's mercy bears long with His wayward children. He gives them every chance to repent. He sends His Spirit to individual hearts. He sends prophetic warnings and makes urgent appeals, but He gives to all the freedom of choice.

Babylon's sins have "reached to heaven" (verse 5). This wording points us back to the origins of Babylon at the Tower of Babel in Genesis 11, where the people said, "Let us build ourselves . . . a tower whose top is in the heavens; let us make a name for ourselves" (verse 4).

The emphasis is on the pronoun *ourselves*, suggesting their insistence on being independent of God. The builders of the Tower of Babel intended to create a godless community in direct contradiction to the plain word of God. They disbelieved God and so turned to their own human wisdom.

The Hebrew word for "tower" is *migdal*. It is related to the word *gadal*, which means "great." It implies the ideas of ambition and self-glorification. The purpose of the builders is obviously a spiritual ambition to replace God and glorify themselves. They push themselves upward because they refuse to believe in the God who comes down to be with His people.

This word *gadal*, which is associated with the Tower of Babel and spiritual "Babylon the great" (Revelation 18:2), is also the very word used to describe the little-horn power of Daniel 7. Like the builders of Babel, this little horn also attempts to exalt itself to the heavens, placing its authority above that of God, casting down God's truth, and changing His law. In this, the tower builders, the little horn, and Babylon the great are like Satan, who sought to "ascend above the heights of the clouds" and "above the stars of God" (Isaiah 14:14, 13).

Babylon and all false religions seek to exalt themselves above God. Genuine Christianity exalts Christ and His Word.

Babylon and all false religions speak of my reputation, my honor. Genuine Christianity speaks of Christ's reputation and Christ's honor.

Babylon and all false religions exalt human works. Genuine Christianity exalts Christ's work in humans.

Babylon and all false religions speak of what I am doing for Christ. Genuine Christianity speaks of what Christ has done for me.

Babylon and all false religions are based on a distortion of biblical truth founded in human opinion. Genuine Christianity is based on biblical truth as it is in Jesus, anchored in God's Word.

It is this gratitude for all that Christ has done for us that motivates our behavior and leads us to commit the entirety of our lives to Him.

The last message to be proclaimed to a world engulfed in spiritual darkness carried by three angels in the midst of heaven is, "Fear God and give glory to Him." There is no glory in our works, no glory in our righteousness, and no glory in our good deeds.

"Come out of her, my people"

The angel of Revelation 18 proclaims God's appeal: "Come out of her [Babylon], my people, lest you share in her sins, and lest you receive of her plagues" (verse 4). Where are most of God's people today? According to this verse, they must be in Babylon, since God is calling them to come out.

Jesus' statement to His disciples in the first century is just as true today. "Other sheep I have which are not of this fold; them also I must bring, and they will hear My voice; and there will be one flock and one shepherd" (John 10:16). Tens of thousands of God's people are in religious systems the Bible terms Babylon. Christ's final appeal to His people in all false religious systems and to those who have rejected religion altogether is "Come out of her, my people." Christ never asks us to leave something without offering something else. He invites us to become part of His Bible-believing, Christ-centered, commandment-keeping, last-day movement.

The appeal to come out of Babylon is God's gracious message of salvation. Here at the end time, every person on earth must choose a side in the great controversy between Christ and Satan. This is the message that God's people, energized by the Holy Spirit, will take to the world with great power.

All this comes about through the power of God's appeal, "Come out of her, my people." Many respond and do come out and prepare to meet their soon-coming Savior. Jesus says, "My sheep hear My voice, . . . and they follow Me" (John 10:27).

Babylon falls because "her sins have reached to heaven, and God has remembered her iniquities" (Revelation 18:5). God "remembers" her iniquities because she refuses to give them up. In contrast, He says to those who surrender their sins and ask His forgiveness, "Their sins and their lawless deeds I will remember no more" (Hebrews 8:12).

Kings and merchants mourn Babylon's fall

In its self-glory, Babylon unites with the "kings of the earth" and the "merchants of the earth" (Revelation 18:3). The picture is of a union of apostate false religions, political powers, and financial or economic interests. This threefold union forms a confederacy of evil to persecute the people of God.

While God is appealing to His people to come out of her, Babylon "says in her heart, 'I sit as queen, and am no widow, and will not see sorrow.' Therefore her plagues will come in one day—death and mourning and famine. And she will be utterly burned with fire, for strong is the Lord God who judges her" (verses 7, 8).

"The kings of the earth who committed fornication and lived luxuriously with her will weep and lament for her, when they see the smoke of her burning, standing at a distance for fear of her torment, saying, 'Alas, alas, that great city Babylon, that mighty city! For in one hour your judgment has come.'

"And the merchants of the earth will weep and mourn over her. . . . The merchants . . . , who became rich by her, will stand at a distance for fear of her torment, weeping and wailing, and saying, 'Alas, alas, that great city that was clothed in fine linen, purple and scarlet, and adorned with gold and precious stones and pearls! For in one hour such great riches came to nothing' " (verses 9–17).

Babylon has attempted to unite humanity around a counterfeit day of worship. In an attempt to usher in world peace and security, she has established a confederacy of religious, political, and economic powers. Natural disasters, economic collapse, political conflicts, and social chaos only harden her heart and make her more determined to accomplish her purposes.

Revelation 18 predicts a sudden economic collapse that stuns the world. Our text says the merchants of the earth are weeping because in "one hour such great riches came to nothing." Verse 19 adds, "In one hour she is made desolate." The great confederacy of evil persists in its opposition and is blind to what is about to happen. These verses indicate that the seven last plagues that fall on Babylon are sudden and last only a relatively short time before Babylon is totally destroyed.

The kings and the merchants—the political and economic interests that have united themselves to Babylon—mourn her fall. They committed spiritual fornication with her and lived luxuriously because of her as they exercised power over the earth. Now they fall with her and mourn as they suffer God's punishment. They do not mourn for their sins and their rebellion against God. They mourn because of the consequences of their sins.

The finality of Babylon's fall

Then a mighty angel took up a stone like a great millstone and threw it into the sea, saying, "Thus with violence the great city Babylon shall be thrown down, and shall not be found anymore. The sound of harpists, musicians, flutists, and trumpeters shall not be heard in you anymore. No craftsman of any craft shall be found in you anymore, and the sound of a millstone shall not be heard in you anymore. The light of a lamp shall not shine in you anymore, and the voice of the bridegroom and the bride shall not be heard in you anymore. For your merchants were the great men of the earth, for by your sorcery all the nations were deceived. And in her was found the blood of prophets and saints, and of all who were slain on the earth" (verses 21–24).

John draws on the experience of Jeremiah to introduce his vivid description of the complete and final destruction of end-time Babylon. Jeremiah 51 tells how the prophet wrote in a book all the punishments and disasters that God had pronounced against Old Testament Babylon. Jeremiah then gave the book to a man named Seraiah, who was going to Babylon, and told him to read the words of the book when he arrived in the city. He told Seraiah, "It shall be, when you have finished reading this book, that you shall tie a stone to it and throw it out into the Euphrates. Then you shall say, 'Thus Babylon shall sink and not rise from the catastrophe that I will bring upon her' " (Jeremiah 51:63, 64).

Notice how John has intensified Jeremiah's picture-lesson. A stone tied to a book and thrown into the Euphrates river has now become a "great millstone" thrown into the sea! In this way, John graphically pictures the final and total destruction of spiritual Babylon at the end of time.

> The theme running through these chapters is Christ's victory over the beasts, dragons, and false prophets who will unite in a vast confederacy of evil to fight against God and destroy His people.

John goes on to describe a deserted city, devoid of the sights and sounds of everyday life. The city is silent and dead. The finality of Babylon's destruction is complete, for "in her was found the blood of prophets and saints, and of all who were slain on the earth" (Revelation 18:24).

The finality of God's victory

For the most part, chapters 13–18 of Revelation have powerfully detailed the end-time conflict between good and evil. Although difficulty and oppression are ahead for God's people, we have the assurance that Christ is with us in every trial, and in the end, He will be victorious over the forces of evil. These chapters are filled with verses reassuring us that the Lamb will overcome and that God is King of kings and Lord of lords.

The theme running through these chapters is Christ's victory over the beasts, dragons, and false prophets who will unite in a vast confederacy of evil to fight against God and destroy His people. The chapters have a secondary focus on an evil confederacy of religious, political, and economic powers who will oppress God's people—because, unfortunately, that is a true picture of what will be taking place at the end of time.

The apostle Paul adds this insight, "Know this, that in the last days perilous times will come: For men will be lovers of themselves, lovers of money, boasters, proud, blasphemers, disobedient to parents, unthankful, unholy, unloving, unforgiving, slanderers, without self-control, brutal, despisers of good, traitors, headstrong, haughty, lovers of pleasure rather than lovers of God" (2 Timothy3:1–4).

Where are we in the stream of time? Where are we in the panorama of last-day events? Where are we in the march of history? There are "perilous times" ahead. As some translations state it, "dangerous times." In His marvelous sermon on the signs of His return, Jesus states, "Men's hearts [will be] failing them for fear and the expectation of those things which are coming on the earth, for the powers of the heavens will be shaken. Then they will see the Son of Man coming in a cloud with power and great glory" (Luke 21:26, 27).

The apostle Paul adds, "When they say, 'Peace and safety!' then sudden destruction comes upon them, as labor pains upon a pregnant woman. And they shall not escape. But you, brethren, are not in darkness, so that this Day should overtake you as a thief. You are all sons of light and sons of the day. We are not of the night nor of darkness. Therefore, let us not sleep, as others do, but let us watch and be sober" (1 Thessalonians 5:3–6). Now is the time to awake from our spiritual lethargy. This is no time for playing religious games.

We are poised on the verge of a religious, political, and economic union. The accumulated figures of sin are rapidly reaching their limit in God's record book. Economic, political, and natural disasters are coming. There will be a time of trouble such as this world has never seen. Where are we in the stream of time?

God is now preparing a people to proclaim the marvels of His grace, the greatness of His love, the goodness of His character, the righteousness of His law, and the beauty of His truth.

Bathed in His righteousness, they are justified by His grace and sanctified through His power. They love His truth, live His truth, and proclaim His truth. They count all things but loss for Christ. He is their all in all. They care not for earthly fame or human accolades. Position, prestige, and human praise mean little to them. With the apostle Paul they say, "For me, to live is Christ" (Philippians 1:21). Empowered by His Spirit, they proclaim His love and share His grace. The earth is lightened with the glory—the character—of God. The Holy Spirit is poured out in latter-rain power. Hearts are touched. Lives are changed. The world is reached, and Jesus comes again.

In the next chapter, we will study in detail the coming of Jesus and His final triumph over Satan and the powers of hell.

THE CONQUERING CHRIST

Revelation 19

1 After these things I heard a loud voice of a great multitude in heaven, saying, "Alleluia! Salvation and glory and honor and power belong to the Lord our God! **2** For true and righteous are His judgments, because He has judged the great harlot who corrupted the earth with her fornication; and He has avenged on her the blood of His servants shed by her." **3** Again they said, "Alleluia! Her smoke rises up forever and ever!" **4** And the twenty-four elders and the four living creatures fell down and worshiped God who sat on the throne, saying, "Amen! Alleluia!" **5** Then a voice came from the throne, saying, "Praise our God, all you His servants and those who fear Him, both small and great!"

6 And I heard, as it were, the voice of a great multitude, as the sound of many waters and as the sound of mighty thunderings, saying, "Alleluia! For the Lord God Omnipotent reigns! **7** Let us be glad and rejoice and give Him glory, for the marriage of the Lamb has come, and His wife has made herself ready." **8** And to her it was granted to be arrayed in fine linen, clean and bright, for the fine linen is the righteous acts of the saints.

9 Then he said to me, "Write: 'Blessed are those who are called to the marriage supper of the Lamb!' " And he said to me, "These are the true sayings of God." **10** And I fell at his feet to worship him. But he said to me, "See that you do not do that! I am your fellow servant, and of your brethren who have the testimony of Jesus. Worship God! For the testimony of Jesus is the spirit of prophecy."

11 Now I saw heaven opened, and behold, a white horse. And He who sat on him was called Faithful and True, and in righteousness He judges and makes war. **12** His eyes were like a flame of fire, and on His head were many crowns. He had a name written that no one knew except Himself. **13** He was clothed with a robe dipped in blood, and His name is called The Word of God. **14** And the armies in heaven, clothed in fine linen, white and clean, followed Him on white horses. **15** Now out of His mouth goes a sharp sword, that with it He should strike the nations. And He Himself will rule them with a rod of iron. He Himself treads the winepress of the fierceness and wrath of Almighty God. **16** And He has on His robe and on His thigh a name written:

KING OF KINGS
AND LORD OF LORDS.

17 Then I saw an angel standing in the sun; and he cried with a loud voice, saying to all the birds that fly in the midst of heaven, "Come and gather together for the supper of the great God, **18** that you may eat the flesh of kings, the flesh of captains, the flesh of mighty men, the flesh of horses and of those who sit on them, and the flesh of all people, free and slave, both small and great."

19 And I saw the beast, the kings of the earth, and their armies, gathered together to make war against Him who sat on the horse and against His army. **20** Then the beast was captured, and with him the false prophet who worked signs in his presence, by which he deceived those who received the mark of the beast and those who worshiped his image. These two were cast alive into the lake of fire burning with brimstone. **21** And the rest were killed with the sword which proceeded from the mouth of Him who sat on the horse. And all the birds were filled with their flesh.

During America's long and bloody civil war, James Russel Lowell wrote a moving poem, titled *The Present Crisis*. The poem focuses especially on the triumph of truth over evil and making the right decision regarding slavery when the nation was at the crossroads of destiny. Lowell writes, "Once to every man and nation comes the moment to decide, in the strife of truth and falsehood, for the good or evil side."

Although these lines were written at another time, in another place, for another purpose, they certainly resonate with the book of Revelation. Revelation is a book about eternal choices. When the rebellion against God began in heaven, every angel had to make a choice for truth or falsehood. Down through the ages, men and women were confronted with that same choice, and in the last days, the conflict between truth and error comes to a climax over the mark of the beast and the seal of God. Once again, all humanity is faced with eternal choices.

In Revelation 13, 17, and 18, John's angelic messenger has emphasized an international confederacy of church, state, and economic powers that seeks world control and domination. As the mark of the beast is enforced, along with its oppressive decrees forbidding those who do not receive the mark from buying or selling and eventually condemning them to death, the picture appears grim for the faithful people of God.

Once again, we are reminded of James Russel Lowell's poem,

Truth forever on the scaffold,
Wrong forever on the throne—
Yet that scaffold sways the future,
And behind the dim unknown,
Standeth God within the shadow
Keeping watch above His own.

Revelation 19 lifts our eyes from what is happening on earth to the throne room of the universe. There we see heavenly beings singing praises to God for His defeat of Babylon and the powers of evil. All of heaven is filled with rejoicing. Truth has triumphed over error. Righteousness has defeated falsehood. Christ is the victor, and all heaven shouts, "Alleluia!"

A glimpse of heaven: Rejoicing over the fall of Babylon

Revelation 19 grows out of verse 20 of the previous chapter. Revelation 18:20 appears in the midst of the description of Babylon's fall, and it says, "Rejoice over her, O heaven, and you holy apostles and prophets, for God has avenged you on her!"

Chapter 19 begins with a response to the angel's instruction. John writes, "After these things I heard a loud voice of a great multitude in heaven, saying, 'Alleluia! Salvation and glory and honor and power belong to the Lord our God! For true and righteous are His judgments, because He has judged the great harlot who corrupted the earth with her fornication; and He has avenged on her the blood of His servants shed by her!' Again they said, 'Alleluia! Her smoke rises up forever and ever!' " (Revelation 19:1–3).

All heaven rejoices. The power of evil is broken. Babylon, the oppressor of God's people, is defeated. The long night of sin has come to an end. This rejoicing comes from "a great multitude in heaven." We have already seen two such multitudes in the book of Revelation. In Revelation 7:9, there is a "great multitude which no one could number, of all nations, tribes, peoples, and tongues." We identified those in that multitude as the saved who had died before the return of Jesus. Then there is a vast throng of angels around the throne of God in Revelation 5:11. "The number of them was ten thousand times ten thousand, and thousands of thousands."

John continues,

> Then a voice came from the throne, saying, "Praise our God, all you His servants and those who fear Him, both small and great!"
> And I heard, as it were, the voice of a great multitude, as the sound of many waters and as the sound of mighty thunderings, saying, "Alleluia! For the Lord God Omnipotent reigns!" (Revelation 19:5, 6).

Perhaps we are to understand from these verses that John heard two different multitudes praising God—the first chorus of praise coming from the multitude of innumerable angels who surround God's throne, and the second from the vast multitude of the saved from all ages of the earth. At any rate, the sound of praise coming from these multitudes of voices must have been impressive beyond imagining.

What a chorus of jubilation! Think of the thrill of singing praise to God with a thousand times ten thousand other voices. Our voices unite in a crescendo of praise. Our hearts rejoice that the enemy has been defeated. The last foe and all his followers are overcome. The plague of sin is blotted out of the universe forever. John compares this hallelujah song of rejoicing to the sound of "mighty thunderings." It echoes and reechoes throughout the universe. It reverberates to the farthest corners of space, and this chorus will be sung through the ceaseless ages of eternity. "Alleluia! Salvation and glory and honor and power belong to the Lord our God!"

The chorus of praise from both groups begins with the word *alleluia*, or *hallelujah*. This is a very common word in religious terminology, but it occurs in the Bible only four times and only in this chapter (verses 1, 3, 4, and 6). It means "Praise God!" Psalms 113–118 all begin with the phrase "Praise the Lord!" They are known as the "Hallel" psalms—the "Praise God" psalms.

The multitudes in heaven praise God because salvation, glory, honor, and power belong to Him (Revelation 19:1). They praise Him because His judgments against the "great harlot," Babylon, are true and righteous. They praise Him because the blood of the saints has been "avenged" (verse 2). This doesn't mean that God seeks revenge against sinners or that He takes pleasure in punishing them. Avenging the blood of the saints involves demonstrating to the universe the injustice caused by sin and setting it right. That is why His judgments are "true and righteous."

The four living creatures and the twenty-four elders, whom we met in Revelation

4, also join in the chorus of praise and adoration. "The twenty-four elders and the four living creatures fell down and worshiped God who sat on the throne, saying, 'Amen! Alleluia!' " (Revelation 19:4). All heaven—angels and redeemed human beings—join their voices to rejoice at the final fall of Babylon and to praise God for the way He has dealt with sin.

The marriage supper of the Lamb

Another reason for the rejoicing in heaven is that "the marriage of the Lamb has come, and His wife has made herself ready" (verse 7). There is a supper connected with this marriage—"Blessed are those who are called to the marriage supper of the Lamb!" (verse 9). The marriage supper of the Lamb is contrasted later in this chapter with the "supper of the great God" (verse 17). They are very different events.

What is the marriage supper of the Lamb, and who is the Lamb's "wife" who has made herself ready?

As Jesus ate the Passover supper with His disciples shortly before the Cross, "He said to them, 'With fervent desire I have desired to eat this Passover with you before I suffer; for I say to you, I will no longer eat of it until it is fulfilled in the kingdom of God' " (Luke 22:15, 16). The Passover meal harkened back to the great deliverance of Israel from Egypt when the firstborn son in every Egyptian household died, but the firstborn sons of the Israelites were spared. A lamb was killed in their place, and it was eaten with unleavened bread and bitter herbs (Exodus 12:1–8).

The Passover became one of the primary religious ceremonies of the Jews commemorating their deliverance from Egyptian bondage. It symbolized the spiritual deliverance God provides for His people through the death of His Son. Jesus told His disciples that He would eat the Passover meal with them again in the kingdom of heaven. This is the marriage supper of the Lamb referred to here in Revelation 19.

There is also a passing reference in Matthew 8:11 to the redeemed sitting down at the table in the kingdom with Abraham, Isaac, and Jacob. Imagine yourself in heaven at the marriage supper of the Lamb, fellowshiping with the patriarchs, prophets, and apostles. Imagine being there with Jesus and the righteous of all ages. The marriage supper of the Lamb is in honor of the Christ, who has given His all for us in the plan of salvation. There we, who have been delivered from this planet in rebellion, scarred with sin, are introduced as sons and daughters of God to the unfallen worlds. We are worthy of heaven because of His worthiness. We are accepted in the beloved, redeemed by grace, clothed in His righteousness.

Who is the Lamb's "wife" who has made herself ready? John says, "I, John, saw the holy city, New Jerusalem, coming down out of heaven from God, prepared as a

bride adorned for her husband" (Revelation 21:2).

"Then one of the seven angels . . . talked with me, saying, 'Come, I will show you the bride, the Lamb's wife.' And he carried me away in the Spirit to a great and high mountain, and showed me the great city, the holy Jerusalem, descending out of heaven from God" (Revelation 21:9, 10).

So according to these verses, the New Jerusalem is the Lamb's bride, His wife. But isn't His true church the bride of Jesus? The apostle Paul writes to the Corinthian Christians, "I have betrothed you to one husband, that I may present you as a chaste virgin to Christ" (2 Corinthians 11:2). And to the Christians at Ephesus, Paul wrote, "Husbands, love your wives, just as Christ also loved the church and gave Himself for her" (Ephesians 5:25). In Revelation 12, we identified the pure woman standing on the sun as a symbol of the church, God's faithful people. The Bible often compares the relationship between God and His people to the marriage relationship.

There is an easy solution to this apparent contradiction. The wife, the bride of Christ, is not a city, but the people who live in that city. Who lives in the New Jerusalem? The redeemed from the earth. Revelation 21:27 says that those who enter the city are "those who are written in the Lamb's Book of Life." So the bride of Christ, His wife, who makes herself ready for the great marriage supper, is His church, His people, the inhabitants of the New Jerusalem. This identification is confirmed in Revelation 19:8, which says that the Lamb's "wife" is "arrayed in fine linen, clean and bright, for the fine linen is the righteous acts of the saints."

We do not want to pass over this expression too quickly. John clearly identifies the fine linen as the "righteous acts" of the people of God. The expression "righteous acts" comes from the Greek word *dikaioma*. This word has to do with the way we live, the sanctified deeds of our lives. These righteous acts are the result of a righteous character. The indwelling Christ empowers us to live godly lives. We do good deeds because of who we are in Christ. If we are in Christ, we will do good deeds. To paraphrase the words of Martin Luther, apple trees do not produce apples in order to become apple trees; they produce apples because they are apple trees. Christians do not develop righteous characters to be Christians; they develop righteous characters because they are Christians. Those eating with Christ in intimate fellowship at the marriage supper of the Lamb have supped with Him in intimate fellowship on earth. His Holy Spirit has transformed them, so the fruits of the Spirit are manifest in their lives (Galatians 5:22–25).

In heaven, we will join Jesus, and all the redeemed—the prophets, the apostles, the martyrs, and the faithful unknown followers of God from every age—to eat, fellowship, and rejoice together at the great marriage supper of the Lamb!

It is important to remember that chapter 19 begins in the predictable pattern of Revelation. The result is often pictured before the events leading up to it. Here, the people of God are pictured in heaven, rejoicing with the heavenly beings before Jesus returns to defeat the enemy and take them home. There are at least two reasons for this. First, people in Bible times did not necessarily think like Westerners today. They wanted to know the end of the story. They were not as concerned about each logical event that led up to the conclusion. They were interested in knowing how the story would end. That *is* the most important thing to know, isn't it? A second reason God tells the end of the story first in these prophecies is that He always wants to encourage us that one day we will live with Him in eternity. He is sovereign, and soon, the long night of sin will be over. We find this sequence of the outcome, then the cause, in Revelation 14, 15, 18, and 19.

The testimony of Jesus

Overwhelmed by the majestic scenes he saw in the vision, John twice fell at the feet of the angel to "worship" him. "But he said to me, 'See that you do not do that! I am your fellow servant, and of your brethren who have the testimony of Jesus. Worship God! For the testimony of Jesus is the spirit of prophecy' " (Revelation 19:10).

"He said to me, 'See that you do not do that. For I am your fellow servant, and of your brethren the prophets, and of those who keep the words of the prophecy of this book' " (Revelation 22:9).

The two experiences are virtually the same, and the angel's response is quite similar. But if we compare the two texts, we see that the phrase, "your brethren who have the testimony of Jesus" in Revelation 19:10 has become the phrase, "your brethren the prophets" in Revelation 22:9. So the testimony of Jesus has to do with the prophets.

We saw in Revelation 12:17 that the saints, God's last-day people, "keep the commandments of God and have the testimony of Jesus." So God's last-day people will have "the spirit of prophecy." This phrase, *the spirit of prophecy*, appears nowhere else in the Bible.

The apostle Paul speaks of the Holy Spirit giving "gifts" to individuals as He chooses, and one of these gifts is the gift of prophecy (1 Corinthians 12:8–10). Both Ephesians 4:8–13 and 1 Corinthians 1:4–9 clearly indicate that the gift of prophecy would remain in God's commandment-keeping church to guide, sustain, strengthen, instruct, and nurture it until the return of Jesus in glory. All these gifts are not given to every member of the church. And, of course, not every church member has the gift of prophecy. The gift of prophecy is a special gift given by God to prepare His people for the coming of Jesus. In the Old Testament, when Israel disobeyed God repeatedly and entered into open rebellion and apostasy, God withdrew the prophetic gift. Lamentations 2:9 puts it this way, "The Law is no more, and her prophets find no vision from the LORD." But according to Revelation 12:17, God would restore the gift of prophecy to His last-day church. His church will have the gifts of the spirit, including the gift of prophecy. It will keep God's commandments, and it will be guided by His prophetic voice, both in the Scriptures and in the gift of prophecy He has placed within His church.

The conquering Christ

John now launches into a powerful description of the conquering Christ and the ultimate destruction of Babylon and all the forces of wickedness:

> I saw heaven opened, and behold, a white horse. And He who sat on him was called Faithful and True, and in righteousness He judges and makes war. His eyes were like a flame of fire, and on His head were many crowns. He had a name written that no one knew except Himself. He was clothed with a robe dipped in blood, and His name is called The Word of God. And the armies in heaven, clothed in fine linen, white and clean, followed Him on white horses. Now out of His mouth goes a sharp sword, that with it He should strike the nations. And He Himself will rule them with a rod of iron. He Himself treads the winepress of the fierceness and wrath of Almighty God. And He has on His robe and on His thigh a name written:
>
> KING OF KINGS AND
> LORD OF LORDS (Revelation 19:11–16).

This is one of the more dramatic pictures in Revelation, a book that is filled with vivid, dramatic imagery. These verses pick up images from a number of places elsewhere in the book. The conquering rider on a white horse brings to mind the white horse of the first seal (Revelation 6:2). His eyes, like flames of fire, are found in Revelation 1:14. His name that no one knows but Himself also appears in the promise to the church of Pergamos (Revelation 2:17). The rod of iron with which He rules is mentioned in Revelation 12:5. Altogether, these symbols make up a magnificent image of the conquering Christ who rides forth from heaven as King of kings and Lord of lords!

Heaven has been rejoicing at the fall of Babylon. It has been praising God for His righteous judgments against sin. Now the rejoicing and praise spill over into an intense preview of the Second Coming. Jesus will ride down the corridors of the sky with a retinue of glorious angels in power and great glory to redeem His people! He rides a white horse and is followed by "the armies of heaven," also riding white horses.

The white horse is a symbol of a conqueror. White horses have traditionally been the favorite of kings and ancient military leaders. Roman generals rode white horses through the streets of Rome when they celebrated their triumphs in war. Through the Cross, Christ has "disarmed principalities and powers, [and] He made a public spectacle of them, triumphing over them" (Colossians 2:15). He has defeated Satan and is the rightful ruler of this world. The kingdoms of this world belong to Him. Now He appears, symbolically, as a warrior riding a white horse to claim what is lawfully His and escort His people back home.

After Peter tried to defend Jesus in the Garden of Gethsemane and succeeded only in cutting off the ear of the high priest's servant, Jesus told him to put away his sword, because if need be, the Father would send "more than twelve legions of angels" to protect Him (Matthew 26:53). A Roman "legion" in the first century consisted of about five thousand soldiers. So twelve legions would be sixty thousand soldiers. But twelve legions of angels are a mere fraction of the "armies in heaven." The angels on white horses who accompany the conquering Christ number ten thousand times ten thousand and thousands of thousands!

The conquering Christ has eyes like flames of fire that seem to pierce to the very heart of every person on earth. He knows their innermost thoughts and words—every action of their lives.

It is important as well to notice the titles of Christ in this passage. According to Revelation 19:11, He is "Faithful and True." He fulfills His promise from John 14:1–3 that He would return. The delay has been long, but Christ is faithful to His word and returns to take His people home. He is also known as the "Word of God" in verse 13. Jesus is the living Word, revealing in His life what God is like. He is the Word made flesh, and John declares, "And the Word became flesh and dwelt among us, and we beheld His glory, the glory as of the only begotten of the Father, full of grace and truth" (John 1:14). The glory of God is revealed in Christ, and when Jesus returns, He returns in the glory of the Father with all His angels (Matthew 16:27). Our finite human minds cannot possibly grasp the magnificence of the glory of God when Christ returns.

The conquering Christ is clothed in "a robe dipped in blood" (Revelation 19:13). It is natural to assume that this refers to the blood He shed on Calvary to redeem humanity. But it is possible that this is pointing to the phrase appearing two verses later—"He Himself treads the winepress of the fierceness and wrath of Almighty God" (verse 15). The blood on His robe may not be His blood, but the blood of His enemies.

Revelation 14:17–20 pictures the final harvest of the lost as grapes being trampled in the winepress of God's wrath and blood coming out of the winepress. The blood on Jesus' robe may well represent the absolute destruction of the wicked in fulfillment of Isaiah's prediction:

> "For I have trodden them in My anger
> And trampled them in My fury;
> Their blood is sprinkled upon My garments,
> And I have stained all My robes.
> For the day of vengeance is in My heart,
> And the year of My redeemed has come" (Isaiah 63:3, 4).

God's anger, or wrath, is His judgment upon sin. This passage portraying Jesus on a white horse depicts Him as a conqueror over His enemies. The symbolic picture in these verses is not the one of Jesus who is the lamb slain from the foundation of the world but Jesus as King of kings, and Lord of all, conquering, triumphing, and defeating the powers of evil.

His eyes are flames of fire, and a sharp sword goes out of His mouth as He rides forth to make war. Heaven has declared His judgments to be true and righteous (Revelation 19:2), and His name to be "Faithful and True" (verse 11). This image of the conquering Christ is set in the context of His righteous judgments against sin and sinners at the end of time. In this context, the blood on His robe may well be the blood of those who refuse His offer of salvation, reject His loving appeals, turn their backs on His initiative to save them, and choose to rebel against His commands. The logical result of their decision is eternal loss. Christ longed to save them, but they refused to respond. Their choice seals their destiny.

The supper of the great God

John records the final scene of this chapter. "Then I saw an angel standing in the sun; and he cried with a loud voice, saying to all the birds that fly in the midst of heaven, 'Come and gather together for the supper of the great God, that you may eat the flesh of kings, the flesh of captains, the flesh of mighty men, the flesh of horses and of those who sit on them, and the flesh of all people, free and slave, both small and great' " (verses 17, 18).

The supper of the great God stands in stark contrast to the marriage supper of the Lamb. At one, the redeemed sit around a vast table in heaven, sharing a meal that is a reminder of their deliverance from the bondage of sin. At the other, vultures and other birds of prey are beckoned from every quarter of the sky to come and glut themselves on the fallen bodies of the slain!

For the redeemed, the scene is one of rejoicing. For the wicked, the scene is one of weeping and sad lament. For one group, there is a new beginning; for the other, there is a tragic end. For one group, the joys of eternity lie ahead of them, for the other, darkness and total annihilation.

The scene John next describes is one of the saddest in all the Bible:

> And I saw the beast, the kings of the earth, and their armies, gathered together to make war against Him who sat on the horse and against His army. Then the beast was captured, and with him the false prophet who worked signs in his presence, by which he deceived those who received the mark of the beast and those who worshiped his image. These two were cast alive into the lake of fire burning with brimstone. And the rest were killed with the sword which proceeded from the mouth of Him who sat on the horse. And all the birds were filled with their flesh (verses 19–21).

Satan and the hosts of those who have followed him in his rebellion against God make a final stand. They gather together to make war against the conquering Christ. The war that began in heaven so long before (Revelation 12:7–9) has reached its last battle. Satan and his angels lost that first battle in heaven, and they will lose this last battle as well.

The beast and the false prophet are destroyed in the lake of fire "prepared for the devil and his angels" (Matthew 25:41). The rest are "killed with the sword which proceeded from the mouth of Him who sat on the horse" (Revelation 19:21). The Word of God is sharper than a two-edged sword. It lays bare the thoughts and intents of the heart (Hebrews 4:12). The truths of God's Word condemn those who have rejected them and fought against them. The supper of the great God is a graphic representation of the awful doom of Satan, his angels, and those who follow him.

These final scenes of earth's history are an urgent appeal to each one of us to respond to God's grace, accept by faith the salvation He so freely offers, and live lives of godly obedience so we, too, can rejoice with the saved of all ages, wearing the white robes of righteousness at the marriage supper of the Lamb.

In the next chapter, we move a thousand years beyond the Second Coming.

THE MILLENNIUM: THE REAL TRUTH ABOUT REVELATION'S 1,000 YEARS

Revelation 20

1 Then I saw an angel coming down from heaven, having the key to the bottomless pit and a great chain in his hand. **2** He laid hold of the dragon, that serpent of old, who is the Devil and Satan, and bound him for a thousand years; **3** and he cast him into the bottomless pit, and shut him up, and set a seal on him, so that he should deceive the nations no more till the thousand years were finished. But after these things he must be released for a little while.

4 And I saw thrones, and they sat on them, and judgment was committed to them. Then I saw the souls of those who had been beheaded for their witness to Jesus and for the word of God, who had not worshiped the beast or his image, and had not received his mark on their foreheads or on their hands. And they lived and reigned with Christ for a thousand years. **5** But the rest of the dead did not live again until the thousand years were finished. This is the first resurrection. **6** Blessed and holy is he who has part in the first resurrection. Over such the second death has no power, but they shall be priests of God and of Christ, and shall reign with Him a thousand years.

7 Now when the thousand years have expired, Satan will be released from his prison **8** and will go out to deceive the nations which are in the four corners of the earth, Gog and Magog, to gather them together to battle, whose number is as the sand of the sea. **9** They went up on the breadth of the earth and surrounded the camp of the saints and the beloved city. And fire came down from God out of heaven and devoured them. **10** The devil, who deceived them, was cast into the lake of fire and brimstone where the beast and the false prophet are. And they will be tormented day and night forever and ever.

11 Then I saw a great white throne and Him who sat on it, from whose face the earth and the heaven fled away.

And there was found no place for them. **12** And I saw the dead, small and great, standing before God, and books were opened. And another book was opened, which is the Book of Life. And the dead were judged according to their works, by the things which were written in the books. **13** The sea gave up the dead who were in it, and Death and Hades delivered up the dead who were in them. And they were judged, each one according to his works. **14** Then Death and Hades were cast into the lake of fire. This is the second death. **15** And anyone not found written in the Book of Life was cast into the lake of fire.

❧

Revelation 19 ends with a dramatic portrayal of the return of Jesus and the destruction of the wicked. But the story is not over. Satan's rebellion is defeated but not ended. There is yet one more scene in the great controversy before harmony reigns throughout the universe forever. That scene is known as the "millennium"—a period lasting one thousand years. The millennium is the subject of Revelation 20.

The term comes from two Latin words, *mille* (thousand) and *annus* (year). The word *millennium* does not appear anywhere in the Bible, and the topic is dealt with only here in Revelation 20. Nevertheless, the millennium, or Revelation's thousand years, is an important and fascinating subject.

Bible students have many different ideas concerning the millennium—what it is and when it will occur. Some believe the millennium will take place *before* Jesus returns. They believe that increasing success in spreading the gospel will eventually result in righteousness and peace filling the earth, and a golden age of one thousand years will follow. Then Jesus will return to usher in eternity. Others believe that the millennium will take place *after* Jesus returns. Many of those holding this view also believe that Jesus will set up His kingdom on earth during this thousand-year period. A third group believes that the millennium in Revelation 20 is symbolic imagery and not an actual time period of a thousand years at all.

Let's see what Revelation has to say about this thousand-year period.

Satan bound in the bottomless pit

John says, "Then I saw an angel coming down from heaven, having the key to the bottomless pit and a great chain in his hand. He laid hold of the dragon, that serpent of old, who is the Devil and Satan, and bound him for a thousand years; and he cast him into the bottomless pit, and shut him up, and set a seal on him, so that he should deceive the nations no more until the thousand years were finished. But after these things he must be released for a little while" (Revelation 20:1–3).

We have encountered the "bottomless pit" in connection with the fifth trumpet. There, John wrote: "Then the fifth angel sounded: And I saw a star fallen from heaven to the earth. To him was given the key to the bottomless pit. And he opened the bottomless pit, and smoke arose out of the pit like the smoke of a great furnace" (Revelation 9:1, 2). Linking these verses with Revelation 8:10, we identified Satan as the "star" that fell from heaven and as the one who holds the key to the bottomless pit. But here in Revelation 20, John pictures Satan being bound with a chain and cast into the bottomless pit by an angel who holds the key. How do we explain the change? How does Satan go from being in control of the bottomless pit to being held captive in it? Once he held the key; now another has it. What has happened?

The short answer is that the second coming of Jesus has happened. Satan's position before Jesus' second coming is very different from his situation once Jesus has returned. As chapter 19 depicts so dramatically, the conquering Christ has descended to earth at the head of the armies of heaven. Who is saved and who is lost has been made evident to everyone because the wicked have been killed and the righteous have been given immortality. Before the Second Coming, Satan was still working with men and women to oppose God. After the Second Coming, he and his angels are still in rebellion against God, but now Satan has no one on earth to use as his agents in the great controversy. There is no one to tempt and deceive any longer. The righteous dead have been resurrected and, along with the righteous living, have been caught up to meet Christ in the air at His second coming (1 Thessalonians 4:16, 17). The wicked, or unsaved, are destroyed with the brightness of Christ's glorious return (Hebrews 12:29; 1 Thessalonians 1:7–10). Before, Satan could cause the smoke of rebellion to rise out of the bottomless pit. He could cloud minds with the smoke of deception. Now, he is in a bottomless pit of his own making—and he will remain there for a thousand years.

The imagery in Revelation 20:1–3 is symbolic. Satan is not literally bound with a chain and locked in a pit. For a thousand years, he is confined to this desolate, unpopulated earth, bound by the circumstances he himself has created. The "chain" that holds Satan during the millennium is symbolic. In 2 Peter 2:4, we read that Satan and his angels were reserved for punishment by "chains of darkness." Satan will be confined to the earth by a chain of circumstances with no one to tempt. For one thousand years, he will see the devastation, destruction, and disaster that his rebellion has created.

The Greek word translated "bottomless pit" is the same word from which we get our English word *abyss.* It is also the same word used in the Septuagint, the Greek version of the Old Testament, to describe the earth at the beginning of Creation. "The earth was without form, and void; and darkness was on the face of the deep" (Genesis 1:2). The word translated "deep" is this same Greek word—*abussos*, "abyss." It describes a desolate earth. The "bottomless pit" is not some subterranean cavern or some yawning chasm somewhere out there in the universe. The tremendous chaos on earth preceding the Second Coming—the great earthquakes and hail storms and flattening of the mountains—has brought the earth back to a dark, disorganized mass like its condition at the beginning of Creation.

The prophet Jeremiah described the earth's condition during the millennium in these words:

> I beheld the earth, and indeed it was without form, and void;
> And the heavens, they had no light.
> I beheld the mountains, and indeed they trembled,
> And all the hills moved back and forth.
> I beheld, and indeed there was no man,
> And all the birds of the heavens had fled.
> I beheld, and indeed the fruitful land was a wilderness,
> And all its cities were broken down (Jeremiah 4:23–26).

This is the "bottomless pit" where Satan must remain for one thousand years. All around him are the results of his rebellion, and he has ample time to reflect on the desolation he has caused. It is also significant that Jeremiah uses the expressions "indeed there was no man, and all the birds of the heaven fled." "The fruitful land was a wilderness, and all the cities were broken down." The prophet here emphasizes the catastrophic destruction at the second coming of Christ and that no person is left alive on earth during this thousand-year period. He confirms this

> God is dealing with the sin problem in a way that will assure the universe that sin will never rise a second time.

fact by using even more dramatic language in Jeremiah 25:33: "And at that day the slain of the LORD shall be from one end of the earth even to the other end of the earth. They shall not be lamented, or gathered, or buried; they shall become refuse on the ground." The earth will be utterly depopulated at Christ's return. Satan is left alone to see the havoc caused by His rebellion. The entire universe looking at a desolate earth recognizes anew that the wages of sin is death.

God is dealing with the sin problem in a way that will assure the universe that sin will never rise a second time (Nahum 1:9). God does this in three primary ways: First, He reveals His limitless love, passionate desire, and relentless efforts to save all humanity. Second, He reveals His justice, fairness, and righteousness. Finally, He allows the universe to see the ultimate results of sin and rebellion.

Reigning in heaven

At the Second Coming, the redeemed are taken to heaven. While Satan is languishing on an uninhabited earth for a thousand years, they are living and reigning with Jesus in heaven. John says, "I saw thrones, and they [the redeemed] sat on them, and judgment was committed to them. Then I saw the souls of those who had been beheaded for their witness to Jesus and for the word of God, who had not worshiped the beast or his image, and not received his mark on their foreheads or on their hands. And they lived and reigned with Christ for a thousand years" (Revelation 20:4).

What will the saved do in heaven for a thousand years? It will take some time just to become accustomed to the sights and sounds of heaven, don't you think? The two final chapters of Revelation attempt to describe what heaven and eternal life will be like. We will soon examine those chapters, but even after doing so, we still can have only a very imperfect understanding of the reality of living and reigning with Jesus in heaven. Yes, heaven will take some getting used to!

Nevertheless, the saved of the earth will be occupied with a number of activities in heaven during the thousand years. Verse 4 says the saints will live and reign with Christ during this time. What does this mean?

It means that during the millennium, the righteous will have an opportunity to observe firsthand God's justice and love in the way He has dealt with the problem of sin. In a new way, more forcefully than ever before, the saved will grasp God's powerful attempts to save everyone who has ever lived. They will realize anew that everyone who is lost has missed out on heaven because of his or her own personal rejection of the appeals of Christ. If there is a loved one or a close friend who is absent from heaven, the saved will have an opportunity to understand more fully all that Jesus did to draw that person to Himself—and why that didn't happen. God will patiently answer any questions.

The apostle Paul wrote to the Christians at Corinth, "Do you not know that we shall judge angels?" (1 Corinthians 6:3). As the righteous live and reign with Christ in heaven during the millennium, we will review the final judgment of Satan and his angels that will occur at the close of the thousand years. All this openness and review will demonstrate beyond any possible doubt that God has been fair and just in all His dealings with sin and sinners. He will be vindicated in the face of all of Satan's charges against Him. The entire universe will see more clearly than ever before God's wisdom in dealing with the great controversy. They will more fully understand God's love and God's justice. In one great celestial refrain, they will exclaim,

> "Great and marvelous are your works,
> Lord God Almighty!
> Just and true are your ways,
> O King of the saints!" (Revelation 15:3).

However, the final chapter in the great controversy is yet to be played out. John states, "After these things he (Satan) must be released for a little while" (Revelation 20:3).

When does the millennium begin and end?

"But the rest of the dead did not live again until the thousand years were finished. This is the first resurrection. Blessed and holy is he who has part in the first resurrection. Over such the second death has no power, but they shall be priests of God and of Christ and shall reign with Him a thousand years" (verses 5, 6).

These verses have confused some Bible students, so let's look at them carefully. If we look just at the two sentences of verse 5, it might seem that the "first resurrection" is the resurrection of "the rest of the dead" and that it takes place at the close of the thousand years. The opposite is true! You see, we must not look at verses 5 and 6 in isolation from verse 4 that precedes them. So let's take a close look at these three verses—4, 5, and 6—and determine exactly what they are saying:

1. There is a "first resurrection." Those raised to life in this first resurrection are "blessed and holy" (verse 6). They "reign with Him [Christ] for a thousand years" (verse 6). Those living and reigning with Christ for a thousand years include the martyrs and those who have overcome the beast and his image and his mark (verse 4). It is clear, then, that the "first resurrection" is the resurrection of the righteous at the second coming of Christ (see 1 Thessalonians 4:16, 17; 1 Corinthians 15:51–57).

2. A "first resurrection" implies that there is a second resurrection. Jesus spoke of two resurrections—a resurrection of life and a resurrection of condemnation

(John 5:28, 29). Revelation 20:6 says that those raised in the first resurrection are blessed and holy, so the first resurrection is the resurrection of life that Jesus talked about. The second resurrection, then, must be the resurrection of condemnation. Those raised in this second resurrection must be the wicked.

3. "The rest of the dead" (verse 5) refers to the wicked. Verse 4 has been describing the saved who live in heaven with Jesus for a thousand years. Then verse 5 follows, saying, "The rest of the dead did not live again until the thousand years were finished." So "the rest of the dead" are those not raised to life in the first resurrection—the wicked. The unsaved are raised to life at the end of the millennium in the resurrection of condemnation Jesus spoke of.

Let's summarize what we have learned from these verses considering when the millennium begins and ends:

1. The millennium begins at the Second Coming when the righteous dead are raised to life and taken to heaven along with the righteous living. All the saved live and reign with Christ in heaven during the millennium.
2. At the Second Coming, the living wicked are destroyed by the brightness of Christ's coming (2 Thessalonians 2:8). The wicked who have died before Jesus returns remain unconscious in the grave. So during the millennium, all the wicked are dead on the earth. They ("the rest of the dead") are raised to life in the resurrection of condemnation at the close of the millennium.
3. During the millennium, Satan and his angels are confined to this earth—desolate and uninhabited by human beings.

Thus, the millennium begins with the resurrection of the righteous at the second coming of Jesus and ends a thousand years later with the resurrection of the wicked. What purpose is there to resurrect the wicked? Why not just leave them in their graves? Everything God does has an eternal purpose. The resurrection of the wicked clearly demonstrates that they come out of their graves with the same characteristics of greed, selfishness, and rebellion with which they went in. A second chance at salvation is unnecessary because their hearts are thoroughly hardened in rebellion against God.

The final battle
John writes,

Now when the thousand years have expired, Satan will be released from his prison and will go out to deceive the nations which are in the four corners of the earth, Gog and Magog, to gather them together to battle, whose number is as the sand of the sea. They went up on the breadth of the earth and surrounded the camp of the saints and the beloved city. And fire came down from God out of heaven and devoured them. The devil, who deceived them, was cast into the lake of fire and brimstone where the beast and the false prophet are. And they will be tormented day and night forever and ever (Revelation 20:7–10).

Satan is released from his prison at the end of the thousand years because the wicked are raised to life. For a thousand years, he has had no one to tempt or deceive. He and his angels have been alone to reflect on where their rebellion against God has taken them. Now, however, Satan has a vast army of followers. Their number is like the sands of the sea (verse 8). All the wicked who have ever lived are now alive once more on the earth.

Notwithstanding the fact that Satan has suffered defeat after defeat in the great controversy, he is not yet ready to end his rebellion. He goes out to deceive "the nations"—all that huge throng of the lost. There are great generals in that multitude; there are masterminds of evil. There are talented, energetic persons with great qualities of leadership. Prior to the millennium, they used those energies and talents to oppose God. Now, they are no more willing to submit to Him than they ever were. Satan inspires them to make one last great effort to overthrow God and set up their own kingdom.

The expression "Gog and Magog" symbolizes the multitudes of unsaved who are in rebellion against God. You can read more about this phrase in Ezekiel 38:1, 2. Gog of the land of Magog is depicted as an enemy of God's people who would attempt to attack and destroy them. God uses this literary symbol to depict Satan and the unsaved of all the ages in their attack upon Christ's holy city, the New Jerusalem, at the end of the millennium. Satan and his followers surround "the camp of the saints and the beloved city" (Revelation 20:9).

At the close of the millennium, all the wicked are raised to life, and the holy city, New Jerusalem, descends to earth from heaven! John says, "Then I, John, saw the holy city, New Jerusalem, coming down out of heaven from God, prepared as a bride adorned for her husband" (Revelation 21:2). The saints have been living and reigning with Christ in the New Jerusalem for the millennium. Now, at the end of the thousand years, the city descends to earth along with God, Jesus, the angels, and all the redeemed. Everyone is present for the final battle of the great controversy. Sin is about to be eradicated once and for all!

The "great white throne" judgment

John continues:

> Then I saw a great white throne and Him who sat on it, from whose face the earth and the heaven fled away. And there was no place found for them. And I saw the dead, small and great, standing before God, and books were opened. And another book was opened, which is the Book of Life. And the dead were judged according to their works, by the things which were written in the books. The sea gave up the dead who were in it, and Death and Hades delivered up the dead who were in them. And they were judged, each one according to his works. Then Death and Hades were cast into the lake of fire. This is the second death. And anyone not found written in the Book of Life was cast into the lake of fire (Revelation 20:11–15).

Satan and his vast army of the wicked surround the holy city. They intend to fight one final battle for supremacy—win or lose. The last chapter in the great controversy is coming to its conclusion. Just as the army of the wicked is preparing to storm the holy city, they are stopped in their tracks by the sight of a great white throne on which God sits.

This is the picture of the judgment that we often have in mind when we think of Judgment Day. But as we have seen previously in the books of Daniel and Revelation, judgment has been going on in heaven since 1844, determining who has accepted God's gracious offer of salvation and who has refused. This "great white throne" judgment is not designed to determine who is saved and who is lost. That has already been decided. This judgment is designed to end sin once and for all. This judgment is intended to establish in the mind of every individual in the universe that God is just and fair. Each lost person in that vast army of Satan is shown exactly the charges for which he or she is condemned. They see their life choices in all their reality. They are convinced that God's judgment is just and that they have made themselves unfit to live in heaven. "As I live, says the LORD, every knee shall bow to Me, and every tongue shall confess to God" (Romans 14:11; Philippians 2:9–11). Everyone in that multitude of the lost will kneel and acknowledge that God has dealt with him or her fairly. Even Satan and his angels must confess that God's judgments are just.

The great controversy ended

Finally, fire comes down from God and devours them—everyone not written in the Lamb's book of life (Revelation 20:9, 15). "This is the second death" (verse 14).

This death is final; it is eternal. This death is what the apostle Paul was referring to when he wrote, "The wages of sin is death" (Romans 6:23). Satan and his angels are destroyed in the lake of fire (Revelation 20:10; Matthew 25:41). Sin is completely eradicated from the universe, never to rise again (Nahum 1:9). Death itself and Hades (the grave) are destroyed in the final fire (Revelation 20:14). The great controversy is ended!

The fire that devours the wicked, along with Satan and his angels, also purifies the earth. The apostle Peter speaks of "the day of the Lord" in which "the earth and the works that are in it will be burned up," and even "the elements will melt with fervent heat" (2 Peter 3:10). Out of the ashes of that inferno, God will create a new heaven and a new earth where only righteousness will exist (2 Peter 3:13). That new earth and the New Jerusalem are the subjects of the last two chapters of Revelation. But don't miss this point. When Jesus comes back, there will be only two groups.

A lot of people today wish they could straddle the fence. They are hesitant to make a complete surrender to Christ. They are attracted to the gospel but afraid that if they fully commit their lives to Christ, it may be too restrictive for them. They enjoy the sweet sound of the gospel, but they find it hard to let go of their favorite sins. They do not come to the point of full surrender.

This is a fatal mistake. To be almost saved is to be 100 percent, totally, and completely lost. Millions are deceiving themselves, reasoning that at some future date, they can turn back, and everything will be all right. Among the vast multitudes of the lost when Christ returns will be many who knew and believed the truth—many who heard the Holy Spirit speaking to their hearts. Like King Agrippa, they were "almost persuaded" (Acts 26:28), yet they hesitated and held back.

They will see the holy city coming down from God out of heaven. They will hear the glorious songs of the saved, and they will say, "The harvest is past, the summer is ended, and we are not saved!" (Jeremiah 8:20).

"Today," says Scripture, "if you will hear His voice, do not harden your hearts" (Hebrews 4:7). "Behold, now is the accepted time; behold, now is the day of salvation" (2 Corinthians 6:2). Christ's arms are wide open for you right now. Human probation has not yet closed. He wants you in heaven more than you can ever imagine. He has done everything possible to save you. Will you open your heart to Him right now? Will you respond to His love without reservation and chose to serve Him forever?

THE NEW JERUSALEM

Revelation 21

1 Now I saw a new heaven and a new earth, for the first heaven and the first earth had passed away. Also there was no more sea. **2** Then I, John, saw the holy city, New Jerusalem, coming down out of heaven from God, prepared as a bride adorned for her husband. **3** And I heard a loud voice from heaven saying, "Behold, the tabernacle of God is with men, and He will dwell with them, and they shall be His people. God Himself will be with them and be their God. **4** And God will wipe away every tear from their eyes; there shall be no more death, nor sorrow, nor crying. There shall be no more pain, for the former things have passed away."

5 Then He who sat on the throne said, "Behold, I make all things new." And He said to me, "Write, for these words are true and faithful."

6 And He said to me, "It is done! I am the Alpha and the Omega, the Beginning and the End. I will give of the fountain of the water of life freely to him who thirsts.

7 He who overcomes shall inherit all things, and I will be his God and he shall be My son. **8** But the cowardly, unbelieving, abominable, murderers, sexually immoral, sorcerers, idolaters, and all liars shall have their part in the lake which burns with fire and brimstone, which is the second death."

9 Then one of the seven angels who had the seven bowls filled with the seven last plagues came to me and talked with me, saying, "Come, I will show you the bride, the Lamb's wife." **10** And he carried me away in the Spirit to a great and high mountain, and showed me the great city, the holy Jerusalem, descending out of heaven from God, **11** having the glory of God. Her light was like a most precious stone, like a jasper stone, clear as crystal. **12** Also she had a great and high wall with twelve gates, and twelve angels at the gates, and names written on them, which are the names of the twelve tribes of the children of Israel: **13** three gates on the east, three gates on the north, three gates on the south, and three gates on the west.

14 Now the wall of the city had twelve foundations, and on them were the names of the twelve apostles of the Lamb. **15** And he who talked with me had a gold reed to measure the city, its gates, and its wall. **16** The city is laid out as a square; its length is as great as its breadth. And he measured the city with the reed: twelve thousand furlongs. Its length, breadth, and height are equal. **17** Then he measured its wall: one hundred and forty-four cubits, according to the measure of a man, that is, of an angel. **18** The construction of its wall was of jasper; and the city was pure gold, like clear glass. **19** The foundations of the wall of the city were adorned with all kinds of precious stones: the first foundation was jasper, the second sapphire, the third chalcedony, the fourth emerald, **20** the fifth sardonyx, the sixth sardius, the seventh

chrysolite, the eighth beryl, the ninth topaz, the tenth chrysoprase, the eleventh jacinth, and the twelfth amethyst. **21** The twelve gates were twelve pearls: each individual gate was of one pearl. And the street of the city was pure gold, like transparent glass.

22 But I saw no temple in it, for the Lord God Almighty and the Lamb are its temple. **23** The city had no need of the sun or of the moon to shine in it, for the glory of God illuminated it. The Lamb is its light. **24** And the nations of those who are saved shall walk in its light, and the kings of the earth bring their glory and honor into it. **25** Its gates shall not be shut at all by day (there shall be no night there). **26** And they shall bring the glory and the honor of the nations into it. **27** But there shall by no means enter it anything that defiles, or causes an abomination or a lie, but only those who are written in the Lamb's Book of Life.

❧

Historic Saint Augustine, Florida, lays claim to being the oldest city in the United States. Its Spanish architecture and sandy beaches, such as Saint Augustine Beach and the tranquil Crescent Beach, make it one of Florida's most desired tourist locations. However, its real claim to fame is Ponce de Leon's fountain of youth. The fountain of youth is a legendary spring that supposedly restores the health and vigor of anyone who drinks or bathes in its bubbling waters.

In the sixteenth century, the story of these healing waters became attached to the biography of Spanish explorer Ponce de Leon, and Saint Augustine is home to the

Fountain of Youth Archaeological Park. The park is a tribute to the spot where Ponce de León is said to have first landed, although there's no clear documentation in his own writings that he discovered the magical fountain.

Well-known American writers such as Nathaniel Hawthorne and Orson Welles have used the metaphor of the fountain of youth in their tales. Even the Walt Disney Company in the United States got into the act by creating cartoons based on the legend.

Sagas of such a fountain have been told worldwide for thousands of years, appearing in writings by Herodotus, Alexander the Great, and the stories of Prester John. Legends of similar waters evidently were also prominent among the Caribbean natives, who told tales of the healing powers of the waters in the mythical land of Bimini.

The problem with these fountains of youth, however, is that people who drink the "magical" water and bathe in its mythical fountains still get old, they still get sick, and they still die. Although hundreds of thousands of tourists have visited Saint Augustine's fountain of youth throughout the years, their health hasn't improved.

Millions of people worldwide also pursue their own "fountains" of eternal youth. Whether it's some fad diet, a rigorous exercise regime, positive thinking, or some wonder cream to reduce wrinkles, we all long to discover something that will extend our lives and perpetuate our youthful exuberance. Within each one of us is a divinely placed desire to live a long, healthy, happy life.

It was God's original plan that Adam and Eve and their descendants experience life to the fullest without any sickness, suffering, heartache, or death. The Bible begins with a perfect world in Genesis 1 and 2, and it ends with a perfect world in Revelation 21 and 22. God's plan for His people will be accomplished. His purposes will be fulfilled. The last two chapters of Revelation give us a glimpse of that eternal world.

The new heavens and the new earth

At the end of Revelation 20, the great controversy is ended. Sin and sinners are no more. Never again will sin arise to disrupt the harmony of eternity. Now John's attention is turned to the "new heavens and a new earth in which righteousness dwells" that the apostle Peter wrote about (2 Peter 3:13). The last two chapters of Revelation—chapters 21 and 22—are devoted to the glorious destiny of the redeemed in the earth made new.

In His Word, God has given us a preview of the glories of the new earth as a little appetizer to create within us a desire to be there. Yet He has not answered every question we might have on this subject. We would do well to remember Paul's quotation of Isaiah 64:4 as we study these last two chapters of Revelation—"Eye has not seen, nor ear heard, nor have entered into the heart of man the things which God has prepared for those who love Him" (1 Corinthians 2:9).

Think of the most extravagant beauty in art and nature, or the soaring rapture of a great choir. All of that will seem like dismal gray, like a noisy gong, when we are present among the sights and sounds of heaven. One day, when we gaze on that glory, when we hear that music, we will finally recognize the evil transformation that sin has brought to our world. The amazing wonders of heaven will be far more than the best we can imagine. They will be more beautiful than the most glorious sunset, more spectacular than the most brilliant multicolored flower gardens, and more delightful than the world's greatest symphony. As the ages roll on, there will be new wonders to explore, new heights to gain, and new mysteries to solve. We will never tire of heaven's new discoveries and eternity's new adventures. In the world made new, our knowledge will be ever-expanding and our joy continually increasing.

With that in mind, let's explore Revelation's glorious climax and learn what we can about the destiny of the redeemed. The Bible's last two chapters do not answer all our questions about heaven, but they do give us a glimpse into what heaven is really like.

All things new
John wrote,

> I saw a new heaven and a new earth, for the first heaven and the first earth had passed away. Also there was no more sea. Then I, John, saw the holy city, New Jerusalem, coming down out of heaven from God, prepared as a bride adorned for her husband. And I heard a loud voice from heaven saying, "Behold, the tabernacle of God is with men, and He will dwell with them, and they shall be His people. God Himself will be with them and be their God. And God will wipe away every tear from their eyes; there shall be no more death, nor sorrow, nor crying. There shall be no more pain, for the former things have passed away."
>
> Then He who sat on the throne said, "Behold, I make all things new." And He said to me, "Write, for these words are true and faithful."
>
> And He said to me, "It is done! I am the Alpha and the Omega, the Beginning and the End. I will give of the fountain of the water of life freely to him who thirsts. He who overcomes shall inherit all things, and I will be his God and he shall be My son" (Revelation 21:1–7).

These are some of the most beautiful words in the Bible! There is much to look at in these verses, so let's focus on some of the details John gives us regarding life in eternity.

The first impression we receive from these verses is *newness, freshness.* There is a "new heaven" and a "new earth" (verse 1). The "former things have passed away" (verse 4). God says, "I make all things new" (verse 5). Nothing reflective of the old world of sin remains. All things are new.

A new earth. In chapter 20, the earth is desolate, uninhabited, formless, and void. Then we saw that at the end of the thousand years, the holy city, New Jerusalem, comes down from God out of heaven along with all the redeemed and the angels. John sees that happening in Revelation 21:2.

In general, most Christians think that the redeemed will spend eternity with God and Jesus and the holy angels in *heaven.* It's true, as we saw in the previous chapter, that the redeemed would spend a thousand years in heaven. Then the capital of God's kingdom comes to earth. Revelation 21:3 says, "Behold, the tabernacle of God is with men, and He will dwell with them, and they shall be His people. God Himself will be with them and be their God." Matthew 5:5 says, "Blessed are the meek, for they shall inherit the earth."

You see, God is going to re-create the earth as it was in the beginning before sin. When the earth came from the hand of the Creator, it was beautiful beyond description. He created it to be inhabited (Isaiah 45:18). Sin disrupted God's plans for earth, but now sin has been eradicated forever. God will restore Eden, and this earth will become the capital of His kingdom. His tabernacle will be here. His holy city—the seat of His government—will be here.

It is beyond our comprehension, but it is true. God will take this planet in rebellion, this pockmarked planet filled with sorrow and misery, suffering and death, sin and iniquity, and make it over again. It will become the cosmic center of the entire universe. Best of all, God will be here! The redeemed will live on the earth made new, and God will live here with them and be their God! He will dwell with us through all eternity. Deep within our hearts, there is a yearning to be loved. No matter how much we are loved here, we long for more. Only God can fill that love deficit, and in eternity, our deepest love needs will be met in His presence. He will supply all our physical, mental, social, and spiritual needs—the One who made us knows how to care for us. In His presence, we will be fully satisfied.

God said through the prophet Isaiah, "Behold, I create new heavens and a new earth; and the former shall not be remembered or come to mind" (Isaiah 65:17). The prophet goes on to say about the redeemed on the earth made new,

"They shall plant vineyards and eat their fruit.
They shall not build and another inhabit;
They shall not plant and another eat;
For as the days of a tree, so shall be the days of My people,
And My elect shall long enjoy the work of their hands" (verses 21, 22).

In the earth made new, God's redeemed people will have eternity to carry out their dreams and plans. Nothing will mar the peace and harmony of a world without sin. " 'The wolf and the lamb shall feed together. . . . They shall not hurt nor destroy in all My holy mountain,' says the Lord" (verse 25). All our fears will vanish away. Our minds will be at peace, and our hearts will be at rest. The garden home of our first parents was real. The air was pure, the brooks were clear; the trees blossomed and bore fruit in delightful abundance. Adam and Eve walked hand in hand through the garden with hearts full of joy and gratitude. When God restores all things, "the wilderness and the wasteland shall be glad for them, and the desert shall rejoice and blossom as the rose" (Isaiah 35:1).

One day soon, Jesus will come. And He says, "Behold, I make all things new" (Revelation 21:5). Then the consequences of sin will be gone forever. "And the inhabitant will not say, 'I am sick' " (Isaiah 33:24). "The eyes of the blind shall be opened, and the ears of the deaf shall be unstopped. Then the lame shall leap like a deer, and the tongue of the dumb sing" (Isaiah 35:5, 6). The first thing our deaf friends will hear will be the voice of Jesus, saying, "Well done, good and faithful servant." The first thing our blind friends will see will be the loving face of Jesus. The paralyzed, the crippled, and the lame will run and leap for joy when Jesus releases them from their bonds. All weaknesses and every limitation caused by sin will be gone. Our bodies will be filled with boundless energy and vitality.

No death, sorrow, crying, or pain. It is interesting how much of John's description of the earth made new is phrased in terms of what will *not* be there. No tears, death, sorrow, crying, or pain (Revelation 21:4). No unbelievers, murderers, liars, or idolaters (verse 8). No night (verse 25). Nothing that defiles (verse 27). No curse (Revelation 22:3). In Revelation 21:1, he even says that there will be "no more sea." If you are a sea lover as I am, you may wonder what this phrase means. When he wrote Revelation, John had been exiled by the Roman emperor Domitian to the rocky, barren Isle of Patmos. As he gazed upon the sea from his vantage point on that isolated island, he may have thought about the friends and colleagues he was separated from. For John, the sea meant separation from loved ones. In heaven, we will have the deepest fellowship with those we love. There will be no more separation.

But certainly, there will be wonderful rivers, streams, and lakes. It is impossible for us to imagine what heaven is really like.

Have you ever thought how difficult it would be to describe a South Pacific island to an Eskimo—in the days before television and the internet? You might talk about sandy beaches and palm trees. Or the profusion of flowers and the thick jungles. But the Eskimo wouldn't be able to picture these things or really comprehend what you were talking about. Instead, you would probably find yourself saying things like, "It is never cold there. There is no snow or ice. No polar bears or walruses." You can see what a problem God has in trying to tell us about life in eternity when the only world we have ever known is a world steeped in sin. God says, "Behold, I make all things new." And He assures John that the words He speaks are "true and faithful" (verse 5).

The water of life. God also says, "I will give of the fountain of the water of life freely to him who thirsts" (verse 6). This reminds us of what happened when Moses struck the rock in the wilderness and streams of water gushed forth for the people who were dying of thirst (Exodus 17:1–7). The Rock of Ages struck on the cross became the water of life for a perishing world. Jesus told the Samaritan woman at the well, "Whoever drinks of the water that I shall give him will never thirst. But the water that I shall give him will become in him a fountain of water springing up into everlasting life" (John 4:14). Jesus Himself is the Water of Life. He said, "If anyone thirsts, let him come to Me and drink" (John 7:37). The fountain of the water of life represents the very life of the One who gives us life in all its abundance.

The New Jerusalem

An angel shows John the New Jerusalem:

> He carried me away in the Spirit to a great and high mountain, and showed me the great city, the holy Jerusalem, descending out of heaven from God, having the glory of God. Her light was like a most precious stone, like a jasper stone, clear as crystal. Also she had a great and high wall with twelve gates, and twelve angels at the gates, and names written on them, which are the names of the twelve tribes of the children of Israel: three gates on the east, three gates on the north, three gates on the south, and three gates on the west.
>
> Now the wall of the city had twelve foundations, and on them were the names of the twelve apostles of the Lamb. . . . The city is laid out as a square; its length is as great as its breadth. . . . Its length, breadth, and height are equal. . . . The construction of its wall was of jasper; and the city was pure gold, like

clear glass. The foundations of the wall were adorned with all kinds of precious stones. . . . The twelve gates were twelve pearls: each individual gate was of one pearl. And the street of the city was pure gold, like transparent glass" (Revelation 21:10–21).

This passage reveals numerous eternal truths. First, the holy city, New Jerusalem, is real. It is an actual city that God will bring to earth from heaven. It will be the capital of the kingdom He sets up on earth. The New Jerusalem will become the nerve center of the universe, the place where God dwells with the redeemed from earth. Next, let's consider the dimensions of the holy city and discover some practical spiritual lessons. Everything God does has an eternal purpose. Some have wondered whether these dimensions are symbolic. When we study Scripture, it is always wise to take Scripture as it reads unless an obvious symbol is used and God interprets that prophetic imagery somewhere else in the Bible. One notable thing about these dimensions is that every numerical specification or dimension given is the number twelve or is a multiple of the number twelve. There are twelve gates and twelve foundations (verses 12–14, 21). The city is "twelve thousand furlongs" long, wide, and high (verse 16). The wall is "one hundred and forty-four cubits" high (verse 17).

As we saw when we looked at the 144,000 who are sealed (Revelation 7:4–8), the number 12 represents the totality of the redeemed—12,000 from each of the 12 tribes of Israel. In the same way, the use of the number 12 in the description of the holy city seems to serve the same purpose—to emphasize the city as the dwelling place of the totality of the redeemed. This is supported further by the fact that the 12 gates each carry the name of one of the 12 tribes of Israel, and the 12 foundations of the city are inscribed with the name of one of the 12 apostles. This is a symbolic joining of the Old Testament people of God (the 12 tribes of Israel) with the New Testament people of God (the 12 apostles). It is a way of pointing out that the New Jerusalem will be the city of *all* of God's people from Eden to the second coming of Jesus.

Think about this fact for a moment. The names of the sons of Jacob are inscribed above the gates. Some of Jacob's sons were scoundrels. They could be condemned in a court of law for robbery, adultery, murder, and a host of other crimes. Consider the foundation of the city with the names of the twelve apostles. There is Peter who denied Jesus. Thomas, who doubted Him. James and John, the sons of thunder who selfishly coveted position in the kingdom they thought He came to establish. Why are the names of the twelve tribes of Israel and the twelve apostles on the gates? I believe they are there to remind us that Christ died for all—all men and women can be forgiven, freed from guilt, saved by grace, changed, and enter in through the gates into the holy city. If they enter, we can enter too. Through Jesus Christ, those who are unworthy become worthy. Those who are unrighteous become righteous. Those who are renegades are redeemed. The names above the gates and the names on the foundations of the city beckon us. They speak to us and declare, "If we pass through these gates, you, too, can enter."

The city is said to be "twelve thousand furlongs" in length, breadth, and height—and that these three dimensions are all equal (verse 16). A furlong is one-eighth of a mile. This would make the city 1,500 miles on each side and 1,500 miles high! Again, the emphasis may simply be to underscore that the city is large enough to accommodate all the redeemed from all ages.

The city is said to be 1,500 miles in height, while the height of the wall is only "one hundred and forty-four cubits" (verse 17)—or merely *216 feet* high! The relatively "low" wall symbolizes that God is more eager to bring men and women into His kingdom than He is to keep them out.

Finally, whatever words John uses to describe the city are inadequate to reveal its brilliance. Human language cannot describe the glories of what John was seeing. He says the city was "pure gold, like clear glass," and its street was the same (verses 18, 21). He says, "each individual gate was of one pearl" (verse 21). He talks about the foundations, each being made of a different precious stone (verses 19, 20). John was clearly dazzled by the glory and brilliance of the city he saw in the vision. It's possible that some of these descriptions under the inspiration and guidance of the Holy Spirit are the very best word pictures John could find. But we must remember that human language is always inadequate when it comes to describing the glories of eternity. There will be so much more to discover there beyond what our finite minds can understand. The glories of the earth made new and the New Jerusalem will satisfy beyond our most fervent imaginations.

> The New Jerusalem will become the nerve center of the universe, the place where God dwells with the redeemed from earth.

Things that are not in the holy city

John continues:

> I saw no temple in it [the city], for the Lord God Almighty and the Lamb are its temple. The city had no need of the sun or of the moon to shine in it,

for the glory of God illuminated it. The Lamb is its light. And the nations of those who are saved shall walk in its light, and the kings of the earth bring their glory and honor into it. Its gates shall not be shut at all by day (there shall be no night there). And they shall bring the glory and the honor of the nations into it. But there shall by no means enter it anything that defiles, or causes an abomination or a lie, but only those who are written in the Lamb's Book of Life (verses 22–27).

No temple. "I saw no temple in it," John writes (verse 22). But in verse 3, he writes about the holy city coming down to earth and adds, "I heard a loud voice from heaven saying, 'Behold, the tabernacle of God is with men, and He will dwell with them.' " How do we explain this? Is there a temple (tabernacle) in the New Jerusalem or not?

The Greek word translated "dwell" in verse 3—"He will dwell with them"—is found only in three places in the New Testament—John 1:14; Revelation 7:15; and Revelation 21:3. It literally means "to dwell in a tent." The wilderness sanctuary was a portable tent and is called a "tabernacle." So there is a sort of play on words here. It can be phrased as "The tabernacle of God is with men, and He will tabernacle with them." The fact that God dwells (tabernacles) with men means the same thing as "the tabernacle of God is with men." Thus, the main idea here is that there is no separation between God and His people.

> The dark saga of sin is over, and now God's people live in His glorious presence without the shades of night keeping Him from their view.

In the Old Testament sanctuary, only the high priest could enter the Most Holy Place of the sanctuary, once a year on the Day of Atonement. It was inconceivable for any ordinary Jew to enter the Shekinah glory of God's presence, neither in the wilderness sanctuary nor later in the temple Solomon built. Saying that there is "no temple" there states the amazing truth, the wonderful reality, that each one of us has personal access to the presence of God.

The emphasis of Revelation 21:3 is clear. John says, "And I heard a loud voice from heaven saying, 'Behold the temple of God is with men, and He will dwell with them, and they shall be His people. God Himself will be with them and be their God.' " The greatest joy of heaven is to be present with God forever, to fellowship with Him through the ceaseless ages of eternity.

Verse 22 explicitly says there is no temple in the holy city because "God and the

Lamb are its temple." The temple, or sanctuary, was a picture lesson illustrating the plan of salvation. Isaiah 59:2 says, "Your iniquities have separated you from your God; and your sins have hidden His face from you, so that He will not hear." Sin separates us from God. Before sin, in Eden, Adam and Eve had direct communication with God. The purpose of the plan of salvation was to reveal God's love before the entire universe and restore lost humanity to fellowship with Him again. Revelation 21 points to a time when that plan has been successfully completed. Salvation is accomplished, and there is no longer a need for a temple or sanctuary to illustrate the plan of salvation. God dwells personally with His people in the earth made new.

No need of the sun or moon. Notice that John does not say that there will be no sun or moon in the city or the earth made new. He says there is no *need* for them because God's glory illuminates the city, and the Lamb is its light (verse 23). Jesus is the Light of the world (John 8:12).

No night (verse 25). John may have had Psalm 139:11, 12 in mind:

If I say, "Surely the darkness shall fall on me,"
Even the night shall be light about me;
Indeed, the darkness shall not hide from You,
But the night shines as the day.

The dark saga of sin is over, and now God's people live in His glorious presence without the shades of night keeping Him from their view.

Nothing that defiles (verse 27). John emphasizes, once again, that sin is eradicated forever. Only those whose names were written in the Lamb's book of life will enter God's holy city. All these things will be absent from the New Jerusalem and the earth made new. But John tells us that "the nations of those who are saved" will be there. Kings of the earth will "bring their glory and honor" into the city (verse 24). Heaven is for all peoples, young and old, rich and poor, educated and uneducated, kings and commoners. They will come from the east and west, north and south, to enter through those gates to the holy city.

Most ancient cities had only a very few gates because that made it much easier to guard and keep the enemy out. God's city has multiple gates, twelve in all, because He wants to get as many people in as possible. Every person entering those gates and everything in the universe will praise and honor God and the Lamb forever!

In chapter 22—the last chapter of his book—John continues his description of the city and the new earth.

"EVEN SO, COME, LORD JESUS!"

Revelation 22

1 And he showed me a pure river of water of life, clear as crystal, proceeding from the throne of God and of the Lamb. **2** In the middle of its street, and on either side of the river, was the tree of life, which bore twelve fruits, each yielding its fruit every month. The leaves of the tree were for the healing of the nations. **3** And there shall be no more curse, but the throne of God and of the Lamb shall be in it, and His servants shall serve Him. **4** They shall see His face, and His name shall be on their foreheads. **5** There shall be no night there: They need no lamp nor light of the sun, for the Lord God gives them light. And they shall reign forever and ever.

6 Then he said to me, "These words are faithful and true." And the Lord God of the holy prophets sent His angel to show His servants the things which must shortly take place.

7 "Behold, I am coming quickly! Blessed is he who keeps the words of the prophecy of this book."

8 Now I, John, saw and heard these things. And when I heard and saw, I fell down to worship before the feet of the angel who showed me these things.

9 Then he said to me, "See that you do not do that. For I am your fellow servant, and of your brethren the prophets, and of those who keep the words of this book. Worship God." **10** And he said to me, "Do not seal the words of the prophecy of this book, for the time is at hand. **11** He who is unjust, let him be unjust still; he who is filthy, let him be filthy still; he who is righteous, let him be righteous still; he who is holy, let him be holy still."

12 "And behold, I am coming quickly, and My reward is with Me, to give to every one according to his work. **13** I am the Alpha and the Omega, the Beginning and the End, the First and the Last."

14 Blessed are those who do His commandments, that they may have the right to the tree of life, and may enter through the gates into the city. **15** But outside are dogs and sorcerers and sexually immoral and murderers and idolaters, and whoever loves and practices a lie.

16 "I, Jesus, have sent My angel to testify to you these things in the churches. I am the Root and the Offspring of David, the Bright and Morning Star."

17 And the Spirit and the bride say, "Come!" And let him who hears say, "Come!" And let him who thirsts come. Whoever desires, let him take the water of life freely.

18 For I testify to everyone who hears the words of the prophecy of this book: If anyone adds to these things, God will add to him the plagues that are written in this book; **19** and if anyone takes away from the words of the book of this prophecy, God shall take away his part from the Book of Life, from the holy city, and from the things which are written in this book.

20 He who testifies to these things says, "Surely I am coming quickly."

Amen. Even so, come, Lord Jesus!

21 The grace of our Lord Jesus Christ be with you all. Amen.

The last chapter of Revelation is a fitting climax to the entire book. It contains encouragement, warnings, urgency, and a final appeal. Reading it, we are moved to a deeper commitment to Christ and His message for this crisis hour of earth's history. In this last chapter of the book of Revelation, and of the entire Bible, Jesus assures us of His desire to have us with Him through all eternity. He paints a picture of heaven that is irresistible to any mind open to His Spirit and then urges us to respond to His loving invitation to live with Him forever.

A description of the new earth

In the last chapter of his book—Revelation 22, John continues his description of life in the New Jerusalem and on the earth made new. In fact, there is no discernible break in the flow of thought from chapter 21 to chapter 22. There really is no good reason to think of these as separate chapters.

Today, we are used to having the Bible divided into chapters and verses. It certainly makes it easy to look up a section of Scripture. However, when the books of the Bible were originally written, they did not contain chapter or verse references. They were written as a single piece of writing, just as are most books today. You may wonder how

we came to have the chapters and verse divisions that we find so helpful and familiar.

It happened around 1227, when the archbishop of Canterbury, Stephen Langdon, put them in place. There had been other chapter and verse divisions earlier, but Langdon's version eventually became the most popular. The Wycliffe English Bible (1382) was the first to use his chapter pattern. Since then, nearly all Bible translations have followed Langdon's divisions.

Bible scholars have pointed out that Langdon's choices are not always well thought out. Some have suggested that he did his work while riding horseback, and some of his awkward divisions were caused by his horse stumbling! Whatever the case may be, at times, his chapter divisions often divide content that obviously flows together. The division between Revelation 21 and 22 is certainly one of those instances. The content simply flows from one chapter to the next with no obvious break in the thought.

So let's pick up John's description of the New Jerusalem and life on the earth made new in chapter 22.

The river of life and the tree of life

John continues to tell us what the angel showed him in the vision. "And he showed me a pure river of water of life, clear as crystal, proceeding from the throne of God and of the Lamb. In the middle of its street, and on either side of the river, was the tree of life, which bore twelve fruits, each tree yielding its fruit every month. The leaves of the tree were for the healing of the nations" (verses 1, 2).

John is drawing here from the imagery of Ezekiel's prophecy. Ezekiel was shown a river flowing from the temple. He says, "Along the bank of the river, on this side and that, will grow all kinds of trees used for food. . . . They will bear fruit every month, because their water flows from the sanctuary. Their fruit will be for food, and their leaves for medicine" (Ezekiel 47:12).

The parallels are obvious, although there are some differences. This theme of a river of water of life flowing from God in blessings to His people is a common one in the Old Testament. The psalmist sings, "There is a river whose streams shall make glad the city of God" (Psalm 46:4). The prophet Joel prophesied, "It will come to pass in that day that . . . a fountain shall flow from the house of the LORD" (Joel 3:18). The prophet Zechariah wrote, "And in that day it shall be that living waters shall flow from Jerusalem. . . . And the LORD shall be King over all the earth" (Zechariah 14:8, 9).

This river of life flowing from God's throne also reminds us of Eden. Genesis says, "A river went out of Eden to water the garden" (Genesis 2:10). Water is the very essence of life. Societies experiencing drought face disease, disaster, and death. The rivers flowing through Eden constantly provided fresh water. Babbling brooks; clear, crystal streams; and gently flowing rivers wound their way through the land. The vegetation flourished. The crops grew. The animals gathered at their banks, and Adam and Eve were nourished and refreshed by the life-giving water of Eden.

In Jesus' discussion with the Samaritan woman in John 4, He used the illustration of water to symbolize the eternal life that only He can provide. Referring to Jacob's well, He said, "Whoever drinks of this water will thirst again, but whoever drinks of the water that I shall give him will never thirst. But the water that I shall give him will become in him a fountain of water springing up into everlasting life" (John 4:13, 14). The river of life flowing through Eden represents the very life of God, given to us in Christ, and there is an abundant supply for all. The life of God is exhaustless, everlasting, never-ending, and offered to us freely.

The tree of life described in Revelation 22:2 was in the Garden of Eden as well. The new earth is Eden restored. In the new earth, the tree of life is placed beside the river of life, and there is no tree of the knowledge of good and evil as there was in the original Eden. The tree of life bears a different fruit each month, and its leaves have healing properties.

We will discover much more about the meaning of this imagery when we are on the new earth, but here are some encouraging things that we do know, making the imagery more meaningful. This picture is one of a vibrant, wholesome life, free from illness of any kind. Given the fact that many of the redeemed will have gone through martyrdom, persecution, and severe trials of all kinds, restoration into the image of God will need to take place on the earth made new. The Greek word for healing in this passage is *therapeia*. You may have guessed—it is the root of the word *therapy*. Could it be that the leaves of the tree of life are our therapy to live the most abundant life possible and to be continually restored in the image of God? Perhaps this peaceful scene of the tree of life with its healing properties situated beside the river of the water of life is designed to depict a soothing environment in which those who have come out of great trials can find peace. The word also has the connotation of service, care, and nurture. The leaves of the tree symbolize God's intimate care for us in supplying our every need. There is abundance for all. There, by the river of life, eating the fruits of the tree of life, nourished by the leaves of that tree, we will be fully satisfied. Our minds will be at peace, and our bodies will radiant with the glow of health.

No more curse

"And there shall be no more curse, but the throne of God and of the Lamb shall be in it, and His servants shall serve Him. They shall see His face, and His name shall be on their foreheads. There shall be no night there: They need no lamp nor light of the sun, for the Lord God gives them light. And they shall reign forever and ever" (Revelation 22:3–5).

When Adam and Eve disobeyed God in the Garden of Eden, the curse of sin fell on them, their descendants, and on the earth itself (Genesis 3). Now that curse has been lifted. Sin is no more.

The redeemed will "see His [God's] face" (verse 4). The promise of Matthew 5:8 will come true—"Blessed are the pure in heart, for they shall see God." Even Moses, when he asked to see God, was told, "You cannot see My face; for no man shall see Me, and live" (Exodus 33:20). But in verse 11, Scripture declares, "The LORD spoke to Moses face to face, as a man speaks to his friend." How do we reconcile these two seemingly contradictory passages? The expression "face to face" in verse 11 is an idiom meaning direct, open, intimate communication.

In the new heavens and the new earth with sin no longer a barrier, we will both see God and enjoy the most intimate fellowship with Him possible. As Moses spoke to God personally and shared his needs, concerns, and the secrets of his heart, we too will enjoy these personal times of one-on-one fellowship with God. We are accepted as His sons and daughters in Christ, heirs of the kingdom, and God loves to talk to His children. On that day, the redeemed who have on the robe of Christ's righteousness will see God's face. What a wonderful privilege, indeed!

> The new earth is Eden restored. In the new earth, the tree of life is placed beside the river of life, and there is no tree of the knowledge of good and evil as there was in the original Eden.

The redeemed have God's name on their foreheads (verse 4). This is the seal of God presented in chapter 7 and contrasts with the mark of the beast that its followers have on their foreheads (Revelation 13:16). God's seal is the outward sign of our loyalty to Christ. It is manifest in keeping the Sabbath, in earth's last hours, when the mark of the beast is enforced. The seal of God, however, is much more than merely keeping the Sabbath. It is settling into the truth so that we can be moved neither spiritually nor intellectually.

The Father's name, or seal, in our foreheads, placed there by the Holy Spirit, is the symbol of a mind totally in harmony with the will of God. The apostle Paul stated in Philippians 2:5, "Let this mind be in you which was also in Christ Jesus."

When we have the mind of Christ, we reflect the character of Christ. God's name represents God's character. It defines who He is. First John 3:2 reveals God's glorious ideal for His children in these words: "Beloved, now we are children of God; and it has not yet been revealed what we shall be, but we know that when He is revealed, we shall be like Him, for we shall see Him as He is." The Father's name on our foreheads identifies us as fully His. We have made our decision. Our choice is fixed. Our destiny is settled. Throughout all eternity, we will reflect His character and, in every thought, feeling, impulse, and action, reveal that we belong to Him.

John repeats what he said earlier (Revelation 21:23, 25) about there being no night in the New Jerusalem. When we remember that, in John's day and for many centuries thereafter, when the sun went down, it became extremely dark, we can better understand how important it was to John that there would be no night in the New Jerusalem. In our modern world of electricity, we can scarcely conceive of what nighttime meant to the world before. Artificial lighting was limited to candles, feeble lamps and lanterns, bonfires, and other low-light sources. John's vision of eternity was one of light, not darkness.

In some of the extreme northern latitudes where the sun does not rise in the winter months, depression is much more prevalent. You may know someone who struggles in parts of the world where the nights are long and the days are dark and gloomy. In John's vision of the new earth, he saw only light, cheer, and joy. The darkness of night with all its gloom was over. For John, it was a big deal that there would be no night in the city and that the Lord God would provide so much light that there would be no need for the sun or moon!

The time is near

> The Lord God of the holy prophets sent His angel to show His servants the things which must shortly take place.
>
> "Behold, I am coming quickly! Blessed is he who keeps the words of the prophecy of this book." . . .
>
> And he [the angel] said to me, "Do not seal the words of the prophecy of this book, for the time is at hand. He who is unjust, let him be unjust still; he who is filthy, let him be filthy still; he who is righteous, let him be righteous still; he who is holy, let him be holy still" (Revelation 22:6–11).

In verse 7, Jesus is the One who is speaking. He repeats the blessing pronounced in Revelation 1:3 on those who keep "the words of the prophecy of this book."

Notice that the angel tells John, "Do not seal the words of the prophecy of this book, for the time is at hand" (verse 10). In contrast, at the close of Daniel's book, the angel Gabriel tells him, "Shut up the words, and seal the book until the time of the end" (Daniel 12:4; cf. verse 9). Daniel lived in the sixth century before Christ. John is writing at the close of the first century after Christ. In Daniel's day, the prophecy was to be sealed, but now "the time is at hand" (Revelation 22:10).

Now, we are living almost two thousand years past the time John wrote. In what sense is the time "at hand"? Ever since Jesus returned to heaven (Acts 1:9–11), His followers have expected His soon return. The apostle Paul told the Roman Christians, "Now it is high time to awake out of sleep; for now, our salvation is nearer than when we first believed. The night is far spent, the day is at hand" (Romans 13:11, 12). Jesus Himself tells John, "Behold, I am coming quickly!" (Revelation 22:7).

William Miller was the leading preacher of the Advent movement, the one who had first worked out from the prophecies of Daniel that Jesus would return to earth in 1844. When that failed to happen, and the Advent people were so terribly disappointed, it is said that someone asked Miller whether he had fastened on another date for Jesus to come. He replied, "Although I have been twice disappointed, I am not yet cast down or discouraged. . . . I have fixed my mind on another time and here I mean to stand until God gives me more light—and that is today, today, and today, until He comes, and I see Him for whom my soul yearns."[1]

> The decisions we are making every day will seal our eternal destiny. The importance of those decisions cannot be overestimated. Every day Christ appeals to our hearts through His Holy Spirit to make each decision in the light of eternity.

That is the position all of Jesus' true followers should take. As we see the prophetic signs being fulfilled all around us, our hearts yearn for His coming. They beat with eager anticipation. We know it must be soon, but we know neither the exact day nor hour of His return, so we continue to cling to the promise—the blessed hope and glorious appearing of our Lord—until He comes (Matthew 24:36; Titus 2:11–13). He has promised to come quickly.

In Revelation 22:11 is the pronouncement, "He who is unjust, let him be unjust still" and "he who is righteous, let him be righteous still." Of course, chronologically, the eternal self-determination of each person has already taken place by the time of chapter 22. This pronouncement is a restatement of the fact that each person makes his or her own choices until a point where there is no possibility of change. That decision is made evident at the Second Coming.

The decisions we are making every day will seal our eternal destiny. The importance of those decisions cannot be overestimated. Every day Christ appeals to our hearts through His Holy Spirit to make each decision in the light of eternity. The decisions we make either are hardening our hearts and leading us further from Jesus or softening them and leading us closer to Him.

The wonderful invitation

"Behold, I am coming quickly, and My reward is with Me, to give to every one according to his work. I am the Alpha and the Omega, the Beginning and the End, the First and the Last."

Blessed are those who do His commandments, that they may have the right to the tree of life, and may enter through the gates into the city. . . .

"I, Jesus, have sent My angel to testify to you these things in the churches. I am the Root and the Offspring of David, the Bright and Morning Star."

And the Spirit and the bride say, "Come!" And let him who hears say, "Come!" And let him who thirsts come. Whoever desires, let him take the water of life freely (verses 12–17).

Jesus here repeats His promise to come quickly. His reward is with Him when He comes (Matthew 16:27). He repeats the description of Himself as the "Alpha and the Omega . . . the First and the Last" (Revelation 1:11; cf. verse 17). Jesus encompasses all things from the beginning to the end. He is the Author and Finisher of our faith (Hebrews 12:1, 2). We can be confident that "He who has begun a good work in you will complete it until the day of Jesus Christ" (Philippians 1:6). What an assurance! If we let Him, He will finish what He started in us and get us home.

The expression "Blessed are they that do His commandments," in verse 14, can also be translated as "wash their robes." The expressions are very close in the original Greek manuscripts. There is harmony between these two ideas. The outward evidence of being clothed with Christ's righteousness is obedience to His commands. Our robes cannot possibly be clean if we cherish known sin in our lives. Christ's righteousness does not cover intentional rebellion against His will. When we are saved by His grace, and His grace alone, our deepest longing is to please Him. Those who walk through the gates into that holy city are clothed in His righteousness—captivated by

His love and transformed by His power to live obedient lives throughout all eternity.

Then is extended the great, all-inclusive invitation to be an inhabitant of the holy city, a citizen of the earth made new. "The Spirit and the bride say, 'Come!' And let him who hears say, 'Come!' And let him who thirsts come. Whoever desires, let him take the water of life freely" (verse 17). All are invited; all are welcome. The only requirement is that you thirst, that you desire to drink the water of life freely.

We find echoes of this great invitation in the words of the prophet Isaiah:

"Everyone who thirsts,
Come to the waters;
And you who have no money,
Come, buy and eat.
Yes, come, buy wine and milk
Without money and without price" (Isaiah 55:1).

How could God make it any plainer? What more could He do to draw men and women to Himself and to eternal life in a world without sin?

Conclusion

I testify to everyone who hears the words of the prophecy of this book: If anyone adds to these things, God will add to him the plagues that are written in this book; and if anyone takes away from the words of the book of this prophecy, God shall take away his part from the Book of Life, from the holy city, and from the things that are written in this book.

He who testifies to these things says, "Surely I am coming quickly!"

Amen. Even so, come, Lord Jesus!

The grace of our Lord Jesus Christ be with you all. Amen (Revelation 22:18–21).

These verses contain a concluding statement common to many ancient writings—a sort of equivalent to our modern copyright notices in books. In John's time, books were handwritten, and copies were also made by hand. That is the literal meaning of the word *manuscript*. It comes from two Latin words, *manus* (hand) and *scriptus* (to write). When copying a book, it was easy to make a change accidentally. It was also easy to make changes on purpose. That is what is behind John's warning against adding or taking away any of the words of his book. Similar "copyright" warnings appear in other Bible books (Deuteronomy 4:2; Proverbs 30:5, 6).

The book of Revelation ends with yet another assurance that Jesus is coming soon (Revelation 22:20). From the depths of his heart, this apostle whom Jesus loved (John 13:23; 19:26; 20:2) responds, "Amen. Even so, come, Lord Jesus!"

John's response finds an echoing chord in our own hearts. We, too, say, "Even so, come, Lord Jesus. Come into my heart. Come into my life. Draw me into Your loving embrace so that I will live for You every day until You come to earth again, and I can live with You in that glorious city on the earth made new."

Our study of the book of Revelation tells us that the end time will be a time of trial and difficulty for God's people. As we draw closer to His coming, perilous times will increase until they may appear overwhelming. Nevertheless, we can keep moving forward, together with Jesus, knowing that the bright city lies ahead. He has never lost a battle with Satan, and He will triumph in this final conflict between good and evil.

Every prophecy in Revelation ultimately ends in the same place—with Christ as the victor. He is the Almighty conqueror. He is our triumphant Lord. He is the King of kings and Lord of lords. We are on the winning side. In Him, and through Him, and with Him, and because of Him, we can triumph. We will live with Him in the earth made new forever. Deep within our hearts, in the very fabric of our beings, we cry out with John, "Even so, come, Lord, Jesus!"

---

1. William Miller to Joshua V. Himes, November 10, 1844, in "Letter From Wm. Miller," *The Midnight Cry!* December 5, 1844.